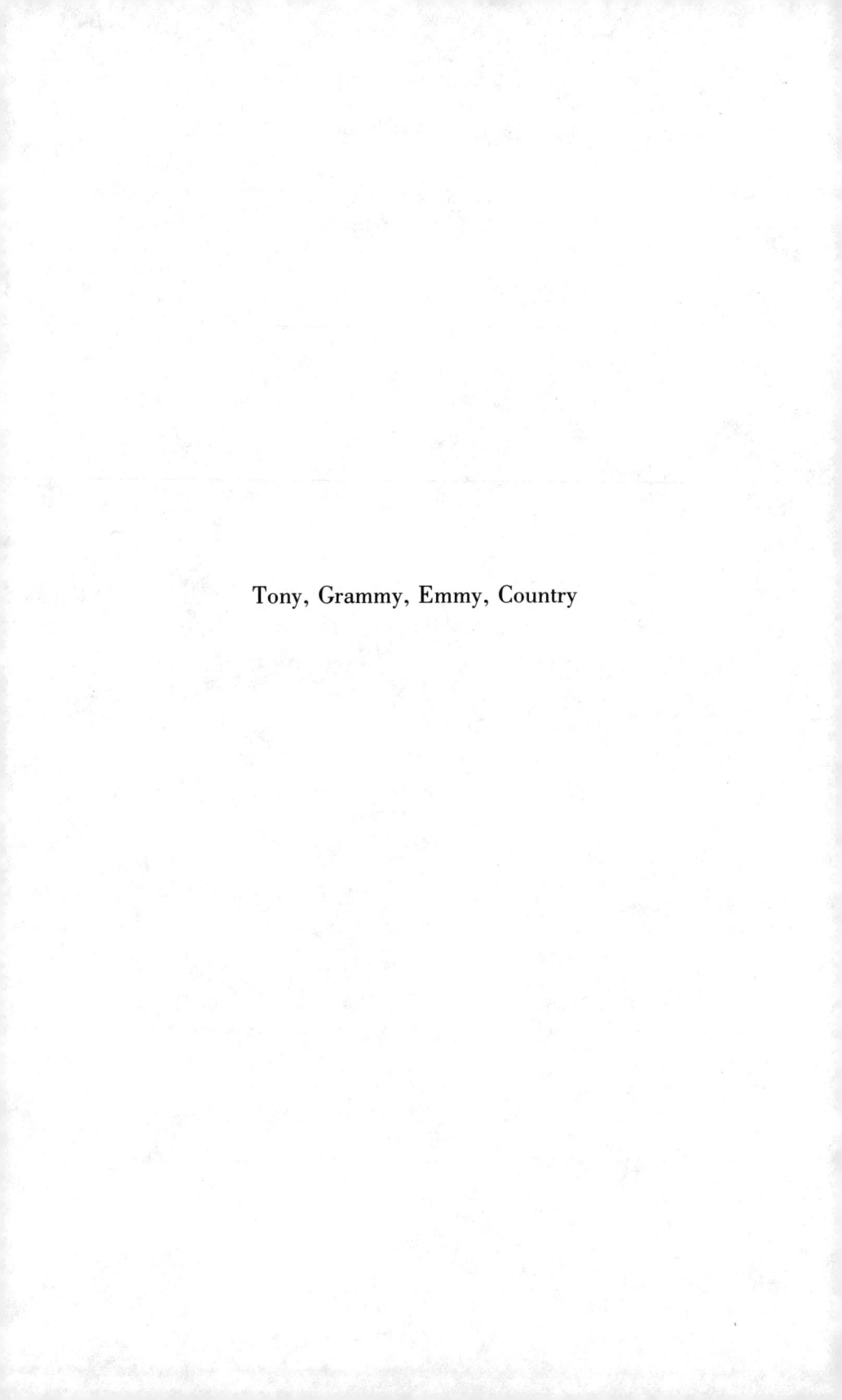

Tony, Grammy, Emmy, Country

To my father

Tony, Grammy, Emmy, Country

A BROADWAY, TELEVISION AND RECORDS AWARDS REFERENCE

Compiled by
DON FRANKS

Poynter Institute for Media Studies
Library

SEP 25

McFarland & Company, Inc., Publishers
Jefferson, North Carolina, and London

Acknowledgments

I wish to acknowledge the help I received in putting this book together from Amy Lovell and Beverly S. Voelbel of the American Theatre Wing, Rolene Naveja, Bernice Tysand and Aida Scorza from the National Academy of Recording Arts & Sciences, Kathy Gurley and Pablo LaPrelle with the Country Music Association, and James L. Loper at the Academy of Television Arts & Sciences. And special thanks to Lynn.

This book is not an official publication of, nor is it endorsed by, the League of New York Theatres and Producers, the National Academy of Recording Arts & Sciences, the Country Music Association, the Academy of Television Arts & Sciences, or the National Academy of Television Arts and Sciences.

Library of Congress Cataloguing-in-Publication Data

Franks, Don, 1945–
Tony, Grammy, Emmy, Country.

Includes index.
1. Performing arts–United States–Awards. I. Title.
PN2270.A93F7   1986   790.2'079   85-43577

ISBN 0-89950-204-0 (acid-free natural paper)

© 1986 Don Franks. All rights reserved.

Manufactured in the United States of America.

McFarland & Company, Inc., Publishers
Box 611, Jefferson, North Carolina 28640

Table of Contents

Acknowledgments	iv
Introduction	vi
Tony Awards	1
Grammy Awards	19
Country Music Association Awards	55
Emmy Awards	61
Index	133

Introduction

Most fields of endeavor enjoy the prestige and reward of recognition. Many take the form of awards in little-known fields such as the Bradford Washburn Award given by the Boston Museum of Science or the Splendid American Award administered by the Thomas A. Dooley Foundation. Writers of cookbooks may be rewarded by receiving the Tastemakers Award given by the R.T. French Company. You may possibly be lucky enough to be the recipient of the Edwin Sutherland Award for your contribution to the field of criminology theory.

Aside from people in these specific fields, few have ever heard of the Splendid American Award or most of the thousand other achievement awards given each year. If the award is televised though, chances are that you not only have heard of it but that you probably cheer for a specific person to receive the award.

Over the years, the big three television networks (ABC, NBC and CBS) have given us many different award shows. This book will deal with a few of the larger ones: the American Theatre Wing's Antoinette Perry Awards (called the Tonys), given by the League of New York Theatres and Producers annually since 1947; the Grammy Awards given every year since 1958 by the National Academy of Recording Arts & Sciences; the Country Music Association Awards presented since 1967 by the Country Music Association; and television's own Emmy Awards given by the National Academy of Television Arts and Sciences since 1948. The awarding agencies are:

Tony Award
American Theatre Wing
250 W 57th St
New York NY 10107

Grammy Award
National Academy of Recording Arts
 & Sciences
303 N Glenoaks Blvd
Suite 140
Burbank CA 91502

CMA Award
Country Music Association
POB 22299
Seven Music Circle N
Nashville TN 37202

Prime-Time Emmy Award
Academy of Television Arts
 & Sciences
4605 Lankershim Blvd
Suite 800
North Hollywood CA 91602

Daytime Emmy Award
National Academy of Television Arts
 & Sciences
110 W 57th St
New York NY 10019

Tony Awards

Antoinette Perry died in 1946 following many years of service as chairwoman of the board and secretary of the American Theatre Wing. A member of the men's executive committee for the American Theatre Wing suggested that the Wing initiate a series of awards for theatrical excellence in memory of Antoinette Perry.

The first awards were given on Easter Sunday in 1947. They consisted of a scroll along with either a cigarette lighter or a compact. The familiar silver medallion did not make its first appearance for another two years.

The 1947 awards were broadcast locally on WOR radio and carried nationally on the Mutual Broadcasting System. They were first telecast locally on New York's Channel 5 in 1956. In 1966, another chairwoman of the American Theatre Wing, Helen Menken, died. Although a solemn presentation of the awards was held in April of that year, the Tony Awards were in danger of disappearing.

In 1967, the Wing authorized the League of New York Theatres to plan and carry out the award ceremonies and present the awards. For almost 20 years the ceremonies had been held in the ballroom of a New York hotel. The League recognized them as an important vehicle advertising New York theatres. So they moved to a Broadway theatre and producer Alexander H. Cohen has handled the national telecasting ever since.

The Tony Awards represent a high point in the history of televised award presentations. Each show is carefully planned and tightly produced. A lot of the waiting for recipients to come to the stage is eliminated by seating the nominees on the aisles.

When arriving at the podium, an unofficial policy is followed keeping the acceptance speech brief. This helps keep the awards presented in a professional manner. The star's Uncle Oscar in Mermentau, Louisiana, does not get thanked but not many viewers remain interested during personal thank-you's anyway.

The Tony Awards do not use up a lot of broadcast time on relatively obscure awards the television audience probably does not understand or even care about. Throughout the years, the categories have changed, new ones replacing ones no longer applicable. This allows the awards to recognize the various achievements each season. It also lets the viewer see some of that year's best productions.

1947 Tony Awards

1. **Dramatic Actors**: Jose Ferrer in *Cyrano de Bergerac*; Fredric March in *Years Ago*
2. **Dramatic Actresses**: Ingrid Bergman in *Joan of Lorraine*; Helen Hayes in *Happy Birthday*
3. **Supporting or Featured Dramatic Actress**: Patricia Neal in *Another Part of the Forest*
4. **Director**: Elia Kazan for *All My Sons*

5. **Supporting or Featured Musical Actor**: David Wayne in *Finian's Rainbow*
6. **Choreographers**: Agnes de Mille for *Brigadoon*; Michael Kidd for *Finian's Rainbow*
7. **Costumes**: Lucinda Ballard for *Happy Birthday, Street Scene, John Loves Mary, The Chocolate Soldier* and *Another Part of the Forest*; David Ffolks for *Henry VIII*
8. **Special Awards**: Dora Chamberlain; Mr. and Mrs. Ira Katzenberg; Jules Leventhal; Burns Mantle; P.A. MacDonald; Arthur Miller; Vincent Sardi, Sr.; Kurt Weill

1948 Tony Awards

1. **Play**: *Mister Roberts* based on the novel by Thomas Heggen
2. **Dramatic Actors**: Henry Fonda in *Mister Roberts*; Paul Kelly in *Command Decision*; Basil Rathbone in *The Heiress*
3. **Dramatic Actresses**: Judith Anderson in *Medea*; Katherine Cornell in *Antony and Cleopatra*; Jessica Tandy in *A Streetcar Named Desire*
4. **Producer**: Leland Hayward for *Mister Roberts*
5. **Authors**: Thomas Heggen and Joshua Logan for *Mister Roberts*
6. **Musical Actor**: Paul Hartman in *Angel in the Wings*
7. **Musical Actress**: Grace Hartman in *Angel in the Wings*
8. **Choreographer**: Jerome Robbins for *High Button Shoes*
9. **Costumes**: Mary Percy Schenck for *The Heiress*
10. **Scenic Designer**: Horace Armistead for *The Medium*
11. **Stage Technicians**: George Gebhardt; George Pierce
12. **Special Awards**: Vera Allen; Paul Beisman; Joe E. Brown; Robert Dowling; Rosamond Gilder; June Lockhart; Mary Martin; Robert Porterfield; James Whitmore; Experimental Theatre, Inc.

1949 Tony Awards

1. **Play**: *Death of a Salesman*
2. **Dramatic Actor**: Rex Harrison in *Anne of the Thousand Days*
3. **Supporting or Featured Dramatic Actor**: Arthur Kennedy in *Death of a Salesman*
4. **Dramatic Actress**: Martita Hunt in *The Madwoman of Chaillot*
5. **Supporting or Featured Dramatic Actress**: Shirley Booth in *Goodbye, My Fancy*
6. **Director**: Elia Kazan for *Death of a Salesman*
7. **Dramatic Producers**: Kermit Bloomgarden and Walter Fried for *Death of a Salesman*
8. **Author**: Arthur Miller for *Death of a Salesman*
9. **Musical**: *Kiss Me Kate*
10. **Musical Actor**: Ray Bolger in *Where's Charley?*
11. **Musical Actress**: Nanette Fabray in *Love Life*
12. **Musical Authors**: Bella and Samuel Spewack for *Kiss Me Kate*
13. **Composer and Lyricist**: Cole Porter for *Kiss Me Kate*
14. **Musical Producers**: Saint-Subber and Lemuel Ayers for *Kiss Me Kate*
15. **Scenic Designer**: Jo Mielziner for *Sleepy Hollow, Summer and Smoke, Death of a Salesman, Anne of the Thousand* and *South Pacific*
16. **Costumes**: Lemuel Ayers for *Kiss Me Kate*
17. **Choreographer**: Gower Champion for *Lend an Ear*
18. **Conductor and Musical Director**: Max Meth for *As the Girls Go*

1950 Tony Awards

1. **Play**: *The Cocktail Party*
2. **Dramatic Actor**: Sidney Blackmer in *Come Back, Little Sheba*
3. **Dramatic Actress**: Shirley Booth in *Come Back, Little Sheba*
4. **Director**: Joshua Logan for *South Pacific*
5. **Dramatic Author**: T.S. Eliot for *The Cocktail Party*
6. **Dramatic Producer**: Gilbert Miller for *The Cocktail Party*
7. **Musical**: *South Pacific*
8. **Musical Actor**: Ezio Pinza in *South Pacific*
9. **Supporting or Featured Musical Actor**: Myron McCormick in *South Pacific*

10. **Musical Actress**: Mary Martin in *South Pacific*
11. **Supporting or Featured Musical Actress**: Juanita Hall in *South Pacific*
12. **Musical Authors**: Joshua Logan and Oscar Hammerstein II for *South Pacific*
13. **Composer**: Richard Rodgers for *South Pacific*
14. **Conductor and Musical Director**: Maurice Abravanel for *Regina*
15. **Musical Producers**: Richard Rodgers, Oscar Hammerstein II, Leland Hayward and Joshua Logan for *South Pacific*
16. **Choreographer**: Helen Tamiris for *Touch and Go*
17. **Scenic Designer**: Jo Mielziner for *The Innocents*
18. **Costumes**: Aline Bernstein for *Regina*
19. **Stage Technicians**: Joe Lynn, master propertyman for *Miss Liberty*
20. **Special Awards**: Maurice Evans, volunteer worker from the hospital program of the American Theatre Wing

1951 Tony Awards

1. **Play**: *The Rose Tattoo*
2. **Dramatic Actor**: Claude Rains in *Darkness at Noon*
3. **Supporting or Featured Dramatic Actor**: Eli Wallach in *The Rose Tattoo*
4. **Dramatic Actress**: Uta Hagen in *The Country Girl*
5. **Supporting or Featured Dramatic Actress**: Maureen Stapleton in *The Rose Tattoo*
6. **Dramatic Author**: Tennessee Williams for *The Rose Tattoo*
7. **Director**: George S. Kaufman for *Guys and Dolls*
8. **Dramatic Producer**: Cheryl Crawford for *The Rose Tattoo*
9. **Musical**: *Guys and Dolls*
10. **Musical Actor**: Robert Alda in *Guys and Dolls*
11. **Supporting or Featured Musical Actor**: Russell Nype in *Call Me Madam*
12. **Musical Actress**: Ethel Merman in *Call Me Madam*
13. **Supporting or Featured Musical Actress**: Isabel Bigley in *Guys and Dolls*
14. **Musical Authors**: Jo Swerling and Abe Burrows for *Guys and Dolls*
15. **Composer and Lyricist**: Frank Loesser for *Guys and Dolls*
16. **Choreographer**: Michael Kidd for *Guys and Dolls*
17. **Musical Producers**: Cy Feuer and Ernest H. Martin for *Guys and Dolls*
18. **Conductor and Musical Director**: Lehman Engel for *The Consul*
19. **Scenic Designer**: Boris Aronson for *The Rose Tattoo*, *The Country Girl*, *Season in the Sun*
20. **Costumes**: Miles White for *Bless You All*
21. **Stage Technician**: Richard Raven for *The Autumn Garden*
22. **Special Award**: Ruth Green

1952 Tony Awards

1. **Play**: *The Fourposter* by Jan de Hartog
2. **Dramatic Actor**: Jose Ferrer in *The Shrike*
3. **Supporting or Featured Dramatic Actor**: John Cromwell in *Point of No Return*
4. **Dramatic Actress**: Julie Harris in *I Am a Camera*
5. **Supporting or Featured Dramatic Actress**: Marian Winters in *I Am a Camera*
6. **Director**: Jose Ferrer for *The Shrike*, *Stalag 17* and *The Fourposter*
7. **Musical**: *The King & I* book and lyrics by Oscar Hammerstein II, music by Richard Rodgers
8. **Musical Actor**: Phil Silvers in *Top Banana*
9. **Supporting or Featured Musical Actor**: Yul Brynner in *The King & I*
10. **Musical Actress**: Gertrude Lawrence in *The King & I*
11. **Supporting or Featured Musical Actress**: Helen Gallagher in *Pal Joey*
12. **Conductor and Musical Director**: Max Meth for *Pal Joey*
13. **Choreographer**: Robert Alton for *Pal Joey*
14. **Scenic Designer**: Jo Mielziner for *The King & I*
15. **Costumes**: Irene Sharaff for *The King & I*

Tony Awards 1953

16. **Stage Technician**: Peter Feller, master carpenter for *Call Me Madam*
17. **Special Awards**: Edward Kook; Judy Garland; Charles Boyer

1953 Tony Awards

1. **Play**: *The Crucible*
2. **Dramatic Actor**: Tom Ewell in *The Seven Year Itch*
3. **Supporting or Featured Dramatic Actor**: John Williams in *Dial M for Murder*
4. **Dramatic Actress**: Shirley Booth in *Time of the Cuckoo*
5. **Supporting or Featured Dramatic Actress**: Beatrice Straight in *The Crucible*
6. **Dramatic Author**: Arthur Miller for *The Crucible*
7. **Director**: Joshua Logan for *Picnic*
8. **Dramatic Producer**: Kermit Bloomgarden for *The Crucible*
9. **Musical**: *Wonderful Town* lyrics by Betty Comden and Adolph Green
10. **Musical Actor**: Thomas Mitchell in *Hazel Flagg*
11. **Supporting or Featured Musical Actor**: Hiram Sherman in *Two's Company*
12. **Musical Actress**: Rosalind Russell in *Wonderful Town*
13. **Supporting or Featured Musical Actress**: Sheila Bond in *Wish You Were Here*
14. **Musical Authors**: Joseph Fields and Jerome Chodorov for *Wonderful Town*
15. **Composer**: Leonard Bernstein for *Wonderful Town*
16. **Choreographer**: Donald Saddler for *Wonderful Town*
17. **Conductor and Musical Director**: Lehman Engel for *Wonderful Town* and the Gilbert and Sullivan season
18. **Musical Producer**: Robert Fryer for *Wonderful Town*
19. **Scenic Designer**: Raoul Pene du Bois for *Wonderful Town*
20. **Costume Designer**: Miles White for *Hazel Flagg*
21. **Stage Technician**: Abe Kurnit for *Wish You Were Here*
22. **Special Awards**: Beatrice Lillie; Danny Kaye; Equity Community Theatre

1954 Tony Awards

1. **Play**: *The Teahouse of the August Moon*
2. **Dramatic Actor**: David Wayne in *The Teahouse of the August Moon*
3. **Supporting or Featured Dramatic Actor**: John Kerr in *Tea and Sympathy*
4. **Dramatic Actress**: Audrey Hepburn in *Ondine*
5. **Supporting or Featured Dramatic Actress**: Jo Van Fleet in *The Trip to Bountiful*
6. **Dramatic Author**: John Patrick for *The Teahouse of the August Moon*
7. **Director**: Alfred Lunt for *Ondine*
8. **Dramatic Producer**: Maurice Evans and George Shaefer for *The Teahouse of the August Moon*
9. **Musical**: *Kismet* music adapted with lyrics by Robert Wright and George Forrest
10. **Musical Actor**: Alfred Drake in *Kismet*
11. **Supporting or Featured Musical Actor**: Harry Belafonte in *John Murray Anderson's Almanac*
12. **Musical Actress**: Dolores Gray in *Carnival in Flanders*
13. **Supporting or Featured Musical Actress**: Gwen Verdon in *Can-Can*
14. **Musical Authors**: Charles Lederer and Luthur Davis for *Kismet*
15. **Composer**: Alexander Borodin for *Kismet*
16. **Choreographer**: Michael Kidd for *Can-Can*
17. **Musical Conductor**: Louis Adrian for *Kismet*
18. **Musical Producer**: Charles Lederer for *Kismet*
19. **Scenic Designer**: Peter Larkin for *Ondine* and *The Teahouse of the August Moon*
20. **Costume Designer**: Richard Whorf for *Ondine*
21. **Stage Technician**: John Davis for *Picnic*

1955 Tony Awards

1. **Play**: *The Desperate Hours*
2. **Dramatic Author**: Alfred Lunt for *Quadrille*
3. **Supporting or Featured Drama-

tic **Actor**: Francis L. Sullivan in *Witness for the Prosecution*
4. **Dramatic Actress**: Nancy Kelly in *The Bad Seed*
5. **Supporting or Featured Dramatic Actress**: Patricia Jessel in *Witness for the Prosecution*
6. **Dramatic Author**: Joseph Hayes for *The Desperate Hours*
7. **Director**: Robert Montgomery for *The Desperate Hours*
8. **Dramatic Producers**: Howard Erskine and Joseph Hayes for *The Desperate Hours*
9. **Musical**: *The Pajama Game*
10. **Musical Actor**: Walter Slezak in *Fanny*
11. **Supporting or Featured Musical Actor**: Cyril Ritchard in *Peter Pan*
12. **Musical Actress**: Mary Martin in *Peter Pan*
13. **Supporting or Featured Musical Actress**: Carol Haney in *The Pajama Game*
14. **Musical Authors**: George Abbott and Richard Bissell for *The Pajama Game*
15. **Composer and Lyricist**: Richard Adler and Jerry Ross for *The Pajama Game*
16. **Choreographer**: Bob Fosse for *The Pajama Game*
17. **Conductor and Musical Director**: Thomas Schippers for *The Saint of Bleecker Street*
18. **Musical Producers**: Frederick Brisson, Robert Griffith and Harold S. Prince for *The Pajama Game*
19. **Scenic Designer**: Oliver Messel for *House of Flowers*
20. **Costume Designer**: Cecil Beaton for *Quadrille*
21. **Stage Technician**: Richard Rodda for *Peter Pan*
22. **Special Award**: Proscenium Productions

1956 Tony Awards

1. **Play**: *The Diary of Anne Frank*
2. **Dramatic Actor**: Paul Muni in *Inherit the Wind*
3. **Supporting or Featured Dramatic Actor**: Ed Begley in *Inherit the Wind*
4. **Dramatic Actress**: Julie Harris in *The Lark*

5. **Supporting or Featured Dramatic Actress**: Una Merkel in *The Ponder Heart*
6. **Dramatic Authors**: Francis Goodrich and Albert Hackett for *The Diary of Anne Frank*
7. **Director**: Tyrone Guthrie for *The Matchmaker, Six Characters in Search of an Author* and *Tamburlaine the Great*
8. **Dramatic Producer**: Kermit Bloomgarden for *The Diary of Anne Frank*
9. **Musical**: *Damn Yankees*
10. **Musical Actor**: Ray Walston in *Damn Yankees*
11. **Supporting or Featured Musical Actor**: Russ Brown in *Damn Yankees*
12. **Musical Actress**: Gwen Verdon in *Damn Yankees*
13. **Supporting or Featured Musical Actress**: Lotte Lenya in *The Threepenny Opera*
14. **Musical Authors**: George Abbott and Douglas Wallop for *Damn Yankees*
15. **Composer and Lyricist**: Richard Adler and Jerry Ross for *Damn Yankees*
16. **Conductor and Musical Director**: Hal Hastings for *Damn Yankees*
17. **Choreographer**: Bob Fosse for *Damn Yankees*
18. **Musical Producers**: Frederick Brisson, Robert Griffith and Harold S. Prince in association with Albert B. Taylor for *Damn Yankees*
19. **Scenic Designer**: Peter Larkin for *Inherit the Wind* and *No Time for Sergeants*
20. **Costume Designer**: Alvin Colt for *Pipe Dream, The Lark* and *Phoenix '55*
21. **Stage Technician**: Harry Green, electrician and sound man for *Middle of the Night* and *Damn Yankees*
22. **Special Awards**: *The Threepenny Opera*; The Theatre Collection of the New York Public Library

1957 Tony Awards

1. **Play**: *Long Day's Journey Into Night*
2. **Dramatic Actor**: Fredric March in *Long Day's Journey Into Night*
3. **Supporting or Featured Dramatic Actor**: Frank Conroy in *The Potting Shed*
4. **Dramatic Actress**: Margaret Leighton in *Separate Tables*
5. **Supporting or Featured Drama-

tic **Actress**: Peggy Cass in *Auntie Mame*
6. **Dramatic Author**: Eugene O'Neill for *Long Day's Journey Into Night*
7. **Dramatic Producers**: Leigh Connell, Theodore Mann and Jose Quintero for *Long Day's Journey Into Night*
8. **Musical**: *My Fair Lady*
9. **Musical Actor**: Rex Harrison in *My Fair Lady*
10. **Supporting or Featured Musical Actor**: Sidney Chaplin in *Bells Are Ringing*
11. **Musical Actress**: Judy Holiday in *Bells Are Ringing*
12. **Supporting or Featured Musical Actress**: Edith Adams in *Li'l Abner*
13. **Musical Author and Lyricist**: Alan Jay Lerner for *My Fair Lady*
14. **Composer**: Frederick Loewe for *My Fair Lady*
15. **Conductor and Musical Director**: Franz Allers for *My Fair Lady*
16. **Choreographer**: Michael Kidd for *Li'l Abner*
17. **Director**: Moss Hart for *My Fair Lady*
18. **Musical Producer**: Herman Levin for *My Fair Lady*
19. **Scenic Designer**: Oliver Smith for *My Fair Lady, A Clearing in the Woods, A Visit to a Small Planet, Eugenia, Candide* and *Auntie Mame*
20. **Costume Designer**: Cecil Beaton for *My Fair Lady, Little Glass Clock*
21. **Stage Technician**: Howard McDonald, carpenter for *Major Barbara*
22. **Special Awards**: American Shakespeare Festival; Jean-Louis Barrault—French Repertory; Robert Russell Bennett; William Hammerstein; Paul Shyre

6. **Dramatic Author**: Dore Schary for *Sunrise at Campobello*
7. **Dramatic Director**: Vincent J. Donehue for *Sunrise at Campobello*
8. **Dramatic Producers**: Lawrence Langner, Theresa Helburn, Armina Marshall and Dore Schary for *Sunrise at Campobello*
9. **Musical**: *The Music Man*
10. **Musical Actor**: Robert Preston in *The Music Man*
11. **Supporting or Featured Musical Actor**: David Burns in *The Music Man*
12. **Musical Actresses**: Thelma Ritter in *New Girl in Town*; Gwen Verdon in *New Girl in Town*
13. **Supporting or Featured Musical Actress**: Barbara Cook in *The Music Man*
14. **Musical Author**: Meredith Willson and Franklin Lacey for *The Music Man*
15. **Composer and Lyricist**: Meredith Willson for *The Music Man*
16. **Conductor and Musical Director**: Herbert Greene for *The Music Man*
17. **Choreographer**: Jerome Robbins for *West Side Story*
18. **Musical Producers**: Kermit Bloomgarden, Herbert Greene and Frank Productions for *The Music Man*
19. **Scenic Designer**: Oliver Smith for *West Side Story*
20. **Costume Designer**: Motley for *The First Gentleman*
21. **Stage Technician**: Harry Romar for *Time Remembered*
22. **Special Awards**: New York Shakespeare Festival; Mrs. Martin Beck

1959 Tony Awards

1. **Play**: *J.B.*
2. **Dramatic Actor**: Jason Robards, Jr. in *The Disenchanted*
3. **Supporting or Featured Dramatic Actor**: Charlie Ruggles in *The Pleasure of His Company*
4. **Dramatic Actress**: Gertrude Berg in *A Majority of One*
5. **Supporting or Featured Dramatic Actress**: Julie Newmar in *The Marriage-Go-Round*
6. **Dramatic Author**: Archibald MacLeish for *J.B.*
7. **Director**: Elia Kazan for *J.B.*

1958 Tony Awards

1. **Play**: *Sunrise at Campobello*
2. **Dramatic Actor**: Ralph Bellamy in *Sunrise at Campobello*
3. **Supporting or Featured Dramatic Actor**: Henry Jones in *Sunrise at Campobello*
4. **Dramatic Actress**: Helen Hayes in *Time Remembered*
5. **Supporting or Featured Dramatic Actress**: Anne Bancroft in *Two for the Seesaw*

Tony Awards 1960 T

8. **Dramatic Producer**: Alfred de Liagre, Jr. for *J.B.*
9. **Musical**: *Redhead* lyrics by Dorothy Fields
10. **Musical Actor**: Richard Kiley in *Redhead*
11. **Supporting or Featured Musical Actors**: Russell Nype in *Goldilocks*; Cast of *La Plume de Ma Tante*
12. **Musical Actress**: Gwen Verdon in *Redhead*
13. **Supporting or Featured Musical Actresses**: Pat Stanley in *Goldilocks*; Cast of *La Plume de Ma Tante*
14. **Musical Authors**: Herbert and Dorothy Fields, Sidney Sheldon and David Shaw for *Redhead*
15. **Composer**: Albert Hague for *Redhead*
16. **Conductor and Musical Director**: Salvatore Dell'Isola for *Flower Drum Song*
17. **Choreographer**: Bob Fosse for *Redhead*
18. **Musical Producers**: Robert Fryer and Lawrence Carr for *Redhead*
19. **Scenic Designer**: Donald Oenslager in *A Majority of One*
20. **Costume Designer**: Rouben Ter-Arutunian for *Redhead*
21. **Stage Technician**: Sam Knapp for *The Music Man*
22. **Special Awards**: John Gielgud; Howard Lindsay and Russel Crouse

1960 Tony Awards

1. **Play**: *The Miracle Worker*
2. **Dramatic Actor**: Melvyn Douglas in *The Best Man*
3. **Supporting or Featured Dramatic Actor**: Roddy McDowall in *The Fighting Cock*
4. **Dramatic Actress**: Anne Bancroft in *The Miracle Worker*
5. **Supporting or Featured Dramatic Actress**: Anne Revere in *Toys in the Attic*
6. **Dramatic Author**: William Gibson for *The Miracle Worker*
7. **Dramatic Director**: Arthur Penn for *The Miracle Worker*
8. **Dramatic Producer**: Fred Coe for *The Miracle Worker*
9. **Musicals**: *Fiorello!* lyrics by Sheldon Harnick; *The Sound of Music* lyrics by Oscar Hammerstein II
10. **Musical Actor**: Jackie Gleason in *Take Me Along*
11. **Supporting or Featured Musical Actor**: Tom Bosley in *Fiorello!*
12. **Musical Actress**: Mary Martin in *The Sound of Music*
13. **Supporting or Featured Musical Actress**: Patricia Neway in *The Sound of Music*
14. **Musical Authors**: Jerome Weidman and George Abbot for *Fiorello!*; Howard Lindsay and Russel Crouse for *The Sound of Music*
15. **Musical Director**: George Abbot for *Fiorello!*
16. **Composers**: Richard Rodgers for *The Sound of Music*; Jerry Bock for *Fiorello!*
17. **Conductor and Musical Director**: Frederick Dvnoch for *The Sound of Music*
18. **Choreographer**: Michael Kidd for *Destry Rides Again*
19. **Musical Producers**: Robert E. Griffith and Harold S. Prince for *Fiorello!*; Leland Hayward, Richard Halliday and Rodgers and Hammerstein for *The Sound of Music*
20. **Dramatic Scenic Designer**: Howard Bay for *Toys in the Attic*
21. **Scenic Designer**: Oliver Smith for *The Sound of Music*
22. **Costume Designer**: Cecil Beaton for *Saratoga*
23. **Stage Technician**: John Walters, chief carpenter for *The Miracle Worker*
24. **Special Awards**: John D. Rockefeller III; James Thurber and Burgess Meredith for *A Thurber Carnival*

1961 Tony Awards

1. **Play**: *Becket* translated by Lucienne Hill
2. **Dramatic Actor**: Zero Mostel in *Rhinoceros*
3. **Supporting or Featured Dramatic Actor**: Martin Gabel in *Big Fish, Little Fish*
4. **Dramatic Actress**: Joan Plowright in *A Taste of Honey*
5. **Supporting or Featured Dramatic Actress**: Colleen Dewhurst in *All the Way Home*

6. **Dramatic Author**: Jean Anouilh for *Becket*
7. **Dramatic Director**: Sir John Gielgud for *Big Fish, Little Fish*
8. **Dramatic Producer**: David Merrick for *Becket*
9. **Musical**: *Bye, Bye Birdie* music by Charles Strouse, lyrics by Lee Adams
10. **Musical Actor**: Richard Burton in *Camelot*
11. **Supporting or Featured Musical Actor**: Dick Van Dyke in *Bye, Bye Birdie*
12. **Musical Actress**: Elizabeth Seal in *Irma la Douce*
13. **Supporting or Featured Musical Actresses**: Tammy Grimes in *The Unsinkable Molly Brown*
14. **Musical Author**: Michael Stewart for *Bye, Bye Birdie*
15. **Musical Director**: Gower Champion for *Bye, Bye Birdie*
16. **Conductor and Musical Director**: Franz Allers for *Camelot*
17. **Choreographer**: Gower Champion for *Bye, Bye Birdie*
18. **Musical Producer**: Edward Padula in association with L. Slade Brown for *Bye, Bye Birdie*
19. **Musical Scenic Designer**: Oliver Smith for *Camelot*
20. **Dramatic Scenic Designer**: Oliver Smith for *Becket*
21. **Dramatic Costume Designer**: Motley for *Becket*
22. **Musical Costume Designer**: Adrian and Tony Duquette for *Camelot*
23. **Stage Technician**: Teddy Van Bemmel for *Becket*
24. **Special Awards**: David Merrick; The Theatre Guild

1962 Tony Awards

1. **Play**: *A Man for All Seasons*
2. **Dramatic Actor**: Paul Scofield in *A Man for All Seasons*
3. **Supporting or Featured Dramatic Actor**: Walter Matthau in *A Shot in the Dark*
4. **Dramatic Actress**: Margaret Leighton in *Night of the Iguana*
5. **Supporting or Featured Dramatic Actress**: Elizabeth Ashley in *Take Her, She's Mine*
6. **Dramatic Author**: Robert Bolt for *A Man for All Seasons*
7. **Dramatic Director**: Noel Willman for *A Man for All Seasons*
8. **Dramatic Producer**: Robert Whitehead and Roger L. Stevens for *A Man for All Seasons*
9. **Musical**: *How to Succeed in Business Without Really Trying* music and lyrics by Frank Loesser
10. **Musical Actor**: Robert Morse in *How to Succeed in Business Without Really Trying*
11. **Supporting or Featured Musical Actor**: Charles Nelson Reilly in *How to Succeed in Business Without Really Trying*
12. **Musical Actresses**: Anna Maria Alberghetti in *Carnival*; Diahann Carroll in *No Strings*
13. **Supporting or Featured Musical Actresses**: Phyllis Newman in *Subways Are for Sleeping*
14. **Musical Authors**: Abe Burrows, Jack Weinstock and Willie Gilbert for *How to Succeed in Business Without Really Trying*
15. **Musical Director**: Abe Burrows for *How to Succeed in Business Without Really Trying*
16. **Composer**: Richard Rodgers for *No Strings*
17. **Choreographers**: Agnes de Mille for *Kwamina*; Joe Layton for *No Strings*
18. **Conductor and Musical Director**: Elliot Lawrence for *How to Succeed in Business Without Really Trying*
19. **Musical Producers**: Cy Feuer and Ernest Martin for *How to Succeed in Business Without Really Trying*
20. **Scenic Designer**: Will Steven Armstrong for *Carnival*
21. **Costume Designer**: Lucinda Ballard for *The Gay Life*
22. **Stage Technician**: Michael Burns for *A Man for All Seasons*
23. **Special Awards**: Brooks Atkinson; Franco Zeffirelli; Richard Rodgers

1963 Tony Awards

1. **Play**: *Who's Afraid of Virginia Woolf?* by Edward Albee
2. **Dramatic Actor**: Arthur Hill in *Who's Afraid of Virginia Woolf?*

3. **Supporting or Featured Dramatic Actor**: Alan Arkin in *Enter Laughing*
4. **Dramatic Actress**: Uta Hagen in *Who's Afraid of Virginia Woolf?*
5. **Supporting or Featured Dramatic Actress**: Sandy Dennis in *A Thousand Clowns*
6. **Dramatic Director**: Alan Schneider for *Who's Afraid of Virginia Woolf?*
7. **Dramatic Producers**: Theater 1963, Richard Barr and Clinton Wilder for *Who's Afraid of Virginia Woolf?*
8. **Musical**: *A Funny Thing Happened on the Way to the Forum* music and lyrics by Stephen Sondheim
9. **Musical Actor**: Zero Mostel in *A Funny Thing Happened on the Way to the Forum*
10. **Supporting or Featured Musical Actor**: David Burns in *A Funny Thing Happened on the Way to the Forum*
11. **Musical Actress**: Vivien Leigh in *Tovarisch*
12. **Supporting or Featured Musical Actress**: Anna Quayle in *Stop the World—I Want to Get Off*
13. **Musical Authors**: Burt Shevelove and Larry Gelbart for *A Funny Thing Happened on the Way to the Forum*
14. **Composer and Lyricist**: Lionel Bart for *Oliver!*
15. **Conductor and Musical Director**: Donald Pippin for *Oliver!*
16. **Choreographer**: Bob Fosse for *Little Me*
17. **Musical Director**: George Abbott for *A Funny Thing Happened on the Way to the Forum*
18. **Musical Producer**: Harold Prince for *A Funny Thing Happened on the Way to the Forum*
19. **Scenic Designer**: Sean Kenny for *Oliver!*
20. **Costume Designer**: Anthony Powell for *The School for Scandal*
21. **Stage Technicians**: Solly Pernick for *Mr. President*; Milton Smith for *Beyond the Fringe*
22. **Special Awards**: W. McNeil Lowry; Irving Berlin; Alan Bennett; Peter Cook; Dudley Moore; Johnathan Miller

1964 Tony Awards

1. **Play**: *Luther* produced by David Merrick
2. **Dramatic Actor**: Alec Guinness in *Dylan*
3. **Supporting or Featured Dramatic Actor**: Hume Cronyn in *Hamlet*
4. **Dramatic Actress**: Sandy Dennis in *Any Wednesday*
5. **Supporting or Featured Dramatic Actress**: Barbara Loden in *After the Fall*
6. **Dramatic Author**: John Osborne for *Luther*
7. **Dramatic Director**: Mike Nichols for *Barefoot in the Park*
8. **Dramatic Producer**: Herman Shumlin for *The Deputy*
9. **Musical**: *Hello, Dolly!*
10. **Musical Actor**: Bert Lahr in *Foxy*
11. **Supporting or Featured Musical Actor**: Jack Cassidy in *She Loves Me*
12. **Musical Actress**: Carol Channing in *Hello, Dolly!*
13. **Supporting or Featured Musical Actress**: Tessie O'Shea in *The Girl Who Came to Supper*
14. **Musical Author**: Michael Stewart for *Hello, Dolly!*
15. **Musical Director**: Gower Champion for *Hello, Dolly!*
16. **Composer and Lyricist**: Jerry Herman for *Hello, Dolly!*
17. **Conductor and Musical Director**: Shepard Coleman for *Hello, Dolly!*
18. **Choreographer**: Gower Champion for *Hello, Dolly!*
19. **Musical Producer**: David Merrick for *Hello, Dolly!*
20. **Scenic Designer**: Oliver Smith for *Hello, Dolly!*
21. **Costume Designer**: Freddy Wittop for *Hello, Dolly!*
22. **Special Awards**: Eve Le Gallienne

1965 Tony Awards

1. **Play**: *The Subject Was Roses* by Frank Gilroy, produced by Edgar Lansbury
2. **Dramatic Actor**: Walter Matthau in *The Odd Couple*
3. **Supporting or Featured Dramatic Actor**: Jack Albertson in *The Subject was Roses*

T Tony Awards 1966

4. **Dramatic Actress**: Irene Worth in *Tiny Alice*
5. **Supporting or Featured Dramatic Actress**: Alice Ghostley in *The Sign in Sidney Brustein's Window*
6. **Dramatic Author**: Neil Simon for *The Odd Couple*
7. **Dramatic Director**: Mike Nichols for *Luv* and *The Odd Couple*
8. **Dramatic Producer**: Claire Nictern for *Luv*
9. **Musical**: *Fiddler on the Roof*
10. **Musical Actor**: Zero Mostel in *Fiddler on the Roof*
11. **Supporting or Featured Musical Actor**: Victor Spinetti in *Oh, What a Lovely War*
12. **Musical Actress**: Liza Minelli in *Flora, The Red Menace*
13. **Supporting or Featured Musical Actress**: Maria Karnilova in *Fiddler on the Roof*
14. **Musical Author**: Joseph Stein for *Fiddler on the Roof*
15. **Composer and Lyricist**: Jerry Bock and Sheldon Harnick for *Fiddler on the Roof*
16. **Choreographer**: Jerome Robbins for *Fiddler on the Roof*
17. **Musical Director**: Jerome Robbins for *Fiddler on the Roof*
18. **Musical Producer**: Harold Prince for *Fiddler on the Roof*
19. **Scenic Designer**: Oliver Smith for *Baker Street, Luv, The Odd Couple*
20. **Costume Designer**: Patricia Zipprodt for *Fiddler on the Roof*
21. **Special Awards**: Gilbert Miller; Oliver Smith

1966 Tony Awards

1. **Play**: *Marat/Sade* by Peter Weiss, English version by Geoffrey Skelton, produced by the David Merrick Arts Foundation
2. **Dramatic Actor**: Hal Holbrook in *Mark Twain Tonight!*
3. **Supporting or Featured Dramatic Actor**: Patrick Magee in *Marat/Sade*
4. **Dramatic Actress**: Rosemary Harris in *The Lion in Winter*
5. **Supporting or Featured Dramatic Actress**: Zoe Caldwell in *Slapstick Tragedy*
6. **Dramatic Director**: Peter Brook for *Marat/Sade*
7. **Musical**: *Man of La Mancha* book by Dale Wasserman, produced by Albert W. Selden and Hal James
8. **Musical Actor**: Richard Kiley in *Man of La Mancha*
9. **Supporting or Featured Musical Actor**: Frankie Michaels in *Mame*
10. **Musical Actress**: Angela Lansbury in *Mame*
11. **Supporting or Featured Musical Actress**: Beatrice Arthur in *Mame*
12. **Composer and Lyricist**: Mitch Leigh and Joe Darion for *Man of La Mancha*
13. **Choreographer**: Bob Fosse for *Sweet Charity*
14. **Musical Director**: Albert Marre for *Man of La Mancha*
15. **Scenic Designer**: Howard Bay for *Man of La Mancha*
16. **Costume Designer**: Gunilla Palmstierna-Weiss for *Marat/Sade*
17. **Special Award**: Helen Menken

1967 Tony Awards

1. **Play**: *The Homecoming* by Harold Pinter, produced by Alexander H. Cohen
2. **Dramatic Actor**: Paul Rogers in *The Homecoming*
3. **Supporting or Featured Dramatic Actor**: Ian Holm in *The Homecoming*
4. **Dramatic Actress**: Beryl Reid in *The Killing of Sister George*
5. **Supporting or Featured Dramatic Actress**: Marian Seldes in *A Delicate Balance*
6. **Dramatic Director**: Peter Hall for *The Homecoming*
7. **Musical**: *Cabaret* book by Joe Masteroff, produced by Harold Prince in association with Ruth Mitchell
8. **Musical Actor**: Robert Preston in *I Do! I Do!*
9. **Supporting or Featured Musical Actor**: Joel Grey in *Cabaret*
10. **Musical Actress**: Barbara Harris in *The Apple Tree*
11. **Supporting or Featured Musical Actress**: Peg Murray in *Cabaret*
12. **Composer and Lyricist**: John Kander and Fred Ebb for *Cabaret*

13. **Choreographer**: Ronald Field for *Cabaret*
14. **Musical Director**: Harold Prince for *Cabaret*
15. **Scenic Designer**: Boris Aronson for *Cabaret*
16. **Costume Designer**: Patricia Zipprodt for *Cabaret*

1968 Tony Awards

1. **Play**: *Rosenkrantz and Guildenstern Are Dead* by Tom Stoppard
2. **Dramatic Actor**: Martin Balsam in *You Know I Can't Hear You When the Water's Running*
3. **Supporting or Featured Dramatic Actor**: James Patterson in *The Birthday Party*
4. **Dramatic Actress**: Zoe Caldwell in *The Prime of Miss Jean Brodie*
5. **Supporting or Featured Dramatic Actress**: Zena Walker in *Joe Egg*
6. **Dramatic Director**: Mike Nichols for *Plaza Suite*
7. **Dramatic Producer**: David Merrick Arts Foundation for *Rosenkrantz and Guildenstern Are Dead*
8. **Musical**: *Hallelujah, Baby!* book by Arthur Laurents
9. **Musical Actor**: Robert Goulet in *The Happy Time*
10. **Supporting or Featured Musical Actor**: Hiram Sherman in *How Now, Dow Jones*
11. **Musical Actresses**: Patricia Routledge in *Darling of the Day*; Leslie Uggams in *Hallelujah, Baby!*
12. **Supporting or Featured Musical Actress**: Lilian Hayman in *Hallelujah, Baby!*
13. **Composer and Lyricist**: Jule Styne, Betty Comden and Adolph Green for *Hallelujah, Baby!*
14. **Choreographer**: Gower Champion for *The Happy Time*
15. **Musical Director**: Gower Champion for *The Happy Time*
16. **Musical Producer**: Albert Selden, Hal James, Jane C. Nusbaum and Harry Rigby for *Hallelujah, Baby!*
17. **Scenic Designer**: Desmond Heeley for *Rosenkrantz and Guildenstern Are Dead*
18. **Costume Designer**: Desmond Heeley for *Rosenkrantz and Guildenstern Are Dead*
19. **Special Awards**: Audrey Hepburn; Carol Channing; Pearl Bailey; David Merrick; Maurice Chevalier; APA-Phoenix Theatre; Marlene Dietrick

1969 Tony Awards

1. **Play**: *The Great White Hope* by Howard Sackler, produced by Herman Levin
2. **Dramatic Actor**: James Earl Jones in *The Great White Hope*
3. **Supporting or Featured Dramatic Actor**: Al Pacino in *Does a Tiger Wear a Necktie?*
4. **Dramatic Actress**: Julie Harris in *Forty Carats*
5. **Supporting or Featured Dramatic Actress**: Jane Alexander in *The Great White Hope*
6. **Dramatic Director**: Peter Dews for *Hadrian VII*
7. **Musical**: *1776* book by Peter Stone, music and lyrics by Sherman Edwards, produced by Stuart Ostrow
8. **Musical Actor**: Jerry Orbach in *Promises, Promises*
9. **Supporting or Featured Musical Actor**: Ronald Holgate in *1776*
10. **Musical Actress**: Angela Lansbury in *Dear World*
11. **Supporting or Featured Musical Actress**: Marian Mercer in *Promises, Promises*
12. **Choreographer**: Joe Layton for *George M!*
13. **Musical Director**: Peter Hunt for *1776*
14. **Costume Designer**: Louden Sainthill for *Canterbury Tales*
15. **Scenic Designer**: Boris Aronson for *Zorba*
16. **Special Awards**: The National Theatre Company of Great Britain; The Negro Ensemble Company; Rex Harrison; Leonard Bernstein; Carol Burnett

1970 Tony Awards

1. **Play**: *Borstal Boy* by Frank McMahon, produced by Michael McAloney and Burton C. Kaiser

2. **Dramatic Actor**: Fritz Weaver in *Child's Play*
3. **Supporting or Featured Dramatic Actor**: Ken Howard in *Child's Play*
4. **Dramatic Actress**: Tammy Grimes in *Private Lives*
5. **Supporting or Featured Dramatic Actress**: Blythe Danner in *Butterflies Are Free*
6. **Dramatic Director**: Joseph Hardy for *Child's Play*
7. **Musical**: *Applause* book by Betty Comden and Adolph Green, music by Charles Strouse, lyrics by Lee Adams, produced by Joseph Kipness and Lawrence Kasha
8. **Musical Actor**: Cleavon Little in *Purlie*
9. **Supporting or Featured Musical Actor**: Rene Auberjonois in *Coco*
10. **Musical Actress**: Lauren Bacall in *Applause*
11. **Supporting or Featured Musical Actress**: Melba Moore in *Purlie*
12. **Choreographer**: Ron Field for *Applause*
13. **Musical Director**: Ron Field for *Applause*
14. **Scenic Designer**: Jo Mielziner for *Child's Play*
15. **Lighting Director**: Jo Mielziner for *Child's Play*
16. **Costume Designer**: Cecil Beaton for *Coco*
17. **Special Awards**: Noel Coward; Alfred Lunt and Lynn Fontanne; New York Shakespeare Festival; Barbra Streisand

1971 Tony Awards

1. **Play**: *Sleuth* by Anthony Schaffer
2. **Dramatic Actor**: Brian Bedford in *The School for Wives*
3. **Supporting or Featured Dramatic Actor**: Paul Sand in *Story Theatre*
4. **Dramatic Actress**: Maureen Stapleton in *Gingerbread Lady*
5. **Supporting or Featured Dramatic Actress**: Rae Allen in *And Miss Reardon Drinks a Little*
6. **Dramatic Director**: Peter Brook for *Midsummer Night's Dream*
7. **Dramatic Producer**: Helen Bonfils, Morton Gottleib and Michael White for *Sleuth*
8. **Musical**: *Company*
9. **Musical Actor**: Hal Linden in *The Rothschilds*
10. **Supporting or Featured Musical Actor**: Keene Curtis in *The Rothschilds*
11. **Musical Actress**: Helen Gallagher in *No, No, Nannette*
12. **Supporting or Featured Musical Actress**: Patsy Kelly in *No, No, Nannette*
13. **Musical Author**: George Furth for *Company*
14. **Composer and Lyricist**: Stephen Sondheim for *Company*
15. **Choreographer**: Donald Saddler for *No, No, Nannette*
16. **Scenic Designer**: Boris Aronson for *Company*
17. **Lighting Director**: H.R. Poindexter for *Story Theatre*
18. **Costume Designer**: Raoul Pene Du Bois for *No, No, Nannette*
19. **Musical Director**: Harold Prince for *Company*
20. **Musical Producer**: Harold Prince for *Company*
21. **Special Awards**: Elliot Norton; Ingram Ash; Playbill; Roger L. Stevens

1972 Tony Awards

1. **Play**: *Sticks and Bones* by David Rabe produced by the New York Shakespeare Festival—Joseph Papp
2. **Dramatic Actor**: Cliff Gorman in *Lenny*
3. **Supporting or Featured Dramatic Actor**: Vincent Gardenia in *The Prisoner of Second Avenue*
4. **Dramatic Actress**: Sada Thompson in *Twigs*
5. **Supporting or Featured Dramatic Actress**: Elizabeth Wilson in *Sticks and Bones*
6. **Dramatic Director**: Mike Nichols for *The Prisoner of Second Avenue*
7. **Musical**: *Two Gentlemen of Verona* produced by the New York Shakespeare Festival—Joseph Papp
8. **Musical Actor**: Phil Silvers in *A Funny Thing Happened on the Way to the Forum*
9. **Supporting or Featured Musical**

Tony Awards 1973

Actor: Larry Blyden in *A Funny Thing Happened on the Way to the Forum*
10. **Musical Actress**: Alexis Smith in *Follies*
11. **Supporting or Featured Musical Actress**: Linda Hopkins in *Inner City*
12. **Musical Author**: John Guare and Mel Shapiro for *Two Gentlemen of Verona*
13. **Composer and Lyricist**: Stephen Sondheim for *Follies*
14. **Choreographer**: Michael Bennett for *Follies*
15. **Musical Director**: Harold Prince and Michael Bennett for *Follies*
16. **Scenic Designer**: Boris Aronson for *Follies*
17. **Lighting Director**: Tharon Musser for *Follies*
18. **Costume Designer**: Florence Klotz for *Follies*
19. **Special Awards**: The Theatre Guild-American Theatre Society; Richard Rodgers; *Fiddler on the Roof*; Ethel Merman

1973 Tony Awards

1. **Play**: *That Championship Season* by Jason Miller produced by the New York Shakespeare Festival—Joseph Papp
2. **Dramatic Actor**: Alan Bates in *Butley*
3. **Supporting or Featured Dramatic Actor**: John Lithgow in *The Changing Room*
4. **Dramatic Actress**: Julie Harris in *The Last of Mrs. Lincoln*
5. **Supporting or Featured Dramatic Actress**: Leora Dana in *The Last of Mrs. Lincoln*
6. **Dramatic Director**: A.J. Antoon for *That Championship Season*
7. **Musical**: *A Little Night Music* produced by Harold Prince
8. **Musical Actor**: Ben Vereen in *Pippin*
9. **Supporting or Featured Musical Actor**: George S. Irving in *Irene*
10. **Musical Actress**: Glynis Johns in *A Little Night Music*
11. **Supporting or Featured Musical Actress**: Patricia Elliot in *A Little Night Music*
12. **Musical Author**: Hugh Wheeler for *A Little Night Music*
13. **Composer and Lyricist**: Stephen Sondheim for *A Little Night Music*
14. **Choreographer**: Bob Fosse for *Pippin*
15. **Musical Director**: Bob Fosse for *Pippin*
16. **Scenic Designer**: Tony Walton for *Pippin*
17. **Lighting Designer**: Jules Fisher for *Pippin*
18. **Costume Designer**: Florence Klotz for *A Little Night Music*
19. **Special Awards**: John Lindsay; Actors' Fund of America; Shubert Organization

1974 Tony Awards

1. **Play**: *The River Niger* by Joseph A. Walker, produced by the Negro Ensemble Company, Inc.
2. **Dramatic Actor**: Michael Moriarty in *Find Your Way Home*
3. **Supporting or Featured Dramatic Actor**: Ed Flanders in *A Moon for the Misbegotten*
4. **Dramatic Actress**: Coleen Dewhurst in *A Moon for the Misbegotten*
5. **Supporting or Featured Dramatic Actress**: Frances Sternhagen in *The Good Doctor*
6. **Dramatic Director**: Jose Quintero for *A Moon for the Misbegotten*
7. **Musical**: *Raisin* book by Robert Nemiroff and Charlotte Zaltzberg, music by Judd Woldin, lyrics by Robert Brittan, produced by Robert Nemiroff
8. **Musical Actor**: Christopher Plummer in *Cyrano*
9. **Supporting or Featured Musical Actor**: Tommy Tune in *Seesaw*
10. **Musical Actress**: Virginia Capers in *Raisin*
11. **Supporting or Featured Musical Actress**: Janie Sell in *Over Here!*
12. **Musical Author**: Hugh Wheeler for *Candide*
13. **Composer and Lyricist**: Frederick Loewe and Alan Jay Lerner for *Gigi*
14. **Choreographer**: Michael Bennett for *Seesaw*
15. **Musical Director**: Harold Prince for *Candide*

16. **Scenic Designer**: Franne and Eugene Lee for *Candide*
17. **Lighting Director**: Jules Fisher for *Ulysses in Nighttown*
18. **Costume Designer**: Franne Lee for *Candide*
19. **Special Awards**: Liza Minnelli; Bette Midler; Peter Cook and Dudley Moore in *Good Evening*; *A Moon for the Misbegotten*; *Candide*; Actors' Equity Association; Theatre Development Fund; John F. Wharton; Harold Friedlander

1975 Tony Awards

1. **Play**: *Equus* by Peter Shaffer, produced by Kermit Bloomgarden and Doris Cole Abrahams
2. **Dramatic Actors**: John Kani and Winston Ntshona in *Sizwe Banzi Is Dead* and *The Island*
3. **Supporting or Featured Dramatic Actor**: Frank Langella in *Seascape*
4. **Dramatic Actress**: Ellen Burstyn in *Same Time, Next Year*
5. **Supporting or Featured Dramatic Actress**: Rita Moreno in *The Ritz*
6. **Dramatic Director**: John Dexter for *Equus*
7. **Musical**: *The Wiz* book by William F. Brown, produced by Ken Harper
8. **Musical Actor**: John Cullum in *Shenandoah*
9. **Supporting or Featured Musical Actor**: Ted Ross in *The Wiz*
10. **Musical Actress**: Angela Lansbury in *Gypsy*
11. **Supporting or Featured Musical Actress**: Dee Dee Bridgewater in *The Wiz*
12. **Composer and Lyricist**: Charlie Smalls for *The Wiz*
13. **Choreographer**: George Faison for *The Wiz*
14. **Musical Director**: Geoffrey Holder for *The Wiz*
15. **Scenic Designer**: Carl Toms for *Sherlock Holmes*
16. **Lighting Director**: Neil Patrick Jampolis for *Sherlock Holmes*
17. **Costume Designer**: Geoffrey Holder for *The Wiz*
18. **Special Awards**: Neil Simon; Al Hirschfield

1976 Tony Awards

1. **Play**: *Travesties* by Tom Stoppard, produced by David Merrick, Doris Cole Abrahams and Barry Fredrick in association with S. Spencer Davids and Eddie Kulukundis
2. **Dramatic Actor**: John Wood in *Travesties*
3. **Supporting or Featured Dramatic Actor**: Edward Herrmann in *Mrs. Warren's Profession*
4. **Dramatic Actress**: Irene Worth in *Sweet Bird of Youth*
5. **Supporting or Featured Dramatic Actress**: Shirley Knight in *Kennedy's Children*
6. **Dramatic Director**: Ellis Rabb for *The Royal Family*
7. **Musical**: *A Chorus Line* produced by the New York Shakespeare Festival—Joseph Papp
8. **Musical Actor**: George Rose in *My Fair Lady*
9. **Supporting or Featured Musical Actor**: Sammy Williams in *A Chorus Line*
10. **Musical Actress**: Donna McKechnie in *A Chorus Line*
11. **Supporting or Featured Musical Actress**: Carole Bishop in *A Chorus Line*
12. **Musical Author**: James Kirkwood and Nicholas Dante for *A Chorus Line*
13. **Composer and Lyricist**: Marvin Hamlisch and Edward Kleban for *A Chorus Line*
14. **Choreographers**: Michael Bennett and Bob Avian for *A Chorus Line*
15. **Musical Director**: Michael Bennett for *A Chorus Line*
16. **Scenic Designer**: Boris Aronson for *Pacific Overtures*
17. **Lighting Director**: Tharon Musser for *A Chorus Line*
18. **Costume Designer**: Florence Klotz for *Pacific Overtures*
19. **Special Awards**: Mathilde Pincus for *Circle in the Square*; Thomas H. Fitzgerald for *The Arena Stage*

1977 Tony Awards

1. **Play**: *The Shadow Box* by Michael Christofer, produced by Allan Francis, Ken Marsolais, Lester Osterman and Leonard Soloway

2. **Dramatic Actor**: Al Pacino in *The Basic Training of Pavlo Hummel*
3. **Supporting or Featured Dramatic Actor**: Johnathon Pryce in *Comedians*
4. **Dramatic Actress**: Julie Harris in *The Belle of Amherst*
5. **Supporting or Featured Dramatic Actress**: Trazana Beverly in *For Colored Girls Who Have Considered Suicide/When the Rainbow is Enuf*
6. **Dramatic Director**: Gordon Davidson for *The Shadow Box*
7. **Musical**: *Annie* produced by Lewis Allen, Mike Nichols, Irwin Meyer and Steven R. Friedman
8. **Musical Actor**: Bary Bostwick in *The Robber Bridegroom*
9. **Supporting or Featured Musical Actor**: Lenny Baker in *I Love My Wife*
10. **Musical Actress**: Dorothy Loudon in *Annie*
11. **Supporting or Featured Musical Actress**: Delores Hall in *Your Arm's Too Short to Box with God*
12. **Musical Book**: *Annie* by Thomas Meehan
13. **Composer and Lyricist**: Charles Strouse and Martin Charnin for *Annie*
14. **Choreographer**: Peter Gennaro for *Annie*
15. **Musical Director**: Gene Saks for *I Love My Wife*
16. **Scenic Designer**: David Mitchell for *Annie*
17. **Lighting Director**: Jennifer Tipton for *The Cherry Orchard*
18. **Costume Designers**: Theoni V. Aldredge for *Annie*; Santo Loquasto for *The Cherry Orchard*
19. **Most Innovative Production of a Revival**: *Porgy and Bess* produced by Sherwin M. Goldman and the Houston Grand Opera
20. **Special Awards**: National Theatre for the Deaf; Diana Ross; Lily Tomlin; Barry Manilow; Equity Library Theatre, New York; Mark Taper Forum Theatre, Los Angeles

1978 Tony Awards

1. **Play**: *Da* by Hugh Leonard, produced by Lester Osterman, Marilyn Strauss and Marc Howard

2. **Dramatic Actor**: Barnard Hughes in *Da*
3. **Supporting or Featured Dramatic Actor**: Lester Rawlins in *Da*
4. **Dramatic Actress**: Jessica Tandy in *The Gin Game*
5. **Supporting or Featured Dramatic Actress**: Ann Wedgeworth in *Chapter Two*
6. **Dramatic Director**: Melvin Bernhardt for *Da*
7. **Musical**: *Ain't Misbehavin'* produced by Emanuel Azenberg, Dasha Epstein, The Shubert Organization, Jane Gaynor and Ron Dante
8. **Musical Actor**: John Cullum in *On the Twentieth Century*
9. **Supporting or Featured Musical Actor**: Kevin Kline in *On the Twentieth Century*
10. **Musical Actress**: Liza Minnelli in *The Act*
11. **Supporting or Featured Musical Actress**: Nell Carter in *Ain't Misbehavin'*
12. **Composer and Lyricist**: Cy Coleman, Betty Comden and Adolph Green for *On the Twentieth Century*
13. **Musical Book**: *On the Twentieth Century* by Betty Comden and Adolph Green
14. **Choreographer**: Bob Fosse for *Dancin'*
15. **Musical Director**: Richard Maltby, Jr. for *Ain't Misbehavin'*
16. **Scenic Designer**: Robin Wagner for *On the Twentieth Century*
17. **Lighting Designer**: Jules Fischer for *Dancin'*
18. **Costume Designer**: Edward Gorey for *Dracula*
19. **Most Innovative Production of a Revival**: *Dracula* produced by Jujamcyn Theatre, Elizabeth I. McCann, John Wulp, Victor Lurie, Nelle Nugent and Max Weitzenhoffer
20. **Special Award**: The Long Wharf Theatre

1979 Tony Awards

1. **Play**: *The Elephant Man* by Bernard Pomerance, produced by Richmond Crinkley, Elizabeth I. McCann and Nelle Nugent

T   Tony Awards 1980

2. **Dramatic Actor**: Tom Conti in *Who's Life Is It Anyway?*
3. **Supporting or Featured Dramatic Actor**: Michael Gough in *Bedroom Farce*
4. **Dramatic Actresses**: Constance Cummings in *Wings*; Carole Shelley in *The Elephant Man*
5. **Supporting or Featured Dramatic Actress**: Joan Hickson in *Bedroom Farce*
6. **Dramatic Director**: Jack Hofsiss for *The Elephant Man*
7. **Musical**: *Sweeney Todd* produced by Richard Barr, Charles Woodward, Robert Fryer, Mary Lea Johnson and Martin Richards
8. **Musical Actor**: Len Cariou in *Sweeney Todd*
9. **Supporting or Featured Musical Actor**: Henderson Forsythe in *The Best Little Whorehouse in Texas*
10. **Musical Actress**: Angela Lansbury in *Sweeney Todd*
11. **Supporting or Featured Musical Actress**: Carlin Glynn in *The Best Little Whorehouse in Texas*
12. **Musical Book**: *Sweeney Todd* by Hugh Wheeler
13. **Composer and Lyricist**: Stephen Sondheim for *Sweeney Todd*
14. **Choreographer**: Michael Bennett and Bob Avian for *Ballroom*
15. **Musical Director**: Harold Prince for *Sweeney Todd*
16. **Scenic Designer**: Eugene Lee for *Sweeney Todd*
17. **Lighting Designer**: Roger Morgan for *The Crucifer of Blood*
18. **Costume Designer**: Franne Lee for *Sweeney Todd*
19. **Special Awards**: Henry Fonda; Walter F. Diehl; Eugene O'Neill Memorial Theatre Center; American Conservatory Theatre

1980 Tony Awards

1. **Play**: *Children of a Lesser God* by Mark Medoff
2. **Dramatic Actor**: John Rubinstein in *Children of a Lesser God*
3. **Supporting or Featured Dramatic Actor**: David Rounds in *Morning's at Seven*
4. **Dramatic Actress**: Phyllis Frelich in *Children of a Lesser God*
5. **Supporting or Featured Dramatic Actress**: Dinah Manoff in *I Ought to be in Pictures*
6. **Dramatic Director**: Vivian Matalon for *Morning's at Seven*
7. **Musical**: *Evita* lyrics by Tim Rice
8. **Musical Actor**: Jim Dale in *Barnum*
9. **Supporting or Featured Musical Actor**: Mandy Patinkin in *Evita*
10. **Musical Actress**: Patti LuPone in *Evita*
11. **Supporting or Featured Musical Actress**: Priscilla Lopez in *A Day in Hollywood/A Night in the Ukraine*
12. **Musical Book**: *Evita* by Andrew Lloyd Webber
13. **Score**: *Evita* by Andrew Lloyd Webber
14. **Choreographers**: Tommy Tune and Tommie Walsh for *A Day in Hollywood/A Night in the Ukraine*
15. **Musical Director**: Harold Prince for *Evita*
16. **Scenic Designers**: John Lee Beatty for *Talley's Folly*; David Mitchell for *Barnum*
17. **Lighting Designer**: David Hersey for *Evita*
18. **Costume Designer**: Theoni V. Aldredge for *Barnum*
19. **Play or Musical Reproduction**: *Morning's at Seven* by Paul Osborn
20. **Special Awards**: Mary Tyler Moore; Actors Theatre of Louisville; Godspeed Opera House

1981 Tony Awards

1. **Play**: *Amadeus* by Peter Shaffer, produced by Nelle Nugent, The Shubert Organization, Elizabeth I. McCann and Roger S. Berlind
2. **Dramatic Actor**: Ian McKellen in *Amadeus*
3. **Supporting or Featured Dramatic Actor**: Brian Backer in *The Floating Light Bulb*
4. **Dramatic Actress**: Jane Lapotaire in *Piaf*
5. **Supporting or Featured Dramatic Actress**: Swoosie Kurtz in *Fifth of July*

6. **Dramatic Director**: Peter Hall for *Amadeus*
7. **Musical**: *42nd Street* by Michael Stewart and Mark Bramble, produced by David Merrick
8. **Musical Actor**: Kevin Kline in *The Pirates of Penzance*
9. **Supporting or Featured Musical Actor**: Hinton Battle in *Sophisticated Ladies*
10. **Musical Actress**: Lauren Bacall in *Woman of the Year*
11. **Supporting or Featured Musical Actress**: Marilyn Cooper in *Woman of the Year*
12. **Musical Book**: *Woman of the Year* by Peter Stone
13. **Score**: *Woman of the Year* music by John Kander, lyrics by Fred Ebb
14. **Choreographer**: Gower Champion for *42nd Street*
15. **Musical Director**: Wilford Leach for *The Pirates of Penzance*
16. **Scenic Designer**: John Bury for *Amadeus*
17. **Lighting Designer**: John Bury for *Amadeus*
18. **Costume Designer**: Willa Kim for *Sophisticated Ladies*
19. **Play or Musical Reproduction**: *The Pirates of Penzance* produced by the New York Shakespeare Festival – Joseph Papp
20. **Special Awards**: Lena Horne; Trinity Square Repertory Company

1982 Tony Awards

1. **Play**: *The Life and Adventures of Nicholas Nickleby* by David Edgar, produced by James M. Nederlander, Elizabeth I. McCann, Nelle Nugent and The Shubert Organization
2. **Dramatic Actor**: Roger Rees in *The Life and Adventures of Nicholas Nickleby*
3. **Supporting or Featured Dramatic Actor**: Zakes Mokae in *'Master Harold'... and the Boys*
4. **Dramatic Actress**: Zoe Caldwell in *Medea*
5. **Supporting or Featured Dramatic Actress**: Amanda Plummer in *Agnes of God*
6. **Dramatic Directors**: Trevor Nunn and John Caird for *The Life and Adventures of Nicholas Nickleby*
7. **Musical**: *Nine* produced by Michel Stuart, Harvey J. Klaris, Roger S. Berlind, James M. Nederlander, Francine LeFrak and Kenneth D. Greenblatt
8. **Musical Actor**: Ben Harney in *Dreamgirls*
9. **Supporting or Featured Musical Actor**: Cleavant Derricks in *Dreamgirls*
10. **Musical Actress**: Jennifer Holliday in *Dreamgirls*
11. **Supporting or Featured Musical Actress**: Liliane Montevecchi in *Nine*
12. **Musical Book**: *Dreamgirls* by Tom Eyen
13. **Score**: *Nine* music and lyrics by Maury Yeston
14. **Choreographers**: Michael Bennett and Michael Peters for *Dreamgirls*
15. **Musical Director**: Tommy Tune for *Nine*
16. **Scenic Designers**: John Napier and Dermot Hayes for *The Life and Adventures of Nicholas Nickleby*
17. **Lighting Designer**: Tharon Musser for *Dreamgirls*
18. **Costume Designer**: William Ivey Long for *Nine*
19. **Play or Musical Reproduction**: *Othello* produced by Barry and Fran Weissler and CBS Video Enterprises
20. **Special Awards**: The Guthrie Theatre; The Actors' Fund of America

1983 Tony Awards

1. **Play**: *Torch Song Trilogy* by Harvey Fierstein, produced by Kenneth Waissman, Martin Markinson, Lawrence Lane, John Glines, BetMar and Donald Tick
2. **Dramatic Actor**: Harvey Fierstein in *Torch Song Trilogy*
3. **Supporting or Featured Dramatic Actor**: Matthew Broderick in *Brighton Beach Memoirs*
4. **Dramatic Actress**: Jessica Tandy in *Foxfire*
5. **Supporting or Featured Dramatic Actress**: Judith Ivey in *Steaming*
6. **Dramatic Director**: Gene Saks for *Brighton Beach Memoirs*
7. **Musical**: *Cats* produced by Cameron MacKintosh, David Geffen, the

Shubert Organization and the Really Useful Company, Ltd.
8. **Musical Actor**: Tommy Tune in *My One and Only*
9. **Supporting or Featured Musical Actor**: Charles 'Honi' Coles in *My One and Only*
10. **Musical Actress**: Natalia Makarova in *On Your Toes*
11. **Supporting or Featured Musical Actress**: Betty Buckley in *Cats*
12. **Musical Book**: *Cats* by T.S. Eliot
13. **Score**: *Cats* by Andrew Lloyd Webber and T.S. Eliot
14. **Choreographers**: Tommy Tune and Thommie Walsh for *My One and Only*
15. **Musical Director**: Trevor Nunn for *Cats*
16. **Scenic Designer**: Ming Cho Lee for *K2*
17. **Lighting Designer**: David Hersey for *Cats*
18. **Costume Designer**: John Napier for *Cats*
19. **Play or Musical Reproduction**: *On Your Toes* produced by Alfred de Liagre, Jr., Roger L. Stevens, John Mauceri, Donald R. Seawell and Andre Pastoria
20. **Special Awards**: The Threatre Collection, Museum of the City of New York; Oregon Shakespearean Festival Association

1984 Tony Awards

1. **Play**: *The Real Thing* by Tom Stoppard, produced by Ivan Bloch, Roger Berlind, Emanuel Azenberg, Byron Goldman, Michael Codron, the Shubert Organization and Icarus Productions
2. **Dramatic Actor**: Jeremy Irons in *The Real Thing*
3. **Supporting or Featured Dramatic Actor**: Joe Mantegna in *Glengarry Glen Ross*
4. **Dramatic Actress**: Glenn Close in *The Real Thing*
5. **Supporting or Featured Dramatic Actress**: Christine Baranski in *The Real Thing*
6. **Dramatic Director**: Mike Nichols for *The Real Thing*
7. **Musical**: *La Cage aux Folles* produced by Fritz Holt, Allan Carr, Kenneth D. Greenblatt, Marvin A. Kraus, Stewart F. Lane, James M. Nedlander, Martin Richards and Barry Brown
8. **Musical Actor**: Hinton Battle in *The Tap Dance Kid*
9. **Supporting or Featured Musical Actor**: George Hearn in *La Cage aux Folles*
10. **Musical Actress**: Lila Kedrova in *Zorba*
11. **Supporting or Featured Musical Actress**: Chita Rivera in *The Rink*
12. **Musical Book**: Harvey Fierstein for *La Cage aux Folles*
13. **Score**: Jerry Herman for *La Cage aux Folles*
14. **Choreographers**: Danny Daniels for *The Tap Dance Kid*
15. **Musical Director**: Arthur Laurents for *La Cage aux Folles*
16. **Scenic Designer**: Tony Straigis for *Sunday in the Park with George*
17. **Lighting Designer**: Richard Nelson for *Sunday in the Park with George*
18. **Costume Designer**: Theoni V. Aldredge for *La Cage aux Folles*
19. **Play or Musical Reproduction**: *Death of a Salesman* produced by Robert Whitehead and Roger L. Stevens
20. **Special Awards**: Al Hirschfeld; Joseph Papp for *A Chorus Line*

Grammy Awards

The Grammy Award is presented by the National Academy of Recording Arts & Sciences (NARAS) annually for excellence in the recording industry.

Since early recording machines were called gramophones, the award statuette is a composite of designs for those early recording machines. Both the Award and its name, Grammy, are registered trademarks of the National Academy of Recording Arts & Sciences.

In 1957, the Hollywood Beautification Committee was faced with a problem. They needed names to put in the stars in the sidewalk on Hollywood's "Walk of Fame." So the committee asked a group of recording executives to name the best recording artists who would have their names put into the stars in the sidewalk.

Those same recording executives realized that recognition was needed which was based on excellence rather than merely popular recognition. The National Academy of Recording Arts & Sciences was formed and the Grammy Awards developed out of that meeting.

The first awards, for 1958 achievements, were handed out on May 4, 1959. The 1959 awards ceremonies were broadcast on national television over the NBC television network and included both live and tape portions. The first all-live broadcast on national television began in 1971.

Today's ceremonies are broadcast yearly live on network television on CBS. Some winners are announced early in the evening before the telecast begins. Entertainment by some of the nominated artists complements the televised envelope opening later in the evening.

Members of the National Academy of Recording Arts & Sciences are classified as either active or associate. Active members are involved in the creative aspects of recording and only active members can vote for the Grammy.

Categories for the Grammy Award have always included popular, country and western, rhythm and blues, comedy, jazz, classical and children's records.

As musical tastes change, new categories are added and old ones dropped. Folk Recordings were added at the 1962 ceremonies only to be replaced by Ethnic or Traditional Recordings in 1970. Latin Recordings were added in 1976. At the 1982 ceremonies, the Video of the Year first appeared, and there are now two music video categories.

1959 Grammy Awards

1. **Record of the Year**: *Nel Blu Dipinto di Blu (Volare)*, by Domenico Modugno on Decca

2. **Album of the Year**: *The Music from Peter Gunn*, by Henry Mancini on RCA

3. **Song of the Year (Award to the Songwriter)**: Domenico Modugno for

G Grammy Awards 1960

Nel Blu Dipinto di Blu (Volare) on Decca

4. **Best Male Vocal Performance**: Perry Como for *Catch a Falling Star* on RCA-Victor
5. **Best Female Vocal Performance**: Ella Fitzgerald for *Ella Fitzgerald Sings the Irving Berlin Songbook* on Verve
6. **Best Individual Jazz Performance**: Ella Fitzgerald for *Ella Fitzgerald Sings the Duke Ellington Song Book* on Verve
7. **Best Country & Western Performance**: Kingston Trio for *Tom Dooley* on Capitol
8. **Best Rhythm & Blues Performance**: The Champs for *Tequila* on Challenge
9. **Best Recording for Children**: David Seville for *The Chipmunk Song* on Liberty
10. **Best Comedy Performance**: David Seville for *The Chipmunk Song* on Liberty
11. **Best Performance by an Orchestra**: Billy May for *Billy May's Big Fat Brass* on Capitol
12. **Best Arrangement**: Henry Mancini for *The Music from Peter Gunn* on RCA
13. **Best Jazz Performance by a Group**: Count Basie for *Basie* on Roulette
14. **Best Performance by a Dance Band**: Count Basie for *Basie* on Roulette
15. **Best Original Cast Album, Broadway or TV**: Meredith Willson for *The Music Man* on Capitol
16. **Best Performance by a Vocal Group or Chorus**: Louis Prima and Keely Smith for *That Old Black Magic* on Capitol
17. **Best Performance, Documentary or Spoken Word** Stan Freberg for *The Best of the Stan Freberg Show* on Capitol
18. **Best Composition Over 5 Minutes First Recorded and Released During the Year** Nelson Riddle for *Cross Country Suite* on Dot
19. **Best Soundtrack Album, Dramatic Picture Score or Original Cast**: Andre Previn for *Gigi* on MGM
20. **Best Instrumental Classical Performance (with Concerto Scale Accompaniment)**: Van Cliburn, pianist, and Kiril Kondrashin and his Symphony Orchestra, for *Tchaikovsky: Concerto No. 1 in B-Flat Minor, Op. 23*

21. **Best Instrumental Classical Performance (Other Than Concerto Scale)**: Andres Segovia for *Segovia Golden Jubilee* on Decca
22. **Best Orchestral Classical Performance**: Felix Slatkin and the Hollywood Bowl Symphony Orchestra for *Gaite Parisienne* on Capitol
23. **Best Classical Performance, vocal soloist (with or without Orchestra)**: Renata Tebaldi for *Operatic Recital* on London
24. **Best Classical Performance, Operatic or Choral**: Roger Wagner Chorale for *Virtuoso* on Capitol
25. **Best Classical Performance, Chamber Music (Including Chamber Orchestra)**: Hollywood String Quartet for *Beethoven Quartet 130* on Decca
26. **Best Engineered Record, Non-Classical**: Ted Keep for *The Chipmunk Song* on Liberty
27. **Best Engineered Record, Classical**: Sherwood Hall III for *Duets with a Spanish Guitar* on Capitol
28. **Best Album Cover**: art director: Frank Sinatra for *Only the Lonely* on Capitol

1960 Grammy Awards

1. **Record of the Year**: *Mack the Knife* by Bobby Darin on Atco
2. **Album of the Year**: *Come Dance with Me* by Frank Sinatra on Capitol
3. **Song of the Year (Award to the Songwriter)**: Jimmy Driftwood for *The Battle of New Orleans* on Columbia
4. **Best Male Vocal Performance**: Frank Sinatra for *Come Dance With Me* on Capitol
5. **Best Female Vocal Performance**: Ella Fitzgerald for *But Not For Me* on Verve
6. **Best Jazz Soloist**: Ella Fitzgerald for *Ella Swings Lightly* on Verve
7. **Best Jazz Group**: Jonah Jones for *I Dig Chicks* on Capitol
8. **Best Country & Western**: Johnny Horton for *The Battle of New Orleans*
9. **Best Rhythm & Blues**: Dinah Washington for *What a Diff'rence a Day Makes* on Mercury
10. **Best Album for Children**: *Peter and the Wolf* narrated by Peter Ustinov,

Philharmonia Orchestra conducted by Herbert von Karajan on Angel

11. **Best Comedy, Spoken Word:** Shelly Berman for *Inside Shelly Berman* on Verve

12. **Best Comedy, Musical:** Homer & Jethro for *The Battle of Kookamonga* on RCA

13. **Best Dance Band Performance:** Duke Ellington for *Anatomy of a Murder* on Columbia

14. **Best Orchestra:** Andre Previn conducting the David Rose Orchestra for *Like Young* on MGM

15. **Best Folk:** The Kingston Trio for *The Kingston Trio at Large* on Capitol

16. **Best Documentary or Spoken Word (other than Comedy):** *A Lincoln Portrait* by Carl Sandburg on Columbia

17. **Best Original Cast Soundtrack Album:** *Porgy and Bess* by the motion picture cast on Columbia

18. **Best Broadway Show Albums:** *Gypsy* by Ethel Merman on Columbia, and *Redhead* by Gwen Verdon on RCA

19. **Best Soundtrack Album, Original Cast, Motion Picture or Television:** *Anatomy of a Murder (Motion Picture)* by Duke Ellington on Columbia

20. **Best Over 5 Minute Musical Composition First Recorded and Released This Year:** *Anatomy of a Murder* composed by Duke Ellington on Columbia

21. **Best Choral Performance:** The Mormon Tabernacle Choir conducted by Richard Condie for *Battle Hymn of the Republic* on Columbia

22. **Best Classical Orchestra:** Boston Symphony conducted by Charles Munch for *Debussy: Images for Orchestra* on RCA

23. **Best Classical Instrumental Soloist (Other than Full Orchestral Accompaniment):** Artur Rubinstein, Pianist for *Beethoven: Sonata No. 21, In C, Op. 53, No. 3* on RCA

24. **Best Classical Concerto or Instrumental Soloist (Full Orchestra):** Van Cliburn, pianist accompanying the Symphony of the Air conducted by Kiril Kondrashin for *Rachmaninoff Piano Concerto No. 3* on RCA

25. **Best Classical Chamber Music (Including Chamber Orchestra):** Artur Rubinstein, pianist for *Beethoven Sonata No. 21, In C, Op. 53, Sonata Number 18, In E-Flat, Op. 31, No. 3* on RCA

26. **Best Classical Vocal Soloist (with or without orchestra):** Jussi Bjoerling for *Bjoerling in Opera* on London

27. **Best Classical Opera Cast or Choral:** Vienna Philharmonic Orchestra conducted by Erich Leinsdorf for *Mozart: The Marriage of Figaro* on RCA

28. **Best Engineered Record (Classical):** Lewis W. Layton for *Victory at Sea, Vol. 1* by Robert Russell Bennett on RCA

29. **Best Engineered Record (Novelty):** Ted Keep for *Alvin's Harmonica* on Liberty

30. **Best Engineered Record (Other Than Classical or Novelty):** Robert Simpson for *Bellafonte at Carnegie Hall* on RCA

31. **Best Arrangement:** Billy May for *Come Dance with Me* on Capitol

32. **Best Album Cover:** Robert M. Jones for *Shostakovich Symphony No. 5* on RCA

33. **Best Performance by a "Top-40" Artist:** Nat "King" Cole on *Midnight Flyer* on Capitol

34. **Special National Trustees' Award for Artists and Repertoire Contribution:** Bobby Darin for *Mack the Knife* produced by Ahmet Ertegun on Atco; Frank Sinatra for *Come Dance with Me* produced by Dave Cavanaugh on Capitol

35. **Best New Artist of 1959:** Bobby Darin on Atco

1961 Grammy Awards

1. **Record of the Year:** *Theme from a Summer Place* by Percy Faith on Columbia

2. **Album of the Year:** *Button Down Mind* by Bob Newhart on Warner Brothers

3. **Song of the Year (Award to the Songwriter):** Ernest Gold for *Theme from Exodus* on RCA

4. **Best Male Vocal Single Record Performance:** Ray Charles for *Georgia on My Mind* on RCA

5. **Best Male Vocal Album Performance:** Ray Charles for *Genius of Ray Charles* on RCA

6. **Best Female Vocal Single Record Performance:** Ella Fitzgerald for *Mack the Knife* on Verve

7. **Best Female Vocal Album Performance:** Ella Fitzgerald for *Mack the Knife—Ella in Berlin* on Verve

G Grammy Awards 1962

8. **Best Jazz Solo or Small Group**: Andre Previn for *West Side Story* on Contemporary
9. **Best Jazz Large Group**: Henry Mancini for *Blues and the Beat* on RCA
10. **Best Jazz Composition of More than 5 Minutes**: Miles Davis and Gil Evans for *Sketches of Spain* on Columbia
11. **Best Pop Single Artist**: Ray Charles for *Georgia on My Mind* on ABC
12. **Best Country & Western**: Marty Robbins for *El Paso* on Columbia
13. **Best Rhythm & Blues**: Ray Charles for *Let the Good Times Roll* on Atlantic
14. **Best Album for Children**: *Let's All Sing with the Chipmunks* by David Seville on Liberty
15. **Best Comedy, Spoken Word**: Bob Newhart for *Button Down Mind Strikes Back* on Warner Brothers
16. **Best Comedy, Musical**: Jo Stafford and Paul Weston for *Johnathan and Darlene Edwards in Paris* on Columbia
17. **Best Dance Band Performance**: Count Basie for *Dance with Basie* on Roulette
18. **Best Orchestra**: Henry Mancini for *Mr. Lucky* on RCA
19. **Best Arrangement**: Henry Mancini for *Mr. Lucky* on RCA
20. **Best Folk**: Harry Belafonte for *Swing Dat Hammer* on RCA
21. **Best Spoken Word (Other Than Comedy)**: Robert Bialek for *FDR Speaks on Washington*
22. **Best Original Cast Soundtrack Music Score from Motion Picture or Television**: Ernest Gold for *Exodus* on RCA
23. **Best Show Album (Original Cast)**: Mary Martin in *The Sound of Music* by Richard Rodgers and Oscar Hammerstein II on Columbia
24. **Best Soundtrack Original Cast**: Frank Sinatra in *Can Can* by Cole Porter on Capitol
25. **Best Vocal Group**: Steve Lawrence & Eydie Gorme for *We Got Us* on ABC
26. **Best Chorus**: Norman Luboff Choir for *Songs of the Cowboy* on Columbia
27. **Best Classical Orchestra**: Chicago Symphony conducted by Fritz Reiner for *Bartok: Music for Strings, Percussion and Celeste* on RCA
28. **Best Classical Concerto or Instrumental Soloist**: Sviatoslav Richter, pianist for *Brahms: Piano Concerto No. 2 in B-Flat* on RCA
29. **Best Classical Chamber Music**: Laurindo Almeida for *Conversations with the Guitar* on Capitol
30. **Best Classical Vocal Soloist**: Leontyne Price for *A Program of Song* on RCA
31. **Best Classical Opera**: Erich Leinsdorf conducting the Rome Opera House Orchestra and Chorus in *Puccini: Turandot* on RCA
32. **Best Contemporary Classical Composition**: Aaron Copeland for *Orchestral Suite from Tender Land Suite* on RCA
33. **Best Classical Choral (Including Oratorio)**: Sir Thomas Beecham conducting The Royal Philharmonic Orchestra and Chorus in *Handel: The Messiah* on RCA
34. **Best Classical Instrumentalist Soloist or Duo**: Laurindo Almeida for *The Spanish Guitars of Laurindo Almeida* on Capitol
35. **Best Engineered Record (Classical)**: Hugh Davies for *The Spanish Guitars of Laurindo Almeida* on Capitol
36. **Best Engineered Record (Novelty)**: John Kraus for *The Old Payola Roll Blues* by Stan Freberg on Capitol
37. **Best Engineering (Pop)**: Luis P. Valentin for *Ella Fitzgerald Sings the George and Ira Gershwin Songbook* on Verve
38. **Best Album Cover (Award to Art Director)**: Marvin Schwartz for *Latin Ala Lee* on Capitol
39. **Best New Artist of 1960**: Bob Newhart on Warner Brothers
40. **Special National Trustees' Awards for Artists and Repertoire Contribution**: Ernest Altschuler producer for *Theme from a Summer Place* on Columbia; George Avakian producer for *Button Down Mind* on Warner Brothers

1962 Grammy Awards

1. **Record of the Year**: *Moon River* by Henry Mancini on RCA
2. **Album of the Year**: *Judy at Carnegie Hall* by Judy Garland on Capitol

Grammy Awards 1962

3. **Song of the Year (Award to the Songwriter):** Henry Mancini and Johnny Mercer for *Moon River* on RCA
4. **Classical Album of the Year:** Igor Stravinsky conducting the Columbia Symphony in *Stravinsky Conducts, 1960: Le Sacre Du Pretemps; Petrouchka* on Columbia
5. **Best Male Solo Vocal:** Jack Jones for *Lollipops and Roses* on Kapp
6. **Best Female Solo Vocal:** Judy Garland for *Judy at Carnegie Hall* on Capitol
7. **Best Jazz Solo or Small Group:** Andre Previn for *Andre Previn Plays Harold Arlen* on Contemporary
8. **Best Jazz Large Group:** Stan Kenton for *West Side Story* on Capitol
9. **Best Original Jazz Composition:** Galt MacDermott for *African Waltz* on Roulette
10. **Best Instrumental Theme:** Galt MacDermott for *African Waltz* on Roulette
11. **Best Country & Western:** Jimmy Dean for *Big Bad John* on Columbia
12. **Best Rhythm & Blues:** Ray Charles for *Hit the Road Jack* on Am-Par
13. **Best Album for Children:** Leonard Bernstein conducting the New York Philharmonic Orchestra in *Prokofiev: Peter and the Wolf* on Columbia
14. **Best Comedy:** *An Evening with Mike Nichols and Elaine May* on Mercury
15. **Best Orchestra for Dancing:** Si Zetner for *Up a Lazy River* on Liberty
16. **Best Orchestra Not for Dancing:** Henry Mancini for *Breakfast at Tiffany's* on RCA
17. **Best Spoken Word:** Leonard Bernstein conducting the New York Philharmonic for *Humor in Music* on Columbia
18. **Best Rock & Roll:** Chubby Checker for *Let's Twist Again* on Parkway
19. **Best Folk:** Belafonte Folk Singers for *Belafonte Folk Singers at Home and Abroad* on RCA
20. **Best Gospel or Other Religious:** Mahalia Jackson for *Everytime I Feel the Spirit* on Columbia
21. **Best Original Cast Show Album:** Frank Loesser for *How to Succeed in Business without Really Trying* on RCA
22. **Best Soundtrack Score:** Henry Mancini for *Breakfast at Tiffany's* on RCA
23. **Best Soundtrack Original Cast:** Johnny Green, Saul Chaplin, Sid Ramin and Irwin Kostal for *West Side Story* on Columbia
24. **Best Arrangement:** Henry Mancini for *Moon River* on RCA
25. **Best Vocal Group:** Lambert, Hendricks and Ross for *High Flying* on Columbia
26. **Best Chorus:** Johnny Mann Singers with the Si Zetner Orchestra for *Great Band with Great Voices* on Liberty
27. **Best Classical Orchestra:** Boston Symphony Orchestra conducted by Charles Munch for *Ravel: Daphnis Et Chloe* on RCA
28. **Best Classical Chamber Music:** Jascha Heifetz, Gregor Piatigorsky, and William Primrose for *Beethoven: Serenade, Op. 8 Kodaly Duo for Violin and Cello, Op. 7* on RCA
29. **Best Classical Vocal Soloist:** Joan Sutherland for *The Art of the Prima Donna* with Molinari-Pradelli conducting the Royal Opera House Orchestra on London
30. **Best Opera:** Gabriele Santini conducting the Rome Opera Chorus and Orchestra in *Puccini: Madame Butterfly* on Capitol
31. **Best Classical Instrumental Soloist with Orchestra:** Isaac Stern, violinist for *Bartok: Concerto No. 1 for Violin and Orchestra* with Eugene Ormandy conducting the Philharmonic Orchestra on Columbia
32. **Best Classical Choral:** Robert Shaw Chorale for *Bach: B-Minor Mass* on RCA
33. **Best Classical Instrumentalist Soloist or Duo without Orchestra:** Laurindo Almeida for *Reverie for Spanish Guitars* on Capitol
34. **Best Contemporary Classical Compositions:** Laurindo Almeida for *Discantus* on Capitol, and Igor Stravinsky for *Movements for Piano and Orchestra* on Columbia
35. **Best Engineered Record (Classical):** Lewis W. Layton for *Ravel: Daphnis Et Chloe* with Charles Munch conducting the Boston Symphony Orchestra on RCA
36. **Best Engineered Record (Novelty):** John Kraus for *Stan Freberg Presents the United States of America* on Capitol
37. **Best Engineering (Pop):** Robert Arnold for *Judy at Carnegie Hall* on Capitol

G Grammy Awards 1963

38. **Best Album Cover (Award to Art Director)**: Jim Silke for *Judy at Carnegie Hall* on Capitol
39. **Best Album Cover (Classical)**: Marvin Schwartz for *Puccini: Madama Butterfly* on Angel
40. **Best New Artist of 1961**: Peter Nero on RCA

1963 Grammy Awards

1. **Record of the Year**: *I Left My Heart in San Francisco* by Tony Bennett on Columbia
2. **Album of the Year**: *The First Family* by Vaughn Meader on Cadence
3. **Song of the Year (Award to the Songwriter)**: Leslie Bricusse and Anthony Newley for *What Kind of Fool Am I?* on London
4. **Classical Album of the Year**: *Columbia Records Presents Vladimir Horowitz* on Columbia
5. **Best Male Solo Vocal**: Tony Bennett for *I Left My Heart in San Francisco* on Columbia
6. **Best Female Solo Vocal**: Ella Fitzgerald for *Ella Swings Brightly with Nelson Riddle* on Verve
7. **Best Jazz Solo or Small Group**: Stan Getz for *Desafinado* on Verve
8. **Best Jazz Large Group**: Stan Kenton for *Adventures in Jazz* on Capitol
9. **Best Original Jazz Composition**: Vince Guaraldi for *Cast Your Fate to the Winds* on Fantasy
10. **Best Instrumental Theme**: Bobby Scott and Ric Marlow for *A Taste of Honey* on Reprise
11. **Best Country & Western**: Burl Ives for *Funny Way of Laughin'* on Decca
12. **Best Rhythm & Blues**: Ray Charles for *I Can't Stop Loving You* on ABC
13. **Best Album for Children**: Leonard Bernstein conducting the New York Philharmonic Orchestra in *Saint-Saens: Carnival of the Animals/Britten: Young Person's Guide to the Orchestra* on Columbia
14. **Best Comedy**: Vaughn Meader for *The First Family* on Cadence
15. **Best Orchestra for Dancing**: Joe Harnell for *Fly Me to the Moon Bossa Nova* on Kapp
16. **Best Orchestra or Instrumentalist with Orchestra Not for Jazz or Dancing**: *The Colorful Peter Nero* on RCA
17. **Best Spoken Word**: *The Storyteller: A Session with Charles Laughton* on Capitol
18. **Best Rock & Roll**: Bent Fabric for *Alley Cat* on Atco
19. **Best Folk**: Peter, Paul & Mary for *If I Had a Hammer* on Warner Brothers
20. **Best Gospel or Other Religious**: Mahalia Jackson for *Great Songs of Love and Faith* on Columbia
21. **Best Original Cast Show Album**: Richard Rodgers for *No Strings* on Capitol
22. **Best Instrumental Arrangement**: Henry Mancini for *Baby Elephant Walk* on RCA
23. **Best Background Arrangement**: Marty Manning for *I Left My Heart in San Francisco* on Columbia
24. **Best Vocal Group**: Peter, Paul & Mary for *If I Had a Hammer* on Warner Brothers
25. **Best Chorus**: The New Christy Minstrels for *Presenting the New Christy Minstrels* on Columbia
26. **Best Classical Orchestra**: The Columbia Symphony conducted by Igor Stravinsky for *Stravinsky: The Firebird Ballet* on Columbia
27. **Best Classical Chamber Music**: Jascha Heifetz, Gregor Piatigorsky, and William Primrose for *The Heifetz/Piatigorsky Concerts with Primrose, Pennario and Guests* on RCA
28. **Best Classical Vocal Soloist**: Eileen Farrell for *Wagner: Gotterdamerung-Brunhilde's Immolation Scene/Wesendonck Songs* with Leonard Bernstein conducting the N.Y. Philharmonic on Columbia
29. **Best Opera**: George Solti conducting the Rome Opera House Chorus and Orchestra in *Verdi: Aida* on RCA
30. **Best Classical Instrumental Soloist with Orchestra**: Isaac Stern, violinist for *Stravinsky: Concerto in D for Violin* with Igor Stravinsky conducting the Columbia Symphony on Columbia
31. **Best Classical Choral**: Philharmonia Choir with choral director Wilhelm Pitz for *Bach: St. Matthew Passion* with Otto Klemperer conducting the Philharmonia Orchestra on Angel

Grammy Awards 1964 G

32. **Best Classical Instrumentalist Soloist or Duo without Orchestra:** *Columbia Records Presents Vladimir Horowitz* on Columbia
33. **Best Contemporary Classical Compositions:** Igor Stravinsky for *The Flood* on Columbia
34. **Best Engineered Record (Classical):** Lewis W. Layton for *Strauss: Also Sprach Zarathustra Op. 30* with Fritz Reiner conducting the Chicago Symphony Orchestra on RCA
35. **Best Engineered Record (Novelty):** Robert Fine for *The Civil War, Volume 1* on Mercury
36. **Best Engineering (Other Than Novelty or Classical):** Al Schmitt for *Hatari!* on RCA
37. **Best Album Cover (Award to Art Director):** Robert Jones for *Lena ... Lovely and Alive* on RCA
38. **Best Album Cover (Classical):** Marvin Schwartz for *The Intimate Bach* on Capitol
39. **Best New Artist of 1962:** Robert Goulet on Columbia

1964 Grammy Awards

1. **Record of the Year:** *The Days of Wine and Roses* by Henry Mancini on RCA
2. **Album of the Year:** *The Barbra Streisand Album* on Columbia
3. **Song of the Year (Award to the Songwriter):** Henry Mancini and Johnny Mercer for *The Days of Wine and Roses* on RCA
4. **Classical Album of the Year:** *Britten: War Requiem* by Benjamin Britten conducting the London Symphony Orchestra and Chorus on London
5. **Best Male Solo Vocal:** Jack Jones for *Wives and Lovers* on Kapp
6. **Best Female Solo Vocal:** Barbra Streisand for *The Barbra Streisand Album* on Columbia
7. **Best Jazz Solo or Small Group:** Bill Evans for *Conversations with Myself* on Verve
8. **Best Jazz Large Group:** *Encore: Woody Herman, 1963* on Philips
9. **Best Original Jazz Composition:** Steve Allen and Ray Brown for *Gravy Waltz*
10. **Best Instrumental Theme:** Norman Newell, Nino Oliviero, and Riz Ortolani for *More (The Theme from "Mondo Cane")* on United Artists
11. **Best Country & Western:** Bobby Bare for *Detroit City* on RCA
12. **Best Rhythm & Blues:** Ray Charles for *Busted* on ABC/Paramount
13. **Best Album for Children:** Leonard Bernstein conducting the New York Philharmonic Orchestra in *Bernstein Conducts for Young People* on Columbia
14. **Best Comedy:** Allan Sherman for *Hello Mudduh, Hello Faddah* on Warner Brothers
15. **Best Orchestra for Dancing:** Count Basie for *This Time by Basie! Hits of the 50's and 60's* on Reprise
16. **Best Orchestra or Instrumentalist with Orchestra Not for Jazz or Dancing:** Al Hirt for *Java* on RCA
17. **Best Spoken Word:** *Who's Afraid of Virginia Woolf?* by Edward Albee on Warner Brothers
18. **Best Rock & Roll:** Nino Tempo and April Stevens for *Deep Purple* on Atco
19. **Best Folk:** Peter, Paul & Mary for *Blowin' in the Wind* on Warner Brothers
20. **Best Gospel or Other Religious:** Soeur Sourire, the Singing Nun for *Dominique* on Philips
21. **Best Original Cast Show Album:** Jerry Bock and Sheldon Harnick for *She Loves Me* on MGM
22. **Best Original Score:** John Addison for *Tom Jones* on United Artists
23. **Best Instrumental Arrangement:** Quincy Jones for *I Can't Stop Loving You* on Reprise
24. **Best Background Arrangment:** Henry Mancini for *The Days of Wine and Roses* on RCA
25. **Best Vocal Group:** Peter, Paul & Mary for *Blowin' in the Wind* on Warner Brothers
26. **Best Chorus:** The Swingle Singers for *Bach's Greatest Hits* on Philips
27. **Best Classical Orchestra:** The Boston Symphony conducted by Erich Leinsdorf for *Bartok: Concerto for Orchestra* on RCA
28. **Best Classical Chamber Music:** Julian Bream Consort for *Evening of Elizabethan Music* on RCA
29. **Best Classical Vocal Soloist:** Leontyne Price for *Great Scenes from Gershwin's Porgy and Bess* on RCA

30. **Best Opera:** Erich Leinsdorf conducting the RCA Italiana Opera orchestra and chorus in *Puccini: Madama Butterfly* on RCA
31. **Best Classical Instrumental Soloist with Orchestra:** Artur Rubinstein, pianist for *Tchaikovsky: Concerto No. 1 in B-Flat Minor for Piano and Orchestra* with Erich Leinsdorf conducting the Boston Symphony Orchestra on RCA
32. **Best Classical Instrumental Soloist without Orchestra:** Vladimir Horowitz for *The Sound of Horowitz* on Columbia
33. **Best Classical Choral:** David Willcocks director of the Bach Choir, Edward Chapman director of the Highgate School Choir for *Britten: War Requiem* with Benjamin Britten conducting the London Symphony Orchestra and Chorus on London
34. **Best Contemporary Classical Compositions:** Benjamin Britten for *War Requiem* on London
35. **Best Engineered Record (Classical):** Lewis Layton for *Puccini: Madama Butterfly* on RCA
36. **Best Engineered Record (Nonclassical):** James Malloy for *Charade* on RCA
37. **Best Engineering (Novelty):** Robert Fine for *Civil War, Vol. 2* on Mercury
38. **Best Album Cover:** John Berg for *The Barbra Streisand Album* on Columbia
39. **Best Album Notes (Award to Annotator):** Stanley Dance and Leonard Feather for *The Ellington Era* on Columbia
40. **Best Album Cover (Classical):** Robert Jones for *Puccini: Madama Butterfly* on RCA
41. **Most Promising New Classical Recording Artist:** Andre Watts on Columbia
42. **Best New Artist of 1963:** Swingle Singers on Philips

1965 Grammy Awards

1. **Record of the Year:** *The Girl from Ipanema* by Stan Getz and Astrud Gilberto on Verve
2. **Album of the Year:** *Getz/Gilberto* by Stan Getz and Joao Gilberto
3. **Song of the Year (Award to the Songwriter):** Jerry Herman for *Hello Dolly!* on Kapp
4. **Classical Album of the Year:** *Bernstein: Symphony No. 3* by Leonard Bernstein conducting the New York Philharmonic on Columbia
5. **Best Male Solo Vocal:** Louis Armstrong for *Hello Dolly!* on Kapp
6. **Best Female Solo Vocal:** Barbra Streisand for *People* on Columbia
7. **Best Jazz Solo or Small Group:** Stan Getz for *Getz/Gilberto* on Verve
8. **Best Jazz Large Group:** Laurindo Almeida for *Guitar from Ipanema* on Capitol
9. **Best Original Jazz Composition:** Lalo Schifrin for *The Cat* on Verve
10. **Best Instrumental (Nonjazz):** Henry Mancini for *The Pink Panther Theme* on RCA
11. **Best Country & Western Single:** Roger Miller for *Dang Me* on Smash
12. **Best Country & Western Album:** Roger Miller for *Dang Me/Chug-a-Lug* on Smash
13. **Best Country & Western Female Vocal:** Dottie West for *Here Comes My Baby* on RCA
14. **Best Country & Western Male Vocal:** Roger Miller for *Dang Me* on Smash
15. **Best Country & Western Song:** Roger Miller for *Dang Me* on Smash
16. **Best Rhythm & Blues:** Nancy Wilson for *How Glad I Am* on Capitol
17. **Best Album for Children:** Julie Andrews and Dick Van Dyke for *Mary Poppins* on Buena Vista
18. **Best Comedy:** Bill Cosby for *I Started Out as a Child* on Warner Brothers
19. **Best Spoken Word:** *BBC Tribute to John Kennedy* by the Cast of "That Was the Week that Was" on Decca
20. **Best Rock & Roll:** Petula Clark for *Downtown* on Warner Brothers
21. **Best Folk:** Gayle Garnett for *We'll Sing in the Sunshine* on RCA
22. **Best Gospel or Other Religious:** Tennessee Ernie Ford for *Great Gospel Songs* on Capitol
23. **Best Original Score:** Richard M. Sherman and Robert B. Sherman for *Mary Poppins* on Buena Vista
24. **Best Score from an Original Show Album:** Jule Styne and Bob Merrill for *Funny Girl* on Capitol

25. **Best Instrumental Arrangement:** Henry Mancini for *Pink Panther* on RCA
26. **Best Accompaniment Arrangement:** Peter Matz for *People* on Columbia
27. **Best Vocal Group:** The Beatles for *A Hard Day's Night* on Capitol
28. **Best Chorus:** The Swingle Singers for *The Swingle Singers Going Baroque* on Philips
29. **Best Classical Orchestra:** The Boston Symphony conducted by Erich Leinsdorf for *Mahler: Symphony No. 5 in C-Sharp Minor, Berg: "Wozzeck" Excerpts* on RCA
30. **Best Classical Chamber Music:** Jascha Heifetz, Gregor Piatigorsky and Jacob Lateiner for *Beethoven: Trio No. 1 in E-Flat Op. 1, No. 1* on RCA
31. **Best Classical Vocal Chamber Music:** Noah Greenberg conducting the New York Pro Musica for *It Was a Lover and His Lass (Morley, Byrd and Others)* on Decca
32. **Best Performance Instrumental Soloist with Orchestra:** Isaac Stern, violinist for *Prokofiev: Concerto No. 1 in D-Major for Violin* on Columbia
33. **Best Performance Instrumental Soloist without Orchestra:** Vladimir Horowitz Plays Beethoven, Debussy, Chopin *(Beethoven: Sonata No. 8 "Pathetique," Debussy: "Preludes," Chopin: Etudes and Scherzos 1 through 4)* on Columbia
34. **Best Opera:** Herbert von Karajan conducting the Vienna Philharmonic Orchestra and Chorus for *Bezet: Carmen* on RCA
35. **Best Vocal Soloist:** Leontyne Price for *Berlioz: Nuits D'Ete (Song Cycle)/Falla: El Amor Brujo* with Fritz Reiner conducting the Chicago Symphony Orchestra on RCA
36. **Best Classical Choral:** Robert Shaw Chorale for *Britten: A Ceremony of Carols* on RCA
37. **Best Classical Composition:** Samuel Barber for *Piano Concerto* on Columbia
38. **Best Engineered Classical Record:** Douglas Larter for *Britten: Young Person's Guide to the Orchestra* on Angel
39. **Best Engineered Record:** Phil Ramone for *Getz/Gilberto* on Verve
40. **Best Engineered Novelty Record:** Dave Hassinger for *The Chipmunks Sing the Beatles* on Liberty
41. **Best Album Cover (Award to the Art Director):** Robert Cato and Don Bronstein for *People* on Columbia
42. **Best Album Notes (Award to Annotator):** Stanton Catlin and Carleton Beals for *Mexico (Legacy Collection)* on Columbia
43. **Best Album Cover (Classical):** Robert Jones and Jan Balet for *Saint-Saens: Carnival of the Animals/Britten: Young Persons Guide to the Orchestra* on RCA
44. **Best Instrumental Performance (Non-Jazz):** Henry Mancini for *Pink Panther* on RCA
45. **Best New Artist:** The Beatles on Capitol
46. **Best New Country & Western Artist:** Roger Miller on Smash
47. **Most Promising New Recording Artist:** Marilyn Horne on London

1966 Grammy Awards

1. **Record of the Year:** *A Taste of Honey* by Herb Alpert and the Tijuana Brass on A&M
2. **Album of the Year:** *September of My Years* by Frank Sinatra on Reprise
3. **Song of the Year (Award to the Songwriter):** Paul Francis Webster and Johnny Mandel for *The Shadow of Your Smile* on Mercury
4. **Classical Album of the Year:** *Horowitz at Carnegie Hall (An Historic Return)* by Vladimir Horowitz on Columbia
5. **Best Male Solo Vocal:** Frank Sinatra for *It Was a Very Good Year*
6. **Best Female Solo Vocal:** Barbra Streisand for *My Name Is Barbra* on Columbia
7. **Best Jazz Solo or Small Group:** Ramsey Lewis Trio for *The "In" Crowd* on Cadet
8. **Best Jazz Large Group:** Duke Ellington Orchestra for *Ellington '66* on Reprise
9. **Best Original Jazz Composition:** Lalo Schifrin for *Jazz Suite on the Mass Texts* on RCA
10. **Best Instrumental (Non-Jazz):** Herb Alpert and the Tijuana Brass for *A Taste of Honey* on A&M

G Grammy Awards 1966

11. **Best Country & Western Single**: Roger Miller for *King of the Road* on Smash
12. **Best Country & Western Album**: Roger Miller for *The Return of Roger Miller* on Smash
13. **Best Country & Western Female Vocal**: Jodie Miller for *Queen of the House* on Capitol
14. **Best Country & Western Male Vocal**: Roger Miller for *King of the Road* on Smash
15. **Best Country & Western Song**: Roger Miller for *King of the Road* on Smash
16. **Best Rhythm & Blues**: James Brown for *Papas Got a Brand New Bag* on King
17. **Best Album for Children**: Marvin Miller for *Dr. Seuss Presents "Fox in Socks"—"Green Eggs and Ham"* on RCA/Camden
18. **Best Comedy**: Bill Cosby for *Why Is There Air?* on Warner Brothers
19. **Best Spoken Word**: *John F. Kennedy—As We Remember Him* producer Goddard Lieberson on Columbia
20. **Best Folk**: Harry Belafonte and Miriam Makeba for *An Evening with Belafonte/Makeba* on RCA
21. **Best Gospel or Other Religious**: George Beverly Shea and the Anita Kerr Singers for *Southland Favorites* on RCA
22. **Best Original Score**: Johnny Mandel for *The Sandpiper* on Mercury
23. **Best Score from an Original Show Album**: Alan Lerner and Burton Lane for *On a Clear Day* on RCA
24. **Best Instrumental Arrangement**: Herb Alpert and the Tijuana Brass for *A Taste of Honey* on A&M
25. **Best Background Arrangement**: Gordon Jenkins for *It Was a Very Good Year* on Reprise
26. **Best Vocal Group**: Anita Kerr Singers for *We Dig Mancini* on RCA
27. **Best Chorus**: The Swingle Singers for *Anyone for Mozart?* on Philips
28. **Best Contemporary Single**: Roger Miller for *King of the Road* on Smash
29. **Best Single Contemporary Male Vocal**: Roger Miller for *King of the Road* on Smash
30. **Best Single Contemporary Female Vocal**: Petula Clark for *I Know a Place* on Warner Brothers
31. **Best Contemporary Group**: The Statler Brothers for *Flowers on the Wall* on Columbia
32. **Best Classical Orchestra**: American Symphony Orchestra conducted by Leopold Stokowski for *Ives: Symphony No. 4* on Columbia
33. **Best Classical Chamber Music**: Julliard String Quartet for *Bartok: The Six String Quartets* on Columbia
34. **Best Performance Instrumental Soloist with Orchestra**: Artur Rubinstein, pianist for *Beethoven: Concerto No. 4 in G-Major for Piano and Orchestra* with Erich Leinsdorf conducting the Boston Symphony Orchestra on RCA
35. **Best Performance Instrumental Soloist without Orchestra**: Vladimir Horowitz for *Horowitz at Carnegie Hall—An Historic Return* on Columbia
36. **Best Opera**: Karl Bohm conducting the Orchestra of the German Opera, Berlin for *Berg: Wozzeck* on DG
37. **Best Vocal Soloist**: Leontyne Price for *Strauss: Salome (Dance of the Seven Veils, Interlude, Final Scene), The Egyptian Helen (Awakening Scene)* on RCA
38. **Best Classical Choral**: Robert Shaw Chorale for *Stravinsky: Symphony of Psalms/Poulenc: Gloria* with the RCA Victor Symphony on RCA
39. **Best Contemporary Classical Composition**: Charles Ives for *Symphony Number 4* on Columbia
40. **Best Engineered Record (Classical)**: Fred Plaut for *Horowitz at Carnegie Hall—An Historic Return* on Columbia
41. **Best Engineered Record**: Larry Levine for *A Taste of Honey* on A&M
42. **Best Album Cover Photography**: Robert Jones and Ken Whitmore for *Jazz Suite on the Mass Texts* on RCA
43. **Best Album Notes (Award to Annotator)**: Stan Cornyn for *September of My Years* on Reprise
44. **Best Album Cover (Classical)**: George Estes and James Alexander for *Bartok: Concerto No. 2 for Violin/Stravinsky: Concerto for Violin* on RCA
45. **Most Promising New Recording Artist**: Peter Serkin on RCA
46. **Best New Country and Western Artist**: The Statler Brothers on Columbia
47. **Best New Artist**: Tom Jones on Parrot

1967 Grammy Awards

1. **Record of the Year:** *Strangers in the Night* by Frank Sinatra on Reprise
2. **Album of the Year:** *Sinatra a Man and His Music* by Frank Sinatra on Reprise
3. **Song of the Year (Award to the Songwriter):** John Lennon and Paul McCartney for *Michelle* on Capitol
4. **Classical Album of the Year:** *Ives: Symphony Number 1 in D-Minor* Morton Gould conducting the Chicago Symphony Orchestra on RCA
5. **Best Male Solo Vocal:** Frank Sinatra for *Strangers in the Night* on Reprise
6. **Best Female Solo Vocal:** Eydie Gorme for *If He Walked into My Life* on Columbia
7. **Best Instrumental Jazz Group:** Wes Montgomery for *Goin' Out of My Head* on Verve
8. **Best Original Jazz Composition:** Duke Ellington for *In the Beginning God* on RCA
9. **Best Instrumental (Non-Jazz):** Herb Alpert and the Tijuana Brass for *What Now My Love* on A&M
10. **Best Country & Western:** David Houston for *Almost Persuaded* on Epic
11. **Best Country & Western Song:** Billy Sherrill and Glenn Sutton for *Almost Persuaded* on Epic
12. **Best Country & Western Female Vocal:** Jeannie Seely for *Don't Touch Me* on Monument
13. **Best Country & Western Male Vocal:** David Houston for *Almost Persuaded* on Epic
14. **Best Rhythm & Blues:** Ray Charles for *Crying Time* on ABC-Paramount
15. **Best Rhythm & Blues Solo Vocal:** Ray Charles for *Crying Time* on ABC-Paramount
16. **Best Rhythm & Blues Group:** Ramsey Lewis for *Hold It Right There* on Cadet
17. **Best Album for Children:** Marvin Miller for *Dr. Seuss Presents "If I Ran the Zoo" and "Sleep Book"* on RCA-Camden
18. **Best Comedy:** Bill Cosby for *Wonderfulness* on Warner Brothers
19. **Best Spoken Word:** *Edward R. Murrow—A Reporter Remembers, Vol. 1: The War Years* on Columbia
20. **Best Folk:** Cortelia Clark for *Blues in the Street* on RCA
21. **Best Sacred:** Porter Wagoner and the Blackwood Brothers for *Grand Old Gospel* on RCA
22. **Best Original Score:** Maurice Jarre for *Dr. Zhivago* on MGM
23. **Best Score from an Original Cast Show Album:** Jerry Herman for *Mame* on Columbia
24. **Best Instrumental Theme:** Neal Hefti for *Batman* on RCA
25. **Best Instrumental Arrangement:** Herb Alpert for *What Now My Love* on A&M
26. **Best Accompaniment Arrangement:** Ernie Freeman for *Strangers in the Night* on Reprise
27. **Best Vocal Group:** Anita Kerr Singers for *A Man and a Woman* on Warner Brothers
28. **Best Chorus:** Ray Coniff Singers for *Somewhere My Love (Lara's Theme from "Dr. Zhivago")* on Columbia
29. **Best Contemporary Rock & Roll:** New Vaudeville Band for *Winchester Cathedral* on Fontana
30. **Best Contemporary Solo Vocal:** Paul McCartney for *Eleanor Rigby* on Capitol
31. **Best Contemporary Group:** The Mamas and the Papas for *Monday, Monday* on Dunhill
32. **Best Classical Orchestra:** The Boston Symphony Orchestra conducted by Erich Leinsdorf for *Mahler: Symphony No. 6 in A-Minor* on RCA
33. **Best Classical Chamber Music:** Boston Symphony Chamber Players on RCA
34. **Best Performance Instrumental Soloist:** Julian Bream for *Baroque Guitar* on RCA
35. **Best Classical Chorales:** Robert Shaw Chorale and Orchestra for *Handel: Messiah* on RCA, and Gregg Smith Singers and Ithaca College Concert Choir with the Texas Boys Choir for *Ives: Music for Chorus (Gen. Wm. Booth Enters Into Heaven, Serenity, the Circus Band, etc.* on Columbia
36. **Best Opera:** Georg Solti conducting the Vienna Philharmonic for *Wagner: Die Walkure* on London
37. **Best Vocal Soloist:** Leontyne Price for *Prima Donna* on RCA
38. **Best Album Cover (Award to Art

G Grammy Awards 1968

Director): Klaus Voormann for *Revolver* on Capitol
39. **Best Album Cover Photography**: Robert Jones and Les Leverette for *Confessions of a Broken Man* on RCA
40. **Best Album Notes (Award to Annotator)**: Stan Cornyn for *Sinatra at the Sands* on Reprise
41. **Best Engineered Classical**: Anthony Salvatore for *Wagner: Lohengrin* on RCA
42. **Best Engineered Non-Classical**: Eddie Brackett and Lee Herschberg for *Strangers in the Night* on Reprise

1968 Grammy Awards

1. **Record of the Year**: *Up, Up and Away* by the 5th Dimension on Soul City
2. **Album of the Year**: *Sgt. Pepper's Lonely Hearts Club Band* by the Beatles on Capitol
3. **Song of the Year (Award to the Songwriter)**: Jim Webb for *Up, Up and Away* on Soul City
4. **Classical Albums of the Year**: *Mahler: Symphony Number 8 in E-Flat Major (Symphony of a Thousand)* by Leonard Bernstein conducting the London Symphony Orchestra on Columbia, and *Berg: Wozzeck* by Pierre Boulez conducting the Paris National Opera on Columbia
5. **Best Male Solo Vocal**: Glen Campbell for *By the Time I Get to Phoenix* on Capitol
6. **Best Female Solo Vocal**: Bobbie Gentry for *Ode to Billie Joe* on Capitol
7. **Best Instrumental Jazz Small Group**: Cannonball Adderley Quintet for *Mercy, Mercy, Mercy* on Capitol
8. **Best Instrumental Jazz Large Group**: Duke Ellington for *Far East Suite* on RCA
9. **Best Country & Western**: Glen Campbell for *Gentle on My Mind* on Capitol
10. **Best Country & Western Song**: John Hartford for *Gentle on My Mind* on Capitol
11. **Best Country & Western Female Vocal**: Tammy Wynette for *I Don't Wanna Play House* on Epic
12. **Best Country & Western Male Vocal**: Glen Campbell for *Gentle on My Mind* on Capitol
13. **Best Country and Western Duet, Trio or Group**: Johnny Cash and June Carter for *Jackson* on Columbia
14. **Best Rhythm & Blues**: Aretha Franklin for *Respect* on Atlantic
15. **Best Rhythm & Blues Female Solo Vocal**: Aretha Franklin for *Respect* on Atlantic
16. **Best Rhythm & Blues Male Solo Vocal**: Lou Rawls for *Dead End Street* on Capitol
17. **Best Rhythm & Blues Group**: Sam & Dave for *Soul Man* on Stax
18. **Best Album for Children**: Boris Karloff for *Dr. Seuss: How the Grinch Stole Christmas* on MGM
19. **Best Comedy**: Bill Cosby for *Revenge* on Warner Brothers/7 Arts
20. **Best Spoken Word**: *Gallant Men* by Senator Everett M. Dirksen on Capitol
21. **Best Folk**: John Hartford for *Gentle on My Mind* on RCA
22. **Best Sacred**: Elvis Presley for *How Great Thou Art* on RCA
23. **Best Gospel**: Porter Wagoner and the Blackwood Brothers for *More Grand Old Gospel* on RCA
24. **Best Original Score**: Lalo Schifrin for *Mission: Impossible* on Dot
25. **Best Score from an Original Cast Show Album**: Fred Ebb and John Kander for *Cabaret* on Columbia
26. **Best Instrumental Theme**: Lalo Schifrin for *Mission: Impossible* on Dot
27. **Best Instrumental Arrangement**: Burt Bachrach for *Alfie* on A&M
28. **Best Instrumental**: Chet Atkins *Picks the Best* on RCA
29. **Best Accompaniment Arrangement**: Jimmie Haskell for *Ode to Billie Joe* on Capitol
30. **Best Vocal Group**: The 5th Dimension for *Up, Up and Away* on Soul City
31. **Best Chorus**: Johnny Mann Singers for *Up, Up and Away* on Liberty
32. **Best Contemporary Single**: The 5th Dimension for *Up, Up and Away* on Soul City
33. **Best Contemporary Male Vocal**: Glen Campbell for *By the Time I Get to Phoenix* on Capitol
34. **Best Contemporary Female Vocal**: Bobbie Gentry for *Ode to Billie Joe* on Capitol
35. **Best Contemporary Group**: The 5th Dimension for *Up, Up and Away* on Soul City

36. **Best Contemporary Album**: *Sgt. Pepper's Lonely Hearts Club Band* by the Beatles on Capitol
37. **Best Classical Orchestra**: The Columbia Symphony Orchestra conducted by Igor Stravinsky for *Stravinsky: Firebird and Petrouchka Suites* on Columbia
38. **Best Classical Chamber Music**: Ravi Shankar and Yehudi Menuhin for *West Meets East* on Angel
39. **Best Performance Instrumental Soloist**: Vladimir Horowitz for *Horowitz in Concert* on Columbia
40. **Best Classical Chorales**: Temple University Chorus conducted by Robert Page for *Orff: Catulli Carmina* with Eugene Ormandy conducting the Philadelphia Orchestra on Columbia, and Leonard Bernstein conducting the London Symphony Orchestra for *Mahler: Symphony No. 8 in E-Flat Major* on Columbia
41. **Best Opera**: Pierre Boulez conducting the Paris National Opera for *Berg: Wozzeck* on Columbia
42. **Best Vocal Soloist**: Leontyne Price for *Prima Donna, Volume 2* with Molinari-Pradelli conducting the RCA Italian Opera Orchestra on RCA
43. **Best Album Cover (Award to Art Director)**: Peter Blake and Jann Haworth for *Sgt. Pepper's Lonely Hearts Club Band* on Capitol
44. **Best Album Cover Photography**: John Berg, Bob Cato and Roland Scherman for *Bob Dylan's Greatest Hits* on Columbia
45. **Best Album Notes (Award to Annotator)**: John D. Loudermilk for *Suburban Attitudes in Country Verse* on RCA
46. **Best Engineered Classical**: Edward T. Graham for *The Glorious Sound of Brass* on Capitol
47. **Best Engineered Non-Classical**: G.E. Emerick for *Sgt. Pepper's Lonely Hearts Club Band* on Capitol
48. **Best New Artist**: Bobbie Gentry on Capitol

1969 Grammy Awards

1. **Record of the Year**: *Mrs. Robinson* by Simon and Garfunkel on Columbia
2. **Album of the Year**: *By the Time I Get to Phoenix* by Glen Campbell on Capitol
3. **Song of the Year (Award to the Songwriter)**: Bobby Russell for *Little Green Apples* on Columbia
4. **Best Contemporary/Pop Male Solo Vocal**: Jose Feliciano for *Light My Fire* on RCA
5. **Best Contemporary/Pop Female Solo Vocal**: Dionne Warwick for *Do You Know the Way to San Jose?* on Scepter
6. **Best Contemporary/Pop Vocal Duo or Group**: Simon and Garfunkel for *Mrs. Robinson* on Columbia
7. **Best Contemporary/Pop Chorus**: Alan Copeland Singers for *Mission: Impossible/Norwegian Wood* on ABC
8. **Best Instrumental Arrangement**: Mike Post for *Classical Gas* on Warner Brothers
9. **Best Contemporary/Pop Instrumental**: Mason Williams for *Classical Gas* on Warner Brothers/7 Arts
10. **Best Accompaniment Arrangement**: Jim Webb for *MacArthur Park* on Dunhill
11. **Best Instrumental Jazz Small Group**: Bill Evans Trio for *Bill Evans at the Montreux Jazz Festival* on Verve
12. **Best Instrumental Jazz Large Group**: Duke Ellington for *And His Mother Called Him Bill* on RCA
13. **Best Country & Western Song**: Bobby Russell for *Little Green Apples* on Smash
14. **Best Country & Western Female Vocal**: Jeannie C. Riley for *Harper Valley P.T.A.* on Plantation
15. **Best Country & Western Male Vocal**: Johnny Cash for *Folsom Prison Blues* on Columbia
16. **Best Country & Western Duet, Trio or Group**: Flatt and Scruggs for *Foggy Mountain Breakdown* on Columbia
17. **Best Rhythm & Blues Song**: Otis Redding and Steve Cropper for *(Sittin' On) The Dock of the Bay* on Volt
18. **Best Rhythm & Blues Female Solo Vocal**: Aretha Franklin for *Chain of Fools* on Atlantic
19. **Best Rhythm & Blues Male Solo Vocal**: Otis Redding for *(Sitting On) The Dock of the Bay* on Volt
20. **Best Rhythm & Blues Group**: The Temptations for *Cloud Nine* on Soul/Gordy
21. **Best Comedy**: Bill Cosby for *To Russell, My Brother, Whom I Slept With* on Warner Brothers/7 Arts

22. **Best Spoken Word**: *Lonesome Cities* by Rod McKuen on Warner Brothers/7 Arts
23. **Best Folk**: Judy Collins for *Both Sides Now* on Elektra
24. **Best Sacred**: Jake Hess for *Beautiful Isle of Somewhere* on RCA
25. **Best Gospel**: The Happy Goodman Family for *The Happy Gospel of the Happy Goodmans* on Word
26. **Best Soul Gospel**: Dottie Rambo for *The Soul of Me* on Heartwarming
27. **Best Original Score**: Paul Simon with additional music by Dave Grusin for *The Graduate* on Columbia
28. **Best Score from an Original Cast Show Album**: Gerome Ragni, James Rado and Galt MacDermott for *Hair* on RCA
29. **Best Instrumental Theme**: Mason Williams for *Classical Gas* on Warner Brothers/7 Arts
30. **Best Classical Orchestra**: New Philharmonia Orchestra conducted by Pierre Boulez for *Boulez Conducts Debussy* on Columbia
31. **Best Classical Chamber Music**: E. Power Biggs with the Edward Tarr Ensemble and Gabrieli Consort conducted by Vittorio Negri for *Gabrieli: Canzoni for Brass, Winds, Strings and Organ* on Columbia
32. **Best Performance Instrumental Soloist**: Vladimir Horowitz for *Horowitz on Television* on Columbia
33. **Best Classical Chorale**: The Gregg Smith Singers, Texas Boys Choir, George Bragg director, Vittorio Negri conductor for *The Glory of Gabrieli* with E. Power Biggs and the Edward Tarr Ensemble on Columbia
34. **Best Opera**: Erich Leinsdorf conducting the New Philharmonic Orchestra and the Ambrosian Opera Chorus for *Mozart: Cosi Fan Tutte* on RCA
35. **Best Vocal Soloist**: Montserrat Caballe for *Rossini Rarities*, Cillario conducting the RCA Italiana Opera Orchestra and Chorus on RCA
36. **Best Engineered Classical**: Gordon Parry for *Mahler: Symphony No. 9 in D-Major* on London
37. **Best Engineered Non-Classical**: Joe Polito and Hugh Davies for *Wichita Lineman* on Capitol
38. **Best Album Cover (Award to Art Director)**: John Berg and Richard Mantel for *Underground* on Columbia
39. **Best Album Notes**: Johnny Cash for *Johnny Cash at Folsom Prison* on Columbia
40. **Best New Artist of 1968**: Jose Feliciano

1970 Grammy Awards

1. **Record of the Year**: *Aquarius/Let the Sunshine In* by the 5th Dimension on Soul City
2. **Album of the Year**: *Blood, Sweat and Tears* by Blood, Sweat and Tears on Columbia
3. **Song of the Year (Award to the Songwriter)**: Joe South for *Games People Play*
4. **Best Contemporary/Pop Male Solo Vocal**: Harry Nilsson for *Everybody's Talkin'* on United Artists
5. **Best Contemporary/Pop Female Solo Vocal**: Peggy Lee for *Is That All There Is?* on Capitol
6. **Best Contemporary/Pop Vocal Duo or Group**: The 5th Dimension for *Aquarius/Let the Sunshine In* on Soul City
7. **Best Contemporary/Pop Chorus**: Percy Faith Orchestra and Chorus for *Love Theme from Romeo and Juliet* on Columbia
8. **Best Instrumental Arrangement**: Henry Mancini for *Love Theme from Romeo and Juliet* on RCA
9. **Best Contemporary/Pop Instrumental**: Blood, Sweat and Tears for *Variations on a Theme by Eric Satie* on Columbia
10. **Best Contemporary Song**: Joe South for *Games People Play*
11. **Best Accompaniment Arrangement**: Fred Lipsius for *Spinning Wheel* on Columbia
12. **Best Instrumental Jazz Small Group**: Wes Montgomery for *Willow Weep for Me* on Verve
13. **Best Instrumental Jazz Large Group**: Quincy Jones for *Walking in Space* on A&M
14. **Best Country & Western Song**: Shel Silverstein for *A Boy Named Sue*
15. **Best Country & Western Female Vocal**: Tammy Wynette for *Stand by Your Man* on Epic
16. **Best Country & Western Male**

Vocal: Johnny Cash for *A Boy Named Sue* on Columbia

17. **Best Country & Western Duet, Trio or Group:** Waylon Jennings and the Kimberleys for *MacArthur Park* on RCA
18. **Best Country & Western Instrumental:** *The Nashville Brass Featuring Danny Davis Play More Nashville Sounds* on RCA
19. **Best Rhythm & Blues Song:** Richard Spencer for *Color Him Father*
20. **Best Rhythm & Blues Female Solo Vocal:** Aretha Franklin for *Share Your Love With Me* on Atlantic
21. **Best Rhythm & Blues Male Solo Vocal:** Joe Simon for *The Chokin' Kind* on Sound Stage 7
22. **Best Rhythm & Blues Vocal or Duo Blues Group:** The Isley Brothers for *It's Your Thing* on T-neck
23. **Best Rhythm & Blues Instrumental:** King Curtis for *Games People Play* on Atco
24. **Best Comedy:** Bill Cosby for *Bill Cosby* on Uni
25. **Best Spoken Word:** *We Love You, Call Collect* by Art Linkletter and Diane on Word/Cap
26. **Best Folk:** Joni Mitchell for *Clouds* on Warner Brothers
27. **Best Sacred:** Jake Hess for *Ain't That Beautiful Singing?* on RCA
28. **Best Gospel:** Porter Wagoner and the Blackwood Brothers for *In Gospel Country* on RCA
29. **Best Soul Gospel:** The Edwin Hawkins Singers for *Oh Happy Day* on Buddah
30. **Best Original Score:** Burt Bacharach for *Butch Cassidy and the Sundance Kid* on A&M
31. **Best Score from an Original Cast Show Album:** Burt Bachrach and Hal David for *Promises, Promises* on Liberty/United Artists
32. **Best Instrumental Theme:** John Barry for *Midnight Cowboy*
33. **Best Children:** Peter, Paul & Mary for *Peter, Paul & Mommy* on Warner Brothers
34. **Classical Album of the Year:** Walter Carlos for *Switched-On Bach* on Columbia
35. **Best Classical Orchestra:** The Cleveland Orchestra conducted by Pierre Boulez for *Boulez Conducts Debussy, Vol. 2 "Images Pour Orchestre"* on Columbia
36. **Best Classical Chamber Music:** The Philadelphia, Cleveland and Chicago Brass Ensembles for *Gabrieli: Antiphonal Music of Gabrieli (Canzoni for Brass Choirs)* on Columbia
37. **Best Performance Instrumental Soloist:** Walter Carlos for *Switched-On Bach* on Columbia
38. **Best Classical Chorales:** The Swingle Singers for *Berio: Sinfonia* the New York Philharmonic conducted by Luciano Berio on Columbia
39. **Best Opera:** Herbert von Karajan conducting the Berlin Philharmonic for *Wagner: Siegfried* on DG
40. **Best Vocal Soloist:** Leontyne Price for *Barber: Two Scenes from "Antony and Cleopatra"/Knoxville: Summer of 1915* The New Philharmonia Orchestra conducted by Thomas Schippers on RCA
41. **Best Engineered Classical:** Walter Carlos for *Switched-On Bach*
42. **Best Engineered Non-Classical:** Geoff Emerick and Phillip McDonald for *Abbey Road* on Apple
43. **Best Album Cover/Album Package:** Evelyn J. Kelbish and David Stahlberg for *America the Beautiful*
44. **Best Album Notes:** Johnny Cash for *Nashville Skyline* on Columbia
45. **Best New Artist of 1969:** Crosby, Stills & Nash

1971 Grammy Awards

1. **Record of the Year:** *Bridge Over Troubled Water* by Simon and Garfunkel on Columbia
2. **Album of the Year:** *Bridge Over Troubled Water* by Simon and Garfunkel on Columbia
3. **Song of the Year (Award to the Songwriter):** Paul Simon for *Bridge Over Troubled Water* on Columbia
4. **Best Contemporary/Pop Male Solo Vocal:** Ray Stevens for *Everything Is Beautiful* on Barnaby
5. **Best Contemporary/Pop Female Solo Vocal:** Dionne Warwick for *I'll Never Fall in Love Again* on Scepter
6. **Best Contemporary/Pop Vocal Duo or Group:** The Carpenters for *Close to You* on A&M

G Grammy Awards 1971

7. **Best Instrumental Arrangement**: Henry Mancini for *Theme from "Z"* on RCA
8. **Best Contemporary/Pop Instrumental**: Henry Mancini for *Theme from "Z" and Other Films* on RCA
9. **Best Contemporary Song**: Paul Simon for *Bridge Over Troubled Water* on Columbia
10. **Best Accompaniment Arrangement**: Paul Simon, Arthur Garfunkel, Jimmy Haskell, Ernie Freeman and Larry Knechtel for *Bridge Over Troubled Water* on Columbia
11. **Best Instrumental Jazz Small Group**: Bill Evans for *Alone* on MGM
12. **Best Instrumental Jazz Large Group**: Miles Davis for *Bitches Brew* on Columbia
13. **Best Country & Western Song**: Marty Robbins for *My Woman, My Woman, My Wife* on Columbia
14. **Best Country & Western Female Vocal**: Lynn Anderson for *Rose Garden* on Columbia
15. **Best Country & Western Male Vocal**: Ray Price for *For the Good Times* on Columbia
16. **Best Country & Western Duet, Trio or Group**: Johnny Cash and June Carter for *If I Were a Carpenter* on Columbia
17. **Best Country & Western Instrumental**: Chet Atkins and Jerry Reed for *Me & Jerry* on RCA
18. **Best Rhythm & Blues Song**: Ronald Dunbar and General Johnson for *Patches* on Atlantic
19. **Best Rhythm & Blues Female Solo Vocal**: Aretha Franklin for *Don't Play That Song* on Atlantic
20. **Best Rhythm & Blues Male Solo Vocal**: B.B. King for *The Thrill Is Gone* on ABC
21. **Best Rhythm & Blues Vocal or Duo Blues Group**: The Delfonics for *Didn't I (Blow Your Mind This Time)* on Philly Groove
22. **Best Comedy**: Flip Wilson for *The Devil Made Me Buy This Dress* on Little David
23. **Best Spoken Word**: *Why I Oppose the War in Vietnam* by Dr. Martin Luther King, Jr. on Black Forum
24. **Best Sacred**: Jake Hess for *Everything Is Beautiful* on RCA
25. **Best Gospel**: The Oak Ridge Boys for *Talk About the Good Times* on Heart Warming
26. **Best Soul Gospel**: The Edwin Hawkins Singers for *Every Man Wants to Be Free* on Buddah
27. **Best Ethnic or Traditional**: T-bone Walker for *Good Feelin'* on Polydor
28. **Best Original Score**: John Lennon, Paul McCartney, Ringo Starr and George Harrison for *Let It Be* on Apple
29. **Best Score from an Original Cast Show Album**: Stephen Sondheim for *Company* on Columbia
30. **Best Instrumental Composition**: Alfred Newman for *Airport Love Theme* on Decca
31. **Best Children**: Joan Cooney producer of *Sesame Street* on Columbia
32. **Classical Album of the Year**: Colin Davis conducting the Royal Opera House Orchestra and Chorus for *Berlioz: Les Troyens* on Phillips
33. **Best Classical Orchestra**: The Cleveland Orchestra conducted by Pierre Boulez for *Stravinsky: Le Sacre du Printemps* on Columbia
34. **Best Classical Chamber Music**: Eugene Istomin, Isaac Stern and Leonard Rose for *Beethoven: The Complete Piano Trios* on Columbia
35. **Best Performance Instrumental Soloists**: David Oistrakh and Mstislav Rostropovich for *Brahms: Double Concerto (Concerto in A-Minor for Violin and Cello)* on Angel
36. **Best Classical Chorale**: The Gregg Smith Singers and the Columbia Chamber Ensemble for *Ives: New Music of Charles Ives* on Columbia
37. **Best Opera**: Colin Davis conducting the Royal Opera House Chorus and Orchestra for *Berlioz: Les Troyens* on Philips
38. **Best Vocal Soloist**: Dietrich Fischer-Dieskau for *Schubert: Lieder* on DG
39. **Best Engineered Classical**: Fred Plaut, Ray Moore and Arthur Kendy for *Stravinsky: Le Sacre du Printemps* with Pierre Boulez conducting the Cleveland Orchestra on Columbia
40. **Best Engineered Non-Classical**: Roy Halee for *Bridge Over Troubled Water* on Columbia
41. **Best Album Cover/Album Package**: Robert Lockart and Ivan Nagy

for *Indianola Mississippi Seeds* on ABC
42. **Best Album Notes**: Chris Albertson for *The World's Greatest Blues Singer* on Columbia
43. **Best New Artist of the Year**: The Carpenters on A&M

1972 Grammy Awards

1. **Record of the Year**: *It's Too Late* by Carole King on Ode
2. **Album of the Year**: *Tapestry* by Carole King on Ode
3. **Song of the Year (Award to the Songwriter)**: Carole King for *You've Got a Friend* on Ode
4. **Best Contemporary/Pop Male Solo Vocal**: James Taylor for *You've Got a Friend* on Warner Brothers
5. **Best Contemporary/Pop Female Solo Vocal**: Carole King for *Tapestry* on Ode
6. **Best Contemporary/Pop Vocal Duo or Group**: The Carpenters for *The Carpenters* on A&M
7. **Best Instrumental Arrangement**: Isaac Hayes and Johnny Allen for *Theme from Shaft* on Enterprise
8. **Best Contemporary/Pop Instrumental**: Quincy Jones for *Smackwater Jack* on A&M
9. **Best Accompaniment Arrangement**: Paul McCartney for *Uncle Albert/Admiral Halsey* on Apple
10. **Best Instrumental Jazz Small Group**: Bill Evans Trio for *The Bill Evans Album* on Columbia
11. **Best Instrumental Jazz Large Group**: Duke Ellington for *New Orleans Suite* on Atlantic
12. **Best Jazz Soloist**: Bill Evans for *The Bill Evans Album* on Columbia
13. **Best Country & Western Song**: Kris Kristofferson for *Help Me Make It Through the Night*
14. **Best Country & Western Female Vocal**: Sammi Smith for *Help Me Make It Through the Night* on Mega
15. **Best Country & Western Male Vocal**: Jerry Reed for *When You're Hot, You're Hot* on RCA
16. **Best Country & Western Duet, Trio or Group**: Conway Twitty & Loretta Lynn for *After the Fire Is Gone* on Decca
17. **Best Country & Western Instrumental**: Chet Atkins for *Snowbird* on RCA
18. **Best Rhythm & Blues Song**: Bill Withers for *Ain't No Sunshine* on Sussex
19. **Best Rhythm & Blues Female Solo Vocal**: Aretha Franklin for *Bridge Over Troubled Water* on Atlantic
20. **Best Rhythm & Blues Male Solo Vocal**: Lou Rawls for *A Natural Man* on MGM
21. **Best Rhythm & Blues Vocal or Duo Blues Group**: Ike and Tina Turner for *Proud Mary* on United Artists
22. **Best Comedy**: Lily Tomlin for *This Is a Recording* on Polydor
23. **Best Spoken Word**: *Desiderata* by Les Crane on Warner Brothers
24. **Best Sacred**: Charley Pride for *Did You Think to Pray?* on RCA
25. **Best Gospel**: Charley Pride for *Let Me Live* on RCA
26. **Best Soul Gospel**: Shirley Caesar for *Put Your Hand in the Hand of the Man from Galilee* on Hob
27. **Best Ethnic**: Muddy Waters for *They Call Me Muddy Waters* on Chess
28. **Best Original Motion Picture Score**: Isaac Hayes for *Shaft* on Enterprise
29. **Best Score from an Original Cast Show Album**: Stephen Schwartz for *Godspell* on Bell
30. **Best Instrumental Composition**: Michel Legrand for *Theme from Summer of '42* on Warner Brothers
31. **Best Children**: Bill Cosby for *Bill Cosby Talks to Kids About Drugs* on Uni
32. **Classical Album of the Year**: Vladimir Horowitz, pianist for *Horowitz Plays Rachmaninoff* on Columbia
33. **Best Classical Orchestra**: Carlo Maria Giulini conducting the Chicago Symphony Orchestra for *Mahler: Symphony No. 1 in D-Major* on Angel
34. **Best Classical Chamber Music**: Julliard Quartet for *Debussy: Quartet in G-Minor/Ravel: Quartet in F-Major* on Columbia
35. **Best Performance Instrumental Soloists (with Orchestra)**: Julian Bream for *Villa-Lobos: Concerto for Guitar* Andre Previn conducting the London Symphony on RCA
36. **Best Performance Instrumental Soloists (without Orchestra)**: Vladimir

Horowitz for *Horowitz Plays Rachmaninoff* on Columbia
37. **Best Opera**: Erich Leinsdorf conducting the London Symphony Orchestra for *Verdi: Aida* on RCA
38. **Best Vocal Soloist**: Leontyne Price for *Leontyne Price Sings Robert Shumann* on RCA
39. **Best Classical Chorale**: Russell Burgess conducting the Wadsworth School Boys Choir, and Arthur Oldham conducting the London Symphony Chorus for *Berlioz: Requiem* with Colin Davis conducting the London Symphony Orchestra on Philips
40. **Best Engineered Classical**: Vittorio Negri for *Berlioz: Requiem* on Philips
41. **Best Engineered Non-Classical**: David Purple, Ron Capone and Henry Bush for *Theme from Shaft* on Enterprise
42. **Best Album Cover (Award to Art Director)**: Dean O. Torrence and Gene Brownell for *Pollution* on Prophesy
43. **Best Album Notes (Award to Annotator)**: Sam Samudio for *Sam, Hard and Heavy* on Atlantic
44. **Best New Artist of the Year**: Carly Simon on Elekta

1973 Grammy Awards

1. **Record of the Year**: *The First Time Ever I Saw Your Face* by Roberta Flack on Atlantic
2. **Album of the Year**: *The Concert for Bangla Desh* by George Harrison, Ravi Shankar, Bob Dylan, Leon Russell, Eric Clapton, Ringo Starr, Billy Preston and Klaus Voormann on Apple
3. **Song of the Year (Award to the Songwriter)**: Ewan MacColl for *The First Time Ever I Saw Your Face*
4. **Best Contemporary/Pop Male Solo Vocal**: Nilsson for *Without You* on RCA
5. **Best Contemporary/Pop Female Solo Vocal**: Helen Reddy for *I Am Woman* on Capitol
6. **Best Contemporary/Pop Vocal Duo or Group**: Roberta Flack and Donny Hathaway for *Where Is the Love?* on Atlantic
7. **Best Instrumental Arrangement**: Don Ellis for *Theme from "The French Connection"* on Columbia
8. **Best Contemporary/Pop Instrumental**: Isaac Hayes for *Black Moses* for Enterprise
9. **Best Pop Instrumental Performer**: Billy Preston for *Out-a-Space* on A&M
10. **Best Accompaniment Arrangement**: Michel Legrand for *What Are You Doing the Rest of Your Life?* on Mainstream
11. **Best Instrumental Jazz Small Group**: Freddy Hubbard for *First Flight* on CTI
12. **Best Instrumental Jazz Large Group**: Duke Ellington for *Toga Brava Suite* on United Artists
13. **Best Jazz Soloist**: Gary Burton for *Alone At Last* on Atlantic
14. **Best Country & Western Song**: Ben Peters for *Kiss an Angel Good Mornin'*
15. **Best Country & Western Female Vocal**: Donna Fargo for *The Happiest Girl in the Whole USA* on Dot
16. **Best Country & Western Male Vocal**: Charlie Pride for *Charley Pride Sings Heart Songs* on RCA
17. **Best Country & Western Duet, Trio or Group**: The Statler Brothers for *Class of '57* on Mercury
18. **Best Country & Western Instrumental**: Charley McCoy for *Charley McCoy/The Real McCoy* on Monument
19. **Best Rhythm & Blues Song**: Barrett Strong and Norman Whitfield for *Papa Was a Rolling Stone*
20. **Best Rhythm & Blues Female Solo Vocal**: Aretha Franklin for *Young, Gifted & Black* on Atlantic
21. **Best Rhythm & Blues Male Solo Vocal**: Billy Paul for *Me & Mrs. Jones* on Philadelphia International
22. **Best Rhythm & Blues Vocal or Duo Blues Group**: The Temptations for *Papa Was a Rolling Stone* on Gordy Motown
23. **Best Rhythm and Blues Instrumental**: Paul Riser conducting the Temptations for *Papa Was a Rolling Stone* on Gordy Motown
24. **Best Comedy**: George Carlin for *FM & AM* on Little David
25. **Best Spoken Word**: *Lenny* produced by Bruce Botnik on Blue Thumb
26. **Best Inspirational**: Elvis Presley for *He Touched Me* on RCA
27. **Best Gospel**: The Blackwood Brothers for *Love* on RCA

Grammy Awards 1974

28. **Best Soul Gospel**: Aretha Franklin for *Amazing Grace* on Atlantic
29. **Best Ethnic or Traditional**: Muddy Waters for *The London Muddy Waters Sessions* on Chess
30. **Best Original Motion Picture Score**: Nino Rota for *The Godfather* on Paramount
31. **Best Score from an Original Cast Show Album**: Micki Grant for *Don't Bother Me, I Can't Cope* on Polydor
32. **Best Instrumental Composition**: Michel Legrand for *Brian's Song*
33. **Best Children**: Producer and music director Joe Raposo for *The Electric Company* project directors Christopher Cerf, Bill Cosby, Rita Moreno and Lee Chamberlain on Warner Brothers
34. **Classical Album of the Year**: Georg Solti conducting the Chicago Symphony Orchestra for *Mahler: Symphony No.8* with the Vienna State Opera Chorus and Vienna Singverein Chorus and Soloists on London
35. **Best Classical Orchestra**: Georg Solti conducting the Chicago Symphony Orchestra for *Mahler, Symphony No. 7* on London
36. **Best Classical Chamber Music**: Julian Bream and John Williams for *Julian & John* on RCA
37. **Best Performance Instrumental Soloists (with Orchestra)**: Artur Rubinstein for *Brahms: Concerto No. 2* on RCA
38. **Best Performance Instrumental Soloists (without Orchestra)**: Vladimir Horowitz for *Horowitz Plays Chopin* on Columbia
39. **Best Opera**: Erik Smith for *Berlioz: Benvenuto Cellini* with Colin Davis conducting the BBC Symphony and the Chorus of the Convent Garden on Philips
40. **Best Vocal Soloist**: Dietrich Fischer-Dieskau for *Brahms: Die Schone Magelone* on Angel
41. **Best Classical Choral**: Georg Solti conductor for *Mahler: Symphony No. 8* on London
42. **Best Engineered Classical**: Gordon Parry and Kenneth Wilkinson for *Mahler: Symphony No. 8* on London
43. **Best Engineered Non-Classical**: Armin Steiner for *Moods* on Uni
44. **Best Album Cover (Award to Art Director)**: Acy Lehman and Harvey Dinerstein for *The Siegel Schwall Band* on Wooden Nickel
45. **Best Album Notes (Award to Annotator)**: Tom T. Hall for *Tom T. Hall's Greatest Hits* on Mercury
46. **Best Album Notes/Classical (Award to Annotator)**: James Lyons for *Vaughan Williams: Symphony No. 2* on RCA
47. **Best New Artist of the Year**: America on Warner Brothers

1974 Grammy Awards

1. **Record of the Year**: *Killing Me Softly with His Song* by Roberta Flack on Atlantic
2. **Album of the Year**: *Innervisions* by Stevie Wonder on Tamla/Motown
3. **Song of the Year (Award to the Songwriter)**: Norman Gimbel and Charles Fox for *Killing Me Softly with His Song*
4. **Best Contemporary/Pop Male Solo Vocal**: Stevie Wonder for *You Are the Sunshine of My Life* on Tamla/Motown
5. **Best Contemporary/Pop Female Solo Vocal**: Roberta Flack for *Killing Me Softly with His Song* on Atlantid
6. **Best Contemporary/Pop Vocal Duo or Group**: Gladys Knight and the Pips for *Neither One of Us (Wants to Be the First to Say Goodbye)* on Soul/Motown
7. **Best Instrumental Arrangement**: Quincy Jones for *Summer in the City* on A&M
8. **Best Contemporary/Pop Instrumental**: Eumir Deodato for *Also Sprach Zarathustra (Used in the Movie "2,001: A Space Odyssey")* on CTI
9. **Best Instrumental Composition**: Gato Barbieri for *Last Tango in Paris*
10. **Best Accompaniment Arrangement**: George Martin for *Live and Let Die* on Apple
11. **Best Instrumental Jazz Small Group**: Supersax for *Supersax Plays Bird* on Capitol
12. **Best Instrumental Jazz Large Group**: Woody Herman for *Giant Steps* on Fantasy
13. **Best Jazz Soloist**: Art Tatum for *God Is in the House* on Onyx
14. **Best Country & Western Song**: Kenny O'Dell for *Behind Closed Doors*

G Grammy Awards 1975

15. **Best Country & Western Female Vocal**: Olivia Newton-John for *Let Me Be There* on MCA
16. **Best Country & Western Male Vocal**: Charlie Rich for *Behind Closed Doors* on Epic/Columbia
17. **Best Country & Western Duo or Group**: Kris Kristofferson and Rita Coolidge for *From the Bottle to the Bottom* on A&M
18. **Best Country & Western Instrumental**: Eric Weissberg and Steve Mandell for *Dueling Banjos* on Warner Brothers
19. **Best Rhythm & Blues Song**: Stevie Wonder for *Superstition*
20. **Best Rhythm & Blues Female Solo Vocal**: Aretha Franklin for *Master of Eyes* on Atlantic
21. **Best Rhythm & Blues Male Solo Vocal**: Stevie Wonder for *Superstition* on Tamla/Motown
22. **Best Rhythm & Blues Vocal or Duo Blues Group**: Gladys Knight and the Pips for *Midnight Train to Georgia* on Buddah
23. **Best Rhythm & Blues Instrumental**: Ramsey Lewis for *Hang on Sloopy* on Columbia
24. **Best Comedy**: Cheech and Chong for *Los Conchinos* on Ode
25. **Best Spoken Word**: *Jonathan Livingston Seagull* by Richard Harris on ABC/Dunhill
26. **Best Inspirational**: The Bill Gaither Trio for *Let's Just Praise the Lord* on Impact
27. **Best Gospel**: The Blackwood Brothers for *Release Me (from My Sin)* on Skylite
28. **Best Soul Gospel**: The Dixie Hummingbirds for *Loves Me Like a Rock* on ABC
29. **Best Ethnic or Traditional**: Doc Watson for *Then and Now* on United Artists
30. **Best Original Motion Picture Score**: Neil Diamond for *Jonathan Livingston Seagull* on Columbia
31. **Best Score from an Original Cast Show Album**: Stephen Sondheim for *A Little Night Music* on Columbia
32. **Best Children**: Joe Raposo producer for *Sesame Street Live* on Columbia
33. **Classical Album of the Year**: Pierre Boulez conducting the New York Philharmonic Orchestra for *Bartok: Concerto for Orchestra* on Columbia
34. **Best Classical Orchestra**: The New York Philharmonic Orchestra conducted by Pierre Boulez for *Bartok: Concerto for Orchestra* on Columbia
35. **Best Classical Chamber Music**: Gunthur Schuller and the New England Conservatory Ragtime Ensemble for *Joplin: The Red Back Book* on Angel
36. **Best Performance Instrumental Soloists (with Orchestra)**: Vladimir Ashkenazy for *Beethoven: Concerti (5) for Piano and Orchestra* with Georg Solti conducting the Chicago Symphony Orchestra on London
37. **Best Performance Instrumental Soloists (without Orchestra)**: Vladimir Horowitz, pianist for *Horowitz Plays Scriabin* on Columbia
38. **Best Opera**: Leonard Bernstein conducting the Metropolitan Opera Chorus for *Bizet: Carmen* on DG
39. **Best Vocal Soloist**: Leontyne Price for *Puccini: heroines (La Boheme, La Rondine, Tosca and Manon Lescaut)* on RCA
40. **Best Classical Chorale**: Andre Previn conducting the London Symphony Orchestra for *Walton: Belshazzar's Feast* with the London Symphony Orchestra Chorus conducted by Arthur Oldham on Angel
41. **Best Engineered Classical**: Edward T. Graham and Raymond Moore for *Bartok: Concerto for Orchestra* on Columbia
42. **Best Engineered Non-Classical**: Robert Margouleff and Malcom Cecil for *Innervisions* on Tamla/Motown
43. **Best Album Cover (Award to Art Director)**: Wilkes and Braun, Inc. for *Tommy* on Ode
44. **Best Album Notes (Award to Annotator)**: Dan Morgenstern for *God Is in the House* on Onyx
45. **Best Album Notes/Classical (Award to Annotator)**: Glenn Gould for *Hindemith: Sonatas for Piano (Complete)* on Columbia
46. **Best New Artist of the Year**: Bette Midler on Atlantic

1975 Grammy Awards

1. **Record of the Year:** *I Honestly Love You* by Olivia Newton-John on MCA

Grammy Awards 1975

2. **Album of the Year:** *Fulfillingness' First Finale* by Stevie Wonder on Tamla/Motown
3. **Song of the Year (Award to the Songwriter):** Marilyn Bergman, Alan Bergman and Marvin Hamlisch for *The Way We Were*
4. **Best Contemporary/Pop Male Solo Vocal:** *Fulfillingness' First Finale* by Stevie Wonder on Tamla/Motown
5. **Best Contemporary/Pop Female Solo Vocal:** Olivia Newton-John for *I Honestly Love You* on MCA
6. **Best Contemporary/Pop Vocal Duo or Group:** Paul McCartney and Wings for *Band on the Run* on Apple/Capitol
7. **Best Instrumental Arrangement:** Pat Williams for *Threshold* on Capitol
8. **Best Contemporary/Pop Instrumental:** *The Entertainer* by Marvin Hamlisch on MCA
9. **Best Instrumental Composition:** Mike Oldfield for *Tubular Bells (Theme from "The Exorcist")*
10. **Best Accompaniment Arrangement:** Joni Mitchell and Tom Scott for *Down to You* on Asylum
11. **Best Instrumental Jazz Small Group:** Oscar Peterson, Joe Pass and Niels Pedersen for *The Trio* on Pablo
12. **Best Instrumental Jazz Large Group:** Woody Herman for *Thundering Herd* on Fantasy
13. **Best Jazz Soloist:** Charlie Parker for *First Recordings* on Onyx
14. **Best Country & Western Song:** Norris Wilson and Billy Sherrill for *A Very Special Love Song*
15. **Best Country & Western Female Vocal:** Anne Murray for *A Love Song* on Capitol
16. **Best Country & Western Male Vocal:** Ronnie Milsap for *Please Don't Tell Me How the Story Ends* on RCA
17. **Best Country & Western Duo or Group:** The Pointer Sisters for *Fairytale* on Blue Thumb
18. **Best Country & Western Instrumental:** Chet Atkins and Merle Travis for *The Atkins-Travis Travelling Show* on ABC
19. **Best Rhythm & Blues Song:** Stevie Wonder for *Living for the City*
20. **Best Rhythm & Blues Female Solo Vocal:** Aretha Franklin for *Ain't Nothing Like the Real Thing* on Atlantic
21. **Best Rhythm & Blues Male Solo Vocal:** Stevie Wonder for *Boogie on Reggae Woman* on Tamla/Motown
22. **Best Rhythm & Blues Vocal or Duo Blues Group:** Rufus for *Tell Me Something Good* on ABC
23. **Best Rhythm and Blues Instrumental:** MFSB for *TSOP (The Sound of Philadelphia)* on Philadelphia International/Epic
24. **Best Comedy:** Richard Pryor for *That Nigger's Crazy* on Partee/Stax
25. **Best Spoken Word:** *Good Evening* by Peter Cook and Dudley Moore on Island
26. **Best Inspirational:** Elvis Presley for *How Great Thou Art* on RCA
27. **Best Gospel:** The Oak Ridge Boys for *The Baptism of Jesse Taylor* on Columbia
28. **Best Soul Gospel:** James Cleveland and the Southern California Community Choir for *In the Ghetto* on Savoy
29. **Best Ethnic or Traditional:** Doc and Merle Watson for *Two Days in November* on United Artists
30. **Best Original Motion Picture Score:** Marvin Hamlisch, Marilyn and Alan Bergman for *The Way We Were* on Columbia
31. **Best Score from an Original Cast Show Album:** Judd Woldin and Robert Brittan for *Raisin* on Columbia
32. **Best Children:** Sebastian Cabot, Sterling Holloway and Paul Winchell for *Winnie the Pooh & Tigger Too* on Disneyland
33. **Classical Album of the Year:** Georg Solti conducting the Chicago Symphony Orchestra for *Berlioz: Symphony Fantastique* on London
34. **Best Classical Orchestra:** The Chicago Symphony conducted by Georg Solti for *Berlioz: Symphony Fantastique* on London
35. **Best Classical Chamber Music:** Artur Rubinstein, Henryk Szeryng and Pierre Fournier for *Brahms and Schumann Trios* on RCA
36. **Best Performance Instrumental Soloists (with Orchestra):** David Oistrakh for *Shostakovich: Violin Concerto No. 1* on Angel

G Grammy Awards 1976

37. **Best Performance Instrumental Soloists (without Orchestra)**: Alicia de Larrocha for *Albeniz: Iberia* on London
38. **Best Opera**: Georg Solti conducting for *Puccini: La Boheme* on RCA
39. **Best Vocal Soloist**: Leontyne Price for *Leontyne Price sings Richard Strauss* on RCA
40. **Best Classical Choral**: Colin Davis conducting for *Berlioz: the Damnation of Faust* on Philips
41. **Best Engineered Classical**: Kenneth Wilkinson for *Berlioz: Symphonie Fantastique* on London
42. **Best Engineered Non-Classical**: Geoff Emerick for *Band on the Run* on Apple/Capitol
43. **Best Album Cover (Award to Art Director)**: Christopher Whorf and Ed Thrasher for *Come and Gone* on Warner Brothers
44. **Best Album Notes (Award to Annotator)**: Charles R. Townsend for *For the Last Time* on United Artists and Dan Morgenstern for *The Hawk Flies* on Milestone
45. **Best Album Notes/Classical (Award to Annotator)**: Rory Guy for *The Classic Erich Wolfgang Korngold* on Angel
46. **Producer of the Year**: Thom Bell
47. **Best New Artist of the Year**: Marvin Hamlisch on MCA

1976 Grammy Awards

1. **Record of the Year**: *Love Will Keep Us Together* by the Captain and Tenille on A&M
2. **Album of the Year**: *Still Crazy After All These Years* by Paul Simon on Columbia
3. **Song of the Year (Award to the Songwriter)**: Stephen Sondheim for *Send in the Clowns*
4. **Best Contemporary/Pop Male Solo Vocal**: Paul Simon for *Still Crazy After All These Years* on Columbia
5. **Best Contemporary/Pop Female Solo Vocal**: *At Seventeen* by Janis Ian on Columbia
6. **Best Contemporary/Pop Vocal Duo or Group**: The Eagles for *Lyin' Eyes* on Asylum
7. **Best Instrumental Arrangement**: Mike Post and Pete Carpenter for *The Rockford Files* on MGM
8. **Best Contemporary/Pop Instrumental**: *The Hustle* by Van McCoy and the Soul City Symphony on AVCO
9. **Best Instrumental Composition**: Michel Legrand for *Images*
10. **Best Accompaniment Arrangement**: Ray Stevens for *Misty* on Barnaby
11. **Best Instrumental Jazz Small Group**: Chick Corea and Return to Forever for *No Mystery* on Polydor
12. **Best Instrumental Jazz Large Group**: Phil Woods with Michel Legrand and his Orchestra for *Images* on Gryphon/RCA
13. **Best Jazz Soloist**: Dizzy Gillespie for *Oscar Peterson and Dizzy Gillespie* on Pablo
14. **Best Country & Western Song**: Chips Moman and Larry Butler for *(Hey Won't You Play) Another Somebody Done Somebody Wrong Song*
15. **Best Country & Western Female Vocal**: Linda Ronstadt for *I Can't Help It (If I'm Still in Love with You)* on Capitol
16. **Best Country & Western Male Vocal**: Willie Nelson for *Blue Eyes Crying in the Rain* on Columbia
17. **Best Country & Western Duo or Group**: Kris Kristofferson and Rita Coolidge for *Lover Please* on Monument
18. **Best Country & Western Instrumental**: Chet Atkins for *The Entertainer* on RCA
19. **Best Rhythm & Blues Song**: Harry Wayne Casey, Richard Finch, Willie Clarke and Betty Wright for *Where Is the Love?*
20. **Best Rhythm & Blues Female Solo Vocal**: Natalie Cole for *This Will Be* on Capitol
21. **Best Rhythm & Blues Male Solo Vocal**: Ray Charles for *Living for the City* on Crossover
22. **Best Rhythm & Blues Vocal or Duo Blues Group**: Earth, Wind & Fire for *Shining Star* on Columbia
23. **Best Rhythm and Blues Instrumental**: Silver Convention for *Fly, Robin Fly* on Midland/RCA
24. **Best Comedy**: Richard Pryor for *Is It Something I Said?* on Reprise
25. **Best Spoken Word**: *Give 'Em Hell, Harry* by James Whitmore on United Artists
26. **Best Inspirational**: The Bill

Gaither Trio for *Jesus, We Just Want to Thank You* on Impact

27. **Best Gospel:** The Imperials for *No Shortage* on Impact

28. **Best Soul Gospel:** Andrae Crouch and the Disciples for *Take Me Back* on Light

29. **Best Ethnic or Traditional:** Muddy Waters for *The Muddy Waters Woodstock Album* on Chess

30. **Best Original Motion Picture Score:** John Williams for *Jaws* on MCA

31. **Best Original Cast:** Jerry Wexler and Charlie Smalls for *The Wiz* on Atlantic

32. **Best Latin:** Eddie Palmieri for *Sun of Latin Music* on Coco

33. **Best Children:** Richard Burton for *The Little Prince* on PIP

34. **Classical Album of the Year:** Georg Solti conducting the Chicago Symphony Orchestra for *Beethoven: Symphonies (9) Complete* on London

35. **Best Classical Orchestra:** Pierre Boulez conducting the New York Philharmonic Orchestra for *Ravel: Daphnis et Chloe (Complete Ballet)* on Columbia

36. **Best Classical Chamber Music:** Artur Rubinstein, Henryk Szeryng and Pierre Fournier for *Schubert: Trios No. 1 in B-Flat Major Op. 99 and 2 in E-Flat Major Op. 100 (the Piano Trios)* on RCA

37. **Best Performance Instrumental Soloists (with Orchestra):** Alicia de Larrocha for *Ravel: Concerto for Left Hand and Concerto for Piano in G-Major/Faure: Fantasie for Piano and Orchestra* with De Burgos & Foster conducting the London Philharmonic Orchestra on London

38. **Best Performance Instrumental Soloists (without Orchestra):** Nathan Milstein for *Bach: Sonatas and Partitas for Violin Unaccompanied* on DG

39. **Best Opera:** Colin Davis conducting the Royal Opera House, Covent Garden for *Mozart: Cosi Fan Tutte* on Philips

40. **Best Vocal Soloist:** Janet Baker for *Mahler: Kindertotenlieder* with Leonard Bernstein conducting the Israel Philharmonic Orchestra on Columbia

41. **Best Classical Choral:** Robert Page directing the Cleveland Orchestra Chorus and Boys Choir for *Orff: Carmina Burana* with Michael Tilson Thomas conducting the Cleveland Orchestra on Columbia

42. **Best Engineered (Classical):** Bud Graham, Ray Moore and Milton Cherin for *Ravel: Daphnis et Chloe* on Columbia

43. **Best Engineered (Non-Classical):** Brooks Arthur, Larry Alexander and Russ Payne for *Between the Lines* on Columbia

44. **Best Album Cover (Award to Art Director):** Jim Ladwig for *Honey* on Mercury

45. **Best Album notes (Award to Annotator):** Pete Hamill for *Blood on the Tracks* on Columbia

46. **Best Album Notes/Classical (Award to the Annotator):** Gunthur Schuller for *Footlifters* on Columbia

47. **Best Producer of the Year:** Arif Mardin

48. **Best New Artist of the Year:** Natalie Cole on Capitol

1977 Grammy Awards

1. **Record of the Year:** *This Masquerade* by George Benson on Warner Brothers

2. **Album of the Year:** *Songs in the Key of Life* by Stevie Wonder on Tamla/Motown

3. **Song of the Year (Award to the Songwriter):** Bruce Johnston for *I Write the Songs*

4. **Best Contemporary/Pop Male Solo Vocal:** Stevie Wonder for *Songs in the Key of Life* on Tamla/Motown

5. **Best Contemporary/Pop Female Solo Vocal:** Linda Ronstadt for *Hasten Down the Wind* on Asylum

6. **Best Contemporary/Pop Vocal Duo or Group:** Chicago for *If You Leave Me Now* on Columbia

7. **Best Instrumental Arrangement:** Chick Corea for *Leprechaun's Dream* on Polydor

8. **Best Contemporary/Pop Instrumental:** *Breezin'* by George Benson on Warner Brothesr

9. **Best Arrangement for Voices (Duo, Group or Chorus):** Starland Vocal Band for *Afternoon Delight* on Windsong/RCA

10. **Best Instrumental Composition:** Chuck Mangione for *Bellavia*

11. **Best Accompaniment Arrangement:** Jimmy Haskell and James William

G Grammy Awards 1977

Guerico for *If You Leave Me Now* on Columbia

12. **Best Instrumental Jazz Small Group**: Chick Corea for *The Leprechaun* on Polydor
13. **Best Instrumental Jazz Large Group**: Duke Ellington for *The Ellington Suites* on Pablo
14. **Best Jazz Soloist**: Count Basie for *Basie and Zoot* on Pablo
15. **Best Jazz Vocal**: Ella Fitzgerald for *Fitzgerald & Pass ... Again* on Pablo
16. **Best Country & Western Song**: Larry Gatlin for *Broken Lady*
17. **Best Country & Western Female Vocal**: Emmylou Harris for *Elite Hotel* on Reprise/Warner Brothers
18. **Best Country & Western Male Vocal**: Ronnie Milsap for *(I'm a) Stand by My Woman Man* on RCA
19. **Best Country & Western Duo or Group**: The Amazing Rhythm Aces for *The End Is Not in Sight (The Cowboy Tune)* on ABC
20. **Best Country & Western Instrumental**: Chet Atkins and Les Paul for *Chester and Lester* on RCA
21. **Best Rhythm & Blues Song**: Boz Scaggs and David Paich for *Lowdown*
22. **Best Rhythm & Blues Female Solo Vocal**: Natalie Cole for *Sophisticated Lady (She's a Different Lady)* on Capitol
23. **Best Rhythm & Blues Male Solo Vocal**: Stevie Wonder for *I Wish* on Tamla/Motown
24. **Best Rhythm & Blues Vocal or Duo Blues Group**: Marilyn McCoo and Billy Davis, Jr. for *You Don't Have to Be a Star (To Be in My Show)* on ABC
25. **Best Rhythm and Blues Instrumental**: George Benson for *Theme from Good King Bad* on CIT
26. **Best Comedy**: Richard Pryor for *Bicentennial Nigger* on Warner Brothers
27. **Best Spoken Word**: *Great American Documents* by Orson Welles, Henry Fonda, Helen Hayes and James Earl Jones on CBS
28. **Best Inspirational**: Gary S. Paxton for *The Astonishing, Outrageous, Amazing, Incredible, Unbelievable, Different World of Gary S. Paxton* on Newpax
29. **Best Gospel**: The Oak Ridge Boys for *Where the Soul Never Dies* on Columbia
30. **Best Soul Gospel**: Mahalia Jackson for *How I Got Over* on Columbia
31. **Best Ethnic or Traditional**: John Hartford for *Mark Twang* on Flying Fish
32. **Best Original Motion Picture Score**: Norman Whitfield for *Car Wash* on MCA
33. **Best Original Cast Show Album**: Hugo and Luigi producers for *Bubbling Brown Sugar* on H&L
34. **Best Latin**: Eddie Palmieri for *Unfinished Masterpiece* on Coco
35. **Best Children**: Hermione Gingold for *Prokofiev: Peter and the Wolf/Saint Saens: Carnival of the Animals* on DG
36. **Classical Album of the Year**: Artur Rubinstein and Daniel Barenboim conducting the London Philharmonic Orchestra for *Beethoven: The Five Concertos* on RCA
37. **Best Classical Orchestra**. Georg Solti conducting the Chicago Symphony Orchestra for *Strauss: Also Sprach Zarathustra* on London
38. **Best Classical Chamber Music**: David Munrow conducting the Early Music Consort of London for *The Art of Courtly Love* on Seraphim
39. **Best Performance Instrumental Soloists (with Orchestra)**: Artur Rubinstein for *Beethoven: The Five Concertos* with Daniel Barenboim conducting the London Philharmonic on RCA
40. **Best Performance Instrumental Soloists (without Orchestra)**: Vladimir Horowitz for *Horowitz Concerts 1975/76* on RCA
41. **Best Opera**: Lorin Maazel conducting the Cleveland Orchestra and Chorus for *Gershwin: Porgy and Bess* on London
42. **Best Vocal Soloist**: Beverly Sills for *Herbert: The Music of Victor Herbert* on Angel
43. **Best Classical Choral**: Arthur Oldham chorus master of the London Symphony Chorus for *Rachmaninoff: The Bells* with Andre Previn conducting the London Symphony Orchestra on Angel
44. **Best Engineered (Classical)**: Edward Graham, Ray Moore and Milton Cherin for *Gershwin: Rhapsody In Blue* on Columbia
45. **Best Engineered (Non-Classical)**: Al Schmitt for *Breezin'* on Warner Brothers
46. **Best Album Cover (Award to Art

Director): John Berg for *Chicago X* on Columbia
47. **Best Album Notes (Award to Annotator)**: Dan Morgenstern for *The Changing Face of Harlem, the Savoy Sessions* on Savoy
48. **Producer of the Year**: Stevie Wonder
49. **Best New Artist of the Year**: Starland Vocal Band on Windsong/RCA

1978 Grammy Awards

1. **Record of the Year**: *Hotel California* by the Eagles on Asylum
2. **Album of the Year**: *Rumours* by Fleetwood Mac on Warner Brothers
3. **Songs of the Year (Award to the Songwriter)**: Barbra Streisand and Paul Williams for *Evergreen*, and Joe Brooks for *You Light Up My Life*
4. **Best Contemporary/Pop Male Solo Vocal**: James Taylor for *Handy Man* on Columbia
5. **Best Contemporary/Pop Female Solo Vocal**: Barbra Streisand for *Love Theme from "A Star Is Born" (Evergreen)* on Columbia
6. **Best Contemporary/Pop Vocal Duo or Group**: Bee Gees for *How Deep Is Your Love?* on RSO
7. **Best Instrumental Arrangement**: Harry Betts, Perry Botkin, Jr. and Barry de Vorzan for *Nadia's Theme (The Young and the Restless)* on Arista
8. **Best Contemporary/Pop Instrumental**: *Star Wars* by John Williams conducting the London Symphony Orchestra on 20th Century
9. **Best Arrangement for Voices**: Eagles for *New Kid in Town* on Asylum
10. **Best Instrumental Composition**: John Williams for *Main Title Theme from "Star Wars"*
11. **Best Accompaniment Arrangement**: Ian Freebairn-Smith for *Love Theme from "A Star Is Born" (Evergreen)* on Columbia
12. **Best Instrumental Jazz Small Group**: Phil Woods for *The Phil Woods Six, Live from Showboat* on RCA
13. **Best Instrumental Jazz Large Group**: Count Basie and his orchestra for *Prime Time* on Pablo
14. **Best Jazz Vocal**: Al Jarreau for *Look to the Rainbow* on Warner Brothers
15. **Best Jazz Instrumentalist**: Oscar Peterson for *The Giants* on Pablo
16. **Best Country & Western Song**: Richard Leigh for *Don't It Make My Brown Eyes Blue?*
17. **Best Country & Western Female Vocal**: Crystal Gayle for *Don't It Make My Brown Eyes Blue?* on United Artists
18. **Best Country & Western Male Vocal**: Kenny Rogers for *Lucille* on United Artists
19. **Best Country & Western Duo or Group**: The Kendalls for *Heaven's Just a Sin Away* on Ovation
20. **Best Country & Western Instrumental**: Hargus "Pig" Robbins for *Hargus "Pig" Robbins* on Elektra
21. **Best Rhythm & Blues Song**: Leo Sayer and Vini Poncia for *You Make Me Feel Like Dancing*
22. **Best Rhythm & Blues Female Solo Vocal**: Thelma Houston for *Don't Leave Me This Way* on Motown
23. **Best Rhythm & Blues Male Solo Vocal**: Lou Rawls for *Unmistakably Lou* on PIR/Epic
24. **Best Rhythm & Blues Vocal or Duo Blues Group**: The Emotions for *Best of My Love* on Columbia
25. **Best Rhythm & Blues Instrumental**: The Brothers Johnson for *Q* on A&M
26. **Best Comedy**: Steve Martin for *Let's Get Small* on Warner Brothers
27. **Best Spoken Word**: *The Belle of Amherst* by Julie Harris on Credo
28. **Best Inspirational**: B.J. Thomas for *Home Where I Belong* on Myrrh/Word
29. **Best Traditional Gospel**: The Oak Ridge Boys for *Just a Little Talk with Jesus* on Rockland Road
30. **Best Contemporary Gospel**: The Imperials for *Sail On* on Dayspring/Word
31. **Best Contemporary Soul Gospel**: Edwin Hawkins and the Edwin Hawkins Singers for *Wonderful* on Birthright
32. **Best Traditional Soul Gospel**: James Cleveland for *James Cleveland Live at Carnegie Hall* on Savoy
33. **Best Ethnic or Traditional**: Muddy Waters for *Hard Again* on Blue Sky/CBS

34. **Best Original Motion Picture Score**: John Williams for *Star Wars* on 20th Century
35. **Best Original Cast Show Album**: Charles Strouse and Martin Charnin for *Annie* on Columbia
36. **Best Latin**: Mongo Santamaria for *Dawn* on Vaya
37. **Best Children**: Christopher Cerf and Jim Timmens for *Aren't You Glad You're You?* on Sesame Street
38. **Classical Album of the Year**: *Concert of the Century* with Leonard Bernstein, Vladimir Horowitz, Isaac Stern, Mstislav Rostropovich, Dietrich Fischer-Dieskau, Yehudi Menuhin and Lyndon Woodside on Columbia
39. **Best Classical Orchestra**: Carlo Maria Guilini conducting the Chicago Symphony Orchestra for *Mahler: Symphony No. 9* on DG
40. **Best Classical Chamber Music**: Julliard Quartet for *Schoenberg: Quartets for Strings* on Columbia
41. **Best Performance Instrumental Soloists (with Orchestra)**: Itzhak Perlman and the London Philharmonic Orchestra for *Vivaldi: The Four Seasons* on Angel
42. **Best Performance Instrumental Soloists (without Orchestra)**: Artur Rubinstein for *Beethoven: Sonata for Piano No. 18/Schumann: Fantasiestucke* on RCA
43. **Best Opera**: John de Main conducting the Sherwin M. Goldman/Houston Grand Orchestra for *Gershwin: Porgy and Bess* on RCA
44. **Best Vocal Soloist**: Janet Baker for *Bach: Arias* on Angel
45. **Best Classical Choral**: Margaret Hillis choral director of the Chicago Symphony Chorus for *Verdi: Requiem* with Georg Solti conducting the Chicago Symphony Orchestra on RCA
46. **Best Engineered (Classical)**: Kenneth Wilkinson for *Ravel: Bolero* on London
47. **Best Engineered (Non-Classical)**: Roger Nichols, Elliot Scheiner, Bill Schnee and Al Schmitt for *AJA* on ABC
48. **Best Album Cover (Award to Art Director)**: Kosh for *Simple Dreams* on Asylum
49. **Best Album Notes (Award to Annotator)**: George T. Simon for *Bing Crosby: A Legendary Performer* on RCA
50. **Producer of the Year**: Peter Asher
51. **Best New Artist of the Year**: Debby Boone on Warner Brothers/Curb

1979 Grammy Awards

1. **Record of the Year**: *Just the Way You Are* by Billy Joel on Columbia
2. **Album of the Year**: *Saturday Night Fever* by the Bee Gees, David Shire, Yvonne Elliman, Tavares, Kool and the Gang, K.C. and the Sunshine Band, MFSB, the Trammps, Walter Murphy and Ralph MacDonald on RSO
3. **Song of the Year (Award to the Songwriter)**: Billy Joel for *Just the Way You Are*
4. **Best Contemporary/Pop Male Solo Vocal**: Barry Manilow for *Copacabana (At the Copa)* on Arista
5. **Best Contemporary/Pop Female Solo Vocal**: Anne Murray for *You Need Me* on Capitol
6. **Best Contemporary/Pop Vocal Duo or Group**: Bee Gees for *Saturday Night Fever* on RSO
7. **Best Instrumental Arrangement**: Quincy Jones and Robert Freedman for *The Main Title (Overture Part One)* from "The Wiz Original Soundtrack" on MCA
8. **Best Contemporary/Pop Instrumental**: Chuck Mangione Group for *Children of Sanchez* on A&M
9. **Best Arrangement for Voices (Duo, Group or Chorus)**: The Bee Gees for *Stayin' Alive* on RSO
10. **Best Instrumental Composition**: John Williams for *Close Encounters of the Third Kind*
11. **Best Accompaniment Arrangement**: Maurice White for *Got To Get You into My Life* on RSO
12. **Best Instrumental Jazz Small Group**: Chick Corea for *Friends* on Polydor
13. **Best Instrumental Jazz Large Group**: Thad Jones and Mel Lewis for *Live in Munich* on Horizon/A&M
14. **Best Jazz Vocal**: Al Jarreau for *All Fly Home* on Warner Brothers
15. **Best Jazz Instrumentalist**: Oscar Peterson for *Montreux '77 – Oscar Peterson Jam* on Pablo

Grammy Awards 1979 G

16. **Best Country & Western Song**: Don Schlitz for *The Gambler*
17. **Best Country & Western Female Vocal**: Dolly Parton for *Here You Come Again* on RCA
18. **Best Country & Western Male Vocal**: Willie Nelson for *Georgia On My Mind* on Columbia
19. **Best Country & Western Duo or Group**: Waylon Jennings and Willie Nelson for *Mamas Don't Let Your Babies Grow Up to Be Cowboys* on RCA
20. **Best Country & Western Instrumental**: Asleep at the Wheel for *One O'Clock Jump* on Capitol
21. **Best Rhythm & Blues Song**: Paul Jabara for *Last Dance*
22. **Best Rhythm & Blues Female Solo Vocal**: Donna Summer for *Last Dance* on Casablanca
23. **Best Rhythm & Blues Male Solo Vocal**: George Benson for *On Broadway* on Warner Brothers
24. **Best Rhythm & Blues Vocal or Duo Blues Group**: Earth, Wind & Fire for *All 'n All* on Columbia
25. **Best Rhythm & Blues Instrumental**: Earth, Wind & Fire for *Runnin'* on Columbia
26. **Best Comedy**: Steve Martin for *A Wild and Crazy Guy* on Warner Brothers
27. **Best Spoken Word**: *Citizen Kane Soundtrack* by Orson Welles on Mark 56
28. **Best Inspirational**: B.J. Thomas for *Happy Man* on Myrrh
29. **Best Traditional Gospel**: The Happy Goodman Family for *Refreshing* on Canaan
30. **Best Contemporary Gospel**: Larry Hart for *What a Friend* on Genesis
31. **Best Contemporary Soul Gospel**: Andrae Crouch and the Disciples for *Live in London* on Light
32. **Best Traditional Soul Gospel**: Mighty Clouds of Joy for *Live and Direct* on ABC
33. **Best Ethnic or Traditional**: Muddy Waters for *I'm Ready* on Blue Sky
34. **Best Original Motion Picture Score**: John Williams for *Close Encounters of the Third Kind* on Arista
35. **Best Original Cast Show Album**: Thomas Z. Shepard for *Ain't Misbehavin'* on RCA Red Seal
36. **Best Latin**: Tito Puente for *Homenaje a Beny More* on Tico
37. **Best Children**: Jim Henson for *The Muppet Show* on Arista
38. **Classical Album of the Year**: *Brahms: Concerto for Violin in D-Major* Itzhak Perlman with Carlo Maria Guilini conducting the Chicago Symphony Orchestra on Angel
39. **Best Classical Orchestra**: Herbert von Karajan conducting the Berlin Philharmonic Orchestra for *Beethoven: Symphonies (9)* on DG
40. **Best Classical Chamber Music**: Itzhak Perlman and Vladimir Ashkenazy for *Beethoven: Sonatas for Violin and Piano* on London
41. **Best Performance Instrumental Soloists (with Orchestra)**: Vladimir Horowitz for *Rachmaninoff: Concerto No. 3 in D-Minor for Piano* with Eugene Ormandy conducting the Philadelphia Orchestra on RCA
42. **Best Performance Instrumental Soloists (without Orchestra)**: Vladimir Horowitz for *The Horowitz Concerts 1977/78* on RCA
43. **Best Opera**: Julius Rudel conducting the New York City Opera Orchestra and Chorus for *Lehar: The Merry Widow* on Angel
44. **Best Vocal Soloist**: Luciano Pavarotti for *Luciano Pavarotti: Hits from Lincoln Center* on London
45. **Best Classical Choral**: Margaret Hillis choral director of the Chicago Symphony Chorus for *Beethoven: Missa Solemnis* with Georg Solti conducting the Chicago Symphony Orchestra on London
46. **Best Engineered (Classical)**: Bud Graham, Arthur Kendy and Ray Moore for *Varese: Ameriques/Arcana/Ionisation (Boulez Conducts Varese)* on Columbia
47. **Best Engineered (Non-Classical)**: Roger Nichols and Al Schmitt for *FM (No Static At All)* on MCA
48. **Best Album Cover (Award to Art Director)**: Johnny Lee and Tony Lane for *Boys in the Trees* on Elektra
49. **Best Album Notes (Award to Annotator)**: Michael Brooks for *A Bing Crosby Collection, Vols. I and II*
50. **Producer of the Year**: Bee Gees, Albhy Galuten and Karl Richardson
51. **Best New Artist of the Year**: A Taste of Honey on Capitol

1980 Grammy Awards

1. **Record of the Year**: *What a Fool Believes* by the Doobie Brothers on Warner Brothers
2. **Album of the Year**: *52nd Street* by Billy Joel on Columbia
3. **Song of the Year (Award to the Songwriter)**: Kenny Loggins and Michael McDonald for *What a Fool Believes*
4. **Best Contemporary/Pop Male Solo Vocal**: Billy Joel for *52nd Street* on Columbia
5. **Best Contemporary/Pop Female Solo Vocal**: Dionne Warwick for *I'll Never Love This Way Again* on Arista
6. **Best Contemporary/Pop Vocal Duo or Group**: The Doobie Brothers for *Minute by Minute* on Warner Brothers
7. **Best Instrumental Arrangement**: Claus Ogerman for *Soulful Strut* on Warner Brothers
8. **Best Contemporary/Pop Instrumental**: Herb Alpert for *Rise* on A&M
9. **Best Rock Performance for Voices (Duo, Group or Chorus)**: The Eagles for *Heartbreak Tonight* on Asylum
10. **Best Rock Instrumental Performance**: Wings for *Rockstra Theme* on Columbia
11. **Best Female Rock Performance**: Donna Summer for *Hot Stuff* on Casablanca
12. **Best Male Rock Performance**: Bob Dylan for *Gotta Serve Somebody* on Columbia
13. **Best Instrumental Composition**: John Williams for *Main Title Theme from "Superman"*
14. **Best Accompaniment Arrangement**: Michael McDonald for *What a Fool Believes* on Warner Brothers
15. **Best Instrumental Jazz Small Group**: Gary Burton and Chick Corea for *Duet* on ECM/Warner Brothers
16. **Best Instrumental Jazz Large Group**: Duke Ellington for *At Fargo, 1940 Live* on Book-of-the-Month Records
17. **Best Jazz Vocal**: Ella Fitzgerald for *Fine and Mellow* on Pablo
18. **Best Jazz Instrumentalist**: Oscar Peterson for *Jousts* on Pablo
19. **Best Jazz Fusion Performance**: Weather Report for *8:30* on ARC/CBS
20. **Best Country & Western Song**: Debbie Hupp and Bob Morrison for *You Decorated My Life*
21. **Best Country & Western Female Vocal**: Emmylou Harris for *Blue Kentucky Girl* on Warner Brothers
22. **Best Country & Western Male Vocal**: Kenny Rogers for *The Gambler* on United Artists
23. **Best Country & Western Duo or Group**: The Charlie Daniels Band for *The Devil Went Down to Georgia* on Epic
24. **Best Country & Western Instrumental**: Doc and Merle Watson for *Big Sandy/Leather Britches* on United Artists
25. **Best Rhythm & Blues Song**: David Foster, Jay Graydon and Bill Champlin for *After the Love Has Gone*
26. **Best Rhythm & Blues Female Solo Vocal**: Dionne Warwick for *Deja Vu* on Arista
27. **Best Rhythm & Blues Male Solo Vocal**: Michael Jackson for *Don't Stop Till You Get Enough* on Epic
28. **Best Rhythm & Blues Vocal, Duo or Blues Group**: Earth, Wind & Fire for *After the Love Has Gone* on ARC/CBS
29. **Best Rhythm & Blues Instrumental**: Earth, Wind & Fire for *Boogie Wonderland* on ARC/CBS
30. **Best Disco Recording**: Gloria Gaynor for *I Will Survive* on Polydor
31. **Best Comedy**: Robin Williams for *Reality ... What a Concept* on Casablanca
32. **Best Spoken Word**: *Ages of Man (Readings from Shakespeare)* by John Gielgud on Caedmon
33. **Best Inspirational**: B.J. Thomas for *You Gave Me Love (When Nobody Gave Me a Prayer)* on Myrrh
34. **Best Traditional Gospel**: The Blackwood Brothers for *Lift Up the Name of Jesus* on Skylite
35. **Best Contemporary Gospel**: The Imperials for *Heed the Call* on Dayspring
36. **Best Contemporary Soul Gospel**: Andrae Crouch for *I'll Be Thinking of You* on Light
37. **Best Traditional Soul Gospel**: Mighty Clouds of Joy for *Changing Times* on Epic
38. **Best Ethnic or Traditional**: Muddy Waters for *Muddy "Mississippi" Waters Live* on Blue Sky/CBS
39. **Best Original Motion Picture Score**: John Williams for *Superman* on Warner Brothers

40. **Best Original Cast Show Album:** Stephen Sondheim for *Sweeney Todd* on RCA
41. **Best Latin:** Irakere for *Irakere* on Columbia
42. **Best Children:** Jim Henson for *The Muppet Movie* on Atlantic
43. **Classical Album of the Year:** *Brahms: Symphonies Complete* by the Chicago Symphony Orchestra conducted by Sir Georg Solti on London
44. **Best Classical Orchestra:** The Chicago Symphony Orchestra conducted by Sir Georg Solti for *Brahms: Symphonies Complete* on London
45. **Best Classical Chamber Music:** Dennis Russell Davies conducting the St. Paul Chamber Orchestra for *Copland: Appalachian Spring* on Sound 80
46. **Best Performance Instrumental Soloists (with Orchestra):** Maurizio Pollini for *Bartok: Concertos for Pianos Nos. 1 and 2* on DG
47. **Best Performance Instrumental Soloists (without Orchestra):** Vladimir Horowitz for *The Horowitz Concerts 1978-79* on RCA
48. **Best Classical Vocal Soloist:** Luciano Pavarotti for *O Sole Mio* on London
49. **Best Opera:** Colin Davis conducting the Orchestra and Chorus of the Royal Opera House for *Britten: Peter Grimes* on Philips
50. **Best Classical Choral:** Margaret Hillis choral director of the Chicago Symphony Chorus for *Brahms: A German Requiem* with Sir Georg Solti conducting the Chicago Symphony Orchestra on London
51. **Best Engineered (Classical):** Anthony Salvatore for *Sondheim: Sweeney Todd* on RCA
52. **Best Engineered (Non-Classical):** Peter Henderson for *Breakfast in America* on A&M
53. **Best Album Cover (Award to Art Director):** Mike Doud and Mick Haggerty for *Breakfast in America* on A&M
54. **Best Album Notes (Award to Annotator):** Bob Porter and James Patrick for *Charlie Parker: The Complete Savoy Sessions* on Savoy
55. **Best Historical Reissue:** Michael Brooks and Jerry Korn for *Billie Holliday (Giants of Jazz)* on Time Life
56. **Non-Classical Producer of the Year:** Larry Butler
57. **Classical Producer of the Year:** James Mallinson
58. **Best New Artist of the Year:** Ricky Lee Jones on Warner Brothers

1981 Grammy Awards

1. **Record of the Year:** *Sailing* by Christopher Cross on Warner Brothers
2. **Album of the Year:** *Christopher Cross* by Christopher Cross on Warner Brothers
3. **Song of the Year (Award to the Songwriter):** Christopher Cross for *Sailing*
4. **Best Contemporary/Pop Male Solo Vocal:** Kenny Loggins for *This Is It* on Columbia
5. **Best Contemporary/Pop Female Solo Vocal:** Bette Midler for *The Rose* on Atlantic
6. **Best Contemporary/Pop Vocal Duo or Group:** Barbra Streisand and Barry Gibb for *Guilty* on Columbia
7. **Best Instrumental Arrangement:** Quincy Jones and Jerry Hey for *Dinorah, Dinorah* on Warner Brothers
8. **Best Contemporary/Pop Instrumental:** Bob James and Earl Klugh for *One on One* on Columbia
9. **Best Arrangement for Voices (Duo, Group or Chorus):** Janis Siegel for *Birdland* on Atlantic
10. **Best Rock Instrumental Performance:** The Police for *Regatta de Blanc* on A&M
11. **Best Female Rock Performance:** Pat Benatar for *Crimes of Passion* on Chrysalis
12. **Best Male Rock Performance:** Billy Joel for *Glass Houses* on Columbia
13. **Best Rock Performance by a Duo or Group with Vocal:** Bob Seger and the Silver Bullet Band for *Against the Wind* on Capitol
14. **Best Instrumental Composition:** John Williams for *The Empire Strikes Back*
15. **Best Accompanying Arrangement:** Michael Omartian and Christopher Cross for *Sailing* on Warner Brothers
16. **Best Instrumental Jazz Small Group:** Bill Evans for *We Shall Meet Again* on Warner Brothers
17. **Best Instrumental Jazz Large**

G Grammy Awards 1981

Group: Count Basie and his Orchestra for *On the Road* on Pablo

18. **Best Female Jazz Vocal**: Ella Fitzgerald for *A Perfect Match/Ella and Basie* on Pablo

19. **Best Male Jazz Vocal**: George Benson for *Moody's Mood* on Q West/Warner Brothers

20. **Best Jazz Instrumentalist**: Bill Evans for *I Will Say Goodbye* on Warner Brothers

21. **Best Jazz Fusion Performance**: Manhattan Transfer for *Birdland* on Atlantic

22. **Best Country & Western Song**: *On the Road Again* by Willie Nelson

23. **Best Country & Western Female Vocal**: *Could I Have This Dance* by Anne Murray on Capitol

24. **Best Country & Western Male Vocal**: *He Stopped Loving Her Today* by George Jones on Epic

25. **Best Country & Western Duo or Group**: Roy Orbison and Emmylou Harris for *That Lovin' You Feelin' Again* on Warner Brothers

26. **Best Country & Western Instrumental**: Gilley's "Urban Cowboy" Band for *Orange Blossom Special/Hoedown* on Full Moon/Asylum

27. **Best Rhythm & Blues Song**: Reggie Lucas and James Mtume for *Never Knew Love Like This Before*

28. **Best Rhythm & Blues Female Solo Vocal**: Stephanie Mills for *Never Knew Love Like This Before* on 20th Century

29. **Best Rhythm & Blues Male Solo Vocal**: George Benson for *Give Me the Night* on Q West/Warner Brothers

30. **Best Rhythm & Blues Vocal or Duo Blues Group**: The Manhattans for *Shining Star* on Columbia

31. **Best Rhythm & Blues Instrumental**: George Benson for *Off Broadway* on Q West/Warner Brothers

32. **Best Comedy**: Rodney Dangerfield for *No Respect* on Casablanca

33. **Best Spoken Word**: *Gertrude Stein, Gertrude Stein, Gertrude Stein* by Pat Carroll on Caedmon

34. **Best Inspirational**: Debby Boone for *With My Song I Will Praise Him* on Lamb & Lion

35. **Best Traditional Gospel**: The Blackwood Brothers for *We Come to Worship* on Voice Box

36. **Best Contemporary Gospel**: Reba Rambo, Dony McGuire, B.J. Thomas, Andrae Crouch, the Archers, Cynthia Clawson, Walter and Tremaine Hawkins for *The Lord's Prayer* on Light

37. **Best Contemporary Soul Gospel**: Shirley Caesar for *Rejoice* on Myrrh

38. **Best Traditional Soul Gospel**: James Cleveland and the Charles Ford Singers for *Lord, Let Me Be an Instrument* on Savoy

39. **Best Ethnic or Traditional**: Dr. Isiah Ross, Big Joe Williams, Maxwell Street Jimmy, Son House, Rev. Robert Wilkins, Little Brother Montgomery and Sunnyland Slim for *Rare Blues* on Takoma

40. **Best Original Motion Picture Score**: John Williams for *The Empire Strikes Back* on RSO

41. **Best Original Cast Show Album**: Andrew Lloyd Webber and Tim Rice for *Evita—Premiere American Recording* on MCA

42. **Best Latin**: Cal Tjader for *La Onda Va Bien* on Concord Jazz

43. **Best Children**: The Doobie Brothers, James Taylor, Carly Simon, Bette Midler, the Muppets, Al Jarreau, Linda Ronstadt, Wendy Waldman, Libby Titus & Dr. John, Livingston Taylor, George Benson & Pauline Wilson, Lucy Simon, Kate Taylor and the Simon/Taylor Family for *In Harmony/A Sesame Street Record* on Sesame Street/Warner Brothers

44. **Classical Album of the Year**: *Berg: Lulu (Complete Version)* with Pierre Boulez conducting the Orchestre de l'Opera de Paris on DG

45. **Best Classical Orchestra**: The Chicago Symphony Orchestra conducted by Sir Georg Solti for *Bruckner: Symphony No. 6 in A-Major* on London

46. **Best Classical Chamber Music**: Itzhak Perlman and Pinchas Zuckerman for *Music for Two Violins (Moszkowski: Suite for Two Violins/Shostokovich: Duets/Prokofiev: Sonata for Two Violins)* on Angel

47. **Best Performance Instrumental Soloists (with Orchestra)**: Itzhak Perlman for *Berg: Concerto for Violin and Orchestra/Stravinsky: Concerto in D-Major for Violin and Orchestra* with Seiji Ozawa conducting the Boston Symphony Orchestra on DG and Itzhak Perlman and Mstislav

Rostropovich for *Brahms: Concerto in A-Minor for Violin and Cello (Double Concerto)* with Haitink conducting the Concertgebouw Orchestra on Angel

48. **Best Performance Instrumental Soloists (without Orchestra)**: Itzhak Perlman for *The Spanish Album* on Angel

49. **Best Classical Vocal Soloist**: Leontyne Price for *Prima Donna, Volume 5 Great Soprano Arias from Handel to Britten* with Henry Lewis conducting the Philharmonia Orchestra on RCA

50. **Best Opera**: Pierre Boulez conducting the Orchestre de l'Opera de Paris for *Berg: Lulu (Complete Version)* on DG

51. **Best Classical Choral**: Norbert Balatsch chorus master of the Philharmonia Orchestra and Chorus for *Mozart: Requiem* with Carlo Maria Guillini conducting on Angel

52. **Best Engineered (Classical)**: Karl-August Naegler for *Berg: Lulu (Complete Version)* on DG

53. **Best Engineered (Non-Classical)**: James Guthrie for *The Wall* on Columbia

54. **Best Album Cover (Award to Art Director)**: Roy Kohara for *Against the Wind* on Capitol

55. **Best Album Notes (Award to Annotator)**: David McClintock for *Trilogy: Past, Present and Future* on Reprise/Warner Brothers

56. **Best Historical Reissue**: Keith Hardwick for *Segovia—The EMI Recordings 1927-39* on Angel

57. **Non-Classical Producer of the Year**: Phil Ramone

58. **Classical Producer of the Year**: Robert Woods

59. **Best New Artist of the Year**: Christopher Cross on Warner Brothers

1982 Grammy Awards

1. **Record of the Year**: *Bette Davis Eyes* by Kim Carnes on EMI/America
2. **Album of the Year**: *Double Fantasy* by John Lennon and Yoko Ono on Warner Brothers/Geffen
3. **Song of the Year (Award to the Songwriter)**: Donna Weiss and Jackie DeShannon for *Bette Davis Eyes*
4. **Best Contemporary/Pop Male Solo Vocal**: Al Jarreau for *Breakin' Away* on Warner Brothers
5. **Best Contemporary/Pop Female Solo Vocal**: Lena Horne for *Lena Horne: The lady and Her Music Live on Broadway* on Q West/Warner Brothers
6. **Best Contemporary/Pop Vocal Duo or Group with Vocal**: The Manhattan Transfer for *Boy from New York City* on Atlantic
7. **Best Instrumental Arrangement**: Quincy Jones and Johnny Mandel for *Velas* on A&M
8. **Best Contemporary/Pop Instrumental**: Mike Post featuring Larry Carlton for *Theme from Hill Street Blues* on Elektra/Asylum
9. **Best Arrangement for Voices (Duo, Group or Chorus)**: Quincy Jones and Jerry Hey for *Al No Corrida* on A&M
10. **Best Rock Instrumental Performance**: The Police for *Behind My Camel* on A&M
11. **Best Female Rock Performance**: Pat Benatar for *Fire and Ice* on Chrysalis
12. **Best Male Rock Performance**: Rick Springfield for *Jessie's Girl* on RCA
13. **Best Rock Performance by a Duo or Group with Vocal**: The Police for *Don't Stand So Close to Me* on A&M
14. **Best Instrumental Arrangement Accompanying Vocals**: Mike Post for *The Theme from Hill Street Blues*
15. **Best Vocal Arrangement for Two or More Voices**: Gene Puerling for *A Nightingale Sang in Berkeley Square* on Atlantic
16. **Best Instrumental Jazz Small Group**: Chick Corea and Gary Burton for *Chick Corea and Gary Burton in Concert, Zurich, October 28, 1979* on ECM
17. **Best Instrumental Jazz Large Group**: Gerry Mulligan and his Orchestra for *Walk on the Water* on DRG
18. **Best Female Jazz Vocal**: Ella Fitzgerald for *Digital III at Montreux* on Pablo Live
19. **Best Male Jazz Vocal**—Al Jarreau for *Blue Rondo a la Turk* on Warner Brothers
20. **Best Jazz Instrumentalist**: John Coltrane for *Bye Bye Blackbird* on Pablo
21. **Best Duo or Group Jazz Vocal Performance**: The Manhattan Transfer

for *Until I Met You (Corner Pocket)* on Atlantic
22. **Best Jazz Fusion Performance**: Grover Washington, Jr. for *Winelight* on Elektra/Asylum
23. **Best Country & Western Song**: *9 to 5* by Dolly Parton
24. **Best Country & Western Female Vocal**: *9 to 5* by Dolly Parton
25. **Best Country & Western Male Vocal**: Ronnie Milsap for *(There's) No Gettin' Over Me* on RCA
26. **Best Country & Western Duet, Trio or Group**: The Oak Ridge Boys for *Elvira* on MCA
27. **Best Country & Western Instrumental**: Chet Atkins for *Country—After All These Years* on RCA
28. **Best Rhythm & Blues Song**: Bill Withers, William Salter and Ralph MacDonald for *Just the Two of Us*
29. **Best Rhythm & Blues Female Solo Vocal**: Aretha Franklin for *Hold On I'm Comin'* on Arista
30. **Best Rhythm & Blues Male Solo Vocal**: James Ingram for *One Hundred Ways* on A&M
31. **Best Rhythm & Blues Vocal or Duo Blues Groups**: Quincy Jones for *The Dude* on A&M
32. **Best Rhythm & Blues Instrumental**: David Sanborn for *All I Need Is You* on Warner Brothers
33. **Best Comedy**: Richard Pryor for *Rev. Du Rite* on Laff
34. **Best Spoken Word**: *Donovan's Brain* by Orson Welles on Radiola
35. **Best Inspirational**: B.J. Thomas for *Amazing Grace* on Myrrh/Word
36. **Best Traditional Gospel**: J.D. Sumner, Hovie Lister, James Blackwood, Rosie Rozell and Jake Hess for *The Masters V* on Skylight
37. **Best Contemporary Gospel**: The Imperials for *Priority* on Dayspring/Word
38. **Best Contemporary Soul Gospel**: Andrae Crouch for *Don't Give Up* on Warner Brothers
39. **Best Traditional Soul Gospel**: Al Green for *The Lord Will Make a Way* on Hi-Myrrh/Word
40. **Best Ethnic or Traditional**: B.B. King for *There Must Be a Better World Somewhere* on MCA
41. **Best Original Motion Picture Score**: John Williams for *Raiders of the Lost Ark*
42. **Best Original Cast Show Album**: Quincy Jones for *Lena Horne: The Lady and Her Music Live on Broadway*
43. **Best Latin**: Clare Fischer for *Guajira Pa' la Jeva* on Pause
44. **Best Children**: The Muppets, Glen Campbell, Crystal Gayle, Loretta Lynn, Tanya Tucker and Jim Henson for *Sesame Street* on Sesame Street
45. **Classical Album of the Year**: *Mahler: Symphony No. 2 in C-Minor* with Sir Georg Solti conducting the Chicago Symphony Orchestra on London
46. **Best Classical Orchestra**: The Chicago Symphony Orchestra conducted by Sir Georg Solti for *Mahler: Symphony No. 2 in C-Minor* on London
47. **Best Classical Chamber Music**: Itzhak Perlman, Lynn Harrell and Vladimir Ashkenazy for *Tchaikovsky: Piano Trio in A-Minor* on Angel
48. **Best Performance Instrumental Soloists (with Orchestra)**: Itzhak Perlman, Isaac Stern and Pinchas Zukermann for *Isaac Stern 60th Anniversary Celebration* with Zubin Mehta conducting the New York Philharmonic Orchestra on CBS
49. **Best Performance Instrumental Soloists (without Orchestra)**: Vladimir Horowitz for *The Horowitz Concerts 1979–1980* on RCA
50. **Best Opera**: Sir Charles Mackerras conducting the Vienna Philharmonic Orchestra for *Janacek: From the House of the Dead* on London
51. **Best Vocal Soloist**: Joan Sutherland, Marilyn Horne and Luciano Pavarotti for *Live from Lincoln Center—Sutherland—Horne—Pavarotti* on London
52. **Best Classical Choral**: Neville Marriner conducting the Chorus of the Academy of St. Martin-in-the-Fields for *Haydn: The Creation* on Philips
53. **Best Engineered (Classical)**: Bud Graham, Ray Moore and Andrew Kazdan for *Isaac Stern 60th Anniversary Celebration* on CBS
54. **Best Engineered (Non-Classical)**: Bill Schnee and Jerry Garszva for *Gaucho* on MCA
55. **Best Album Cover (Award to Art

Director): Peter Corriston for *Tatoo You* on Rolling Stones/Atlantic
56. **Best Album Notes (Award to Annotator):** Dan Morgenstern for *Errol Garner: Master of the Keyboard* on Book-of-the-Month Records
57. **Best Historical Album:** George Spitzer and Michael Brooks for *Hoagy Carmichael from "Star Dust" to "Ole Buttermilk Sky"* on Book-of-the-Month Records
58. **Non-Classical Producer of the Year:** Quincy Jones
59. **Classical Producer of the Year:** James Mallinson
60. **Best New Artist of the Year:** Sheena Easton on EMI/America
61. **Best Video of the Year:** Michael Nesmith for *Michael Nesmith in Elephant Ears* on Pacific Arts Video

1983 Grammy Awards

1. **Record of the Year:** *Rosanna* by Toto on Columbia
2. **Album of the Year:** *Toto IV* by Toto on Columbia
3. **Song of the Year (Award to the Songwriter):** Johnny Christopher, Mark James and Wayne Carson for *Always on My Mind*
4. **Best Contemporary/Pop Male Solo Vocal:** Lionel Richie for *Truly* on Motown
5. **Best Contemporary/Pop Female Solo Vocal:** Melissa Manchester for *You Should Hear How She Talks About You* on Arista
6. **Best Contemporary/Pop Vocal Duo or Group with Vocal:** Joe Cocker and Jennifer Warnes for *Up Where We Belong*
7. **Best Instrumental Arrangement:** John Williams for *Flying* on MCA
8. **Best Contemporary/Pop Instrumental:** Ernie Watts for the dance version of the *Theme from "Chariots of Fire"* on Q West/Warner Brothers
9. **Best Arrangement for Voices (Duo, Group or Chorus):** David Paich for *Rosanna* on Columbia
10. **Best Rock Instrumental Performance:** A Flock of Seagulls for *D.N.A.* on Jive/Arista
11. **Best Female Rock Perfor-** mance: Pat Benatar for *Shadows of the Night* on Chrysalis
12. **Best Male Rock Performance:** John Cougar for *Hurts So Good* on Riva/Polygram
13. **Best Rock Performance by a Duo or Group with Vocal:** Survivor for *Eye of the Tiger* on Scotti Brothers/CBS
14. **Best Instrumental Arrangement Accompanying Vocals:** Jerry Hey, David Paich and Jeff Porcaro for *Rosanna* on Columbia
15. **Best Instrumental Composition:** John Williams for *Flying (The Theme from E.T., The Extra-Terrestrial)*
16. **Best Instrumental Jazz Small Group:** The Phil Woods Quartet for *"More" Live* on Adelphi
17. **Best Instrumental Jazz Large Group:** Count Basie and his Orchestra for *Warm Breeze* on Pablo Today
18. **Best Female Jazz Vocal:** Sarah Vaughan for *Gershwin Live!* on CBS
19. **Best Male Jazz Vocal:** Mel Torme for *An Evening with George Shearing and Mel Torme* on Concord Jazz
20. **Best Jazz Instrumentalist:** Miles Davis for *We Want Miles* on Columbia
21. **Best Duo or Group Jazz Vocal Performance:** The Manhattan Transfer for *Route 66* on Atlantic
22. **Best Jazz Fusion Performance:** Pat Metheny Group for *Offramp* on ECM/Warner Brothers
23. **Best Country & Western Song:** *Always on My Mind* by Wayne Carson, Johnny Christopher and Mark James
24. **Best Country & Western Female Vocal:** *Break It Gently* by Juice Newton on Capitol
25. **Best Country & Western Male Vocal:** Willie Nelson for *Always on My Mind* on Columbia
26. **Best Country & Western Duet, Trio or Group:** Alabama for *Mountain Music* on RCA
27. **Best Country & Western Instrumental:** Roy Clark for *Alabama Jubilee* on Churchill
28. **Best Rhythm & Blues Song:** Jay Graydon, Steve Lukather and Bill Champlin for *Turn Your Love Around*
29. **Best Rhythm & Blues Female Solo Vocal:** Jennifer Holiday for *And I Am Telling You I'm Not Going* on Geffen/Warner Brothers

G Grammy Awards 1983

30. **Best Rhythm & Blues Male Solo Vocal**: Marvin Gaye for *Sexual Healing* on Columbia
31. **Best Rhythm & Blues Performance by a Vocal or Duo Blues Groups**: Dazz Band for *Let It Whip* on Motown, and Earth, Wind & Fire for *Wanna Be With You* on ARC/CBS
32. **Best Rhythm & Blues Instrumental**: Marvin Gaye for *Sexual Healing* on Columbia
33. **Best Traditional Blues**: Clarence Gatemouth Brown for *Alright Again* on Rounder
34. **Best Comedy**: Richard Pryor for *Live on Sunset Strip* on Warner Brothers
35. **Best Spoken Word, Documentary or Drama Recording**: *Raiders of the Lost Ark: The Movie on Record* by Tom Voegeli on Columbia
36. **Best Inspirational**: Barbara Mandrell for *He Set My Life to Music* on Songbird/MCA
37. **Best Traditional Gospel**: The Blackwood Brothers for *I'm Following You* on Voice Box
38. **Best Contemporary Gospel**: Amy Grant for *Age to Age* on Myrrh/Word
39. **Best Contemporary Soul Gospel**: Al Green for *Higher Plane* on Myrrh/Word
40. **Best Traditional Soul Gospel**: Al Green for *Precious Lord* by Myrrh/Word
41. **Best Ethnic or Traditional Folk**: Queen Ida for *Queen Ida and the Ben Temps Zydeco Band on Tour* on GNP/Crescendo
42. **Best Original Motion Picture Score**: John Williams for *E.T. The Extra-Terrestrial*
43. **Best Original Cast Show Album**: Tom Eyen and Henry Krieger for *Dreamgirls* on Geffen/Warner Brothers
44. **Best Latin**: Machito for *Machito and his Salsa Big Band '82* on Timeless
45. **Best Children**: Billy Joel, Bruce Springsteen, James Taylor, Kenny Loggins, Carly and Lucy Simon, Teddy Pendergrass, Crystal Gayle, Lou Rawls, Deniece Williams, Janis Ian and Dr. John for *In Harmony* on CBS
46. **Classical Album of the Year**: *Bach: The Goldberg Variations* by Glenn Gould on CBS
47. **Best Classical Orchestra**: The Chicago Symphony Orchestra conducted by James Levine for *Mahler: Symphony No. 7 in E-Minor* on RCA
48. **Best Classical Chamber Music**: Richard Stoltzman and Richard Goode for *Brahms: The Sonatas for Clarinet and Piano Op. 120* on RCA
49. **Best Performance Instrumental Soloists (with Orchestra)**: Itzhak Perlman for *Elgar: Concerto for Violin in B-Minor* with Daniel Barenboim conducting the Chicago Symphony Orchestra on DG
50. **Best Performance Instrumental Soloists (without Orchestra)**: Glenn Gould for *Bach: The Goldberg Variations* on CBS
51. **Best Classical Vocal Soloist**: Leontyne Price for *Leontyne Price Sings Verdi* with Zubin Mehta conducting the Israel Philharmonic Orchestra on London
52. **Best Opera**: Pierre Boulez conducting the Bayreuth Festival Orchestra for *Wagner: Der Ring Des Nibelungen* on Philips
53. **Best Classical Choral**: Margaret Hillis chorus director for the Chicago Symphony Chorus for *Berlioz: The Damnation of Faust* with Sir Georg Solti conducting the Chicago Symphony Orchestra on London
54. **Best Engineered (Classical)**: Paul Goodman for *Mahler: Symphony No. 7 in E-Minor* on RCA
55. **Best Engineered (Non-Classical)**: Al Schmitt, Tom Knox, Greg Ladanyi and David Leonard for *Toto IV* on Columbia
56. **Best Album Cover (Award to Art Director)**: Kosh and Ron Larson for *Get Closer* on Elektra/Asylum
57. **Best Album Notes (Award to Annotator)**: John Chilton and Richard Sudhalter for *Bunny Berrigan (Giants of Jazz)* on Time Life
58. **Best Historical Album**: Alan Dell, Ethel Gabriel and Don Wardell on *The Tommy Dorsey/Frank Sinatra Sessions Vols. 1, 2, & 3*
59. **Non-Classical Producer of the Year**: Toto
60. **Classical Producer of the Year**: Robert Woods
61. **Best New Artist of the Year**: Men at Work on Columbia
62. **Best Video of the Year**: Olivia Newton-John for *Olivia Physical* on MCA Video

1984 Grammy Awards

1. **Record of the Year:** *Beat It* by Michael Jackson on Epic/CBS
2. **Album of the Year:** *Thriller* by Michael Jackson on Epic/CBS
3. **Song of the Year (Award to the Songwriter):** Sting for *Every Breath You Take*
4. **Best Contemporary/Pop Male Solo Vocal:** Michael Jackson for *Thriller* on Epic/CBS
5. **Best Contemporary/Pop Female Solo Vocal:** Irene Cara for *Flashdance ... What a Feeling* on Casablanca/Polygram
6. **Best Contemporary/Pop Vocal Duo or Group with Vocal:** The Police for *Every Breath You Take* on A&M
7. **Best Instrumental Arrangement:** Dave Grusin for *Summer Sketches '82* on GRP
8. **Best Contemporary/Pop Instrumental:** George Benson for *Being With You* on Warner Brothers
9. **Best Instrumental Arrangement Accompanying Voices:** Nelson Riddle for *What's New* on Asylum/EA
10. **Best Rock Instrumental Performance:** Sting for *Brimstone & Treacle* on A&M
11. **Best Female Rock Performance:** Pat Benatar for *Love Is a Battlefield* on Chrysalis
12. **Best Male Rock Performance:** Michael Jackson for *Beat It* on Epic/CBS
13. **Best Rock Performance by a Duo or Group with Vocal:** The Police for *Synchronicity* on A&M
14. **Best Vocal Arrangement for Two or More Voices:** Arif Mardin and Chaka Khan for *Be Bop Medley* on Warner Brothers
15. **Best Instrumental Composition:** Giorgio Moroder for *Love Theme from "Flashdance"*
16. **Best Instrumental Jazz Small Group:** The Phil Woods Quartet for *At the Vanguard* on Antilles/Island
17. **Best Instrumental Jazz Large Group:** Bob McConnell and The Boss Brass for *All in Good Time* on Dark Orchid
18. **Best Female Jazz Vocal:** Ella Fitzgerald for *The Best Is Yet to Come* on Pablo Today
19. **Best Male Jazz Vocal:** Mel Torme for *Top Drawer* on Concord Jazz
20. **Best Jazz Instrumentalist:** Wynton Marsalis for *Think of One* on Columbia
21. **Best Duo or Group Jazz Vocal Performance:** The Manhattan Transfer for *Why Not?* on Atlantic
22. **Best Jazz Fusion Performance:** Pat Metheny Group for *Travels* on ECM/Warner Brothers
23. **Best Country & Western Song:** *Stranger in My House* by Mike Reid
24. **Best Country & Western Female Vocal:** *A Little Good News* by Anne Murray on Capitol
25. **Best Country & Western Male Vocal:** Lee Greenwood for *I.O.U.* on MCA
26. **Best Country & Western Duet, Trio or Group:** Alabama for *Alabama* on RCA
27. **Best Country & Western Instrumental:** The New South (Ricky Skaggs, Tony Rice, Jerry Douglas, J.D. Crowe and Todd Philips) for *Fireball* on Sugar Hill
28. **Best Rhythm & Blues Song:** Michael Jackson for *Billie Jean*
29. **Best Rhythm & Blues Female Solo Vocal:** Chaka Khan for *Chaka Khan* on Warner Brothers
30. **Best Rhythm & Blues Male Solo Vocal:** Michael Jackson for *Billie Jean* on Epic/CBS
31. **Best Rhythm & Blues Performance by a Vocal or Duo Blues Group:** Rufus and Chaka Khan for *Ain't Nobody* on Warner Brothers
32. **Best Rhythm & Blues Instrumental:** Herbie Hancock on *Rockit* on Columbia
33. **Best Traditional Blues:** B.B. King for *Blues and Jazz* on MCA
34. **Best Comedy:** Eddie Murphy for *Eddie Murphy: Comedian* on The Entertainment Company/Columbia
35. **Best Spoken Word or Non-Musical Recording:** *Copland: Lincoln Portrait* by William Warfield on Mercury/Philips
36. **Best Inspirational:** Donna Summer for *He's a Rebel* on Mercury/Polygram
37. **Best Female Gospel:** Amy Grant for *Ageless Medley* on Myrrh/Word
38. **Best Male Gospel:** Russ Taff for *Walls of Glass* on Myrrh/Word
39. **Best Gospel Performance by a Duo or Group:** Sandi Patti and Larnelle

Harris for *More Than Wonderful* on Impact/Benson

40. **Best Female Soul Gospel**: Sandra Crouch for *We Sing Praises* on Light/Lexicon

41. **Best Male Soul Gospel**: Al Green for *I'll Rise Again* on Myrrh/Word

42. **Best Soul Gospel by a Duo or Group**: Bobby Jones and New Life with Barbara Mandrell for *I'm So Glad I'm Standing Here Today* on Myrrh/Word

43. **Best Original Motion Picture Score**: Giorgio Morodor, Keith Forsey, Irene Cara, Shandi Sinnamon, Ronald Magness, Douglas Cotler, Richard Gilbert, Michael Boddicker, Jerry Hey, Phil Ramone, Michael Sembello, Kim Carnes, Duane Hitchings, Craig Krampf and Dennis Matosky for *Flashdance* on Casablanca/Polygram

44. **Best Original Cast Show Album**: Andrew Lloyd Webber for *Cats* on Geffen/Warner Brothers

45. **Best Latin**: Jose Feliciano for *Me Enamore* on Profono/TPL

46. **Best Tropical Latin**: Tito Puente and his Latin Ensemble for *On Broadway* on Concord Picante

47. **Best Mexican/American**: Los Lobos for *Anselma* on Slash/Warner Brothers

48. **Best Ethnic or Traditional Folk**: Clifton Chenier and his Red Hot Louisiana Band for *I'm Here* on Alligator

49. **Best Children**: Quincy Jones for *E.T. The Extra-Terrestrial* with Michael Jackson, Narration and Vocals on MCA

50. **Classical Album of the Year**: *Mahler: Symphony No. 9 in D-Major* with Sir Georg Solti conducting the Chicago Symphony Orchestra on London

51. **Best Classical Orchestra**: The Chicago Symphony Orchestra conducted by Sir Georg Solti for *Mahler: Symphony No. 9 in D-Major* on London

52. **Best Classical Chamber Music**: Mstislav Rostropovich and Rudolf Serkin for *Brahms: Sonata for Cello and Piano in E-Minor, Op. 38 & Sonata in F-Major, Op. 99* on DG

53. **Best Performance Instrumental Soloists (with Orchestra)**: Wynton Marsalis for *Haydn: Concerto for Trumpet and Orchestra in E-Flat Major. Mozart: Concerto for Trumpet and Orchestra in D-Major, Hummel: Concerto for Trumpet and Orchestra in E-Flat Major* on CBS

54. **Best Performance Instrumental Soloists (without Orchestra)**: Glenn Gould for *Beethoven: Sonata for Piano No. 12 in A-Flat Major, Op. 26 and No. 13 in E-Flat Major, Op. 27, No. 1* on CBS

55. **Best Classical Vocal Soloist**: Leontyne Price and Marilyn Horne for *Leontyne Price and Marilyn Horne in Concert at the Met* on RCA

56. **Best Opera Recordings**: Sir Georg Solti conducting for *Mozart: Le Nozzi di Figaro* on London and James Levine conducting for *Verdi: La Traviata* on Elektra

57. **Best Classical Choral**: Margaret Hillis chorus director for the Chicago Symphony Chorus for *Haydn: The Creation* with Sir Georg Solti conducting the Chicago Symphony Orchestra on London

58. **Best Engineered (Classical)**: James Lock for *Mahler: Symphony No. 9 in D-Minor* on London

59. **Best Engineered (Non-Classical)**: Bruce Swieden for *Thriller* on Epic/CBS

60. **Best Album Cover (Award to Art Director)**: Robert Rauschenberg for *Speaking in Tongues* on Sire/Warner Brothers

61. **Best Album Notes (Award to Annotator)**: Orin Keepnews for *The "Interplay" Sessions* on Milestone

62. **Best Historical Album**: Stanley Walker and Allan Steckler for *The Greatest Recordings of Arturo Toscanini Symphonies Vol. 1* on Franklin Mint

63. **Non-Classical Producers of the Year**: Quincy Jones and Michael Jackson

64. **Classical Producers of the Year**: Marc J. Aubort and Joanna Nickrenz

65. **Best New Artist of the Year**: Culture Club on Epic/CBS

66. **Best Short Form Video of the Year**: Duran Duran for *Girls on Film/Hungry Like a Wolf* on Picture Music International/Thorne

67. **Best Video Album**: Duran Duran for *Duran Duran* on Picture Music International/Thorne EMI/Pioneer Artists

Country Music Association Awards

The Country Music Association was formed in Nashville in 1958. But the CMA Awards did not come into existence until the Country Music Association was nine years old.

During the 1967 anniversary banquet, country performers and songwriters were presented with the first CMA statuettes. The next year, the Award presentation was separated from the annual banquet.

The second ceremony was held October 19, 1968, at the Grand Ole Opry House. The presentation was videotaped for the NBC television network and later broadcast on the "Kraft Music Hall."

Beginning in 1969 the ceremonies were shown live. By 1971 the Awards were no longer part of the "Kraft Music Hall." "The Fifth Annual CMA Awards Show" also marks the last year they were on NBC. Since 1972, the CBS television network has handled the CMA Awards.

Dale Evans and Roy Rogers hosted the first year. Today various country artists host and present the CMA Awards. Originally there were ten Awards presented. Like the Grammy Awards, some classifications of Awards have remained. Other Awards have been dropped and replaced by new categories.

In 1970, Porter Wagoner and Dolly Parton were named the first winners of the Vocal Duo of the Year. Also in 1970, Roy Clark was awarded the last Comedian of the Year Award.

In 1981, the Horizon Award was introduced. The Horizon Award is for career development by an individual or an act that has never won a CMA Award. The first recipient was Terri Gibbs.

The Song of the Year Award is determined by the national chart listing of the song in music trade magazines in combination with total membership votes. All other Awards are determined by the combined votes of all members of the Country Music Association.

1967 CMA Awards

1. **Entertainer of the Year**: Eddy Arnold
2. **Single of the Year**: *There Goes My Everything* by Jack Greene on Decca
3. **Album of the Year**: *There Goes My Everything* by Jack Greene on Decca
4. **Song of the Year**: *There Goes My Everything* by Dallas Frazier
5. **Female Vocalist of the Year**: Loretta Lynn
6. **Male Vocalist of the Year**: Jack Greene
7. **Vocal Group of the Year**: The Stoneman Family
8. **Instrumental Group or Band of the Year**: The Buckaroos
9. **Instrumentalist of the Year**: Chet Atkins

C Country Awards 1968

10. Comedian of the Year: Don Bowman

1968 CMA Awards

1. Entertainer of the Year: Glen Campbell
2. Single of the Year: *Harper Valley P.T.A.* by Jeannie C. Riley on Plantation
3. Album of the Year: *Johnny Cash at Folsom Prison* by Johnny Cash on Columbia
4. Song of the Year: *Honey* by Bobby Russell
5. Female Vocalist of the Year: Tammy Wynette
6. Male Vocalist of the Year: Glen Campbell
7. Vocal Group of the Year: Porter Wagoner and Dolly Parton
8. Instrumental Group or Band of the Year: The Buckaroos
9. Instrumentalist of the Year: Chet Atkins
10. Comedian of the Year: Ben Colder

1969 CMA Awards

1. Entertainer of the Year: Johnny Cash
2. Single of the Year: *A Boy Named Sue* by Johnny Cash on Columbia
3. Album of the Year: *Johnny Cash at San Quentin Prison* by Johnny Cash on Columbia
4. Song of the Year: *Carroll County Accident* by Bob Ferguson
5. Female Vocalist of the Year: Tammy Wynette
6. Male Vocalist of the Year: Johnny Cash
7. Vocal Group of the Year: Johnny Cash and June Carter
8. Instrumental Group or Band of the Year: Danny Davis and the Nashville Brass
9. Instrumentalist of the Year: Chet Atkins
10. Comedian of the Year: Archie Campbell

1970 CMA Awards

1. Entertainer of the Year: Merle Haggard
2. Single of the Year: *Okie from Muskogee* by Merle Haggard on Capitol
3. Album of the Year: *Okie from Muskogee* by Merle Haggard on Capitol
4. Song of the Year: *Sunday Morning Coming Down* by Kris Kristofferson
5. Female Vocalist of the Year: Tammy Wynette
6. Male Vocalist of the Year: Merle Haggard
7. Vocal Group of the Year: The Glaser Brothers
8. Vocal Duo of the Year: Porter Wagoner and Dolly Parton
9. Instrumental Group or Band of the Year: Danny Davis and The Nashville Brass
10. Instrumentalist of the Year: Jerry Reed
11. Comedian of the Year: Roy Clark

1971 CMA Awards

1. Entertainer of the Year: Charley Pride
2. Single of the Year: *Help Me Make It Through the Night* by Sammi Smith on Mega
3. Album of the Year: *I Won't Mention It Again* by Ray Price on Columbia
4. Song of the Year: *Easy Loving* by Freddy Hart
5. Female Vocalist of the Year: Lynn Anderson
6. Male Vocalist of the Year: Charley Pride
7. Vocal Group of the Year: The Osborne Brothers
8. Vocal Duo of the Year: Porter Wagoner and Dolly Parton
9. Instrumental Group or Band of the Year: Danny Davis and the Nashville Brass
10. Instrumentalist of the Year: Jerry Reed

1972 CMA Awards

1. Entertainer of the Year: Loretta Lynn

Country Awards 1973

2. **Single of the Year**: *The Happiest Girl in the Whole USA* by Donna Fargo on Dot
3. **Album of the Year**: *Let Me Tell You About a Song* by Merle Haggard on Capitol
4. **Song of the Year**: *Easy Loving* by Freddy Hart
5. **Female Vocalist of the Year**: Loretta Lynn
6. **Male Vocalist of the Year**: Charley Pride
7. **Vocal Group of the Year**: The Statler Brothers
8. **Vocal Duo of the Year**: Conway Twitty and Loretta Lynn
9. **Instrumental Group or Band of the Year**: Danny Davis and the Nashville Brass
10. **Instrumentalist of the Year**: Charlie McCoy

1973 CMA Awards

1. **Entertainer of the Year**: Roy Clark
2. **Single of the Year**: *Behind Closed Doors* by Charlie Rich on Epic
3. **Album of the Year**: *Behind Closed Doors* by Charlie Rich on Epic
4. **Song of the Year**: *Behind Closed Doors* by Kenny O'Dell
5. **Female Vocalist of the Year**: Loretta Lynn
6. **Male Vocalist of the Year**: Charlie Rich
7. **Vocal Group of the Year**: The Statler Brothers
8. **Vocal Duo of the Year**: Conway Twitty and Loretta Lynn
9. **Instrumental Group or Band of the Year**: Danny Davis and the Nashville Brass
10. **Instrumentalist of the Year**: Charlie McCoy

1974 CMA Awards

1. **Entertainer of the Year**: Charlie Rich
2. **Single of the Year**: *Country Bumpkin* by Cal Smith on MCA
3. **Album of the Year**: *A Very Special Love Song* by Charlie Rich on Epic
4. **Song of the Year**: *Country Bumpkin* by Don Wayne
5. **Female Vocalist of the Year**: Olivia Newton-John
6. **Male Vocalist of the Year**: Ronnie Milsap
7. **Vocal Group of the Year**: The Statler Brothers
8. **Vocal Duo of the Year**: Conway Twitty and Loretta Lynn
9. **Instrumental Group or Band of the Year**: Danny Davis and the Nashville Brass
10. **Instrumentalist of the Year**: Don Rich

1975 CMA Awards

1. **Entertainer of the Year**: John Denver
2. **Single of the Year**: *Before the Next Teardrop Falls* by Freddy Fender on ABC-Dot
3. **Album of the Year**: *A Legend in My Time* by Ronnie Milsap
4. **Song of the Year**: *Back Home Again* by John Denver
5. **Female Vocalist of the Year**: Dolly Parton
6. **Male Vocalist of the Year**: Waylon Jennings
7. **Vocal Group of the Year**: The Statler Brothers
8. **Vocal Duo of the Year**: Conway Twitty and Loretta Lynn
9. **Instrumental Group or Band of the Year**: Roy Clark and Buck Trent
10. **Instrumentalist of the Year**: Johnny Gimble

1976 CMA Awards

1. **Entertainer of the Year**: Mel Tillis
2. **Single of the Year**: *Good Hearted Woman* by Waylon Jennings and Willie Nelson on RCA
3. **Album of the Year**: *Wanted—The Outlaws* by Waylon Jennings, Willie Nelson, Tompall, and Jessi Colter on RCA
4. **Song of the Year**: *Rhinestone Cowboy* by Larry Weiss
5. **Female Vocalist of the Year**: Dolly Parton

6. **Male Vocalist of the Year**: Ronnie Milsap
7. **Vocal Group of the Year**: The Statler Brothers
8. **Vocal Duo of the Year**: Waylon Jennings and Willie Nelson
9. **Instrumental Group or Band of the Year**: Roy Clark and Buck Trent
10. **Instrumentalist of the Year**: Hargus "Pig" Robbins

1977 CMA Awards

1. **Entertainer of the Year**: Ronnie Milsap
2. **Single of the Year**: *Lucille* by Kenny Rogers
3. **Album of the Year**: *Ronnie Milsap Live* by Ronnie Milsap on RCA
4. **Song of the Year**: *Lucille* by Roger Bowling and Hal Bynum
5. **Female Vocalist of the Year**: Crystal Gayle
6. **Male Vocalist of the Year**: Ronnie Milsap
7. **Vocal Group of the Year**: The Statler Brothers
8. **Vocal Duo of the Year**: Jim Ed Brown and Helen Cornelius
9. **Instrumental Group or Band of the Year**: The Original Texas Playboys
10. **Instrumentalist of the Year**: Roy Clark

1978 CMA Awards

1. **Entertainer of the Year**: Dolly Parton
2. **Single of the Year**: *Heaven's Just a Sin Away* by The Kendalls on Ovation
3. **Album of the Year**: *It Was Almost Like a Song* by Ronnie Milsap on RCA
4. **Song of the Year**: *Don't It Make My Brown Eyes Blue* by Richard Leigh
5. **Female Vocalist of the Year**: Crystal Gayle
6. **Male Vocalist of the Year**: Don Williams
7. **Vocal Group of the Year**: The Oak Ridge Boys
8. **Vocal Duo of the Year**: Kenny Rogers and Dottie West
9. **Instrumental Group or Band of the Year**: The Oak Ridge Boys
10. **Instrumentalist of the Year**: Roy Clark

1979 CMA Awards

1. **Entertainer of the Year**: Willie Nelson
2. **Single of the Year**: *The Devil Went Down to Georgia* by The Charlie Daniels Band on Epic
3. **Album of the Year**: *The Gambler* by Kenny Rogers on UA
4. **Song of the Year**: *The Gambler* by Don Schlitz/Writers Night Music
5. **Female Vocalist of the Year**: Barbara Mandrell
6. **Male Vocalist of the Year**: Kenny Rogers
7. **Vocal Group of the Year**: The Statler Brothers
8. **Vocal Duo of the Year**: Kenny Rogers and Dottie West
9. **Instrumental Group or Band of the Year**: The Charlie Daniels Band
10. **Instrumentalist of the Year**: Charlie Daniels

1980 CMA Awards

1. **Entertainer of the Year**: Barbara Mandrell
2. **Single of the Year**: *He Stopped Loving Her Today* by George Jones on Epic
3. **Album of the Year**: *Coal Miner's Daughter* Original Motion Picture Soundtrack on MCA
4. **Song of the Year**: *He Stopped Loving Her Today* by Bobby Braddock and Curly Putnam/Tree International
5. **Female Vocalist of the Year**: Emmylou Harris
6. **Male Vocalist of the Year**: George Jones
7. **Vocal Group of the Year**: The Statler Brothers
8. **Vocal Duo of the Year**: Moe Bandy and Joe Stampley
9. **Instrumental Group or Band of the Year**: The Charlie Daniels Band
10. **Instrumentalist of the Year**: Roy Clark

1981 CMA Awards

1. **Entertainer of the Year:** Barbara Mandrell
2. **Single of the Year:** *Elvira* by the Oak Ridge Boys
3. **Album of the Year:** *I Belive in You* by Don Williams
4. **Song of the Year:** *He Stopped Loving Her Today* by Bobby Braddock and Curly Putnam/Tree International
5. **Female Vocalist of the Year:** Barbara Mandrell
6. **Male Vocalist of the Year:** George Jones
7. **Vocal Group of the Year:** Alabama
8. **Vocal Duo of the Year:** David Frizzell and Shelly West
9. **Instrumental Group or Band of the Year:** Alabama
10. **Instrumentalist of the Year:** Chet Atkins
11. **Horizon Award:** Terri Gibbs

1982 CMA Awards

1. **Entertainer of the Year:** Alabama
2. **Single of the Year:** *Always on My Mind* by Willie Nelson
3. **Album of the Year:** *Always on My Mind* by Willie Nelson
4. **Song of the Year:** *Always on My Mind* by Johnny Christopher, Wayne Carson, Mark James/Screen Gems, EMI Music, Rose Bridge Music
5. **Female Vocalist of the Year:** Janie Fricke
6. **Male Vocalist of the Year:** Ricky Skaggs
7. **Vocal Group of the Year:** Alabama
8. **Vocal Duo of the Year:** David Frizzell and Shelly West
9. **Instrumental Group of the Year:** Alabama
10. **Instrumentalist of the Year:** Chet Atkins
11. **Horizon Award:** Ricky Skaggs

1983 CMA Awards

1. **Entertainer of the Year:** Alabama
2. **Single of the Year:** *Swingin'* by John Anderson
3. **Album of the Year:** *The Closer You Get* by Alabama
4. **Song of the Year:** *Always on My Mind* by Johnny Christopher, Wayne Carson, Mark James/Screen Gems, EMI Music, Rose Bridge Music
5. **Female Vocalist of the Year:** Janie Fricke
6. **Male Vocalist of the Year:** Lee Greenwood
7. **Vocal Group of the Year:** Alabama
8. **Vocal Duo of the Year:** Merle Haggard and Willie Nelson
9. **Instrumental Group of the Year:** The Ricky Skaggs Band
10. **Instrumentalist of the Year:** Chet Atkins
11. **Horizon Award:** John Anderson

1984 CMA Awards

1. **Entertainer of the Year:** Alabama
2. **Single of the Year:** *A Little Good News* by Anne Murray on Capitol
3. **Album of the Year:** *A Little Good News* by Anne Murray on Capitol
4. **Song of the Year:** *Wind Beneath My Wings* by Jeff Silbar and Larry Henley
5. **Female Vocalist of the Year:** Reba McEntire
6. **Male Vocalist of the Year:** Lee Greenwood
7. **Vocal Group of the Year:** The Statler Brothers
8. **Vocal Duo of the Year:** Willie Nelson and Julio Inglesias
9. **Instrumental Band or Group of the Year:** The Ricky Skaggs Band
10. **Instrumentalist of the Year:** Chet Atkins
11. **Horizon Award:** The Judds

Emmy Awards

An Image Orthicon tube was used in early television cameras. Technicians called the tube an "immy." When the award was made, it was not too far from "immy" to "emmy."

The National Academy of Television Arts & Sciences was formed in 1946. NATAS was organized similarly to the Association of Motion Picture Arts & Sciences which hands out the Oscar Awards. Only six awards were handed out at the first ceremonies. Those first ceremonies were held January 25, 1949, at the Hollywood Athletic Club.

The Seventh Annual Emmy Awards, held on March 7, 1955, was the first televised coast-to-coast. NBC carried the ceremonies through 1966. Since then, a rotating system of coverage has been in effect.

Television has always had a hard time deciding on the categories for the awards. Partially because of the ever changing categories and methods of determining winners, the first major defection among the broadcasters occurred in May 1964. CBS News withdrew from the ceremonies and ABC followed shortly after. To try and overcome the problem, a multiple award system was tried in 1965.

The new structure was not very popular and the Emmy Awards returned to the original method of presentation the next year.

Things went smoothly for several years. Everyone in the Academy voted for all Awards. But most of the prime-time programs were made in Hollywood. So in 1976, the Hollywood Chapter boycotted the ceremonies.

A new organization was formed out of the old Hollywood Chapter. This new organization was called the Academy of Television Arts & Sciences: ATAS got control over the prime-time Emmies and NATAS kept control of Emmys for daytime television.

A labor dispute at the 1980 ceremonies caused the most recent disruption. The 32nd Annual Emmy Awards were handed out September 7, 1980. The Emmy boycott was called by members of the Screen Actor's Guild and the American Federation of Television and Radio Artists.

1948 Emmy Awards

1. **Most Outstanding Television Personality**: Shirley Dinsdale and her puppet Judy Splinters (KTLA)
2. **Most Popular Television Program**: *Pantomime Quiz Time* (KTLA)
3. **Best Film Made for Television**: *The Necklace*
4. **Station Award for Outstanding Overall Achievement**: KTLA (Los Angeles)
5. **Technical Award**: Charles Mesak for the Phase-fader

E Emmy Awards 1949

6. **Special Award:** Louis McManus for original design of the Emmy statuette

1949 Emmy Awards

1. **Most Outstanding Live Personality:** Ed Wynn (KTTV)
2. **Most Outstanding Kinescope Personality:** Milton Berle (KTTV)
3. **Best Live Show:** Ed Wynn, KTTV
4. **Best Kinescope Show:** Texaco Star Theatre (KNBH/NBC)
5. **Best Children's Show:** *Time for Beany* (KTLA)
6. **Best Film Made for and Viewed on Television:** *Life of Riley* (KNBH)
7. **Best Sports Coverage:** Wrestling (KTLA)
8. **Station Achievement:** KTLA (Los Angeles)
9. **Best Public Service, Cultural or Educational Program:** *Crusade in Europe* (KECA-TV and KTTV)
10. **Best Commercial Made for Television:** Lucky Strike/N.W. Ayer
11. **Technical Award:** Harold W. Jury

1950 Emmy Awards

1. **Most Outstanding Personality:** Groucho Marx (KNBH/NBC)
2. **Best Actor:** Alan Young (KTTV/CBS)
3. **Best Acress:** Gertrude Berg (KTTV/CBS)
4. **Best Public Service:** *City at Night* (KTLA)
5. **Best Children's Show:** *Time for Beany* (KTLA)
6. **Best Dramatic Show:** *Pulitzer Prize Playhouse* (KECA-TV)
7. **Best Sports Program:** Rams Football (KNBH)
8. **Station Achievement:** KTLA (Los Angeles)
9. **Best Cultural Show:** *Campus Chorus and Orchestra* (KTSL)
10. **Special Events:** Departure of Marines for Korea (KFMB and KTLA)
11. **Best News Program:** *KTLA Newsreel*
12. **Best Educational Show:** *KFI-TV University*

13. **Best Variety Show:** *The Alan Young Show* (KTTV/CBS)
14. **Best Game and Audience Participation Show:** *Truth or Consequences* (KTTV/CBS)
15. **Technical Award:** KNBH/NBC for Orthogram T.V.

1951 Emmy Awards

1. **Best Comedian or Comedienne:** Red Skelton (NBC)
2. **Best Comedy Show:** *Red Skelton Show* (NBC)
3. **Best Dramatic Show:** *Studio One* (CBS)
4. **Best Actor:** Sid Caesar
5. **Best Actress:** Imogene Coca
6. **Best Variety Show:** *Your Show of Shows* (NBC)
7. **Special Achievement Award:** U.S. Senator Estes Kefauver

1952 Emmy Awards

1. **Best Comedian:** Jimmy Durante
2. **Best Comedienne:** Lucille Ball
3. **Best Situation Comedy:** *I Love Lucy* (CBS)
4. **Best Dramatic Show:** *Robert Montgomery Presents* (NBC)
5. **Best Actor:** Thomas Mitchell
6. **Best Actress:** Helen Hayes
7. **Best Variety Show:** *Your Show of Shows* (NBC)
8. **Best Public Affairs Program:** *See It Now* (CBS)
9. **Best Children's Program:** *Time for Beany* (KTLA)
10. **Best Audience Participation, Quiz or Panel Show:** *What's My Line?* (CBS)
11. **Best Mystery, Action or Adventure Program:** *Dragnet* (NBC)
12. **Most Outstanding Personality:** Bishop Fulton J. Sheen

1953 Emmy Awards

1. **Best Dramatic Show:** *U.S. Steel Hour* (ABC)
2. **Best Situation Comedy:** *I Love Lucy* (CBS)

Emmy Awards 1954 E

3. **Best Variety Program:** *Omnibus* (CBS)
4. **Best Male Star of a Regular Series:** Donald O'Connor on the *Colgate Comedy Hour* (NBC)
5. **Best Female Star of a Regular Series:** Eve Arden on *Our Miss Brooks* (CBS)
6. **Best Series Supporting Actor:** Art Carney on *The Jackie Gleason Show* (CBS)
7. **Most Outstanding Personality:** Edward R. Murrow (CBS)
8. **Best Public Affairs Program:** *Victory at Sea* (NBC)
9. **Best Children's Program:** *Kukla, Fran and Ollie* (NBC)
10. **Best Audience Participation, Quiz or Panel Programs:** *What's My Line?* (CBS), and *This Is Your Life* (NBC)
11. **Best Mystery, Action or Adventure Program:** *Dragnet* (NBC)
12. **Best Program of News or Sports:** *See It Now* (CBS)
13. **Best New Programs:** *Make Room for Daddy* (ABC), and *U.S. Steel Hour* (ABC)

1954 Emmy Awards

1. **Best Dramatic Series:** *U.S. Steel Hour* (ABC)
2. **Best Situation Comedy Series:** *Make Room for Daddy* (ABC)
3. **Best Variety Series Including Musical Varieties:** *Disneyland* (ABC)
4. **Best Male Star of a Regular Series:** Danny Thomas in *Make Room for Daddy* (ABC)
5. **Best Female Star of a Regular Series:** Loretta Young in *The Loretta Young Show* (NBC)
6. **Best Series Supporting Actor:** Art Carney on *The Jackie Gleason Show* (CBS)
7. **Best Series Supporting Actress:** Audrey Meadows on *The Jackie Gleason Show* (CBS)
8. **Most Outstanding New Personality:** George Gobel (NBC)
9. **Best Cultural, Religious or Educational Program:** *Omnibus* (CBS)
10. **Best Sports Program:** *Gillette Cavalcade of Sports* (NBC)
11. **Best Audience Participation, Quiz or Panel Programs:** *This Is Your Life* (NBC)
12. **Best Mystery or Intrigue Series:** *Dragnet* (NBC)
13. **Best Children's Program:** *Lassie* (CBS)
14. **Best Daytime Program:** *Art Linkletter's House Party* (CBS)
15. **Best Male Singer:** Perry Como (CBS)
16. **Best Female Singer:** Dinah Shore (NBC)
17. **Best Actor for Single Performance:** Robert Cummings in "Twelve Angry Men" on *Studio One* (CBS)
18. **Best Actress for Single Performance:** Judith Anderson in "Macbeth" on *Hallmark Hall of Fame* (NBC)
19. **Best News Reporter or Commentator:** John Daly (ABC)
20. **Best Western or Adventure Series:** *Stories of the Century* (syndicated)
21. **Best Individual Program of the Year:** "Operation Undersea" on *Disneyland* (ABC)
22. **Best Written Dramatic Material:** Reginald Rose for "Twelve Angry Men" on *Studio One* (CBS)
23. **Best Written Comedy Material:** James Allardice, Hal Kanter, Harry Winkler and Jack Douglas for *The George Gobel Show* (NBC)
24. **Best Art Direction of a Live Show:** Bob Markel for *Mallory's Tragedy on Mt. Everest* (CBS)
25. **Best Direction of Photography:** Lester Schorr for "I Climb the Stairs" on *Medic* (NBC)
26. **Best Sound Editing:** George Nicholson for *Dragnet* (NBC)
27. **Best Television Film Editing:** Grant Smith and Lynn Harrison for "Operation Undersea" on *Disneyland* (ABC)
28. **Best Direction:** Franklin Schaffner for "Twelve Angry Men" on *Studio One* (CBS)
29. **Best Art Direction of a Filmed Show:** Ralph Berger and Albert Pyke for "A Christmas Carol" on *Shower of Stars* (CBS)
30. **Best Choreographer:** June Taylor for *The Jackie Gleason Show* (CBS)
31. **Best Original Music Composed for TV:** Walter Schumann for *Dragnet* (NBC)

E Emmy Awards 1955

32. **Best Scoring of a Dramatic or Variety Program**: Victor Young for *Diamond Jubilee of Lights* (four networks)
33. **Best Engineering Effects**: Robert Shelby for four quadrant screen for National Election Coverage (NBC)
34. **Best Technical Achievements for Color TV Policy**: John West (NBC)

1955 Emmy Awards

1. **Best Dramatic Series**: *Producer's Showcase* (NBC)
2. **Best Situation Series**: *You'll Never Get Rich* (CBS)
3. **Best Variety Series**: *The Ed Sullivan Show* (CBS)
4. **Best Male Star of a Regular Series**: Phil Silvers on *You'll Never Get Rich* (CBS)
5. **Best Female Star of a Regular Series**: Lucille Ball on *I Love Lucy* (CBS)
6. **Best Series Supporting Actor**: Art Carney on *The Jackie Gleason Show* (CBS)
7. **Best Series Supporting Actress**: Nanette Fabray in *Ceasar's Hour* (NBC)
8. **Best Actor Single Performance**: Lloyd Nolan for "Caine Mutiny Court Martial" on *Ford Star Jubilee* (CBS)
9. **Best Actress Single Performance**: Mary Martin for "Peter Pan" on *Producer's Showcase* (NBC)
10. **Best Comedian**: Phil Silvers (CBS)
11. **Best Comedienne**: Nanette Fabray (NBC)
12. **Best Special Event or News Program**: *A-Bomb Coverage* (CBS)
13. **Best Documentary Program**: *Omnibus* (CBS)
14. **Best Contribution to Daytime Program**: *Matinee Theatre* (NBC)
15. **Best Audience Participation, Quiz or Panel Program**: *$64,000 Question* (CBS)
16. **Best News Commentator or Reporter**: Edward R. Murrow (CBS)
17. **Best Children's Program**: *Lassie* (CBS)
18. **Best M.C. or Program Host**: Perry Como (NBC)
19. **Best Male Singer**: Perry Como (CBS)
20. **Best Female Singer**: Dinah Shore (NBC)
21. **Best Specialty Act**: Marcel Marceau (NBC)
22. **Best Comedy Writing**: Nat Hiken, Barry Blister, Arnold Aurbach, Harry Orkin, Vincent Bogert, Arnold Rosen, Tony Webster, Terry Ryan and Coleman Jacoby for *You'll Never Get Rich* (CBS)
23. **Best Musical Contribution**: "Love and Marriage" from "Our Town" on *Producer's Showcase* (NBC)
24. **Best Television Adaptation**: Paul Gregory and Franklin Schaffner for "Caine Mutiny Court Martial" on *Ford Star Jubilee* (CBS)
25. **Best Live Series Director**: Franklin Schaffner for "Caine Mutiny Court Martial" on *Ford Star Jubilee* (CBS)
26. **Best Film Series Director**: Nat Hiken for *You'll Never Get Rich* (CBS)
27. **Best Original Teleplay Writing**: Rod Serling for *Kraft Television Theatre* (NBC)
28. **Best Live Series Producer**: Fred Coe for *Producer's Showcase* (NBC)
29. **Best Film Series Producer**: Walt Disney for *Disneyland* (ABC)
30. **Best Editing of a Television Film**: Edward Williams for "Breakdown" on *Alfred Hitchcock Presents* (CBS)
31. **Best Cinematography for Television**: William Scikner for "Black Friday" on *Medic* (NBC)
32. **Best Live Show Camerawork**: T. Miller for *Studio One* (CBS)
33. **Best Live Series Art Direction**: Otis Riggs for *Playwrights' '56* and *Producer's Showcase* (NBC)
34. **Best Film Series Art Direction**: William Ferrari for *You Are There* (CBS)
35. **Best Choreographer**: Tony Charmoli for "Show Biz" on *Your Hit Parade* (NBC)
36. **Best Commercial Campaign**: Ford Motor Company
37. **Best Technical Achievement**: RCA tricolor picture tube
38. **Governor's Award**: President Dwight D. Eisenhower for his use and continuing encouragement of television

1956 Emmy Awards

1. **Best Series of One Hour or Longer**: *Caesar's Hour* (NBC)

Emmy Awards 1957 E

2. **Best Series of One Half Hour:** *Phil Silver's Show* (CBS)
3. **Best Single Program:** "Requiem for a Heavyweight" on *Playhouse 90* (CBS)
4. **Best New Program Series:** *Playhouse 90* (CBS)
5. **Best Public Service Series:** *See It Now* (CBS)
6. **Best Coverage of a Newsworthy Event:** Edward R. Murrow for *Years of Crisis* (CBS)
7. **Best Dramatic Actor in a Regular Series:** Robert Young for *Father Knows Best* (NBC)
8. **Best Dramatic Actress in a Regular Series:** Loretta Young for *The Loretta Young Show* (NBC)
9. **Best Comic Actor in a Regular Series:** Sid Caesar in *Caesar's Hour* (NBC)
10. **Best Comedienne in a Regular Series:** Nannette Fabray in *Caesar's Hour* (NBC)
11. **Best Supporting Actor:** Carl Reiner for *Caesar's Hour* (NBC)
12. **Best Supporting Actress:** Pat Caroll for *Caesar's Hour* (NBC)
13. **Best Single Performance by an Actor:** Jack Palance for "Requiem for a Heavyweight" on *Playhouse 90* (CBS)
14. **Best Single Performance by an Actress:** Claire Trevor for "Dodsworth" on *Producer's Showcase* (NBC)
15. **Best Continuing Performance by an Actor:** Perry Como (NBC)
16. **Best Continuing Performance by an Actress:** Dinah Shore (NBC)
17. **Best News Commentator:** Edward R. Murrow (CBS)
18. **Best Hour or Longer Teleplay Writing:** Rod Serling for "Requiem for a Heavyweight" on *Playhouse 90* (CBS)
19. **Best Half Hour Teleplay Writing:** James P. Cavanaugh for "Fog Closing In" on *Alfred Hitchcock Presents* (CBS)
20. **Best Comedy Writing:** Nat Hiken, Tony Webster, Coleman Jacoby, Arnold Rosen, Billy Friedberg and Leonard Stern for *The Phil Silvers Show* (CBS)
21. **Best One Hour or Longer Direction:** Ralph Nelson for "Requiem for a Heavyweight" on *Playhouse 90* (CBS)
22. **Best Half Hour Direction:** Sheldon Leonard for "Danny's Comeback" on *The Danny Thomas Show* (ABC)
23. **Best Editing of a Television Film:** Frank Keller for "Our Mr. Sun" on *A.T.&T. Science Series* (CBS)
24. **Best Cinematography for Television:** Norbert Brodine for "The Pearl" on *The Loretta Young Show* (NBC)
25. **Best Live Show Camerawork:** "A Night to Remember" on *Kraft Television Theatre* (NBC)
26. **Best One Hour or Longer Art Direction:** Albert Hershong for "Requiem for a Heavyweight" on *Playhouse 90* (CBS)
27. **Best Half Hour Art Direction:** Paul Barnes for *Your Hit Parade* (NBC)
28. **Best Musical Contribution for Television:** Leonard Bernstein, composing and conducting on *Omnibus* (CBS)
29. **Best Engineering or Technical Development:** Ampex and CBS for videotape development and applications

1957 Emmy Awards

1. **Best Dramatic Anthology Series:** *Playhouse 90* (CBS)
2. **Best Dramatic Series with Continuing Characters:** *Gunsmoke* (CBS)
3. **Best Single Program:** "The Comedian" on *Playhouse 90* (CBS)
4. **Best New Program Series:** *Seven Lively Arts* (CBS)
5. **Best Comedy:** *The Phil Silvers Show* (CBS)
6. **Best Coverage of an Unscheduled Newsworthy Event:** "Riker's Island Plane Crash" on *World News Roundup* (CBS)
7. **Best Musical Variety, Audience Participation or Quiz Series:** *Dinah Shore Chevy Show* (NBC)
8. **Best Public Service Program or Series:** *Omnibus* (ABC and NBC)
9. **Best Performance by an Actor in a Series:** Robert Young for *Father Knows Best* (NBC)
10. **Best Performance by an Actress in a Series:** Jane Wyatt for *Father Knows Best* (NBC)
11. **Best Single Performance by an Actor:** Peter Ustinov for "The Life of Samuel Johnson" on *Omnibus* (NBC)
12. **Best Single Performance by an Actress:** Polly Bergen for "The Helen Morgan Story" on *Playhouse 90* (CBS)
13. **Best Continuing Support Per-

E Emmy Awards 1958

formance by an Actor: Carl Reiner for *Caesar's Hour* (NBC)

14. **Best Continuing Support Performance by an Actress**: Ann B. Davis for *The Bob Cummings Show* (CBS and NBC)

15. **Best Continuing Performance by an Actor Essentially Playing Himself**: Jack Benny (CBS)

16. **Best Continuing Performance by an Actress Essentially Playing Herself**: Dinah Shore (NBC)

17. **Best News Commentary**: Edward R. Murrow for *See It Now* (CBS)

18. **Best Hour or Longer Teleplay Writing**: Rod Serling for "The Comedian" on *Playhouse 90* (CBS)

19. **Best Half Hour Teleplay Writing**: Paul Monash for "The Lonely Wizard" on *Schlitz Playhouse of Stars* (CBS)

20. **Best Comedy Writing**: Nat Hiken, Tony Webster, Coleman Jacoby, Billy Friedberg, Terry Ryan and Phil Sharp for *The Phil Silvers Show* (CBS)

21. **Best One Hour or Longer Direction**: Bob Banner for *The Dinah Shore Chevy Show* (NBC)

22. **Best Half Hour Direction**: Robert Stevens for "The Glass Eye" on *Alfred Hitchcock Presents* (CBS)

23. **Best Editing of a Television Film**: Moike Pozen for "How to Kill a Woman" on *Gunsmoke* (CBS)

24. **Best Cinematography for Television**: Harold E. Wellman for "Hemo the Magnificent" on *The Bell Telephone Science Series* (CBS)

25. **Best Live Show Camerawork**: *Playhouse 90* (CBS)

26. **Best Art Direction**: Rouben Ter-Arutunian for "Twelfth Night" on *Hallmark Hall of Fame* (NBC)

27. **Best Half Hour Art Direction**: Paul Barnes for *Your Hit Parade* (NBC)

28. **Best Musical Contribution for Television**: Leonard Bernstein conducting and analyzing the music of Johann Sebastian Bach on *Omnibus* (ABC)

29. **Best Engineering or Technical Achievement**: *Wide, Wide World* (NBC)

1958 Emmy Awards

1. **Best One Hour or Longer Dramatic Series**: *Playhouse 90* (CBS)

2. **Best Half Hour Dramatic Series**: *Alcoa-Goodyear Theatre* (NBC)

3. **Best Single Program**: *An Evening with Fred Astaire* (NBC)

4. **Best Comedy Series**: *The Jack Benny Show* (CBS)

5. **Best Western Series**: *Maverick* (ABC)

6. **Best News Reporting Series**: *The Huntley-Brinkley Report* (NBC)

7. **Best Special News Program**: *The Face of Red China* (CBS)

8. **Best Public Service Program or Series**: *Omnibus* (NBC)

9. **Best Musical or Variety Series**: *Dinah Shore Chevy Show* (NBC)

10. **Best Panel, Quiz or Audience Participation Series**: *What's My Line?* (CBS)

11. **Best One Hour or Longer Dramatic Program**: "Little Moon of Alban" on *Hallmark Hall of Fame* (NBC)

12. **Best Continuing Leading Performance by an Actress in a Comedy Series**: Jane Wyatt for *Father Knows Best* (NBC and CBS)

13. **Best Continuing Leading Performance by an Actor in a Comedy Series**: Jack Benny for *The Jack Benny Show* (CBS)

14. **Best Actress in a Leading Role in a Dramatic Series**: Loretta Young in *The Loretta Young Show* (NBC)

15. **Best Actor in a Leading Role in a Dramatic Series**: Raymond Burr in *Perry Mason* (CBS)

16. **Best Supporting Actress in a Dramatic Series**: Barbara Hale in *Perry Mason* (CBS)

17. **Best Supporting Actor in a Dramatic Series**: Dennis Weaver in *Gunsmoke* (CBS)

18. **Best Supporting Actress in a Comedy Series**: Ann B. Davis in *The Bob Cummings Show* (NBC)

19. **Best Supporting Actor in a Comedy Series**: Tom Poston in *The Steve Allen Show* (NBC)

20. **Best Performance by an Actor in a Musical or Variety Series**: Perry Como (CBS)

21. **Best Performance by an Actress in a Musical or Variety Series**: Dinah Shore (NBC)

22. **Best Single Performance by an

Emmy Awards 1959 E

Actor: Fred Astaire in *An Evening with Fred Astaire* (NBC)

23. **Best Single Performance by an Actress**: Julie Harris in "Little Moon of Alban" on *Hallmark Hall of Fame* (NBC)
24. **Best News Commentator or Analyst**: Edward R. Murrow (CBS)
25. **Best One Hour or Longer Direction from a Dramatic Series**: George Schaefer for "Little Moon of Alban" on *Hallmark Hall of Fame* (NBC)
26. **Best Half Hour Direction from a Dramatic Series**: Jack Smight for "Eddie" on *Alcoa-Goodyear Theatre* (NBC)
27. **Best Direction of a Single Musical or Variety Program**: Bud Yorkin for *An Evening with Fred Astaire* (NBC)
28. **Best Direction of a Single Program from a Comedy Series**: Peter Tewksbury for "Medal for Margaret" on *Father Knows Best* (CBS)
29. **Best One Hour or Longer Writing of a Single Dramatic Program**: James Costigan for "Little Moon of Alban" on *Hallmark Hall of Fame* (NBC)
30. **Best Half Hour Writing of a Single Dramatic Program of a Dramatic Series**: Alfred Brenner and Ken Hughes for "Eddie" on *Alcoa-Goodyear Theatre* (NBC)
31. **Best Writing of a Single Program of a Comedy Series**: Sam Perin, Hal Goodman, George Balzer and Al Gordon for "With Ernie Kovacs" on *The Jack Benny Show* (CBS)
32. **Best Editing of a Television Film**: Silvio d'Alisera for "Meet Mr. Lincoln" on *Project 20* (NBC)
33. **Best Cinematography for Television**: Ellis W. Carter for "Alphabet Conspiracy" on *The Bell Telephone Special* (NBC)
34. **Best Live Show Camerawork**: *An Evening with Fred Astaire* (NBC)
35. **Best Art Direction in a Television Film**: Claudio Guzman for "Bernadette" on *Westinghouse Desilu Playhouse* (CBS)
36. **Best Art Direction of a Live Program**: Edward Stephenson for *An Evening with Fred Astaire* (NBC)
37. **Best Musical Contribution for Television**: David Rose for *An Evening with Fred Astaire* (NBC)
38. **Best Choreography**: Hermes Pan for *An Evening with Fred Astaire* (NBC)
39. **Best Spot Coverage of a News Event**: *Cuban Revolution* (CBS)
40. **Best Engineering or Technical Achievement**: Industrywide improvement of editing (ABC, CBS and NBC)
41. **Trustees Award**: Bob Hope

1959 Emmy Awards

1. **Outstanding Achievement in Drama**: *Playhouse 90* (CBS)
2. **Outstanding Achievement in Variety**: *Fabulous Fifties* (CBS)
3. **Outstanding Achievement in Humor**: *Art Carney Special* (NBC)
4. **Outstanding Achievement in News**: *Huntley-Brinkley Report* (NBC)
5. **Outstanding Achievement in Public Affairs and Education**: *Twentieth Century* (CBS)
6. **Outstanding Achievement in Children's Programming**: *Huckleberry Hound* (syndicated)
7. **Outstanding Achievement by a Series Actor**: Robert Stack for *The Untouchables* (ABC)
8. **Outstanding Achievement by a Series Actress**: Jane Wyatt for *Father Knows Best* (CBS)
9. **Outstanding Single Performance by an Actor**: Laurence Olivier in *The Moon and Sixpence* (NBC)
10. **Outstanding Single Performance by an Actress**: Ingrid Bergman in "The Turn of the Screw" on *Ford Startime* (NBC)
11. **Outstanding Performance in a Variety or Musical Program Series**: Harry Belafonte in "Tonight with Belafonte" on *Revlon Revue* (CBS)
12. **Outstanding Achievement in Direction of Drama**: Robert Mulligan for *The Moon and Sixpence* (NBC)
13. **Outstanding Achievement in Direction of Comedy**: Ralph Levy and Bud Yorkin for *The Jack Benny Hour Specials* (CBS)
14. **Outstanding Writing Achievement in Drama**: Rod Serling for *Twilight Zone* (CBS)
15. **Outstanding Writing Achievement in Comedy**: Sam Perrin, George

E Emmy Awards 1960

Balzer, Al Gordon and Hal Goldman for *The Jack Benny Show* (CBS)

16. **Outstanding Writing Achievement in Documentary**: Howard K. Smith and Av Westin for *The Population Explosion* (CBS)

17. **Best Editing of a Television Film**: Ben H. Ray and Robert L. Swanson for *The Untouchables* (ABC)

18. **Best Cinematography for Television**: Charles Straumer for "The Untouchables" on *Westinghouse Desilu Playhouse* (CBS)

19. **Best Live Show Camerawork**: Winter Olympics (CBS)

20. **Best Art Direction and Scenic Design**: Ralph Berger and Frank Smith for "The Untouchables" on *Westinghouse Desilu Playhouse* (CBS)

21. **Outstanding Achievement in Music**: Leonard Bernstein and the New York Philharmonic (CBS)

22. **Best Engineering or Technical Achievement**: General Electric super sensitive camera tube

23. **Trustees' Award**: Frank Stanton

24. **Trustees' Citation**: Michael R. Gargiulo, Richard Gillaspy, Ampex Corporation and the Radio Corporation of America for the Nixon-Khrushchev Debates in Moscow

1960 Emmy Awards

1. **Outstanding Achievement in Drama**: "Macbeth" on *Hallmark Hall of Fame* (NBC)

2. **Outstanding Achievement in Variety**: *Astaire Time* (NBC)

3. **Outstanding Achievement in Humor**: *Jack Benny Show* (CBS)

4. **Outstanding Achievement in News**: *Huntley-Brinkley Report* (NBC)

5. **Outstanding Achievement in Public Affairs and Education**: *Twentieth Century* (CBS)

6. **Outstanding Achievement in Children's Programming**: "Aaron Copeland's Birthday Party" on *Young People's Concert* (CBS)

7. **Outstanding Program of the Year**: "Macbeth" on *Hallmark Hall of Fame* (NBC)

8. **Outstanding Achievement by a Series Actor**: Raymond Burr on *Perry Mason* (CBS)

9. **Outstanding Achievement by a Series Actress**: Barbara Stanwyck on *The Barbara Stanwyck Show* (NBC)

10. **Outstanding Single Performance by an Actor**: Maurice Evans in "Macbeth" on *Hallmark Hall of Fame* (NBC)

11. **Outstanding Single Performance by an Actress**: Judith Anderson in "Macbeth" on *Hallmark Hall of Fame* (NBC)

12. **Outstanding Performance in a Variety or Musical Program Series**: Fred Astaire on *Astaire Time* (NBC)

13. **Outstanding Performance in a Series Supporting Role**: Don Knotts on *The Andy Griffith Show* (CBS)

14. **Outstanding Performance in a Supporting Role**: Roddy McDowall in "Not Without Honor" on *Equitable's American Heritage* (NBC)

15. **Outstanding Achievement in Direction of Drama**: George Schaeffer for "Macbeth" on *Hallmark Hall of Fame* (NBC)

16. **Outstanding Achievement in Direction of Comedy**: Sheldon Leonard for *The Danny Thomas Show* (CBS)

17. **Outstanding Writing Achievement in Drama**: Rod Serling for *Twilight Zone* (CBS)

18. **Outstanding Writing Achievement in Comedy**: Sherwood Schwartz, Dave O'Brien, Al Schwartz, Martin Ragaway and Red Skelton for *The Red Skelton Show* (CBS)

19. **Outstanding Writing Achievement in Documentary**: Victor Wolfson for *Winston Churchill, The Valiant Years* (ABC)

20. **Best Editing of a Television Film**: Harry Coswick, Aaron Nibley and Milton Schifman for *Naked City* (ABC)

21. **Best Cinematography for Television**: George Clemens for *Twilight Zone* (CBS)

22. **Outstanding Achievement in Electronic Camera Work**: "Sounds of America" on *Bell Telephone Hour* (NBC)

23. **Outstanding Achievement in Art Direction and Scenic Design**: John J. Lloyd for *Checkmate* (CBS)

24. **Outstanding Achievement in**

Emmy Awards 1961 E

Music: *Leonard Bernstein and the Philharmonic* (CBS)
25. **Outstanding Engineering or Technical Achievement:** Marconi's Wireless Telegraph Company and the Radio Corporation of America for independent development of the 4½ inch image orthicon tube.
26. **Trustees' Award:** Joyce C. Hall, National Educational Television and Radio Center and its affiliated stations

1961 Emmy Awards

1. **Outstanding Achievement in Drama:** *The Defenders* (CBS)
2. **Outstanding Achievement in Variety:** *Gary Moore Show* (CBS)
3. **Outstanding Achievement in Humor:** *Bob Newhart Show* (CBS)
4. **Outstanding Achievement in News:** *Huntley-Brinkley Report* (NBC)
5. **Outstanding Achievement in Public Affairs and Education:** *David Brinkley's Journal* (NBC)
6. **Outstanding Achievement in Children's Programming:** *New York Philharmonic Young People's Concerts with Leonard Bernstein* (CBS)
7. **Outstanding Program of the Year:** "Victoria Regina" on *Hallmark Hall of Fame* (NBC)
8. **Outstanding Achievement by a Series Actor:** E.G. Marshall in *The Defenders* (CBS)
9. **Outstanding Achievement by a Series Actress:** Shirley Booth in *Hazel* (NBC)
10. **Outstanding Single Performance by an Actor:** Peter Falk in "The Price of Tomatoes" on *The Dick Powell Show* (NBC)
11. **Outstanding Single Performance by an Actress:** Julie Harris in "Victoria Regina" on *Hallmark Hall of Fame* (NBC)
12. **Outstanding Performance in a Variety or Musical Progam Series:** Carol Burnett on *The Gary Moore Show* (CBS)
13. **Outstanding Performance in a Series Supporting Role:** Don Knotts on *The Andy Griffith Show* (CBS)
14. **Outstanding Performance in a Supporting Role by an Actress:** Pamela Brown in "Victoria Regina" on *Hallmark Hall of Fame* (NBC)
15. **Outstanding Achievement in Direction of Drama:** Franklin Schaffner in *The Defenders* (CBS)
16. **Outstanding Achievement in Direction of Comedy:** Nat Hiken for *Car 54, Where Are You?* (NBC)
17. **Outstanding Writing Achievement in Drama:** Reginald Rose for *The Defenders* (CBS)
18. **Outstanding Writing Achievement in Comedy:** Carl Reiner for *Dick Van Dyke Show* (CBS)
19. **Outstanding Writing Achievement in Documentary:** Lou Hazam for *Vincent Van Gogh: A Self Portrait* (NBC)
20. **Best Editing of a Television Film:** Aaron Nibley, Charles L. Freeman and Hugh Chaloupka for *Naked City* (ABC)
21. **Best Cinematography for Television:** John S. Priestly for *Naked City* (ABC)
22. **Outstanding Achievement in Electronic Camera Work:** Ernie Kovacs (ABC)
23. **Outstanding Achievement in Art Direction and Scenic Design:** Gary Smith for *Perry Como's Kraft Music Hall* (NBC)
24. **Outstanding Achievement in Music:** *Leonard Bernstein and the New York Philharmonic in Japan* (CBS)
25. **Outstanding Achievement in Music Composed for Television:** Richard Rodgers for *Winston Churchill: The Valiant Years* (ABC)
26. **Outstanding Daytime Program:** *Purex Specials for Women* (NBC)
27. **Outstanding Engineering or Technical Achievement:** ABC Videotape Expander, slow motion tape developed by Albert Malang
28. **Trustees' Awards:** CBS, NBC and ABC News Department Heads, CBS News and Jacqueline Kennedy for *A Tour of the White House*, and General David Sarnoff

1962 Emmy Awards

1. **Outstanding Achievement in Drama:** *The Defenders* (CBS)
2. **Outstanding Achievement in Variety:** *Andy Williams Show* (NBC)

E Emmy Awards 1963

3. **Outstanding Achievement in Humor**: *Dick Van Dyke Show* (CBS)
4. **Outstanding Achievement in News**: *Huntley-Brinkley Report* (NBC)
5. **Outstanding Achievement in News Commentary or Public Affairs**: *David Brinkley's Journal* (NBC)
6. **Outstanding Achievement in Children's Programming**: *Walt Disney's Wonderful World of Color* (CBS)
7. **Outstanding Program of the Year**: *The Tunnel* (NBC)
8. **Outstanding Achievement of Documentary Programs**: *The Tunnel* (NBC)
9. **Outstanding Achievement for International Reporting or Commentary**: Piers Anderton on *The Tunnel* (NBC)
10. **Outstanding Achievement of Panel, Quiz or Audience Participation**: *G.E. College Bowl* (CBS)
11. **Outstanding Achievement by a Series Actor**: E.G. Marshall in *The Defenders* (CBS)
12. **Outstanding Achievement by a Series Actress**: Shirley Booth in *Hazel* (NBC)
13. **Outstanding Single Performance by an Actor**: Trevor Howard in "The Invincible Mr. Disraeli" on *Hallmark Hall of Fame* (NBC)
14. **Outstanding Single Performance by an Actress**: Kim Stanley in "A Cardinal Act of Mercy" on *Ben Casey* (ABC)
15. **Outstanding Performance in a Variety or Musical Program or Series**: Carol Burnett on *Julie and Carol at Carnegie Hall* (CBS)
16. **Outstanding Performance by an Actor in a Series Supporting Role**: Don Knotts on *The Andy Griffith Show* (CBS)
17. **Outstanding Performance in a Supporting Role by an Actress**: Glenda Farrell for "A Cardinal Act of Mercy" on *Ben Casey* (ABC)
18. **Outstanding Achievement in Direction of Drama**: Stuart Rosenberg for "The Madman" on *The Defenders* (CBS)
19. **Outstanding Achievement in Direction of Comedy**: John Rich for *Dick Van Dyke Show* (CBS)
20. **Outstanding Writing Achievement in Drama**: Robert Thom and Reginald Rose for "The Madman" on *The Defenders* (CBS)
21. **Outstanding Writing Achievement in Comedy**: Carl Reiner for *Dick Van Dyke Show* (CBS)
22. **Outstanding Program Achievement in Music**: *Julie and Carol at Carnegie Hall* (CBS)
23. **Outstanding Achievement for Original Music**: Robert Russell Bennett for "He Is Risen" on *Project 20* (NBC)
24. **Best Editing of a Television Film**: Sid Katz for *The Defenders* (CBS)
25. **Best Cinematography for Television**: John S. Priestly for *Naked City* (ABC)
26. **Outstanding Achievement in Electronic Camera Work**: "The Invincible Mr. Disraeli" on *Hallmark Hall of Fame* (NBC)
27. **Outstanding Achievement in Art Direction and Scenic Design**: Carroll Clark and Marvin Aubrey Davis for *Walt Disney's World of Color* (NBC)
28. **International Award**: *War and Peace* on England's Granada network
29. **Station Award**: WCBS-TV, New York for *Superfluous People*
30. **Trustees' Award**: Dick Powell, the American Telephone and Telegraph Company and President John F. Kennedy

1963 Emmy Awards

1. **Outstanding Achievement in Drama**: *The Defenders* (CBS)
2. **Outstanding Achievement in Variety**: *The Danny Kaye Show* (CBS)
3. **Outstanding Achievement in Humor**: *Dick Van Dyke Show* (CBS)
4. **Outstanding Achievement in News**: *Huntley-Brinkley Report* (NBC)
5. **Outstanding Achievement in News Commentary or Public Affairs**: *David Brinkley's Journal* (NBC)
6. **Outstanding Achievement in Children's Programming**: *Discovery '63–'64* (ABC)
7. **Outstanding Program of the Year**: *Making of the President 1960* (ABC)
8. **Outstanding Achievement of Documentary Programs**: *Making of the President 1960* (ABC)
9. **Outstanding Achievement for News Commentary or Public Affairs**: Cuba Parts I & II, *The Bay of Pigs* and *The Missile Crisis* (NBC)

10. **Outstanding Achievement in Music:** *Bell Telephone Hour* (NBC)
11. **Outstanding Achievement by a Series Actor:** Dick Van Dyke for *Dick Van Dyke Show* (CBS)
12. **Outstanding Achievement by a Series Actress:** Mary Tyler Moore for *Dick Van Dyke Show* (CBS)
13. **Outstanding Single Performance by an Actor:** Jack Klugman for "Blacklist" on *The Defenders* (CBS)
14. **Outstanding Single Performance by an Actress:** Shelley Winters for "Two Is the Number" on *Bob Hope Presents the Chrysler Theatre* (NBC)
15. **Outstanding Performance in a Variety or Musical Program or Series:** Danny Kaye for *The Danny Kaye Show* (CBS)
16. **Outstanding Performance by an Actor in a Supporting Role:** Albert Paulson for "One Day in the Life of Ivan Denisovich" on *Bob Hope Presents the Chrysler Theatre* (NBC)
17. **Outstanding Performance in a Supporting Role by an Actress:** Ruth White for "Little Moon of Alban" on *Hallmark Hall of Fame* (NBC)
18. **Outstanding Writing Achievement in Drama Adaptation:** Rod Serling for "It's Mental Work" on *Bob Hope Presents the Chrysler Theatre* (NBC)
19. **Outstanding Writing Achievement in Original Drama:** Ernest Kinoy for "Blacklist" on *The Defenders* (CBS)
20. **Outstanding Writing Achievement in Comedy or Variety:** Carl Reiner, Sam Denoff and Bill Persky for *Dick Van Dyke Show* (CBS)
21. **Outstanding Achievement in Direction for Drama:** Tom Gries for "Who Do You Kill?" on *East Side/West Side* (CBS)
22. **Outstanding Achievement in Direction for Comedy:** Jerry Paris for *Dick Van Dyke Show* (CBS)
23. **Outstanding Achievement in Direction for Variety or Music:** Robert Sheerer for *The Danny Kaye Show* (CBS)
24. **Outstanding Achievement for Original Music:** Elmer Bernstein for *The Making of the President 1960* (ABC)
25. **Best Editing of a Television Film:** William T. Cartwright for *The Making of the President 1960* (ABC)
26. **Best Cinematography for Television:** J. Baxter Peters for *The Kremlin* (ABC)
27. **Outstanding Achievement in Electronic Camera Work:** *The Danny Kaye Show* (CBS)
28. **Outstanding Achievement in Art Direction and Scenic Design:** Warren Clymer for *Hallmark Hall of Fame* (NBC)
29. **International Award:** *Les Raisins Verts* Radiodiffusion Television Francais
30. **Station Award:** KPIX, San Francisco for *Operation Challenge—A Study in Hope*

1964 Emmy Awards

1. **Outstanding Program Achievement in Entertainment:** *Dick Van Dyke Show* (CBS)
2. **Outstanding Program Achievement in Entertainment:** "The Magnificent Yankee" on *Hallmark Hall of Fame* (NBC)
3. **Outstanding Program Achievement in Entertainment:** *My Name is Barbra* (CBS)
4. **Outstanding Program Achievement in Entertainment:** "What Is Sonata Form?" on *New York Philharmonic Young People's Concert with Leonard Bernstein* (CBS)
5. **Outstanding Individual Achievement of an Actor or Performer in Entertainment:** Leonard Bernstein for *New York Philharmonic Young People's Concert with Leonard Bernstein* (CBS)
6. **Outstanding Individual Achievement of an Actor or Performer in Entertainment:** Lynn Fontanne in "The Magnificent Yankee" on *Hallmark Hall of Fame* (NBC)
7. **Outstanding Individual Achievement of an Actor or Performer in Entertainment:** Alfred Lunt in "The Magnificent Yankee" on *Hallmark Hall of Fame* (NBC)
8. **Outstanding Individual Achievement of an Actor or Performer in Entertainment:** Barbra Streisand for *My Name is Barbra* (CBS)
9. **Outstanding Individual Achievement of an Actor or Performer in Entertainment:** Dick Van Dyke for *Dick Van Dyke Show* (CBS)

E Emmy Awards 1965

10. **Outstanding Program Achievement in News, Documentaries or Sports**: "I, Leonardo" on *Saga of Western Man* (ABC)
11. **Outstanding Program Achievement in News, Documentaries or Sports**: *The Louvre* (NBC)
12. **Outstanding Individual Achievement in News, Documentaries or Sports**: Richard Basehart for *Let My People Go* (syndicated)
13. **Outstanding Individual Writing Achievement in News, Documentaries or Sports**: Sidney Carroll for *The Louvre* (NBC)
14. **Outstanding Individual Film Editing Achievement in News, Documentaries or Sports**: Aram Boyajian for *The Louvre* (NBC)
15. **Outstanding Individual Directing Achievement in News, Documentaries or Sports**: John J. Sughrue for *The Louvre* (NBC)
16. **Outstanding Individual Achievement in Cinematography in News, Sports or Documentaries**: Tom Priestly for *The Louvre* (NBC)
17. **Outstanding Individual Achievement in Music for News, Documentaries or Sports**: Norman Fello Joio for *The Louvre* (NBC)
18. **Outstanding Individual Achievement in Cinematography in Entertainment**: William Spencer for *Twelve O'Clock High* (ABC)
19. **Outstanding Individual Music Achievement in Entertainment**: Peter Matz for *My Name is Barbra* (CBS)
20. **Outstanding Individual Achievement in Directing Entertainment**: Paul Bogert for "The 700 Year Old Gang" on *The Defenders* (CBS)
21. **Outstanding Individual Writing Achievement in Entertainment**: David Karp for "The 700 Year Old Gang" on *The Defenders* (CBS)
22. **Outstanding Individual Achievement in Costume Design in Entertainment**: Noel Taylor for "The Magnificent Yankee" on *Hallmark Hall of Fame* (NBC)
23. **Outstanding Individual Achievement in Lighting Direction in Entertainment**: Henry Berman, Joseph Dervin and Will Glock for *The Man from U.N.C.L.E.* (NBC)
24. **Outstanding Individual Achievement in Lighting Direction in Entertainment**: Phil Hymes for "The Magnificent Yankee" on *Hallmark Hall of Fame* (NBC)
25. **Outstanding Individual Achievement in Choreography in Entertainment**: Joe Layton for *My Name is Barbra* (CBS)
26. **Outstanding Individual Achievement in Set Decoration in Entertainment**: Warren Clymer for "The Holy Terror" on *Hallmark Hall of Fame* (NBC)
27. **Outstanding Individual Achievement in Art and Set Direction in Entertainment**: Bill Harp and Tom John for *My Name is Barbra* (CBS)
28. **Outstanding Individual Achievement in Make-up in Entertainment**: Robert O'Bradovich for "The Magnificent Yankee" on *Hallmark Hall of Fame* (NBC)
29. **Outstanding Individual Achievement in Special Photographic Effects in Entertainment**: L.B. Abbott for *Voyage to the Bottom of the Sea* (ABC)
30. **Outstanding Individual Achievement in Special Effects in Entertainment**: Production Team from *Man from U.N.C.L.E.* (NBC)
31. **Outstanding Individual Achievement in Color Consulting in Entertainment**: Edward Acona for *Bonanza* (NBC)
32. **Outstanding Individual Achievement in Technical Directing in Entertainment**: Clair McCoy for *The Wonderful World of Burlesque* (NBC)
33. **International Award**: *Le Barber de Seville* Canadian Broadcasting Company
34. **Station Award**: WDSU-TV, New Orleans for *Ku Klux Klan*

1965 Emmy Awards

1. **Outstanding Comedy Series**: *The Dick Van Dyke Show* (CBS)
2. **Outstanding Variety Series**: *The Andy Williams Show* (NBC)
3. **Outstanding Dramatic Series**: *The Fugitive* (ABC)
4. **Outstanding Children's Program**: *A Charlie Brown Christmas* (CBS)

Emmy Awards 1965 E

5. **Outstanding Musical Program**: *Frank Sinatra: A Man and His Music* (NBC)
6. **Outstanding Variety Special**: *Chrysler Presents the Bob Hope Christmas Special* (NBC)
7. **Outstanding Dramatic Program**: *Ages of Man* (CBS)
8. **Outstanding Single Performance by a Dramatic Actor**: Cliff Robertson in "The Game" on *Bob Hope Presents the Chrysler Theatre* (NBC)
9. **Outstanding Single Performance by a Dramatic Actress**: Simone Signoret in "A Small Rebellion" on *Bob Hope Presents the Chrysler Theatre* (NBC)
10. **Outstanding Continuing Performance by a Dramatic Actor**: Bill Cosby in *I Spy* (NBC)
11. **Outstanding Continuing Performance by a Dramatic Actress**: Barbara Stanwyk in *The Big Valley* (ABC)
12. **Outstanding Supporting Performance by a Dramatic Actor**: James Daly on "Eagle in a Cage" on *Hallmark Hall of Fame* (NBC)
13. **Outstanding Supporting Performance by a Dramatic Actress**: Lee Grant on *Peyton Place* (ABC)
14. **Outstanding Continuing Performance by a Comic Actor**: Dick Van Dyke on *Dick Van Dyke Show* (CBS)
15. **Outstanding Continuing Performance by a Comic Actress**: Mary Tyler Moore on *The Dick Van Dyke Show* (CBS)
16. **Outstanding Supporting Performance by a Comic Actor**: Don Knotts on *The Andy Griffith Show* (CBS)
17. **Outstanding Supporting Performance by a Comic Actress**: Alice Pearce on *Bewitched* (ABC)
18. **Outstanding Directing of Drama**: Sidney Pollack for "The Game" on *Bob Hope Presents the Chrysler Theatre* (NBC)
19. **Outstanding Directing of Comedy**: William Asher for *Bewitched* (ABC)
20. **Outstanding Directing of Music or Variety**: Alan Handley for *The Julie Andrews Show* (NBC)
21. **Outstanding Writing in Drama**: Millard Lampell for "Eagle in a Cage" on *Hallmark Hall of Fame* (NBC)
22. **Outstanding Writing in Comedy**: Bill Persky and Sam Denoff for "Coast to Coast Big Mouth" on *Dick Van Dyke Show* (CBS)
23. **Outstanding Writing on Variety**: Al Gordon, Hal Goodman and Sheldon Keller for *An Evening with Carol Channing* (CBS)
24. **Outstanding Individual Achievement in Film Editing**: David Blewitt and William T. Cartwright for *The Making of the President 1964* (CBS)
25. **Outstanding Individual Achievement in Film Editing**: Marvin Coil, Everett Douglass and Ellsworth Hoagland for *Bonanza* (NBC)
26. **Outstanding Individual Achievement in Videotape Editing**: Craig Curtis and Art Schneider for *The Julie Andrews Show* (NBC)
27. **Outstanding Achievement in News and Documentaries**: *American White Paper: United States Foreign Policy* (NBC)
28. **Outstanding Achievement in News and Documentaries**: *KKK—The Invisible Empire* (CBS)
29. **Outstanding Achievement in News and Documentaries**: *Senate Hearings on Vietnam* (NBC)
30. **Outstanding Achievement in Daytime Programs**: *Camera Three* (CBS)
31. **Outstanding Achievement in Daytime Programs**: *Mutual of Omaha's Wild Kingdom* (NBC)
32. **Outstanding Achievement in Sports**: *CBS Golf Classic* (CBS)
33. **Outstanding Achievement in Sports**: *ABC Wide World of Sports* (ABC)
34. **Outstanding Achievement in Sports**: *Shell's Wonderful World of Gold* (NBC)
35. **Outstanding Individual Achievement in Educational Television**: Julia Child in *The French Chef* (NET)
36. **Outstanding Individual Achievement in Music**: Laurence Rosenthal for *Michelangelo: The Last Giant* (NBC)
37. **Outstanding Individual Achievement in Technical Directing**: O. Tamburri for "Inherit the Wind" on *Hallmark Hall of Fame* (NBC)
38. **Outstanding Individual Achievement in Lighting**: Lon Stucky for *Frank Sinatra: A Man and His Music* (NBC)
39. **Outstanding Individual**

E Emmy Awards 1966

Achievement in Art Direction: James Trittipo for *The Hollywood Palace* (ABC)
40. **Outstanding Individual Achievement in Special Photographic Effects**: L.B. Abbott and Howard Lydecker in *Voyage to the Bottom of the Sea* (ABC)
41. **Outstanding Individual Achievement in Cinematography**: Winston C. Hoch for *Voyage to the Bottom of the Sea* (ABC)
42. **Outstanding Individual Achievement in Audio Engineering**: Laurence Schneider for "Seventh Annual Young Performer's Concert" on *The New York Philharmonic with Leonard Bernstein* (CBS)
43. **Outstanding Individual Achievement in Engineering**: Hughes Aircraft Corporation and Communications Satellite Corporation for the Early Bird Satellite
44. **Outstanding Individual Achievement in Engineering**: MVR Corporation and CBS for Stop Action Playback
45. **Outstanding Individual Achievement in Engineering**: Burr Tillstrom for "Berlin Wall" on *That Was the Week That Was* (NBC)
46. **International Award**: "Breakout" on *Wyvern at War No. 2* (Westwood Television Limited, Plymouth, England)
47. **Station Award**: WBBM, Chicago for *I See Chicago*
48. **Trustees' Awards**: Edward R. Murrow and the Xerox Corporation

1966 Emmy Awards

1. **Outstanding Comedy Series**: *The Monkees* (NBC)
2. **Outstanding Variety Series**: *The Andy Williams Show* (NBC)
3. **Outstanding Dramatic Series**: *Mission: Impossible* (CBS)
4. **Outstanding Children's Program**: *Jack and the Beanstalk* (CBS)
5. **Outstanding Musical Program**: *Brigadoon* (ABC)
6. **Outstanding Variety Special**: *The Sid Caesar, Imogene Coca, Carl Reiner, Howard Morris Special* (NBC)
7. **Outstanding Program Achievement in News and Documentaries**: *Hall of Kings* (ABC)
8. **Outstanding Program Achievement in News and Documentaries**: *The Italians* (CBS)
9. **Outstanding Program Achievement in News and Documentaries**: *China: The Roots of Madness* (syndicated)
10. **Outstanding Achievement in Daytime Programming**: *Mutual of Omaha's Wild Kingdom* (NBC)
11. **Outstanding Achievement in Daytime Programming**: *The Mike Douglas Show* (syndicated)
12. **Outstanding Achievement in Sports Programming**: *ABC's Wide World of Sports* (ABC)
13. **Outstanding Single Performance by a Dramatic Actor**: Peter Ustinov in "Barefoot in Athens" on *Hallmark Hall of Fame* (NBC)
14. **Outstanding Single Performance by a Dramatic Actress**: Geraldine Page in "A Christmas Memory" on *ABC Stage 67* (ABC)
15. **Outstanding Continuing Performance by a Dramatic Actor**: Bill Cosby on *I Spy* (NBC)
16. **Outstanding Continuing Performance by a Dramatic Actress**: Barbara Bain on *Mission: Impossible* (CBS)
17. **Outstanding Continuing Performance by a Comic Actor**: Don Adams for *Get Smart* (NBC)
18. **Outstanding Continuing Performance by a Comic Actress**: Lucille Ball in *The Lucy Show* (CBS)
19. **Outstanding Supporting Performance by a Comic Actor**: Don Knotts on *The Andy Griffith Show* (CBS)
20. **Outstanding Supporting Performance by a Comic Actress**: Frances Bavier on *The Andy Griffith Show* (CBS)
21. **Outstanding Supporting Performance by a Dramatic Actor**: Eli Wallach on "The Poppy Is Also a Flower" on *Xerox Special* (ABC)
22. **Outstanding Supporting Performance by a Dramatic Actress**: Agnes Morehead on "Hight of the Vicious Valentine" on *Wild, Wild West* (CBS)
23. **Outstanding Achievement in Directing of Drama**: Alex Segal for *Death of a Salesman* (CBS)
24. **Outstanding Achievement in**

Emmy Awards 1967 E

Directing of Comedy: James Frawley for "Royal Flush" on *The Monkees* (NBC)

25. **Outstanding Directing of Music or Variety**: Fielder Cook for *Brigadoon* (ABC)

26. **Outstanding Writing in Drama**: Bruce Geller for *Mission: Impossible* (CBS)

27. **Outstanding Writing in Comedy**: Buck Henry and Leonard Stern for "Ship of Spies" on *Get Smart* (NBC)

28. **Outstanding Writing on Variety**: Mel Brooks, Sam Denoff, Carl Reiner, Bill Persky and Mel Tonkin for *The Sid Caesar, Imogene Coca, Carl Reiner, Howard Morris Special* (CBS)

29. **Outstanding Individual Achievement in Film Editing**: Paul Krasny and Robert Watts for *Mission: Impossible* (CBS)

30. **Outstanding Individual Achievement in Sound Editing**: Don Hall, Dick Legrand, Daniel Mandell for *Voyage to the Bottom of the Sea* (ABC)

31. **Outstanding Costume Design**: Ray Aghayan for *Alice Through the Looking Glass* (NBC)

32. **Outstanding Make-Up**: Dick Smith for *Mark Twain Tonight!* (CBS)

33. **Outstanding Lighting Direction**: Leard Davis for *Brigadoon* (ABC)

34. **Outstanding Audio Engineering**: Bill Cole for *Frank Sinatra: A Man and His Music, Part II* (CBS)

35. **Outstanding Individual Achievement in Photographic Special Effects**: L.B. Abbott for *The Time Tunnel* (ABC)

36. **Outstanding Achievement in News or Documentaries**: Theodore H. White for *China: The Roots of Madness* (syndicated)

37. **Outstanding Individual Achievement in Technical Directing**: A.J. Cunningham for *Brigadoon* (ABC)

38. **Outstanding Achievement in Electronic Camerawork**: Robert Dunn, Gorm Erickson, Ben Wolf and Nick Demos for *Brigadoon* (ABC)

39. **Outstanding Achievement in Engineering Development**: Ampex Company for High-Band Videotape Recorder

40. **Outstanding Achievement in Engineering Development**: A.C. Philips Gloelampenfabrieken for the Plumbicon Tube

41. **Special Award**: Truman Capote and Eleanor Perry for "A Christmas Memory" on *ABC Stage 67* (ABC)

42. **Special Award**: Arthur Miller for *Death of a Salesman* (CBS)

43. **Special Award**: Art Carney for *The Jackie Gleason Show* (CBS)

44. **International Award**: *Big Deal at Gothenburg* (Tyne Tees Television Limited, Newcastle-upon-Tyne, England)

45. **Station Award**: KLZ-TV, Denver for *The Road to Nowhere*

46. **Trustees' Award**: Sylvester L. "Pat" Weaver, Jr.

1967 Emmy Awards

1. **Outstanding Comedy Series**: *Get Smart* (NBC)

2. **Outstanding Variety or Music Series**: *Rowan and Martin's Laugh-In* (NBC)

3. **Outstanding Variety or Music Program**: *Rowan and Martin's Laugh-In Special* (NBC)

4. **Outstanding Dramatic Series**: *Mission: Impossible* (CBS)

5. **Outstanding Dramatic Program**: "Elizabeth the Queen" on *Hallmark Hall of Fame* (NBC)

6. **Outstanding News Documentary Program**: *Africa* (ABC)

7. **Outstanding News Documentary Program**: *Crisis in the Cities* (NET)

8. **Outstanding News Documentary Program**: *Summer 67: What We Learned* (NBC)

9. **Outstanding Cultural Documentary**: *Eric Hoffer: The Passionate State of Mind* (CBS)

10. **Outstanding Cultural Documentary**: *John Steinbeck's America and Americans* (NBC)

11. **Outstanding Cultural Documentary**: *Gauguin in Tahiti: The Search for Paradise* (CBS)

12. **Outstanding Cultural Documentary**: *Dylan Thomas: The World I Breathe* (NET)

13. **Other News Documentary Program**: *The 21st Century* (CBS)

14. **Other News Documentary Program**: *Science and Religion: Who Will Play God?* (CBS)

E Emmy Awards 1967

15. **Outstanding Sports Program**: *ABC's Wide World of Sports* (ABC)
16. **Outstanding Daytime Program**: *Today* (NBC)
17. **Outstanding Dramatic Actor in a Single Performance**: Melvyn Douglas in "Do Not Go Gentle into that Good Night" on *CBS Playhouse* (CBS)
18. **Outstanding Dramatic Actress in a Single Performance**: Maureen Stapleton in "Among the Paths to Eden" on *Xerox Special* (ABC)
19. **Outstanding Dramatic Actor in a Series**: Bill Cosby in *I Spy* (NBC)
20. **Outstanding Dramatic Actress in a Series**: Barbara Bain in *Mission: Impossible* (CBS)
21. **Outstanding Supporting Dramatic Actor**: Milburn Stone in *Gunsmoke* (CBS)
22. **Outstanding Supporting Dramatic Actress**: Barbara Anderson in *Ironside* (NBC)
23. **Outstanding Comic Actor in a Series**: Don Adams in *Get Smart* (NBC)
24. **Outstanding Comic Actress in a Series**: Lucille Ball in *The Lucy Show* (CBS)
25. **Outstanding Supporting Comic Actor**: Werner Klemperer in *Hogan's Heroes* (CBS)
26. **Outstanding Supporting Comic Actress**: Marion Lorne in *Bewitched* (ABC)
27. **Outstanding Individual Achievement in Sports Programming**: Jim McKay in *ABC's Wide World of Sports* (ABC)
28. **Special Individual Achievement**: Pat Paulson on *The Smothers Brothers Comedy Hour* (CBS)
29. **Special Individual Achievement**: Art Carney on *The Jackie Gleason Show* (CBS)
30. **Outstanding Individual Achievement in News and Documentaries**: Harry Reasoner for "What About Ronald Reagan" on *CBS Reports* (CBS)
31. **Outstanding Individual Achievement in News and Documentaries**: John Laurence and Keith Kay, correspondent and cameraman for "Con Thien," "1st Cavalry" and other stories on *CBS Evening News with Walter Cronkite* (CBS)
32. **Outstanding Individual Achievement in Special Events**: Frank McGee for satellite coverage of Konrad Adenauer's funeral (NBC)
33. **Outstanding Dramatic Writing**: Loring Mandell for "Do Not Go Gentle into that Good Night" on *CBS Playhouse* (CBS)
34. **Outstanding Comic Writing**: Alan Burns and Chris Hayward for "The Coming Out Party" on *He and She* (CBS)
35. **Outstanding Music or Variety Writing**: Chris Beard, Phil Hahn, Jack Hanrahan, Paul Keyes, Marc London, Hugh Wedlock, Digby Wolf, David Panich, Coslough Johnson and Allan Mannings for *Rowan and Martin's Laugh-In* (NBC)
36. **Outstanding Writing for Cultural Documentaries**: Harry Morgan for *Who, What, When, Where, Why with Harry Reasoner* (CBS)
37. **Outstanding Comedy Director**: Bruce Billson for "Maxwell Smart, Private Eye" on *Get Smart* (NBC)
38. **Outstanding Dramatic Director**: Paul Bogert for "Dear Friends" on *CBS Playhouse* (CBS)
39. **Outstanding Music or Variety Director**: Jack Haley, Jr. for *Movin' with Nancy* (NBC)
40. **Outstanding Film Editing**: Peter Johnson for "The Sounds of Chicago" on *Bell Telephone Hour* (NBC)
41. **Outstanding Individual Achievement in Electronic Production**: Arthur Schneider, videotape editor for *Rowan and Martin's Laugh-In Special* (NBC)
42. **Outstanding Achievement Cultural Documentaries**: Thomas A. Priestly and Robert Loweree, director of photography and editor for *John Steinbeck's America and Americans* (NBC)
43. **Outstanding Cinematography**: Ralph Woolsey for "A Thief Is a Thief" on *It Takes a Thief* (ABC)
44. **Outstanding Electronic Camerawork**: Edward Chaney, Robert Fonorow, Harry Tatarian and Ben Wolf (cameramen) and A.J. Cunningham (Technical Director) for "Do Not Go Gentle into that Good Night" on *CBS Playhouse* (CBS)
45. **Outstanding Camerawork for News and Documentaries**: Vo Huynh for *Same Mud, Same Blood* (NBC)
46. **Outstanding Art Photography for Cultural Documentaries**: Nathaniel

Dorsky for *Gauguin in Tahiti: The Search for Paradise* (CBS)

47. Outstanding Music Composition: Earle Hagen for "Laya" on *I Spy* (NBC)

48. Outstanding Music Composition for News and Documentaries: Georges Delerue for *Our World* (NET)

49. Outstanding Art Direction and Scenic Design: James W. Trittipo for *The Fred Astaire Show* (NBC)

50. Outstanding Achievement in Engineering Development: British Broadcasting Corporation for electronic field/store colour television standards concerter

51. Trustees' Award: Donald McGannon

52. Station Award: WCAU-TV, Philadelphia for *Now Is the Time*

53. Special Citation: WRC-TV, Washington for *The Other Washington*

54. Special Citation: WLW-TV, New Orleans for *The Other Side of the Shadow*

55. International Award (Documentary): *La Section Anderson* (Office de Radiodiffusion Television Francais, O.R.T.F., Paris, France)

56. International Award (Entertainment): "Call Me Daddy" on *Armchair Theatre* (ABC Television Limited, Middlesex, Great Britain)

1968 Emmy Awards

1. **Outstanding Comedy Series**: *Get Smart* (NBC)
2. **Outstanding Variety or Music Series**: *Rowan and Martin's Laugh-In* (NBC)
3. **Outstanding Variety or Music Program**: *The Bill Cosby Special* (NBC)
4. **Outstanding Dramatic Series**: *NET Playhouse* (NET)
5. **Outstanding Dramatic Program**: "Teacher, Teacher" on *Hallmark Hall of Fame* (NBC)
6. **Outstanding Series Comic Actor**: Don Adams for *Get Smart* (NBC)
7. **Outstanding Series Comic Actress**: Hope Lange for *The Ghost and Mrs. Muir* (NBC)
8. **Outstanding Series Dramatic Actor**: Carl Betz for *Judd for the Defense* (ABC)
9. **Outstanding Series Dramatic Actress**: Barbara Bain for *Mission: Impossible* (CBS)
10. **Outstanding Individual Performance by Dramatic Actor**: Paul Scofield in "Male of the Species" on *Prudential's On-Stage* (NBC)
11. **Outstanding Individual Performance by Dramatic Actress**: Geraldine Page in *The Thanksgiving Visitor* (ABC)
12. **Outstanding Continuing Performance by Supporting Actor**: Werner Klemperer in *Hogan's Heroes* (CBS)
13. **Outstanding Individual Performance by Supporting Actress**: Anna Calder-Marshall in "The Male of the Species" on *Prudential's On-Stage* (NBC)
14. **Outstanding Continuing Performance by Supporting Actress**: Susan St. James in *The Name of the Game* (NBC)
15. **Outstanding Daytime Program**: *The Dick Cavett Show* (ABC)
16. **Outstanding Sports Program**: *19th Summer Olympic Games* (ABC)
17. **Outstanding Individual Achievement in Sports Programming**: Robert Ringer, Bill Bennington, Mike Freedman, Mac Memion, Andy Sidaris, Marv Schenkler, Lou Volpicelli and Doug Wilson for *19th Summer Olympic Games* (ABC)
18. **Outstanding News Documentary Program**: *CBS Reports: Hunger in America* (CBS)
19. **Outstanding News Documentary Program**: *Law and Order* (NET)
20. **Outstanding Special Event Coverage**: Coverage of Martin Luther King's assassination and aftermath (CBS)
21. **Outstanding Achievement within Regularly Scheduled New Program**: James Wilson, Charles Kuralt and Robert Funk for "On the Road" series on *CBS Evening News* (CBS)
22. **Outstanding Achievement within Regularly Scheduled News Program**: Coverage of hunger in America on *The Huntley-Brinkley Report* (NBC)
23. **Outstanding News Documentary Individual Achievement**: Andy Rooney and Perry Wolff for "Black History: Lost, Stolen or Strayed" on *CBS News Hour* (CBS)
24. **Outstanding Cultural Documentary and Magazine-type Program**:

E Emmy Awards 1969

"Don't Count the Candles" on *CBS News Hour* (CBS)

25. **Outstanding Cultural Documentary and Magazine-type Program**: "The Great American Novel" on *CBS News Hour* (CBS)

26. **Outstanding Cultural Documentary and Magazine-type Program**: "Man Who Dances: Edward Villella" on *Bell Telephone Hour* (NBC)

27. **Outstanding Cultural Documentary and Magazine-type Program**: "Justice Black and the Bill or Rights" on *CBS News Hour* (CBS)

28. **Outstanding Cultural Documentary and Magazine-type Program**: Walter Dombrow and Jerry Sims, cinematographers for "The Great American Novel" on *CBS News Hour* (CBS)

29. **Outstanding Cultural Documentary and Magazine-type Program**: Lord Snowdown, cinematographer for "Don't Count the Candles" on *CBS News Hour* (CBS)

30. **Outstanding Cultural Documentary and Magazine-type Program**: Tom Pettit, producer for "CBW: The Secrets of Secrecy" on *First Tuesday* (NBC)

31. **Outstanding Achievement in Film Editing**: Bill Mosher for "An Elephant in a Cigar Box" on *Judd for the Defense* (ABC)

32. **Outstanding Dramatic Director**: David Green for "The People Next Door" on *CBS Playhouse* (CBS)

33. **Outstanding Dramatic Writer**: J.P. Miller for "The People Next Door" on *CBS Playhouse* (CBS)

34. **Outstanding Comedy Writing**: Mason Williams, Allan Blye, Bob Einstein, Murray Roman, Carl Gottlieb, Steve Martin, Jerry Music, Cecil Tuck, Paul Wayne and Cy Howard for *The Smothers Brothers Comedy Hour* (CBS)

35. **Outstanding Cinematography**: George Folsey for *Here's Peggy Fleming* (NBC)

36. **Outstanding Electronic Camerawork**: Nick Demos, Bob Fonarow, Fred Gough, Jack Jennings, Dick Nelson, Rick Tanzi and Ben Wolf. A.J. Cunningham, technical director for "The People Next Door" for *CBS Playhouse* (CBS)

37. **Outstanding Achievement in Art Direction and Scenic Design**: William P. Ross and Lou Hafley for "The Bunker" on *Mission: Impossible* (CBS)

38. **Outstanding Achievement in Musical Composition**: John T. Williams for *Heidi* (NBC)

39. **Outstanding Individual Achievement in Music**: Mort Lindsey for *Barbra Streisand: A Happening in Central Park* (CBS)

40. **Special Classification Program Achievement**: *Firing Line with William F. Buckley, Jr.* (syndicated)

41. **Special Classification Program Achievement**: *Mutual of Omaha's Wild Kingdom* (NBC)

42. **Special Variety Performance Classification**: Harvey Korman in *The Carol Burnett Show* (CBS)

43. **Special Variety Performance Classification**: Arte Johnson in *Rowan and Martin's Laugh-In* (NBC)

44. **Trustees' Awards**: William R. McAndrew and the Apollo VII, VIII, IX and X astronauts

45. **Special Citations**: The Columbia Broadcasting System, Billy Schulman and WFIL-TV, Philadelphia for *Assignment: The Young Greats*

46. **Station Award**: WHA-TV, Madison, Wisconsin for *Pretty Soon Runs Out*

47. **International Documentary Award**: *The Last Campaign of Robert Kennedy* (Swiss Broadcasting and Television, Zurich)

48. **International Entertainment Award**: *A Scent of Flowers* (Canadian Broadcasting Corporation, Ontario)

1969 Emmy Awards

1. **Outstanding Comedy Series**: *My World and Welcome To It* (NBC)

2. **Outstanding Variety or Music Series**: *The David Frost Program* (syndicated)

3. **Outstanding Variety or Music Program**: *Annie, the Women in the Life of a Man* (CBS)

4. **Outstanding Classical Variety or Music Program**: *Cinderella* (NET)

5. **Outstanding Dramatic Series**: *Marcus Welby, M.D.* (ABC)

6. **Outstanding Dramatic Program**: "A Storm in Summer" in *Hallmark Hall of Fame* (NBC)

7. **Outstanding New Series:** *Room 222* (ABC)
8. **Outstanding Series Comic Actor:** William Windom for *My World and Welcome to It* (NBC)
9. **Outstanding Series Comic Actress:** Hope Lange for *The Ghost and Mrs. Muir* (NBC)
10. **Outstanding Series Dramatic Actor:** Robert Young for *Marcus Welby, M.D.* (ABC)
11. **Outstanding Series Dramatic Actress:** Susan Hampshire in *The Forsythe Saga* (NET)
12. **Outstanding Individual Performance by Dramatic Actor:** Peter Ustinov in "A Storm in Summer" on *Hallmark Hall of Fame* (NBC)
13. **Outstanding Individual Performance by Dramatic Actress:** Patty Duke in "My Sweet Charlie" on *World Premiere* (NBC)
14. **Outstanding Continuing Dramatic Performance by Supporting Actor:** James Brolin in *Marcus Welby, M.D.* (ABC)
15. **Outstanding Continuing Dramatic Performance by Supporting Actress:** Gail Fisher in *Mannix* (CBS)
16. **Outstanding Continuing Comic Performance by Supporting Actor:** Michael Constantine in *Room 222* (ABC)
17. **Outstanding Continuing Comic Performance by Supporting Actress:** Karen Valentine in *Room 222* (ABC)
18. **Outstanding Daytime Program:** *Today* (NBC)
19. **Outstanding Sports Programs:** *The NFL Games* (CBS), and *ABC's Wide Wide World of Sports* (ABC)
20. **Special Classification of Outstanding Program Achievement:** *Mutual of Omaha's Wild Kingdom* (NBC)
21. **Outstanding Children's Program:** *Sesame Street* (NET)
22. **Outstanding Program Achievement in News Documentary Programming:** *Hospital* (NET)
23. **Outstanding Program Achievement in Magazine-type Programming:** *Black Journal* (NET)
24. **Outstanding Program Achievement in Cultural Documentary Programming:** "Fathers and Sons" on *CBS News Hour* (CBS)
25. **Outstanding Program Achievement in Cultural Documentary Programming:** "The Japanese" on *CBS News Hour* (CBS)
26. **Outstanding Program Achievements within Regularly Scheduled News Programs:** "An Investigation of Teenage Drug Addiction: Odyssey House" on *The Huntley-Brinkley Report* (NBC), and "Can the World Be Saved?" on *CBS Evening News with Walter Cronkite* (CBS)
27. **Outstanding Program Achievements in Coverage of Special Events:** "Apollo: A Journey to the Moon" on *Apollo X, XI and XII* (NBC), and *Solar Eclipse: A Darkness at Noon* (NBC)
28. **Outstanding Individual Achievement in Special Events Coverage:** Walter Cronkite for *Man on the Moon: The Epic Journey of Apollo XI* (CBS)
29. **Outstanding Individual Achievement in News Documentary Programming:** Frederick Wiseman, director of *Hospital* (NET)
30. **Outstanding Program Achievement in Cultural Documentary Programming:** Arthur Rubinstein (NBC)
31. **Outstanding Individual Achievements in Cultural Documentary Programming:** Arthur Rubinstein for *Arthur Rubinstein* (NBC), and Edwin O. Reischauer for "The Japanese" on *CBS News Hour* (CBS)
32. **Outstanding Individual Achievement in Magazine-type Programming:** Tom Pettit for "Some Footnotes to 25 Nuclear Years" on *First Tuesday* (NBC)
33. **Outstanding Drama Director:** Paul Bogert for "Shadow Game" on *CBS Playhouse* (CBS)
34. **Outstanding Comedy, Variety or Music Director:** Dwight A. Hemion for "The Sound of Burt Bachrach" on *Kraft Music Hall* (NBC)
35. **Outstanding Achievement in Film Editing for Entertainment Program in Series:** Bill Mosher for "Sweet Smell of Failure" on *Bracken's World* (NBC)
36. **Outstanding Achievement in Film Editing for Entertainment Program Specially Made for Television:** Edward R. Abroms for "My Sweet Charlie" on *World Premiere* (NBC)
37. **Outstanding Achievement in Film Editing for Individual News and**

E Emmy Awards 1969

Documentary Programming: Michael C. Shugrue for "The High School Profile" on *The Huntley-Brinkley Report* (NBC)

38. **Outstanding Achievement in Film Editing for Magazine-type or Documentary Program**: John Soh for "The Desert Whales" on *The Undersea World of Jacques Cousteau* (ABC)

39. **Outstanding Individual Achievement in Sports Programming**: Robert R. Forte, film editor for *Pre Game Program* (CBS)

40. **Outstanding Achievement in Film/Sound Editing**: Richard E. Raderman and Norman Karlin for "Charlie Noon" on *Gunsmoke* (CBS)

41. **Outstanding Achievement in Film/Sound Mixing**: Gordon L. Day and Dominick Gaffney for "The Submarine" on *Mission: Impossible* (CBS)

42. **Outstanding Achievement in Film/Sound Editing**: Douglas H. Grindstaff, Alex Bamattre, Michael Colgan, Bill Lee, Joe Kavigan and Josef von Stroheim for "The Immortal" on *Movie of the Week* (ABC)

43. **Outstanding Achievement in Video Tape Editing**: John Shultis for "The Sound of Burt Bachrach" on *Kraft Music Hall* (NBC)

44. **Outstanding Achievement in Live or Tape Sound Mixing**: Bill Cole and Dave Williams for *The Switched-On Symphony* (NBC)

45. **Outstanding Achievement in Entertainment Series Cinematography**: Walter Strenge for "Hello, Goodbye, Hello" on *Marcus Welby, M.D.* (ABC)

46. **Outstanding Achievement in Entertainment Cinematography of Made for Television Program**: Lionel Lindon for "Ritual of Evil" on *NBC Monday Night Movies* (NBC)

47. **Outstanding Achievement in Regularly Scheduled News and Documentary Cinematography**: Edward Winkle for "Model Hippie" on *The Huntley-Brinkley Report* (NBC)

48. **Outstanding Achievement in Documentary or Magazine-type Cinematography**: Thomas B. Priestly for *Sahara: La Caravanne du Sel* (NBC)

49. **Outstanding Achievement in Technical Direction and Electronic Camerawork**: Heino Ripp, Al Camoin, Gene Martin, Donald Mulvaney and Cal Shadwell for "The Sound of Burt Bachrach" on *Kraft Music Hall* (NBC)

50. **Outstanding Dramatic Writing Achievement**: Richard Levinson and William Link for "My Sweet Charlie" on *World Premiere* (NBC)

51. **Outstanding Comedy, Variety or Music Writing**: Gary Belkin, Peter Bellwood, Herb Sargent, Thomas Meehan and Judith Viorst for *Annie, the Women in the Life of a Man* (CBS)

52. **Outstanding Achievement in Music, Lyrics and Special Material**: Arnold Margolin and Charles Fox for *Love, American Style* (ABC)

53. **Outstanding Music Direction of a Variety, Musical or Dramatic Program**: Peter Matz for "The Sound of Burt Bachrach" on *Kraft Music Hall* (NBC)

54. **Outstanding Special Program Musical Composition**: Pete Rugolo for "The Challengers" on *CBS Friday Night Movies* (CBS)

55. **Outstanding First Year Series Musical Composition**: Morton Stevens for "A Thousand Pardons, You're Dead" on *Hawaii Five-O* (CBS)

56. **Outstanding Choreography**: Norman Maen for *This Is Tom Jones* (ABC)

57. **Outstanding Dramatic Art Direction or Scenic Design**: Jan Scott and Earl Carlson for "Shadow Game" on *CBS Playhouse* (CBS)

58. **Outstanding Music or Variety Art Direction or Scenic Design**: E. Jay Krause for *Mitzi's 2nd Special* (NBC)

59. **Outstanding Achievement in Costume Design**: Bob Mackie for *Diana Ross and the Supremes and the Temptations on Broadway* (NBC)

60. **Outstanding Achievement in Lighting Direction**: Leard Davis and Ed Hill for "Appalachian Autumn" on *CBS Playhouse* (CBS)

61. **Outstanding Achievement in Make-Up**: Louis A. Phillippi and Ray Sebastian for *The Don Adams Special: Hooray for Hollywood* (CBS)

62. **Outstanding Individual Achievements in Children's Programming**: Joe Raposo and Jeffrey Moss for "This Way to Sesame Street" (NBC), and John Stone, Jeffrey Moss, Ray Sipherd, Jerry Juhl, Dan Wilcox, Dave Connell, Bruce Hart, Carole Hart and Virginia

Schone for "Sally Sees Sesame Street" on *Sesame Street* (NET)

63. **Outstanding Engineering Development**: Video Communications Division of NASA and Westinghouse Corporation for Apollo color television from space

64. **Citation**: Ampex Corporation for development of HS-200 color television production system

65. **Trustees' Awards**: Presidents of the three network news division, NASA and 3M Company

66. **Station Award**: KNBC-TV, Los Angeles for *The Slow Guillotine*

67. **Special Citation**: WJZ-TV, Baltimore, Maryland for *The Other Americans*

1970 Emmy Awards

1. **Outstanding Comedy Series**: *All in the Family* (CBS)
2. **Outstanding Musical Variety Series**: *The Flip Wilson Show* (NBC)
3. **Outstanding Talk Variety Series**: *The David Frost Show* (syndicated)
4. **Outstanding Variety or Music Program**: *Singer Presents Burt Bacharach* (CBS)
5. **Outstanding Classical Variety or Music Program**: Leopold Stokowski (PBS)
6. **Outstanding New Series**: *All in the Family* (CBS)
7. **Outstanding Dramatic Series**: *The Senator—The Bold Ones* (NBC)
8. **Outstanding Drama or Comedy Program**: *The Andersonville Trial* (PBS)
9. **Outstanding Series Comic Actor**: Jack Klugman for *The Odd Couple* (ABC)
10. **Outstanding Series Comic Actress**: Jean Stapleton for *All in the Family* (CBS)
11. **Outstanding Series Dramatic Actor**: Hal Holbrook for *The Senator—The Bold Ones* (NBC)
12. **Outstanding Series Dramatic Actress**: Susan Hampshire in "The First Churchills" on *Masterpiece Theatre* (PBS)
13. **Outstanding Individual Performance by Dramatic Actor**: George C. Scott in "The Price" on *Hallmark Hall of Fame* (NBC)
14. **Outstanding Individual Performance by Dramatic Actress**: Lee Grant in "The Neon Ceiling" on *World Premiere NBC Monday Night at the Movies* (NBC)
15. **Outstanding Dramatic Performance by Supporting Actor**: David Burns in "The Price" on *Hallmark Hall of Fame* (NBC)
16. **Outstanding Dramatic Performance by Supporting Actress**: Margaret Leighton in "Hamlet" on *Hallmark Hall of Fame* (NBC)
17. **Outstanding Continuing Comic Performance by Supporting Actor**: Edward Asner in *The Mary Tyler Moore Show* (CBS)
18. **Outstanding Continuing Comic Performance by Supporting Actress**: Valerie Harper in *The Mary Tyler Moore Show* (CBS)
19. **Outstanding Daytime Program**: *Today* (NBC)
20. **Outstanding Sports Program**: *ABC's Wide Wide World of Sports* (ABC)
21. **Outstanding Children's Program**: *Sesame Street* (PBS)
22. **Outstanding Program Achievement in News Documentary Programming**: "The World of Charlie Company," correspondent John Laurence on "The World of Charlie Company," "The Selling of the Pentagon" on *CBS News* (CBS)
23. **Outstanding Program Achievement in News Documentary Programming**: "Pollution Is a Matter of Choice", and writer Fred Freed for "Pollution Is a Matter of Choice" on *NBC White Paper* (NBC)
24. **Outstanding Program Achievement in Magazine-type Programming**: *The Great American Dream Machine* (PBS)
25. **Outstanding Program Achievement in Magazine-type Programming**: "Gulf of Tonkin" segment on *60 Minutes* (CBS)
26. **Outstanding Program Achievement in Magazine-type Programming**: Correspondent Mike Wallace for *60 Minutes* (CBS)
27. **Outstanding Program Achievement in Cultural Documentary Programming**: *The Everglades* and *The Making of "Butch Cassidy and the Sundance Kid"* (NBC)
28. **Outstanding Individual Achievements in Cultural Documen-

E   Emmy Awards 1970

tary Programming: narrator Nana Mahomo for *A Black View of South Africa* (CBS), writers Robert Guenette and Theodore H. Strauss for *They've Killed President Lincoln* (NBC), and director Robert Young for *The Eskimo: Fight for Life* (CBS)

29. **Outstanding Program Achievement in Special Event Coverage**: "CBS News Space Coverage for 1970–71", and correspondent Walter Cronkite for "CBS News Space Coverage for 1970–71" (CBS)

30. **Outstanding Program Achievement Within Regularly Scheduled News Programs**: "Five Part Investigation of Welfare" on *NBC Nightly News* (NBC)

31. **Outstanding Individual Achievement Within Regularly Scheduled News Programs**: Correspondent Bruce Morton for "Reports from the Lt. Calley Trial" on *CBS Evening News with Walter Cronkite* (CBS)

32. **Outstanding Director of Comedy Series Program**: Jay Sandrich for "Toulouse Lautrec Is One of My Favorite Artists" on *The Mary Tyler Moore Show* (CBS)

33. **Outstanding Achievement as Director of Comedy, Variety or Music Special Program**: Sterling Johnson for *Timex Presents Peggy Flemming at Sun Valley* (NBC)

34. **Outstanding Director of Drama Series Program**: Daryl Duke for "The Day the Lion Died" on *The Bold Ones – The Senator* (NBC)

35. **Outstanding Achievement as Director of Single Drama**: Fielder Cook for "The Price" on *Hallmark Hall of Fame* (NBC)

36. **Outstanding Achievement as Director of Series Variety or Music Program**: Mark Warren for *Rowan and Martin's Laugh-In* (NBC)

37. **Outstanding Achievement in Film Editing for Entertainment Series Programming**: Michael Economou for "A Continual Roar of Musketry" on *The Bold Ones – The Senator* (NBC)

38. **Outstanding Achievement in Film Editing for Special or Feature Made-for-Television**: George J. Nicholson for "Longstreet" on *ABC Movie of the Week* (ABC)

39. **Outstanding Achievement in Film Editing for News or Documen-

tary Program or Program Segment**: George L. Johnson for "Prisons Parts I through IV" on *NBC Nightly News* (NBC)

40. **Outstanding Achievement in Film Editing for Magazine-type or Mini-Documentary News and Documentary Programming**: Robert B. Loweree and Henry J. Grennon for *Cry Help! An NBC White Paper on Mentally Disturbed Youth* (NBC)

41. **Outstanding Achievement in Film Sound Editing**: Don Hall, Jack Johnson, Bob Weatherford and Dick Jensen for "Tribes" on *Movie of the Week* (ABC)

42. **Outstanding Achievement in Video Tape Editing**: Marco Zappia for *Hee Haw* (CBS)

43. **Outstanding Achievement in Film Sound Mixing**: Theodore Sonderberg for "Tribes" on *Movie of the Week* (ABC)

44. **Outstanding Achievement in Live or Tape Sound Mixing**: Henry Bird for "Hamlet" on *Hallmark Hall of Fame* (NBC)

45. **Outstanding Achievement in Choreography**: Ernest O. Flatt for *The Carol Burnett Show* (CBS)

46. **Outstanding Achievement in Dramatic Writing for Single Program in Series**: Joel Oliansky for "To Taste of Death But Once" on *The Bold Ones – The Senator* (NBC)

47. **Outstanding Achievement in Original Teleplay Writing**: Tracy Keenan Wynn and Marvin Schwartz for "Tribes" on *Movie of the Week* (ABC)

48. **Outstanding Achievement in Drama Adaptation Writing**: Saul Levitt for "The Andersonville Trial" on *Hollywood Television Theatre* (PBS)

49. **Outstanding Achievement in Writing for Program in Comedy Series**: James L. Brooks and Allan Burns for "Support Your Local Mother" on *The Mary Tyler Moore Show* (CBS)

50. **Outstanding Achievement in Writing for Program in Variety or Music**: Herbert Baker, Hal Goodman, Larry Klein, Bob Weiskopf, Norman Steinberg, Bob Schiller and Flip Wilson for *The Flip Wilson Show* (NBC)

51. **Outstanding Achievement in Special Program Comedy, Variety or

Music: Bob Ellison and Marty Farrell for *Singer Presents Burt Bachrach* (CBS)

52. **Outstanding Individual Achievement in Children's Programming**: Burr Tillstrom on *Kukla, Fran and Ollie* (PBS)

53. **Outstanding Individual Achievements in Sports Programming**: Jim McKay for *Wide World of Sports* (ABC), and Don Meredith for *NFL Monday Night Football* (ABC)

54. **Outstanding Achievement in Lighting Direction**: John Rook for "Hamlet" on *Hallmark Hall of Fame* (NBC)

55. **Outstanding Achievement in Technical Direction and Electronic Camerawork**: Gordon Baird, Tom Ancell, Rick Bennewitz, Larry Bentley and Jack Reader for "The Andersonville Trial" on *Hollywood Television Theatre* (PBS)

56. **Outstanding Achievement in Series Entertainment Cinematography**: Jack Marta for "Cynthia Is Alive and Living in Avalon" on *The Name of the Game* (NBC)

57. **Outstanding Achievements in Special Entertainment Cinematography**: Lionel Lindon for "Vanished Parts I and II" on *Movie of the Week* (ABC), and Bob Collins for *Timex Presents Peggy Fleming at Sun Valley* (NBC)

58. **Outstanding Achievement in Regularly Scheduled News Cinematography**: Larry Travis for "Los Angeles—Earthquake" on *CBS Evening News with Walter Cronkite* (CBS)

59. **Outstanding Achievement in News and Documentary Cinematography**: Jacques Renoir for "Tragedy of the Red Salmon" on *The Undersea World of Jacques Cousteau* (ABC)

60. **Outstanding Achievements in Any Area of Creative Technical Crafts**: Lenwood B. Abbott and John C. Caldwell for "City Beneath the Sea" on *World Premiere NBC Monday Night at the Movies* (NBC), and Gene Widhoff for courtroom sketches at the Manson trial on *The Huntley-Brinkley Report* (NBC)

61. **Outstanding Achievement in Dramatic Program Art Direction or Scenic Design**: Peter Roden for "Hamlet" on *Hallmark Hall of Fame* (NBC)

62. **Outstanding Achievement in Music or Variety Art Direction or Scenic Design**: James W. Trittipo and George Gaines for *Robert Young the Family* (CBS)

63. **Outstanding Achievement in Make-Up**: Robert Down for "Catafalque" on *Mission: Impossible* (CBS)

64. **Outstanding Achievement in Costume Design**: Martin Baugh and David Walker for "Hamlet" on *Hallmark Hall of Fame* (NBC)

65. **Outstanding Achievement in Series Music Composition**: David Rose for "The Love Child" on *Bonanza* (CBS)

66. **Outstanding Achievement in Special Program Music Composition**: Walter Scharf for "Tragedy of the Red Salmon" on *The Undersea World of Jacques Cousteau* (ABC)

67. **Outstanding Achievement in Music Direction for Drama, Variety or Music**: Dominick Frontiere for *Swing Out, Sweet Land* (NBC)

68. **Outstanding Achievement in Music, Lyrics or Special Material**: Ray Charles for *The First Months Are the Hardest* (NBC)

69. **Outstanding Achievement in Engineering Developments**: Columbia Broadcasting System for the Color Corrector and American Broadcasting Company for open-loop synchronizing system

70. **Trustees' Award**: Ed Sullivan, first President of Academy

71. **Citations**: General Electric for Portable Earth Station Transmitter, and Stefan Kudelski for design of NAGRA IV recorder

72. **Station Award**: KNXT, Los Angeles for *If You Turn On*

1971 Emmy Awards

1. **Outstanding Comedy Series**: *All in the Family* (CBS)
2. **Outstanding Musical Variety Series**: *The Carol Burnett Show* (CBS)
3. **Outstanding Talk Variety Series**: *The Dick Cavett Show* (ABC)
4. **Outstanding Variety or Music Program**: "Jack Lemmon in 'S Wonderful, 'S Marvelous, 'S Gershwin" on *Bell System Family Theatre* (NBC)
5. **Outstanding Classical Variety or Music Program**: *Beethoven's Birthday: A Celebration in Vienna with Leonard Bernstein* (CBS)

E Emmy Awards 1971

6. **Outstanding New Series**: *Elizabeth R* (PBS)
7. **Outstanding Dramatic Series**: *Elizabeth R* (PBS)
8. **Outstanding Drama or Comedy Program**: *Brian's Song* (ABC)
9. **Outstanding Series Comic Actor**: Carroll O'Connor in *All in the Family* (CBS)
10. **Outstanding Series Comic Actress**: Jean Stapleton for *All in the Family* (CBS)
11. **Outstanding Series Dramatic Actor**: Peter Falk in "Columbo" on *NBC Mystery Movie* (NBC)
12. **Outstanding Series Dramatic Actress**: Glenda Jackson in "Elizabeth R" on *Masterpiece Theatre* (PBS)
13. **Outstanding Individual Performance by Dramatic Actor**: Keith Mitchell in "Catherina Howard" on *The Six Wives of Henry VIII* (PBS)
14. **Outstanding Dramatic Performance by Supporting Actor**: Jack Warden in "Brian's Song" on *Movie of the Week* (ABC)
15. **Outstanding Dramatic Performance by Supporting Actress**: Jenny Agutter in "The Snow Goose" on *Hallmark Hall of Fame* (NBC)
16. **Outstanding Continuing Comic Performance by Supporting Actor**: Edward Asner in *The Mary Tyler Moore Show* (CBS)
17. **Outstanding Continuing Comic Performance by Supporting Actress**: Valerie Harper in *The Mary Tyler Moore Show* (CBS)
18. **Outstanding Comic Performance by a Supporting Actress**: Sally Struthers in *All in the Family* (CBS)
19. **Outstanding Performance in Music or Variety**: Harvey Korman on *The Carol Burnett Show* (CBS)
20. **Outstanding Daytime Drama**: *The Doctors* (NBC)
21. **Outstanding Sports Program**: *ABC's Wide Wide World of Sports* (ABC)
22. **Outstanding Children's Program**: *Sesame Street* (PBS)
23. **Outstanding Cultural Achievements in Documentary Programming**: "Hollywood: The Dream Factory" on *The Monday Night Special* (ABC), "A Sound of Dolphins" on *The Undersea World of Jacques Cousteau* (ABC), and "The Unsinkable Sea Otter" on *The Undersea World of Jacques Cousteau* (ABC)
24. **Outstanding Program Achievement Currently Significant Documentary Programming**: *A Night in Jail, A Day in Court* (CBS), and *This Child Is Rated X: An NBC News White Paper on Juvenile Justice* (NBC)
25. **Outstanding Achievement in Special Event Coverage**: *The China Trip* (ABC), *A Ride on the Moon: The Flight of Apollo 15* (CBS), and *June 30, 1971, A Day in History: The Supreme Court and the Pentagon Papers* (NBC)
26. **Outstanding Program Achievements in Magazine-type Programming**: *Chronolog* (NBC), and *The Great American Dream Magazine* (PBS)
27. **Outstanding Individual Achievement in Magazine-type Programming**: Mike Wallace, reporter on *60 Minutes* (CBS)
28. **Outstanding Program Achievement Within Regularly Scheduled News Programs**: "Defeat at Dacca" on *NBC Nightly News* (NBC)
29. **Outstanding Individual Achievements Within Regularly Scheduled News**: Phil Brady, reporter on "Defeat at Dacca" on *NBC Nightly News* (NBC), and Bob Schieffer, Phil Jones, Don Webster and Bill Plante for "The Air War" on *CBS Evening News with Walter Cronkite* (CBS)
30. **Outstanding Individual Achievements in Documentary Programming**: Louis J. Hazam, writer for *Venice Be Damned* (NBC), and Robert Northshield, writer for *Suffer the Little Children—An NBC News White Paper on Northern Ireland* (NBC)
31. **Outstanding Direction of Single Program in Series**: Alexander Singer for "The Invasion of Kevin Ireland" on *The Bold Ones—The Lawyers* (NBC)
32. **Outstanding Direction of Single Program**: Tom Gries for "The Glass House" on *The CBS Friday Night Movies* (CBS)
33. **Outstanding Direction in Series Comedy**: John Rich for "Sammy's Visit" on *All in the Family* (CBS)
34. **Outstanding Series Music or Variety Direction**: Art Fisher for *The Sonny and Cher Comedy Hour* (CBS)
35. **Outstanding Special Comedy,

Variety or Music Direction: Walter C. Miller and Martin Charnin for "Jack Lemmon in 'S Wonderful, 'S Marvelous, 'S Gershwin" on *Bell System Family Theatre* (NBC)

36. **Outstanding Entertainment Series Film Editing**: Edward R. Abroms for "Death Lends a Hand" on *Columbo* (NBC)

37. **Outstanding Entertainment Special Film Editing**: Bud S. Isaacs for "Brian's Song" on *Movie of the Week* (ABC)

38. **Outstanding Documentary Film Editing**: Spenser David Saxon for "Monkeys, Apes and Man" on *National Geographic Special* (CBS)

39. **Outstanding Regularly Scheduled News Program Film Editing**: Darold Murray for "War Song" on *NBC Nightly News* (NBC)

40. **Outstanding Achievement in Video Tape Editing**: Pat McKenna for "Hogan's Goat" on *Special of the Week* (PBS)

41. **Outstanding Achievement in Film Sound Editing**: Jerry Christian, James Troutman, Ronald LaVine, Sidney Lubow, Richard Raderman, Dale Johnston, Sam Caylor, John Stacy and Jack Kirschner for "Duel" on *Movie of the Week* (ABC)

42. **Outstanding Achievement in Live or Tape Sound Mixing**: Norman H. Dewes for "The Elevator Story" on *All in the Family* (CBS)

43. **Outstanding Achievement in Film Sound Mixing**: Theodore Soderberg and Richard Overton for "Fireball Forward" on *The ABC Sunday Night Movie* (ABC)

44. **Outstanding Achievement in Technical Direction and Electronic Camerawork**: Heino Ripp, Albert Camoin, Frank Gaeta, Gene Martin and Donald Mulvaney for "'S Wonderful, 'S Marvelous, 'S Gershwin" on *Bell System Family Theatre* (NBC)

45. **Outstanding Achievement in Series Entertainment Cinematography**: Lloyd Ahern for "Blue Print for Murder" on *Columbo* (NBC)

46. **Outstanding Achievement in Special Entertainment Programming**: Joseph Biroc for "Brian's Song" on *Movie of the Week* (ABC)

47. **Outstanding Achievement in Regularly Scheduled News Cinematography**: Peter McIntyre and Lim Youn Choul for "Defeat at Dacca" on *NBC Nightly News* (NBC)

48. **Outstanding Achievement in Documentary Cinematography**: Thomas Priestly for *Venice Be Damned* (NBC)

49. **Outstanding Achievement in Lighting Direction**: John Freschi for "Gideon" on *Hallmark Hall of Fame* (NBC)

50. **Special Classification of Outstanding Docu-Drama Programming**: *The Search for the Nile, Parts I–IV* (NBC)

51. **Special Classification of Outstanding General Programming**: *The Pentagon Papers* (PBS)

52. **Outstanding Choreography**: Alan Johnson for "'S Wonderful, 'S Marvelous, 'S Gershwin" on *Bell System Family Theatre* (NBC)

53. **Outstanding Achievement in Musical or Variety Art Direction or Scenic Design**: E. Jay Krause for *Diana* (ABC)

54. **Outstanding Achievement in Feature Length Art Direction or Scenic Design**: Jan Scott for "Scarecrow" on *Hollywood Television Theatre* (PBS)

55. **Outstanding Costume Design**: Elizabeth Waller for "Lion's Club" on *Elizabeth R* (PBS)

56. **Outstanding Make-Up**: Frank Westmore for "Kung Fu" on *Movie of the Week* (ABC)

57. **Outstanding Individual Achievements in Sports Programming**: William P. Kelley, Jim Culley, Jack Bennett, Buddy Joseph, Mario Ciarlo, Frank Manfredi, Corey Leible, Gene Martin, Cal Shadwell, Billy Barnes and Ron Charbonneau for *The AFC Championship* (NBC)

58. **Outstanding Achievement in Dramatic Writing for Single Program in Series**: Richard Levinson and William Link for "Death Lends a Hand" on *Columbo* (NBC)

59. **Outstanding Achievement in Original Teleplay Writing**: Allan Sloane for *To All My Friends on Shore* (CBS)

60. **Outstanding Achievement in Drama Adaptation Writing**: William Blinn for "Brian's Song" on *Movie of the Week* (ABC)

61. **Outstanding Achievement in**

Writing for Program in Comedy Series: Burt Styler for "Edith's Problem" on *All in the Family* (CBS)

62. **Outstanding Achievement in Writing for Series Program in Variety or Music**: Don Hinkley, Stan Hart, Larry Siegel, Woody Kling, Art Baer, Robert Beatty, Ben Joelson, Stan Burns, Mike Marmer and Arnie Rosen for *The Carol Burnett Show* (CBS)

63. **Outstanding Achievement in Writing for Special Program in Variety or Music**: Anne Howard Bailey for "The Trial of Mary Lincoln" on *NET Opera Theatre* (PBS)

64. **Special Classification for Outstanding Individual Achievement**: Michael Hastings and Derek Marlow, writers for *Search for the Nile, Parts I–VI* (NBC)

65. **Outstanding Achievement in Series Music**: Peter Rugolo for "In Defense of Ellen McKay" on *The Bold Ones — The Lawyers* (NBC)

66. **Outstanding Achievement in Special Music**: John T. Williams for "Jane Eyre" on *Bell System Family Theatre* (NBC)

67. **Outstanding Musical Direction for Musical, Variety or Dramatic Program**: Elliot Lawrence for "'S Wonderful, 'S Marvelous, 'S Gershwin" on *Bell System Family Theatre* (NBC)

68. **Outstanding Achievement in Music, Lyrics and Special Material**: Ray Charles for *The Funny Side of Marriage* (NBC)

69. **Outstanding Individual Achievements in Religious Programming**: Alfredo Antonini, music director for *And David Wept* (CBS), and Lon Stuckey, lighting director for *A City of the King* (syndicated)

70. **Outstanding Achievements in Any Area of Creative Technical Crafts**: Pierre Goupil, Michael Deloire and Yves Omer for underwater camerawork on "Secrets of the Sunken Caves" on *The Undersea World of Jacques Cousteau* (ABC)

71. **Trustees' Awards**: Bill Lawrence, national affairs editor of ABC News and Frank Stanton, president of CBS

72. **Outstanding Achievement for Engineering Development**: Lee Harrison for Scanimate Electronic Animation

73. **Citations**: National Broadcasting Company for Hum Bucker means of correcting remote pickup transmission defects and Richard E. Hill and the Electronic Engineering Company of California for editing equipment for video tape editing

74. **Station Award**: WZZM-TV, Grand Rapids for *Sickle Cell Disease: Paradox of Neglect*

1972 Emmy Awards

1. **Outstanding Comedy Series**: *All in the Family* (CBS)
2. **Outstanding Musical Variety Series**: *The Julie Andrews Hour* (ABC)
3. **Outstanding Variety or Popular Music Program**: *Singer Presents Liza with a Z* (NBC)
4. **Outstanding Classical Music Program**: *The Sleeping Beauty* (PBS)
5. **Outstanding New Series**: *America* (NBC)
6. **Outstanding Continuing Dramatic Series**: *The Waltons* (CBS)
7. **Outstanding Limited Episode Dramatic Series**: *Tom Brown's Schooldays, Parts I–V* (PBS)
8. **Outstanding Drama or Comedy Program**: "A War of Children" on *The New CBS Tuesday Night Movie* (CBS)
9. **Outstanding Daytime Drama**: *The Edge of Night* (CBS)
10. **Outstanding Daytime Program**: *Dinah's Place* (NBC)
11. **Outstanding Children's Entertainment/Fictional Programming**: *Sesame Street* (PBS), *Zoom* (PBS), Tom Whedon, John Boni, Sara Compton, Tom Dunsmuir, Thad Mumford, Jeremy Stevens and Jim Thurman writers for *The Electric Company* (PBS)
12. **Outstanding Children's Informational/Factual Programming**: "Last of the Curlews" on *The ABC Afterschool Special* (ABC), and Shari Lewis performer in "A Picture of Us" on *NBC Children's Theatre* (ABC)
13. **Outstanding Sports Programming**: *ABC's Wide World of Sports* (ABC), and *1972 Summer Olympic Games* (ABC)
14. **Outstanding Series Comic Actor**: Jack Klugman in *The Odd Couple* (ABC)
15. **Outstanding Religious Program**: *Duty Bound* (NBC)

Emmy Awards 1972 E

16. **Special Classification of Outstanding Program**: *The Advocates* (PBS), and *VD Blues* (PBS)
17. **Outstanding Series Comic Actress**: Mary Tyler Moore in *The Mary Tyler Moore Show* (CBS)
18. **Outstanding Series Dramatic Actor**: Richard Thomas in *The Waltons* (CBS)
19. **Outstanding Series Dramatic Actress**: Michael Learned in *The Waltons* (CBS)
20. **Outstanding Individual Performance by Actor**: Laurence Olivier in *Long Day's Journey Into Night* (ABC)
21. **Outstanding Individual Performance by Actress**: Cloris Leachman in "A Brand New Life" on *Movie of the Week* (ABC)
22. **Outstanding Limited Episode Leading Actor in a Comic or Dramatic Performance**: Anthony Murphy in *Tom Brown's Schooldays* (PBS)
23. **Outstanding Limited Episode Leading Actress in a Comic or Dramatic Performance**: Susan Hampshire in "Vanity Fair, Parts I-V" on *Masterpiece Theatre* (PBS)
24. **Outstanding Continuing Comic Performance by Supporting Actress**: Valerie Harper in *The Mary Tyler Moore Show* (CBS)
25. **Outstanding Continuing Comic Performance by Supporting Actor**: Ted Knight in *The Mary Tyler Moore Show* (CBS)
26. **Outstanding Dramatic Performance by a Supporting Actor**: Scott Jacoby in "That Certain Summer" on *Wednesday Night Movie of the Week* (ABC)
27. **Outstanding Dramatic Performance by a Supporting Actress**: Ellen Corby in *The Waltons* (CBS)
28. **Outstanding Performance in Music or Variety**: Tim Conway on *The Carol Burnett Show* (CBS)
29. **Outstanding Daytime Performer**: Mary Fickett in *All My Children* (ABC)
30. **Outstanding Dramatic Series Director**: Jerry Thorpe for "An Eye for an Eye" on *Kung Fu* (ABC)
31. **Outstanding Single Program Director**: Joseph Sargent for "The Marcus-Nelsen Murders" on *The CBS Thursday Night Movies* (CBS)
32. **Outstanding Comedy Series Director**: Jay Sandrich for "It's Whether You Win or Lose" on *The Mary Tyler Moore Show* (CBS)
33. **Outstanding Series Variety or Music Director**: Bill Davis for *The Julie Andrews Hour* (ABC)
34. **Outstanding Single Program Variety or Music Director**: Bob Fosse for *Singer Presents Liza with a Z* (NBC)
35. **Outstanding Entertainment Series Film Editing**: Gene Fowler, Jr., Marjorie Fowler and Anthony Wollner for "The Literary Man" on *The Waltons* (CBS)
36. **Outstanding Single Program Entertainment Film Editing**: Peter C. Johnson and Ed Spiegel for *Surrender at Appomattox: Appointment with Destiny* (CBS)
37. **Outstanding Video Tape Editing**: Nick Giordano and Arthur Schneider for *The Julie Andrews Hour* (ABC)
38. **Outstanding News Film Editing**: Patrick Minerva, Martin Sheppard, George Johnson, William J. Freeda, Miguel E. Portillo, Albert J. Helias, Irwin Graf, Jean Venable, Rick Hessel, Loren Berry, Nick Wilkins, Gerry Breese, Michael Shugrue, K. Su, Edwin Einarsen, Thomas Dunphy, Russell Moore and Albert Mole for *NBC Nightly News* (NBC)
39. **Outstanding Documentary Film Editing**: Les Parry for *The Incredible Flight of the Snow Geese* (NBC)
40. **Outstanding Sports Programming**: John Croak, Charles Gardner, Jakob Hierl, Conrad Kraus, Edward McCarthy, Nick Mazur, Alex Moskovic, James Parker, Louis Rende, Ross Skipper, Robert Steinbeck, John de Lisa, George Boettscher, Merrit Roesser, Leo Scharf, Randy Cohen, Vito Geraldi, Harold Byers, Winfield Gross, Paul Scoskie, Peter Fritz, Leo Stephan, Gerber McBeath, Louis Torino, Michael Wenig, Tom Wight and James Kelly, videotape editors for *The 1972 Summer Olympic Games* (ABC)
41. **Outstanding Film Sound Editing**: Ross Taylor, Fred Brown and David Marshall for "The Red Pony" on *Bell System Family Theatre* (NBC)
42. **Outstanding Film Sound Mixing**: Richard Wagner, George E. Porte, Eddie Nelson and Fred Leroy Granville for

E   Emmy Awards 1972

Surrender at Appomattox: Appointment with Destiny (CBS)

43. **Outstanding Live or Tape Sound Mixing:** Al Gramaglia and Mahlon Fox for *Much Ado About Nothing* (CBS)

44. **Outstanding Series Entertainment Cinematography:** Jack Wolf for "An Eye for an Eye" on *Kung Fu* (ABC)

45. **Outstanding Single Program Entertainment Cinematography:** Howard Schwartz for "Night of Terror" on *Tuesday Movie of the Week* (ABC)

46. **Outstanding Documentary Cinematography:** Des and Jen Bartlett for *The Incredible Flight of the Snow Geese* (NBC)

47. **Outstanding News and Special Event Cinematography:** Laurens Pierce for coverage of the shooting of Governor George Wallace on *The CBS Evening News with Walter Cronkite* (CBS)

48. **Outstanding Technical Direction and Electronic Camerawork:** Ernie Buttelman, Robert A. Kemp, James Angel, James Balden and David Hilmer for *The Julie Andrews Hour* (ABC)

49. **Outstanding Lighting Direction:** John Freschi and John Casagrande for *The 44th Oscar Awards* (NBC) and Trucke Krone for *The Julie Andrews Christmas Hour* (ABC)

50. **Outstanding Costume Design:** Jack Bear for *The Julie Andrews Hour* (ABC)

51. **Outstanding Make-Up:** Del Armstrong, Ellis Burman and Stan Winston for "Jayoupes" on *The New CBS Tuesday Night Movies* (CBS)

52. **Outstanding Original Dramatic Teleplay:** Abby Mann for "The Marcus-Nelson Murders" on *The CBS Thursday Night Movies* (CBS)

53. **Outstanding Dramatic Adaptation:** Eleanor Perry for *The House Without a Christmas Tree* (CBS)

54. **Outstanding Choreography:** Bob Fosse for *Singer Presents Liza with a Z* (NBC)

55. **Outstanding Series Music Composition:** Charles Fox for *Love, American Style* (ABC)

56. **Outstanding Single Program Musical Composition:** Jerry Goldsmith for "The Red Pony" on *Bell System Family Theatre* (NBC)

57. **Outstanding Variety, Dramatic or Musical Program Music Direction:** Peter Matz for *The Carol Burnett Show* (CBS)

58. **Outstanding Music, Lyrics and Special Material:** Fred Ebb and John Kander for *Singer Presents Liza with a Z* (NBC)

59. **Outstanding Dramatic Program Art Direction or Scenic Direction:** Tom John for *Much Ado About Nothing* (CBS)

60. **Outstanding Music or Variety Series Art Direction or Scenic Design:** Brian Bartholomew and Keaton S. Walker for *The Julie Andrews Hour* (ABC)

61. **Outstanding Series Comedy Writing:** Michael Ross, Bernie West and Lee Kalcheim for "The Bunkers and the Swingers" on *All in the Family* (CBS)

62. **Outstanding Special Program Writing in Comedy, Variety or Music:** Renee Taylor and Joseph Bologna for *Acts of Love and Other Comedies* (ABC)

63. **Outstanding Series Writing in Comedy, Variety or Music:** Stan Hart, Larry Siegel, Gail Parent, Woody Kling, Robert Beatty, Tom Patchett, Jay Tarses, Robert Hilliard, Arnie Kogen, Bill Angelos and Buz Kohan for *The Carol Burnett Show* (CBS)

64. **Outstanding Cultural Achievements in Documentary Programming:** *America* (NBC), and *Jane Goodall and the World of Animal Behavior* (ABC)

65. **Outstanding Program Achievement Currently Significant Documentary Programming:** "The Blue Collar Trap" in *NBC White Paper* (NBC), "The Mexican Connection" on *CBS Reports* (CBS), and *One Billion Dollar Weapon; And Now the War is Over, The American Military in the '70s* (NBC)

66. **Outstanding Program Achievement in Special Event Coverage:** Jim McKay commentator and ABC for coverage of the Munich Olympic tragedy (ABC)

67. **Outstanding Program Achievements in Magazine-type Programming:** *60 Minutes* (CBS), "The Selling of Colonel Herbert" on *60 Minutes* (CBS), and "The Poppy Fields in Turkey – The Heroin Labs of Marseilles – The New York Connection" on *60 Minutes* (CBS)

68. **Outstanding Individual

Achievement in Magazine-type Programming: Mike Wallace, reporter on "The Selling of Colonel Herbert" on *60 Minutes* (CBS), and Mike Wallace for correspondent for *60 Minutes* (CBS)

69. **Outstanding Program Achievement Within Regularly Scheduled News Programs**: "The U.S./Soviet Wheat Deal" on *CBS Evening News with Walter Cronkite* (CBS)

70. **Outstanding Individual Achievements Within Regularly Scheduled News**: Eric Sevaried, correspondent for "L.B.J. the Man and the President" on *CBS Evening News with Walter Cronkite* (CBS), Joel Blocker, Walter Cronkite, Dan Rather and Daniel Schorr correspondents for "The Watergate Affair" on *CBS Evening News with Walter Cronkite* (CBS), and David Dick, Dan Rather, Roger Mudd and Walter Cronkite correspondents for the coverage of the shooting of Governor George Wallace on *CBS Evening News with Walter Cronkite* (CBS)

71. **Outstanding Individual Achievements in Documentary Programming**: Alistair Cooke, narrator for *America* (NBC), Alistair Cooke, writer for "A Fireball in the Night" on *America* (NBC), and Hugo Van Lawick, director for *Jane Goodall and the World of Animal Behavior* (ABC)

72. **Outstanding Achievements in Any Area of Creative Technical Crafts**: Donald Feldstein, Robert Fontana and Joe Zuckerman for the animation layout of Leonardo da Vinci art for *Leonardo: To Know How to See* (NBC)

73. **Outstanding Engineering Development**: Sony for trinitron picture tube and CBS Systems for computer video tape editing system

74. **National Community Service Award**: KDIN-TV, Des Moines, Iowa for *Take Des Moines ... Please*

1973 Emmy Awards

1. **Outstanding Comedy Series**: *M*A*S*H* (CBS)
2. **Outstanding Musical Variety Series**: *The Carol Burnett Show* (CBS)
3. **Outstanding Variety or Popular Music Program**: *Lily* (CBS)
4. **Outstanding Limited Series**: *Columbo* (NBC)
5. **Outstanding Dramatic Series**: "Upstairs, Downstairs" on *Masterpiece Theatre* (PBS)
6. **Outstanding Drama or Comedy Special**: *The Autobiography of Jane Pittman* (CBS)
7. **Outstanding Daytime Drama**: *The Doctors* (NBC)
8. **Outstanding Drama Special**: *The Other Woman* (ABC)
9. **Outstanding Game Show**: *Password* (ABC)
10. **Outstanding Talk, Service or Variety Series**: *The Merv Griffin Show* (syndicated)
11. **Outstanding Children's Entertainment Series**: *Zoom* (PBS)
12. **Outstanding Children's Entertainment Special**: "Rookie of the Year" on *The ABC Afterschool Special* (ABC)
13. **Outstanding Children's Informational Series**: *Make a Wish* (ABC)
14. **Outstanding Children's Informational Special**: *The Runaways* (ABC)
15. **Outstanding Children's Instructional Programming**: *Inside/Out* (syndicated)
16. **Outstanding Children's Special**: *Marlo Thomas and Friends in Free to Be ... You and Me* (ABC)
17. **Outstanding Sports Program**: *ABC's Wide World of Sports* (ABC)
18. **Special Award for Outstanding Program and Individual Achievement**: Tom Snyder for *Tomorrow* (NBC) and *The Dick Cavett Show* (ABC)
19. **Outstanding Series Comic Actor**: Alan Alda in *M*A*S*H* (CBS)
20. **Outstanding Series Comic Actress**: Mary Tyler Moore in *The Mary Tyler Moore Show* (CBS)
21. **Outstanding Series Dramatic Actor**: Telly Savalas in *Kojak* (CBS)
22. **Outstanding Series Dramatic Actress**: Michael Learned in *The Waltons* (CBS)
23. **Outstanding Limited Series Actor**: William Holden in *The Blue Knight* (NBC)
24. **Outstanding Limited Series Actress**: Mildred Natwick in "The Snoop Sisters" on *NBC Tuesday Night Mystery Movie* (NBC)
25. **Outstanding Special Dramatic**

E Emmy Awards 1973

Actor: Hal Holbrook in "Pueblo" on *ABC Theatre* (ABC)

26. **Outstanding Special Dramatic Actress**: Cecily Tyson in *The Autobiography of Miss Jane Pittman* (CBS)

27. **Series Actor of the Year**: Alan Alda in *M*A*S*H* (CBS)

28. **Series Actress of the Year**: Mary Tyler Moore in *The Mary Tyler Moore Show* (CBS)

29. **Special Actor of the Year**: Hal Holbrook in "Pueblo" on *ABC Theatre* (ABC)

30. **Special Actress of the Year**: Cecily Tyson in *The Autobiography of Miss Jane Pittman* (CBS)

31. **Best Supporting Comedy Actor**: Rob Reiner in *All in the Family* (CBS)

32. **Best Supporting Comedy Actress**: Cloris Leachman in "The Lars Affair" on *The Mary Tyler Moore Show* (CBS)

33. **Best Supporting Dramatic Actor**: Michael Moriarty in *The Glass Menagerie* (ABC)

34. **Best Supporting Dramatic Actress**: Joanna Miles in *The Glass Menagerie* (ABC)

35. **Best Supporting Variety Actor**: Harvey Korman in *The Carol Burnett Show* (CBS)

36. **Best Supporting Variety or Music Actress**: Brenda Vaccaro in *The Shape of Things* (CBS)

37. **Supporting Actor of the Year**: Michael Moriarty in *The Glass Menagerie* (ABC)

38. **Supporting Actress of the Year**: Joanna Miles in *The Glass Menagerie* (ABC)

39. **Best Daytime Dramatic Series Actor**: MacDonald Carey in *Days of Our Lives* (NBC)

40. **Best Daytime Dramatic Series Actress**: Elizabeth Hubbard in *The Doctors* (NBC)

41. **Best Daytime Dramatic Special Actor**: Pat O'Brien in *The Other Woman* (ABC)

42. **Best Daytime Dramatic Special Actress**: Cathleen Nesbitt in "The Mask of Love" on *ABC Matinee Today* (ABC)

43. **Daytime Actor of the Year**: Pat O'Brien in "The Other Woman" on *ABC Matinee Today* (ABC)

44. **Daytime Actress of the Year**: Cathleen Nesbitt in "The Mask of Love" on *ABC Matinee Today* (ABC)

45. **Best Game Show Host or Hostess**: Peter Marshall in *The Hollywood Squares* (NBC)

46. **Best Variety Host or Hostess**: Dinah Shore in *Dinah's Place* (NBC)

47. **Daytime Host of the Year**: Peter Marshall in *The Hollywood Squares* (NBC)

48. **Outstanding Comedy Series Director**: Jackie Cooper for "Carry On, Hawkeye" on *M*A*S*H* (CBS)

49. **Outstanding Series Variety or Music Director**: Dave Powers for "The Australia Show" on *The Carol Burnett Show* (CBS)

50. **Outstanding Single Program Variety or Music Director**: Dwight Hemion for *Barbra Streisand ... and Other Musical Instruments* (CBS)

51. **Best Series Dramatic Director**: Robert Butler for *The Blue Knight, Part III* (NBC)

52. **Best Special Dramatic Director**: John Korty for *The Autobiography of Miss Jane Pittman* (CBS)

53. **Best Daytime Drama Series Director**: H. Wesley Kenney for *Days of Our Lives* (NBC)

54. **Best Game Show Director**: Mike Garguilo for *Jackpot!* (NBC)

55. **Best Special Director**: H. Wesley Kenney for *Miss Kline, We Love You* (ABC)

56. **Best Variety Director**: Dick Carson for *The Merv Griffin Show* (syndicated)

57. **Daytime Director of the Year**: H. Wesley Kenney for *Miss Kline, We Love You* (ABC)

58. **Series Director of the Year**: Robert Butler for *The Blue Knight* (NBC)

59. **Special Director of the Year**: Dwight Hemion for *Barbra Streisand ... Other Musical Instruments* (CBS)

60. **Outstanding Entertainment Series Film Editing**: Gene Fowler, Jr., Marjorie Fowler and Samuel E. Beetley for *The Blue Knight* (NBC)

61. **Outstanding Single Program Entertainment Film Editing**: Frank Morris for "The Execution of Private Slovak" on *NBC Wednesday Night at the Movies* (NBC)

62. **Film Editor of the Year**: Frank Morris for "The Execution of Private Slovak" on *NBC Wednesday Night at the Movies* (NBC)

Emmy Awards 1973 E

63. **Outstanding Special Video Tape Editing**: Alfred Muller for "Pueblo" on ABC Theatre (ABC)
64. **Best Video Tape Editing**: Gary Anderson for *Paramount Presents ... ABC Wide World of Entertainment* (ABC)
65. **Outstanding Daytime Editing**: Gary Anderson for *Miss Kline, We Love You* (ABC)
66. **Outstanding News Film Editing**: William J. Freeda for "Profile of Poverty in Appalachia" on *NBC Nightly News* (NBC)
67. **Outstanding Documentary Film Editing**: Ann Chegwidden for "The Babboons of Gombe" on *Jane Goodall and the World of Animal Behavior* (ABC)
68. **Outstanding Film Sound Editing**: Bud Nolan for "Pueblo" on *ABC Theatre* (ABC)
69. **Outstanding Film or Tape Sound Mixing**: Robert A. Gramaglia and Michael Schnidler for "Pueblo" on *ABC Theatre* (ABC)
70. **Best Film or Tape Sound Editing**: Charles L. Campbell, Robert Cornett, Larry Caron, Larry Kaufman, Colin Moria, Don Warner and Frank R. White for "The Baboons of Gombe" on *Jane Goodall and the World of Animal Behavior* (ABC)
71. **Best Film or Tape Sound Mixing**: Peter Pilafian, George R. Porter, Eddie J. Nelson and Robert L. Harman for "Journey to the Outer Limits" on *National Geographic Special* (ABC)
72. **Outstanding Daytime Sound Mixing**: Ernest Dellutri for *Days of Our Lives* (NBC)
73. **Best Series Entertainment Cinematography**: Harry Wolf in "Any Old Port in a Storm" on *Columbo* (NBC)
74. **Best Special Entertainment Cinematography**: Ted Voigtlander for "It's Good to Be Alive" on *GE Theatre* (CBS)
75. **Cinematographer of the Year**: Ted Voigtlander for "It's Good to Be Alive" on *GE Theatre* (CBS)
76. **Outstanding Technical Direction and Electronic Camerawork**: Gerry Bucci, Kenneth Tamburri, Dave Hilmer, Dave Smith, Jim Balden and Ron Brooks for "In Concert with Cat Stevens" on *ABC Wide World of Entertainment* (ABC)
77. **Outstanding Daytime Technical Direction and Electronic Camerawork**: Lou Marchand, Gerald M. Dowd, Frank Melchiorre and John Morris for *One Life to Live* (ABC)
78. **Outstanding Achievement in Sports Programming**: Jim McKay, host for *ABC's Wide World of Sports* (ABC)
79. **Best Series Dramatic Writing**: Joanna Lee for "The Thanksgiving Story" on *The Waltons* (CBS)
80. **Best Original Teleplay Dramatic Writing**: Fay Kanin for "Tell Me Where It Hurts" on *GE Theatre* (CBS)
81. **Best Adaptation Dramatic Writing**: Tracy Keenan Wynn for *The Autobiography of Miss Jane Pittman* (CBS)
82. **Best Series Comedy Writing**: Treva Silverman for "The Lou and Edie Story" on *The Mary Tyler Moore Show* (CBS)
83. **Best Series Variety Writing**: Ed Simmons, Gary Belkin, Robert Beatty, Arnie Kogen, Bill Richmond, Gene Perret, Rudy de Luca, Barry Levinson, Dick Clair, Jenna McMahon and Barry Harmon for *The Carol Burnett Show* (CBS)
84. **Best Special Variety Writing**: Herb Sargent, Rosalyn Drexler, Lorne Michaels, Richard Pryor, Jim Rusk, James R. Stein, Robert Illes, Lily Tomlin, George Yanok, Jane Wagner, Rod Warren, Ann Elder and Karyl Geld for *Lily* (CBS)
85. **Series Writer of the Year**: Treva Silverman for *The Mary Tyler Moore Show* (CBS)
86. **Special Writer of the Year**: Fay Kanin for "Tell Me Where It Hurts" on *GE Theatre* (CBS)
87. **Best Daytime Dramatic Writing**: Henry Slesar for *The Edge of Night* (CBS)
88. **Best Daytime Special Dramatic Writing**: Lila Garrett and Sandy Krinski for "Mother of the Bride" on *ABC Afternoon Playbreak* (ABC)
89. **Best Daytime Game Show Writing**: Jay Reack, Harry Friedman, Harold Schneider, Gary Johnson, Steve Levitch, Rick Kellard and Rowby Goren for *The Hollywood Squares* (NBC)
90. **Best Daytime Variety Writing**: Tony Grafalo, Bob Murphy and Merv Griffin for *The Merv Griffin Show* (syndicated)
91. **Best Daytime Writer of the Year**: Lila Garrett and Sandy Krinski for

"Mother of the Bride" on *ABC Playbreak* (ABC)
92. Outstanding Choreography: Tony Charmoli for *Mitzi ... A Tribute to the American Housewife* (CBS)
93. Best Series Music Composition: Morton Stevens for "Hookman" on *Hawaii Five-O* (CBS)
94. Best Special Music Composition: Fred Karlin for *The Autobiography of Miss Jane Pittman* (CBS)
95. Best Song or Theme: Marty Paich and David Paich for "Light the Way" on *Ironside* (NBC)
96. Best Music Direction of Musical Program: Jack Parnell, Ken Welch and Mitzi Welch for *Barbra Streisand ... and Other Musical Instruments* (CBS)
97. Musician of the Year: Jack Parnell, Ken Welch and Mitzi Welch for *Barbra Streisand ... and Other Musical Instruments* (CBS)
98. Outstanding Daytime Musical Direction: Richard Clements for "A Special Act of Love" on *ABC Afternoon Playbreak* (ABC)
99. Outstanding Lighting Direction: William M. Klages for "The Lie" on *CBS Playhouse* (CBS)
100. Outstanding Daytime Lighting Direction: Richard Holbrook for *The Young and the Restless* (CBS)
101. Outstanding Individual Achievement in Children's Programming: Charles M. Schulz, writer for *A Charlie Brown Thanksgiving* (CBS), and William Zaharuk and Peter Razmofski for "The Borrowers" on *Hallmark Hall of Fame* (NBC)
102. Best Series Dramatic Art Direction or Scenic Design: Jan Scott and Charles Kreiner for "The Lie" on *CBS Playhouse* (CBS)
103. Best Special Musical Art Direction or Scenic Design: Brian C. Bartholomew for *Barbra Streisand ... and Other Musical Instruments* (CBS)
104. Art Director and Set Decorator of the Year: Jan Scott and Charles Kreiner for "The Lie" on *CBS Playhouse* (CBS)
105. Outstanding Daytime Art Direction or Scenic Design: Tom Trimble and Brock Broughton for *The Young and the Restless* (CBS)

106. Outstanding Costume Design: Bruce Walkup and Sandy Stewart for *The Autobiography of Miss Jane Pittman* (CBS)
107. Outstanding Daytime Costume Design: Bill Jobe for "The Mask of Love" on *ABC Matinee Today* (ABC)
108. Outstanding Make-Up: Stan Winston and Rick Baker for *The Autobiography of Miss Jane Pittman* (CBS)
109. Outstanding Daytime Make-Up: Douglas C. Kelly for "The Mask of Love" on *ABC Matinee Today* (ABC)
110. Outstanding Achievement in Any Area of Creative Technical Craft: Lynda Gurasich, hairstylist for *The Autobiography of Miss Jane Pittman* (CBS)
111. Outstanding Segment in Regularly Scheduled News Program: "The Agnew Resignation" on *CBS Evening News with Walter Cronkite* (CBS), "The Key Biacayne Bank Charter Struggle" on *CBS Evening News with Walter Cronkite* (CBS), "Reports on World Hunger" on *NBC Nightly News* (NBC), and coverage of the October War from Israel's Northern Front on *CBS Evening News with Walter Cronkite* (CBS)
112. Outstanding Achievement in Magazine-type Programming: "America's Nerve Gas Arsenal" on *First Tuesday* (NBC), "A Question of Impeachment" on *Bill Moyer's Journal* (PBS), and "The Adversaries" on *Behind the Lines* (PBS)
113. Outstanding Special Event Coverage: *Watergate Coverage* (PBS), and *Watergate: The White House Transcripts* (CBS)
114. Outstanding Current Interest Documentary: "Fire!" on *ABC News Closeup* (ABC) and *CBS News Special Report: The Senate and the Watergate Affair* (CBS)
115. Outstanding Artistic, Cultural or Historic Documentary: "Journey to the Outer Limits" on *National Geographic Special* (ABC), *CBS Reports: The Rockefellers* (CBS), and *The World at War* (syndicated)
116. Outstanding Interview Program: "Henry Steele Commager" on *Bill Moyers Journal* (PBS), and "Solzhenitsyn" on *CBS News Special* (CBS)
117. Outstanding News Broadcaster: Harry Reasoner on *ABC News* (ABC), and Bill Moyers on "Essay on

Watergate" on *The Bill Moyers Journal* (PBS)

118. **Outstanding News and Documentary Direction**: Pamela Hill for "Fire!" on *ABC News Closeup* (ABC)

119. **Best Magazine-type Program Cinematography**: Walter Dumbrow for "Ballerina" on *60 Minutes* (CBS)

120. **Best Technical Direction and Electronic Camerawork**: Carl Schutzman, Joseph Schwartz and William Bell for *60 Minutes* (CBS)

121. **Best Regularly Scheduled News Cinematography**: Delos Hall for "Clanking Savannah Blacksmith" on *The CBS Evening News with Walter Cronkite* (CBS)

122. **Outstanding Achievement in Any Area of Creative Technical Crafts**: Philippe Cousteau, underwater camerawork on "Beneath the Frozen World" on *The Undersea World of Jacques Cousteau* (ABC), Aggie Whelan, courtroom artist on the Mitchell-Stans Trial on *The CBS Evening News* (CBS), and John Chambers and Tom Burman, Make-Up for *Struggle for Survival: Primal Man* (ABC)

123. **Best Art Direction or Scenic Design**: William Sunshine for *60 Minutes* (CBS)

124. **Best Music Composition**: Walter Scharf for "Beneath the Frozen World" on *The Undersea World of Jacques Cousteau* (ABC)

125. **Oustanding Achievement in Children's Programming**: John Stone, Joseph A. Bailey, Jerry Juhl, Emily Perl, Jeffrey Moss, Ray Sipherd and Norman Stiles, writers for *Sesame Street* (PBS), and The Muppets, performers on *Sesame Street* (PBS)

126. **Outstanding Set Decorating and Art Direction in Children's Programming**: Ronald Baldwin and Nat Mongioi for *The Electric Company* (PBS)

127. **Outstanding Religious Program**: Kan Lamkin, Sam Drummy, Garry Stanton and Robert Hatfield for "Gift of Tears" on *This Is the Life* (syndicated)

128. **National Award for Community Service**: *Through the Looking Glass Darkly* (WKY-TV, Oklahoma City)

129. **Outstanding Achievement in Engineering Achievement**: Consolidated Video Systems, Inc. for portable video tape equipment and RCA for quadraplex video tape cartridge equipment

130. **International Non-fiction Award**: *Horizon: The Making of a Natural History Film* (British Broadcasting Corporation, London)

131. **International Fiction Award**: *La Cabina* (Television Espanola, Madrid)

132. **International Directorate Emmy Award**: Charles Curran, president European Broadcasting Union and director general of the British Broadcasting Corporation

1974 Emmy Awards

1. **Outstanding Comedy Series**: *The Mary Tyler Moore Show* (CBS)
2. **Outstanding Musical Variety Series**: *The Carol Burnett Show* (CBS)
3. **Outstanding Variety or Popular Music Program**: *An Evening with John Denver* (ABC)
4. **Outstanding Limited Series**: *Benjamin Franklin* (CBS)
5. **Outstanding Dramatic Series**: *Benjamin Franklin* (CBS)
6. **Outstanding Drama or Comedy Special**: "The Law" on *NBC World Premiere Movie* (NBC)
7. **Outstanding Classical Music Program**: *Profile in Music: Beverly Sills* (PBS)
8. **Outstanding Daytime Drama**: *The Young and the Restless* (CBS)
9. **Outstanding Drama Special**: *The Girl Who Couldn't Lose* (ABC)
10. **Outstanding Game Show**: *Hollywood Squares* (NBC)
11. **Outstanding Talk, Service or Variety Series**: *Dinah!* (syndicated)
12. **Outstanding Children's Entertainment Series**: *Star Trek* (NBC)
13. **Outstanding Children's Entertainment Special**: "Harlequin" on *The CBS Festival of Lively Arts for Young People* (CBS)
14. **Outstanding Children's Special**: *Yes, Virginia, There Is a Santa Claus* (ABC)
15. **Outstanding Sports Program**: *Wide World of Sports* (ABC)
16. **Outstanding Sports Event**: *Jimmy Connors vs. Rod Laver Tennis Challenge* (CBS)
17. **National Award for Commu-

nity Service: *The Willowbrook Case: The People vs. the State of New York* (WABC-TV, New York)
18. **International Non-fiction Award**: *Aquarius: Hello Dali!* on London Weekend Television (London), and *Inside Story: Marek* on British Broadcasting Corporation (London)
19. **International Fiction Award**: *Mr. Axelford's Angel* on Yorkshire Television Limited (London), and *The Evacuees* on British Broadcasting Corporation (London)
20. **Outstanding Series Comic Actor**: Tony Randall in *The Odd Couple* (ABC)
21. **Outstanding Series Comic Actress**: Valerie Harper in *Rhoda* (CBS)
22. **Outstanding Series Dramatic Actor**: Robert Blake in *Baretta* (ABC)
23. **Outstanding Series Dramatic Actress**: Jean Marsh in "Upstairs, Downstairs" on *Masterpiece Theatre* (PBS)
24. **Outstanding Limited Series Actor**: Peter Falk in "Columbo" on *NBC Sunday Night Mystery Movie* (NBC)
25. **Outstanding Limited Series Actress**: Jessica Walter in "Amy Prentiss" on *NBC Sunday Mystery Movie* (NBC)
26. **Outstanding Special Dramatic Actor**: Laurence Olivier in "Love Among the Ruins" on *ABC Theatre* (ABC)
27. **Outstanding Special Dramatic Actress**: Katherine Hepburn in "Love Among the Ruins" on *ABC Theatre* (ABC)
28. **Outstanding Continuing Supporting Actor in a Comedy Series**: Ed Asner in *The Mary Tyler Moore Show* (CBS)
29. **Outstanding Continuing Supporting Actress in a Comedy Series**: Betty White in *The Mary Tyler Moore Show* (CBS)
30. **Outstanding Continuing Supporting Actor in a Drama Series**: Will Geer in *The Waltons* (CBS)
31. **Outstanding Continuing Supporting Actress in a Drama Series**: Ellen Corby in *The Waltons* (CBS)
32. **Outstanding Supporting Actor in Comedy or Drama Special**: Jack Albertson in *Cher* (CBS)
33. **Outstanding Supporting Actor in Comedy or Drama**: Anthony Quayle in "QB VII, Parts 1 and 2" on *ABC Movie Special* (ABC)
34. **Outstanding Supporting Actor in Comedy or Drama Series**: Patrick McGoohan in "By the Dawn's Early Light" on *Columbo* (NBC)
35. **Outstanding Supporting Actress in Variety or Music Special**: Cloris Leachman in *Cher* (CBS)
36. **Outstanding Supporting Actress in Comedy or Drama**: Juliet Mills in "QB VII, Parts 1 and 2" on *ABC Movie Special* (ABC)
37. **Outstanding Supporting Actress in Comedy or Drama Series**: Cloris Leachman in "Phyllis Whips Inflation" on *The Mary Tyler Moore Show* (CBS)
38. **Outstanding Single Performance by Supporting Actress in Comedy or Drama**: Zohra Lampert in "Queen of the Gypsies" on *Kojak* (CBS)
39. **Outstanding Sports Broadcaster**: Jim McKay on *Wide World of Sports* (ABC)
40. **Outstanding Actor in Daytime Drama Series**: MacDonald Carey in *Days of Our Lives* (NBC)
41. **Outstanding Actress in Daytime Drama Series**: Susan Flannery in *Days of Our Lives* (NBC)
42. **Outstanding Actor in Daytime Drama Special**: Bradford Dillman in "The Last Bride of Salem" on *ABC Afternoon Playbreak* (ABC)
43. **Outstanding Actress in Daytime Drama Special**: Kay Lenz in "Heart in Hiding" on *ABC Afternoon Playbreak* (ABC)
44. **Outstanding Host or Hostess in Talk, Service or Variety Series**: Barbara Walters in *Today* (NBC)
45. **Outstanding Host in Quiz or Audience Participation Show**: Peter Marshall in *The Hollywood Squares* (NBC)
46. **Special Classification of Outstanding Individual Achievement**: Alistair Cooke in *Masterpiece Theatre* (PBS)
47. **Oustanding Directing in a Drama Series**: Bill Bain for *Upstairs, Downstairs* (PBS)
48. **Outstanding Directing in a Comedy Series**: Gene Reynolds for *M*A*S*H* (CBS)
49. **Outstanding Directing in a Comedy/Variety or Music Series**: Dave Powers for *The Carol Burnett Show* (CBS)
50. **Outstanding Directing in a Comedy/Variety or Music Special**: Bill Davis for *An Evening with John Denver* (ABC)
51. **Outstanding Directing in a**

Comedy or Variety Special: George Cukor for "Love Among the Ruins" on *ABC Theatre* (ABC)

52. **Outstanding Directing in a Daytime Drama Series**: Richard Dunlap for *The Young and the Restless* (CBS)

53. **Outstanding Directing in a Daytime Special Program**: Mort Lachman for *The Girl Who Couldn't Lose* (ABC)

54. **Outstanding Directing in a Daytime Variety Program**: Glen Swanson for "Dinah Salutes Broadway" on *Dinah!* (syndicated)

55. **Outstanding Directing in a Game or Audience Participation Show**: Jerome Shaw for *The Hollywood Squares* (NBC)

56. **Outstanding Comedy Series Film Editing**: Douglas Hines for "An Affair to Forget" on *The Mary Tyler Moore Show* (CBS)

57. **Outstanding Drama Series Film Editing**: Donald R. Rode for "Mirror, Mirror on the Wall" on *Petrocelli* (NBC)

58. **Outstanding Special Film Editing**: John A. Martinelli for "The Legend of Lizzie Borden" on *ABC Monday Night Movie* (ABC)

59. **Outstanding Individual Achievement in Sports Programming**: Herb Altman, film editor for *The Baseball World of Joe Garagiola* (NBC)

60. **Outstanding Achievement in Video Tape Editing**: Gary Anderson and Jim McElroy for *Judgement: The Court-Martial of Lt. William Calley* (ABC)

61. **Outstanding Achievement in Film Sound Editing**: Marvin I. Kosberg, Richard Burrow, Milton C. Burrow, Jack Milner, Ronald Ashcroft, James Ballas, Josef von Stroheim, Jerry Rosenthal, William Andrews, Edward Sandlin, David Horton, Alvin Kajita, Tony Garber and Jeremy Hoenack for "QB-VII, Parts 1 and 2" on *ABC Movie Special* (ABC)

62. **Outstanding Achievement in Film or Tape Sound Mixing**: Marshall King for *The American Film Institute Salute to James Cagney* (CBS)

63. **Outstanding Drama Series Writing**: Howard Fast for "The Ambassador" on *Benjamin Franklin* (CBS)

64. **Outstanding Comedy Series Writing**: Ed Weinberger and Stan Daniels for "Mary Richards Goes to Jail" on *The Mary Tyler Moore Show* (CBS)

65. **Outstanding Writing in a Comedy/Variety or Music Series**: Gary Belkin, Robert Beatty, Ed Simmons, Arnie Kogen, Bill Richmond, Gene Perret, Rudy de Luca, Barry Levinson, Dick Clair and Jenna McMahon for *The Carol Burnett Show* (CBS)

66. **Outstanding Writing in a Comedy/Variety or Music Special**: Bob Wells, John Bradford and Cy Coleman for *Shirley MacLaine: If They Could See Me Now* (CBS)

67. **Outstanding Writing in a Drama or Comedy Special Program Original Teleplay**: James Costigan for "Love Among the Ruins" on *ABC Theatre* (ABC)

68. **Outstanding Writing in a Drama or Comedy Special Program Adaptation**: David W. Rintels for *IBM Presents Clarence Darrow* (NBC)

69. **Outstanding Writing for a Daytime Drama Series**: Harding Lemay, Tom King, Charles Kozloff, Jan Merlin and Douglas Marland for *Another World* (NBC)

70. **Outstanding Writing for a Daytime Special**: Audrey Davis Levin for "Heart in Hiding" on *ABC Afternoon Playbreak* (ABC)

71. **Outstanding Series Cinematography**: Richard Glouner for *Columbo* (NBC)

72. **Outstanding Special Cinematography**: David M. Walsh for *Queen of the Stardust Ballroom* (CBS)

73. **Outstanding Technical Direction and Electronic Camerawork**: Ernie Buttelman, technical director and Jim Angel, Jim Balden, Ron Brooks and Art Lacombe, cameramen for "The Missiles of October" on *ABC Theatre* (ABC)

74. **Outstanding Choreography**: Marge Champion for *Queen of the Stardust Ballroom* (CBS)

75. **Outstanding Series Musical Composition**: Billy Goldenberg for "The Rebel" on *Benjamin Franklin* (CBS)

76. **Outstanding Special Musical Composition**: Jerry Goldsmith for "QB-VII, Parts 1 and 2" on *ABC Movie Special* (ABC)

77. **Outstanding Lighting Direction**: John Freschi for *The Perry Como Christmas Show* (CBS)

78. **Outstanding Art Direction or Scenic Design from Comedy/Variety or Music Series**: Robert Kelly, art director and Robert Checchi, set decorator for *Cher* (CBS)

79. **Outstanding Art Direction or Scenic Design from Dramatic Special or Feature-Length Television Production**: Carmen Dillon, art director and Tess Davis, set director for "Love Among the Ruins" on *ABC Theatre* (ABC)

80. **Outstanding Art Direction or Scenic Design from Single Episode of Comedy or Drama Series**: Charles Lisanby, art director and Robert Checchi for "The Ambassador" on *Benjamin Franklin* (CBS)

81. **Outstanding Graphic Design and Title Sequences**: Phil Norman for "QB-VII, Parts 1 and 2" on *ABC Movie Special* (ABC)

82. **Outstanding Costume Design**: Guy Verhille for "The Legend of Lizzie Borden" on *ABC Monday Night Movie* (ABC), and Margaret Furse for "Love Among the Ruins" on *ABC Theatre* (ABC)

83. **Outstanding Individual Achievement in Sports Programming**: Gene Schwarz, technical director for *The 1974 World Series* (NBC), and Corey Leible, Ben Basile, Jack Bennett, Lou Gerard and Ray Figelski, electronic cameramen for *The 1974 Stanley Cup Playoffs* (NBC), John Pumo, Charles D'Onofrio and Frank Florio, technical directors and George Klimcsak, Robert Kania, Harold Hoffmann, Herman Lang, George Drago, Walt Deniear, Stan Gould, Al Diamond, Charles Armstrong, Al Brantley, Sig Meyers, Frank McSpedon, George F. Naeder, Gordon Sweeney, Jo Sidlo, William Hathaway, Gene Pescalek and Curly Fonorow, cameramen for *Masters Tournament* (CBS)

84. **Outstanding Individual Achievement in Children's Programming**: Elinor Bunin, graphic design and title sequences for *Funshine Saturday and Sunday* (ABC)

85. **Outstanding Achievement in Any Area of Television Creative Crafts**: Edie Panda, hair stylist for "The Ambassador" on *Benjamin Franklin* (CBS), and Doug Nelson and Norm Schwartz for double-system sound editing and synchronization for stereo broadcasting on *Wide World Concert* (ABC)

86. **Outstanding Achievement in Engineering Development**: Columbia Broadcasting System for development of Electronic News Gathering System and Nippon Electronic Company for television digital frame synchronizers

87. **Special Classification for Outstanding Program Achievement**: *American Film Institute Salute to James Cagney* (CBS)

88. **International Directorate Award**: Junzo Imamichi, chairman of the board of Tokyo Broadcasting Company

89. **Trustees' Award**: Elmer Lower of American Broadcasting Company and Peter Goldmark of Goldmark Laboratories

1975 Emmy Awards

1. **Outstanding Comedy Series**: *The Mary Tyler Moore Show* (CBS)
2. **Outstanding Comedy/Variety or Music Series**: *NBC's Saturday Night Live* (NBC)
3. **Outstanding Drama Series**: *Police Story* (NBC)
4. **Outstanding Limited Series**: "Upstairs, Downstairs" on *Masterpiece Theatre* (PBS)
5. **Outstanding Classical Music Program**: *Bernstein and the New York Philharmonic* (PBS)
6. **Outstanding Drama or Comedy Special**: "Eleanor and Franklin" on *ABC Theatre* (ABC)
7. **Outstanding Comedy/Variety or Music Special**: *Gypsy in My Soul* (CBS)
8. **Special Classification of Outstanding Program Achievement**: *The Tonight Show Starring Johnny Carson* (NBC), and *Bicentennial Minutes* (CBS)
9. **Outstanding Daytime Drama**: *Another World* (NBC)
10. **Outstanding Daytime Drama Special**: *First Ladies' Diaries: Edith Wilson* (NBC)
11. **Outstanding Daytime Game or Audience Participation Show**: *The $20,000 Pyramid* (ABC)
12. **Outstanding Children's Entertainment Series**: *Big Blue Marble* (syndicated)

13. **Outstanding Children's Informational Series:** *Go* (NBC)
14. **Outstanding Children's Entertainment Special:** "Danny Kaye's Look-In at the Metropolitan Opera" on *The CBS Festival of Lively Arts for Young People* (CBS)
15. **Outstanding Informational Children's Program:** *Happy Anniversary, Charlie Brown* (CBS)
16. **Outstanding Children's Instructional Series or Special:** *Grammar Rock* (ABC)
17. **Outstanding Daytime Talk, Service or Variety Series:** *Dinah!* (syndicated)
18. **Outstanding Children's Special:** *You're a Good Sport, Charlie Brown* (CBS)
19. **Outstanding Live Sports Special:** *1975 World Series* (NBC)
20. **Outstanding Live Sports Special:** *NFL Monday Night Football* (ABC)
21. **Outstanding Edited Sports Special:** *XII Winter Olympic Games* (ABC)
22. **Outstanding Edited Sports Series:** *ABC's Wide World of Sports* (ABC)
23. **Outstanding Series Lead Comedy Actress:** Mary Tyler Moore in *The Mary Tyler Moore Show* (CBS)
24. **Outstanding Series Lead Comedy Actor:** Jack Albertson in *Chico and the Man* (NBC)
25. **Outstanding Series Lead Dramatic Actress:** Michael Learned in *The Waltons* (CBS)
26. **Outstanding Series Lead Dramatic Actor:** Peter Falk in *Columbo* (NBC)
27. **Outstanding Limited Series Lead Actress:** Rosemary Harris in "Notorious Woman" on *Masterpiece Theatre* (PBS)
28. **Outstanding Limited Series Lead Actor:** Hal Holbrook in *Sandburg's Lincoln* (NBC)
29. **Outstanding Lead Actress in Comedy or Drama Special:** Susan Clark in *Babe* (CBS)
30. **Outstanding Lead Actor in Comedy or Drama Special:** Anthony Hopkins in "The Lindbergh Kidnapping Case" on *NBC World Premiere Movie* (NBC)
31. **Outstanding Lead Actress in a Single Performance in a Drama or Comedy Series:** Kathryn Walker in "John Adams, Lawyer" on *The Adams Chronicles* (PBS)
32. **Outstanding Lead Actor in a Single Performance in a Drama or Comedy Series:** Edward Asner in *Rich Man, Poor Man* (ABC)
33. **Outstanding Supporting Actress in Comedy Series:** Betty White in *The Mary Tyler Moore Show* (CBS)
34. **Outstanding Supporting Actor in Comedy Series:** Ted Knight in *Mary Tyler Moore Show* (CBS)
35. **Outstanding Supporting Actress in Drama Series:** Ellen Corby in *The Waltons* (CBS)
36. **Outstanding Supporting Actor in Drama Series:** Anthony Zerbe in *Harry O* (ABC)
37. **Outstanding Supporting Actress in Variety or Music:** Vicki Lawrence in *The Carol Burnett Show* (CBS)
38. **Outstanding Supporting Actor in Variety or Music:** Chevy Chase in *NBC's Saturday Night* (NBC)
39. **Outstanding Supporting Actress in Comedy or Drama Special:** Rosemary Murphy in "Eleanor and Franklin" on *ABC Theatre* (ABC)
40. **Outstanding Supporting Actor in Comedy or Drama Special:** Ed Flanders in *A Moon for the Misbegotten* (ABC)
41. **Outstanding Comedy or Drama Single Performance by a Supporting Actress:** Fionnuala Flanagan in *Rich Man, Poor Man* (ABC)
42. **Outstanding Actor in Daytime Drama Series:** Larry Haines in *Search for Tomorrow* (CBS)
43. **Outstanding Actress in Daytime Drama Series:** Helen Gallagher in *Ryan's Hope* (ABC)
44. **Outstanding Actor in Daytime Drama Special:** Gerald Gordon in *First Ladies' Diaries: Martha Washington* (NBC), and James Luisi in *First Ladies' Diaries: Martha Washington* (NBC)
45. **Outstanding Actress in Daytime Drama Special:** Elizabeth Hubbard in *First Ladies' Diaries: Edith Wilson* (NBC)
46. **Outstanding Host or Hostess in a Game or Audience Participation Show:** Allen Ludden in *Password* (ABC)
47. **Outstanding Host or Hostess in a Talk, Service or Variety Show:** Dinah Shore in *Dinah!* (syndicated)

48. **Outstanding Sports Personality:** Jim McKay in *ABC Wide World of Sports* (ABC)
49. **Outstanding Directing in a Drama Series:** David Greene for *Rich Man, Poor Man* (ABC)
50. **Outstanding Directing in a Comedy Series:** Gene Reynolds for *M*A*S*H* (CBS)
51. **Outstanding Directing in a Comedy, Variety or Music Special:** Dwight Hemion for *Steve and Eydie: Our Love Is Here to Stay* (CBS)
52. **Outstanding Directing in a Comedy, Variety or Music Series:** Dave Wilson for *NBC's Saturday Night Live* (NBC)
53. **Outstanding Directing in a Drama or Comedy Special:** Daniel Petrie for "Eleanor and Franklin" on *ABC Theatre* (ABC)
54. **Outstanding Directing in a Daytime Variety Program:** Glen Swanson for *Dinah!* (syndicated)
55. **Outstanding Directing in a Game or Audience Participation Show:** Mike Garguilo for *The $20,000 Pyramid* (ABC)
56. **Outstanding Directing in a Daytime Drama Series:** David Pressman for *One Life to Live* (ABC)
57. **Outstanding Directing in a Daytime Special:** Nicholas Havinga for *First Ladies' Diaries: Edith Wilson* (NBC)
58. **Outstanding Individual Achievement in Sports Programming:** Andy Sidaris, Don Ohlmeyer, Larry Kamm, Roger Goodman, Ronnie Hawkins and Ralph Melanby, directors for *XII Winter Olympic Games* (ABC)
59. **Outstanding Film Editing in Comedy Series:** Stanford Tischler and Fred W. Berger for "Welcome to Korea" on *M*A*S*H* (CBS)
60. **Outstanding Film Editing in Dramatic or Limited Series:** Samuel Beetley and Ken Zemke for "The Quality of Mercy" on *Medical Story* (NBC)
61. **Outstanding Film Editing in Special Program:** Michael Kahn for "Eleanor and Franklin" on *ABC Theatre* (ABC)
62. **Outstanding Achievement in Series Video Tape Editing:** Grish Bhargava and Manfred Schorn for *The Adams Chronicles* (PBS)
63. **Outstanding Video Tape Editing in a Special:** Nick V. Giordano for "Alice Cooper—The Nightmare" on *Wide, Wide World: In Concert* (ABC)
64. **Outstanding Individual Achievement in Sports Program:** Jeff Cohan, Joe Aceti, John de Lisa, Lou Frederick, Jack Gallivan, Jim Jennett, Carol Lehti, Howard Fritz, Eddie C. Joseph, Ken Klingbeil, Leo Stephan, Michael Wenig, Ted Summers, Ron Ackerman, Michael Bonifazio, Barbara Bowman, Charlie Burnham, John Croak, Charles Gardner, Marvin Gench, Victor Gonzales, Jakob Hierl, Nick Mazur, Ed McCarthy, Alex Moskovic, Arthur Nace, Lou Rende, Erskin Roberts, Merritt Roesser, Arthur Volk, Roger Haenelt, Curt Brand, Phil Mollica, Herb Ohlandt and George Boettcher, video tape editors for *XII Winter Olympic Games* (ABC)
65. **Outstanding Film Sound Editing:** Marvin I. Kosberg, Douglas H. Grindstaff, Al Kajita, Hans Mewman, Leon Selditz, Dick Friedman, Stan Gilbert, Hank Salerno, Larry Singer and William Andrews for "The Quality of Mercy" on *Medical Story* (NBC)
66. **Outstanding Film Sound Mixing:** Don Bassman and Don Johnson for "Eleanor and Franklin" on *ABC Theatre* (ABC)
67. **Outstanding Video Tape Sound Mixing:** Dave Williams for the anniversary show of *The Tonight Show Starring Johnny Carson* (NBC)
68. **Outstanding Individual Achievement in Sports Program:** Dick Roes, Jack Kelly, Bill Sandreuter, Frank Bailey and Jack Kestenbaum, video tape sound mixers for *XII Winter Olympic Games* (ABC)
69. **Outstanding Individual Achievement in Children's Program:** Bud Nolan and Jim Cookman, film sound editors for *Sound of Freedom* (NBC)
70. **Outstanding Entertainment Series Cinematography:** Harry L. Wolf for "Keep Your Eye on the Sparrow" on *Baretta* (ABC)
71. **Outstanding Entertainment Special Cinematography:** Paul Lohmann and Edward R. Brown for *Eleanor and Franklin* (ABC)
72. **Outstanding Technical Direction and Electronic Camerawork:**

Leonard Chumbley, technical director, and Walter Edel, John Fehler and Steve Zink, cameramen for *The Adams Chronicles* (PBS)

73. **Outstanding Drama Series Writing**: Sherman Yellen for *The Adams Chronicles* (PBS)

74. **Outstanding Comedy Series Writing**: David Lloyd for *The Mary Tyler Moore Show* (CBS)

75. **Outstanding Comedy/Variety or Music Series Writing**: Anne Beatts, Chevy Chase, Al Franken, Tom Davis, Lorne Michaels, Suzanne Miller, Michael O'Donoghue, Herb Sargent, Tom Schiller, Rosie Schuster and Alan Zweibel for *NBC's Saturday Night* (NBC)

76. **Outstanding Writing Adaptation for Comedy or Drama**: David W. Rintels for *Fear on Trial* (CBS)

77. **Outstanding Original Teleplay Writing for Comedy or Drama**: James Costigan for "Eleanor and Franklin" on *ABC Theatre* (ABC)

78. **Outstanding Writing for Comedy/Variety of Music Special**: Jane Wagner, Lorne Michaels, Ann Elder, Christopher Guest, Earl Pomerantz, Jim Rusk, Lily Tomlin, Rod Warren and George Yanok for *Lily Tomlin* (ABC)

79. **Outstanding Daytime Drama Series Writing**: Kay Lenard, Pat Falken Smith, William J. Bell, Margaret Stewart, Bill Rega, Sheri Anderson and Wanda Coleman for *Days of Our Lives* (NBC)

80. **Outstanding Daytime Special Writing**: Audrey Davis Levin for *First Ladies' Diaries: Edith Wilson* (NBC)

81. **Outstanding Special Classification of Program Achievement**: Ann Marcus, Jerry Adelman and Daniel Gregory Brown, writers for *Mary Hartman, Mary Hartman* (syndicated)

82. **Outstanding Lighting Direction**: William Krages and Lon Stuckey for *Mitzi and the Hundred Guys* (CBS), and John Freschi for *Mitzi ... Roarin' in the 20's* (CBS)

83. **Outstanding Achievement in Choreography**: Tony Charmoli for *Gypsy in My Soul* (CBS)

84. **Outstanding Series Musical Composition**: Alex North for *Rich Man, Poor Man* (ABC)

85. **Outstanding Special Musical Composition**: Jerry Goldsmith for *Babe* (CBS)

86. **Outstanding Achievement Musical Direction**: Seiji Ozawa for "Central Park in the Dark/A Hero's Life" on *Evening at the Symphony* (PBS)

87. **Special Achievement in Special Musical Material**: Ken Welch, Mitzie Welch and Artie Malvin for *The Carol Burnett Show* (CBS)

88. **Outstanding Comedy or Drama Art Direction or Scenic Design**: Tom John, art direction, and John Wendell and Wes Laws, set decorators, for pilot of *Beacon Hill* (CBS)

89. **Outstanding Comedy/Variety or Music Series Scenic Design and Art Direction**: Raymond Klausen, art director, and Robert Checci, set decorator for *Cher* (CBS)

90. **Outstanding Dramatic Special Art Direction and Scenic Design**: Jan Scott, art direction, and Anthony Mondello, set decorator for *Eleanor and Franklin* (ABC)

91. **Outstanding Individual Achievement in Daytime Program**: Rene Lagler, art director, and Richard Harvey, set decorator for *Dinah!* (syndicated)

92. **Outstanding Make-Up**: Del Armstrong and Mike Westmore for *Eleanor and Franklin* (ABC)

93. **Outstanding Drama or Comedy Series Costume Design**: Jane Robinson and Jill Silverside for "Recover," "Jenny" and "Lady Randolph Churchill" on "Great Performances" (PBS)

94. **Outstanding Music and Variety Costume Design**: Bob Mackie for *Mitzi ... Roarin' in the 20's* (CBS)

95. **Outstanding Hairstylists**: Jean Burt Reilly and Billy Laughridge for *Eleanor and Franklin* (ABC)

96. **Outstanding Achievement in Any Area of Creative Technical Crafts**: Donald Sahlin, Kermit Love, Caroly Wilcox, John Lovelady and Rollie Krewson, costumes and props for the Muppets on *Sesame Street* (PBS)

97. **Outstanding Individual Achievement in Children's Programming**: The Muppets, Jim Hensen, Frank Oz, Jerry Nelson, Carroll Spinney and Richard Hunt, on *Sesame Street* (PBS)

98. **Outstanding Graphic Design**

E Emmy Awards 1976

and Title Sequences: Norman Sunshine for *Addie and the King of Hearts* (CBS)
99. **Outstanding Drama Special Costume Design:** Joe I. Tompkins for *Eleanor and Franklin* (ABC)
100. **Outstanding Achievement in Religious Programming:** Joseph J.H. Valdala, cinematographer for *A Determining Force* (NBC)
101. **National Award for Community Service:** WBBM-TV, Chicago for *Forgotten Children*
102. **Outstanding Engineering Development:** Eastman Kodak for Eastman Ektachrome Video News Film, and Sony Corporation for U-Matic Video Cassette Concept

1976 Emmy Awards

1. **Outstanding Comedy Series:** *The Mary Tyler Moore Show* (CBS)
2. **Outstanding Comedy/Variety or Music Series:** *Dick Van Dyke and Company* (NBC)
3. **Outstanding Drama Series:** "Upstairs, Downstairs" on *Masterpiece Theatre* (PBS)
4. **Outstanding Limited Series:** *Roots* (ABC)
5. **Special Classification of Outstanding Program Achievement:** *The Tonight Show Starring Johnny Carson* (NBC)
6. **Outstanding Comedy, Variety or Music Special:** *The Barry Manilow Special* (ABC)
7. **Outstanding Drama or Comedy Special:** "Eleanor and Franklin: The White House Years" on *ABC Theatre* (ABC), and "Sybil" on *NBC World Premiere Movie: The Big Event* (NBC)
8. **Outstanding Lead Comedy Actor:** Carroll O'Connor in *All in the Family* (CBS)
9. **Outstanding Lead Comedy Actress:** Beatrice Arthur in *Maude* (CBS)
10. **Outstanding Continuing Performance by a Supporting Actor in Comedy Series:** Gary Burghoff in *M*A*S*H* (CBS)
11. **Outstanding Continuing Performance by a Supporting Actress in Comedy Series:** Mary Kay Place in *Mary Hartman, Mary Hartman* (syndicated)
12. **Outstanding Lead Dramatic Actor:** James Garner in *The Rockford Files* (NBC)
13. **Outstanding Lead Dramatic Actress:** Lindsay Wagner in *The Bionic Woman* (ABC)
14. **Outstanding Continuing Performance by a Supporting Actor in a Drama Series:** Gary Frank in *Family* (ABC)
15. **Outstanding Continuing Performance by a Supporting Actress in a Drama Series:** Kristy McNichol in *Family* (ABC)
16. **Outstanding Single Performance by a Supporting Actor in a Comedy or Drama Series:** Edward Asner in *Roots, Part 1* (ABC)
17. **Outstanding Single Performance by a Supporting Actress in a Comedy or Drama Series:** Olivia Cole in *Roots, Part 8* (ABC)
18. **Outstanding Lead Actor for Single Appearance in a Drama or Comedy Series:** Louis Gossett, Jr. in *Roots, Part 2* (ABC)
19. **Outstanding Lead Actress for Single Appearance in a Drama or Comedy Series:** Beulah Bondi in "The Pony Cart" on *The Waltons* (CBS)
20. **Outstanding Continuing or Single Performance by a Supporting Actor in Variety or Music:** Tim Conway in *The Carol Burnett Show* (CBS)
21. **Outstanding Continuing or Single Performance by a Supporting Actress in Variety or Music:** Rita Moreno in *The Muppet Show* (syndicated)
22. **Outstanding Lead Actor in Drama or Comedy Special:** Ed Flanders in *Harry S Truman: Plain Speaking* (PBS)
23. **Outstanding Lead Actress in Drama or Comedy Special:** Sally Field in "Sybil" on *The Big Event* (NBC)
24. **Outstanding Lead Actor in a Limited Series:** Christopher Plummer in "The Moneychangers" on *NBC World Premiere: The Big Event* (NBC)
25. **Outstanding Lead Actress in a Limited Series:** Patty Duke Astin in "Captains and the Kings" on *NBC's Best Seller* (NBC)
26. **Outstanding Performance by a Supporting Actor in a Drama or Comedy Special:** Burgess Meredith in "Tail Gunner Joe" on *The Big Event* (NBC)

Emmy Awards 1976 E

27. **Outstanding Performance by a Supporting Actress in a Drama or Comedy Special**: Diana Hyland in "The Boy in the Plastic Bubble" on *The ABC Friday Night Movie* (ABC)
28. **Outstanding Comedy Directing**: Alan Alda for *M*A*S*H* (CBS)
29. **Outstanding Directing in a Comedy or Drama Special**: Daniel Petrie for "Eleanor and Franklin: The White House Years" on *ABC Theatre* (ABC)
30. **Outstanding Drama Series Direction**: David Greene for *Roots, Part 1* (ABC)
31. **Outstanding Comedy, Variety or Music Special Directing**: Dwight Hemion for *America Salutes Richard Rodgers: The Sound of His Music* (CBS)
32. **Outstanding Comedy, Variety or Music Series Directing**: Dave Powers for *The Carol Burnett Show* (CBS)
33. **Outstanding Individual Achievement in Coverage of Special Events**: John C. Moffitt, director of *The 28th Annual Emmy Awards* (ABC)
34. **Outstanding Children's Special**: "Ballet Shoes, Parts I and II" on *Piccadilly Circus* (PBS)
35. **Outstanding Performing Arts Classical Program**: "American Ballet Theatre: Swan Lake" on *Live from Lincoln Center/Great Performances* (PBS)
36. **Outstanding Comedy Series Film Editing**: Douglas Hines for *The Mary Tyler Moore Show* (CBS)
37. **Outstanding Drama Series Film Editing**: Neil Travis and James Heckert for *Roots, Part 2* (ABC)
38. **Outstanding Special Program Film Editing**: Rita Roland and Michael S. McLean for "Eleanor and Franklin: The White House Years" on *ABC Theatre* (ABC)
39. **Special Classification of Outstanding Individual Achievement**: Allen Brewster, Bob Roethle, William Lorenz, Manuel Martinez, Ron Fleury, Mike Welch, Jerry Burling, Walter Balderson and Chuck Droege, video tape editors for "The First Fifty Years" on *The Big Event* (NBC), and George Pitts, Clay Cassell, film editors for "The First Fifty Years" on *The Big Event* (NBC)
40. **Outstanding Series Video Tape Editing**: Roy Stewart for "The War Window" on *Visions* (PBS)
41. **Outstanding Special Program Video Tape Editing**: Gary H. Anderson for *American Bandstand's 25th Anniversary* (ABC)
42. **Outstanding Series Film Sound Editing**: Larry Carow, Larry Neiman, Don Warner, Colin Mouat, George Fredrick, Dave Pettijohn and Paul Bruce Richardson for *Roots, Part 2* (ABC)
43. **Outstanding Special Program Film Sound Editing**: Bernard F. Pincus, Milton C. Burrow, Gene Eliot, Don Ernst, Tony Garber, Don V. Isaacs, Larry Kaufman, William L. Manger, David Marshall, Richard Oswald, Edward L. Sandlin and Russ Tinsley for "Raid on Entebbe" on *The Big Event* (NBC)
44. **Outstanding Film Sound Mixing**: Alan Bernard, George R. Porter, Eddie J. Nelson and Robert L. Harman for "The Savage Bees" on *NBC Monday Night at the Movies* (NBC)
45. **Outstanding Tape Sound Mixing**: Doug Nelson for *John Denver and Friend* (ABC)
46. **Outstanding Entertainment Series Cinematography**: Ric Waite for "Captains and Kings, Chapter 1" on *NBC's Best Seller* (NBC)
47. **Outstanding Entertainment Special Cinematography**: Wilmer C. Butler for "Raid on Entebbe" on *The Big Event* (NBC)
48. **Outstanding Technical Direction and Electronic Camerawork**: Karl Messerschmidt, technical director, and Jon Olson, Bruce Gray, John Guiterrez, Jim Dodge and Wayne McDonald, cameramen, for *Doug Henning's World of Magic* (NBC)
49. **Outstanding Individual Achievement in Children's Programming**: Jean de Joux and Elizabeth Savel, videoanimation on "Peter Pan" on *Hallmark Hall of Fame: The Big Event* (NBC), Bill Hargate, costume designer, and Jerry Greene, video tape editor, for "Peter Pan" on *Hallmark Hall of Fame: The Big Event* (NBC)
50. **Outstanding Comedy Series Writing**: Allan Burns, James L. Brooks, Ed Weinberger, Stan Daniels, David Lloyd and Bob Ellison for "Ted's Change of Heart" on *The Mary Tyler Moore Show* (CBS)
51. **Outstanding Drama Series

E Emmy Awards 1976

Writing: Ernest Kinoy and William Blinn for *Roots, Part 2* (ABC)

52. **Outstanding Comedy, Variety or Music Series Writing**: Anne Beatts, Dan Aykroyd, Al Franken, Tom Davis, James Downey, Lorne Michaels, Marilyn Suzanne Miller, Michael O'Donoghue, Herb Sargent, Tom Schiller, Rosie Schuster, Alan Zweibel, John Belushi and Bill Murray for *NBC's Saturday Night Live* (NBC)

53. **Outstanding Writing Adaptation in a Drama or Comedy Special**: Stewart Stern for "Sybil" on *The Big Event* (NBC)

54. **Outstanding Original Teleplay Writing for Drama or Comedy**: Lane Slate for "Tail Gunner Joe" on *The Big Event* (NBC)

55. **Outstanding Writing for Comedy, Variety or Music Special**: Alan Buz Kohan and Ted Strauss for *America Salutes Richard Rodgers: The Sound of His Music* (CBS)

56. **Outstanding Comedy Series Art Direction or Scenic Design**: Thomas E. Azzari, art director for *Fish* (ABC)

57. **Outstanding Drama Series Art Direction or Scenic Design**: Tim Harvey, scenic designer for *The Pallisers, Episode 1* (PBS)

58. **Outstanding Art Direction or Scenic Design for Comedy, Variety or Music Series**: Romain Johnston, art director, for *The Mac Davis Show* (NBC)

59. **Outstanding Dramatic Special Art Direction or Scenic Design**: Jan Scott, art director, and Anne D. McCully, set decorator, for "Eleanor and Franklin: The White House Years" on *ABC Theatre* (ABC)

60. **Outstanding Art Direction or Scenic Design for Comedy, Variety or Music Special**: Robert Kelly, art director, for *America Salutes Richard Rodgers: The Sound of His Music* (CBS)

61. **Outstanding Series Music Composition**: Quincy Jones and Gerald Fried for *Roots, Part 1* (ABC)

62. **Outstanding Special Program Music Composition**: Alan Bergman, Marilyn Bergman and Leonard Rosenman for "Sybil" on *The Big Event* (NBC)

63. **Outstanding Musical Direction**: Ian Fraser for *America Salutes Richard Rodgers: The Sound of His Music* (CBS)

64. **Outstanding Graphic Design and Title Sequences**: Stu Bernstein and Eytan Keller for *Bell Telephone Jubilee* (NBC)

65. **Outstanding Drama Special Costume Design**: Joe I. Tompkins for "Eleanor and Franklin: The White House Years" on *ABC Theatre* (ABC)

66. **Outstanding Music/Variety Costume Design**: Jan Skalicky for "The Barber of Seville" on *Live from Lincoln Center: Great Performances* (PBS)

67. **Outstanding Drama or Comedy Series Costume Design**: Raymond Hughes for *The Pallisers, Episode 1* (PBS)

68. **Outstanding Make-Up**: Ken Chase, make-up design, and Joe DiBella, make-up artist, for "Eleanor and Franklin: The White House Years" on *ABC Theatre* (ABC)

69. **Outstanding Choreography**: Ron Field for *America Salutes Richard Rodgers: The Sound of His Music* (CBS)

70. **Outstanding Lighting Direction**: William M. Klages and Peter Edwards for *The Dorothy Hammill Special* (ABC)

71. **Outstanding Achievement in Any Area of Creative Technical Crafts**: Emma di Vittorio and Vivienne Walker, hairstylists, for "Eleanor and Franklin: The White House Years" on *ABC Theatre* (ABC)

72. **Outstanding Individual Achievement in Special Event Coverage**: Brian C. Bartholomew and Keaton S. Walker, Walter Edel, John Fehler and Steve Zink, cameramen, art directors, for *The 28th Annual Emmy Awards* (ABC)

73. **Special Award for Leadership in Establishing Circularly Polarized Transmission to Improve Television Reception**: American Broadcasting Company

74. **Special Citation for Improving the Efficiency of UHF Klystrons**: Varian Associates

75. **Outstanding Achievement in Broadcast Journalism**: *The MacNeil-Lehrer Report*, Eric Sevareid, League of Women Voters, *60 Minutes*

76. **Outstanding Daytime Drama Series**: *Ryan's Hope* (ABC)

77. **Outstanding Daytime Talk, Service or Variety Show**: *The Merv Griffin Show* (syndicated)

78. **Outstanding Game or Audience

Participation Show: *The Family Feud* (ABC)
79. **Outstanding Children's Entertainment Series**: *Zoom* (PBS)
80. **Outstanding Children's Informational Series**: *The Electric Company* (PBS)
81. **Outstanding Children's Instructional Programming**: *Sesame Street* (PBS)
82. **Outstanding Children's Entertainment Special**: "Big Henry and the Polka Dot Kid" on *Special Treat* (NBC)
83. **Outstanding Children's Informational Special**: "My Mom's Having a Baby" on *ABC Afternoon Specials* (ABC)
84. **Outstanding Program and Individual Achievement in Daytime Drama Specials**: Gaby Monet and Anne Grant, writers, and Lois Nettleton, performer, for *The American Woman: Portraits of Courage* (ABC)
85. **Outstanding Daytime Dramatic Actor**: Val Dufor in *Search for Tomorrow* (CBS)
86. **Outstanding Daytime Dramatic Actress**: Helen Gallagher in *Ryan's Hope* (ABC)
87. **Outstanding Host or Hostess in a Talk, Service or Variety Series**: Phil Donahue in *Donahue* (syndicated)
88. **Outstanding Host or Hostess in a Game or Audience Participation Series**: Bert Convy in *Tattletales* (CBS)
89. **Outstanding Daytime Drama Series Director**: Lela Swift for February 8 program of *Ryan's Hope* (ABC)
90. **Outstanding Single Episode Director for Daytime Variety Program**: Donald R. King for "Mike in Hollywood with Ray Charles and Michel Legrand" on *The Mike Douglas Show* (syndicated)
91. **Outstanding Single Episode Director for Game or Audience Participation Show**: Mike Gargiulo for August 10 program of *The $20,000 Pyramid* (ABC)
92. **Outstanding Writing for Daytime Drama Series**: Claire Labine, Paul Avila Mayer and Mary Munisteri for *Ryan's Hope* (ABC)
93. **Original Teleplay Writing for Drama or Comedy Special Program**: Lane Slate for "Tail Gunner Joe" on *The Big Event* (NBC)
94. **Outstanding Live Sports Special**: Roone Arledge, Chuck Howard, Don Ohlmeyer, Chet Forte, Dennis Lewin, Bob Goodrich, Geoffrey Mason, Terry Lastrow, Eleanor Riger, Ned Steckel, Brice Weisman, John Wilcox and Doug Wilson for *1976 Olympic Games* (ABC)
95. **Outstanding Live Sports Series**: Michael Pearl, Hal Classen and Sid Kaufman for *The NFL Today/NFL Football on CBS* (CBS)
96. **Outstanding Sports Personality**: Frank Gifford
97. **Outstanding Directing in Sports Directing**: Chet Forte for *NFL Monday Night Football* (ABC)
98. **Outstanding Edited Sports Series**: Bud Greenspan and Cappy Petrash Greenspan for *The Olympiad* (PBS)
99. **Outstanding Edited Sports Special**: Roone Arledge, Chuck Howard, Don Ohlmeyer, Chet Forte, Dennis Lewin, Bob Goodrich, Geoffrey Mason, Terry Lastrow, Eleanor Riger, Ned Steckel, Bruce Weisman, John Wilcox and Doug Wilson for *A Special Preview of the 1976 Olympic Games from Montreal, Canada* (ABC)
100. **Outstanding Individual Achievement in Sports Film Editing**: John Petersen, Angelo Bernaducci, Irwin Krechaf, Margaret Murphy, Vincent Reda and Anthony Zaccaro for *1976 Olympic Games* (ABC)
101. **Outstanding Individual Achievement in Sports Cinematography**: Peter Henning, Harvey Harrison, Harry Hart, D'Arcy March, Don Shapiro, Don Shoemaker and Joe Valentine for *1976 Olympic Games* (ABC)
102. **National Award for Community Service**: WGBH-TV, Boston, Massachusetts for *Rape*

1977 Emmy Awards

1. **Outstanding Comedy Series**: *All in the Family* (CBS)
2. **Outstanding Drama Series**: *The Rockford Files* (NBC)
3. **Outstanding Comedy-Variety or Music Series**: *The Muppet Show* (ITC syndication)
4. **Outstanding Children's Special**: *Halloween Is Grinch Night* (ABC)

E Emmy Awards 1977

5. **Outstanding Program Achievement**: *The Tonight Show Starring Johnny Carson* (NBC)
6. **Outstanding Comedy, Variety or Music Special**: *Bette Midler—Ole Red Hair Is Back* (NBC)
7. **Outstanding Limited Series**: *Holocaust* (NBC)
8. **Outstanding Informational Series**: *The Body Human* (CBS)
9. **Outstanding Classical Program in the Performing Arts**: American Ballet Theatre's "Giselle" on *Live from Lincoln Center* (PBS)
10. **Outstanding Informational Special**: "The Great Whales" on *National Geographic Special* (PBS)
11. **Outstanding Drama or Comedy Special**: *The Gathering* (ABC)
12. **Outstanding Special Classification Program Achievement**: *Live from Lincoln Center: Recital of Tenor Luciano Pavarotti from the Met* (PBS)
13. **Outstanding Lead Comedy Actress**: Jean Stapleton in *All in the Family* (CBS)
14. **Outstanding Lead Comedy Actor**: Carroll O'Connor in *All in the Family* (CBS)
15. **Outstanding Continuing Performance by a Supporting Actress in a Comedy Series**: Julie Kavner in *Rhoda* (CBS)
16. **Outstanding Continuing Performance by a Supporting Actor in a Comedy Series**: Rob Reiner in *All in the Family* (CBS)
17. **Outstanding Lead Actress in a Drama Series**: Sada Thompson in *Family* (ABC)
18. **Outstanding Lead Actor in a Drama Series**: Edward Asner in *Lou Grant* (CBS)
19. **Outstanding Continuing Performance by a Supporting Actress in a Drama Series**: Nancy Marchand in *Lou Grant* (CBS)
20. **Outstanding Continuing Performance by a Supporting Actor in a Drama Series**: Robert Vaughn in *Washington: Behind Closed Doors* (ABC)
21. **Outstanding Lead Actress in a Limited Series**: Meryl Streep in *Holocaust* (NBC)
22. **Outstanding Lead Actor in a Limited Series**: Michael Moriarity in *Holocaust* (NBC)
23. **Outstanding Continuing or Single Performance by a Supporting Actress in Variety or Music**: Gilda Radner in *NBC's Saturday Night Live* (NBC)
24. **Outstanding Continuing or Single Performance by a Supporting Actor in Variety or Music**: Tim Conway in *The Carol Burnett Show* (CBS)
25. **Outstanding Single Performance by a Supporting Actress in a Comedy or Drama Series**: Blanche Baker in *Holocaust* (NBC)
26. **Outstanding Single Performance by a Supporting Actor in a Comedy or Drama Series**: Ricardo Montalban in *How the West Was Won, Part Two* (ABC)
27. **Outstanding Lead Actress for a Single Appearance in a Drama or Comedy Series**: Rita Moreno in "The Paper Palace" on *The Rockford Files* (NBC)
28. **Outstanding Lead Actor for a Single Appearance in a Drama or Comedy Series**: Barnard Hughes in "Judge" on *Lou Grant* (CBS)
29. **Outstanding Performance by a Supporting Actress in a Comedy or Drama Special**: Eve Le Gallienne in *The Royal Family* (PBS)
30. **Outstanding Performance by a Supporting Actor in a Comedy or Drama Special**: Howard Da Silva in "Verna: USO Girl" on *Great Performances* (PBS)
31. **Outstanding Lead Actress in a Drama or Comedy Special**: Joanne Woodward in "See How She Runs" on *GE Theatre* (CBS)
32. **Outstanding Lead Actor in a Drama or Comedy Special**: Fred Astaire in *A Family Upside Down* (NBC)
33. **Outstanding Directing in a Comedy Series**: Paul Bogart for "Edith's 50th Birthday" on *All in the Family* (CBS)
34. **Outstanding Directing in a Drama Series**: Marvin J. Chomsky for *Holocaust* (NBC)
35. **Outstanding Directing in a Comedy/Variety or Music Series**: Dave Powers for *The Carol Burnett Show* (CBS)
36. **Outstanding Directing in a Comedy/Variety or Music Special**: Dwight

Hemion for *The Sentry Collection Presents Ben Vereen—His Roots* (ABC)

37. Outstanding Directing in a Special Drama or Comedy Program: David Lowell Rich for *The Defection of Simas Kudirka* (CBS)

38. Outstanding Writing in a Comedy Series: Bob Weiskopf, Harve Brosten, Barry Harman and Bob Schiller for "Cousin Liz" on *All in the Family* (CBS)

39. Outstanding Writing in a Drama Series: Gerald Green for *Holocaust* (NBC)

40. Outstanding Writing in a Comedy/Variety or Music Series: Robert Beatty, Tim Conway, Dick Clair, Elias Davis, Rick Hawkins, Jenna McMahan, Gene Perret, Bill Richmond, Liz Sage, David Pollock, Adele Styler, Ed Simmons and Burt Styler for *The Carol Burnett Show* (CBS)

41. Outstanding Writing in a Comedy/Variety or Music Special: Chevy Chase, Al Franken, Tom Davis, Charles Grodin, Lorne Michaels, Lily Tomlin, Paul Simon and Alan Zweibal for *The Paul Simon Special* (NBC)

42. Outstanding Writing in a Special Program, Adaption: Caryl Ledner for *Mary White* (ABC)

43. Outstanding Writing in a Comedy or Drama Special Program, Original Teleplay: George Rubino for *The Last Tenant* (ABC)

44. First Annual ATAS Governor's Award: William S. Paley, Chairman CBS

45. Outstanding Comedy Series Film Editing: Ed Cotter for "Richie Almost Dies" on *Happy Days* (ABC)

46. Outstanding Drama Series Film Editing: Alan Heim, Graig McKay, Robert M. Reitano, Stephen A. Rotter and Brian Smedley-Aston for *Holocaust* (NBC)

47. Outstanding Special Film Editing: John A. Martinelli for *The Defection of Simas Kudirka* (CBS)

48. Outstanding Special Film Sound Editing: James Yant, Donald Higgins, Michael Corrigan, William Jackson, John Strauss, Richard Le Grand, Jerry Pirozzi, John Kline, and Jerry Rosenthal for *The Amazing Howard Hughes* (CBS)

49. Outstanding Series or Special Film Sound Mixing: Robert L. Harman, Eddie J. Nelson, George E. Porter and William Teague for *Young Joe, the Forgotten Kennedy* (ABC)

50. Outstanding Series Videotape Editing: Tucker Wiard for *The Carol Burnett Show* (CBS)

51. Outstanding Special Videotape Editing: Pam Marshall and Andy Zall for *The Sentry Collection Presents Ben Vereen—His Roots* (ABC)

52. Outstanding Entertainment Series Cinematography: Ted Voigtlander for "The Fighter" on *Little House on the Prairie* (NBC)

53. Outstanding Entertainment Special Cinematography: Gerald Perry Finnerman for *Ziegfeld: The Man and His Women* (NBC)

54. Outstanding Series Technical Direction and Electronic Camerawork: Gene Crowe, Larry Heider, Dave Hillmer, Bob Keys and Wayne Orr for *The Sentry Collection Presents Ben Vereen—His Roots* (ABC)

55. Outstanding Series Music Composition: Billy Goldenberg for *King* (NBC)

56. Outstanding Special Music Composition: Jimmie Haskell for "See How She Runs" on *GE Theatre* (CBS)

57. Outstanding Series or Special Music Direction: Ian Fraser for *The Sentry Collection Presents Ben Vereen—His Roots* (ABC)

58. Outstanding Series or Special Tape Sound Mixing: Ron Bryan, Edward J. Greene and Thomas J. Huth for *Bette Midler—Ole Red Hair Is Back* (NBC)

59. Outstanding Series or Special Lighting Direction: Greg Brunton for *Cher* (CBS)

60. Outstanding Special Music Material: Stan Freeman and Arthur Malvin for "High Hat" on *The Carol Burnett Show* (CBS)

61. Outstanding Sound Effects: William F. Brownell and John H. Kantrowe for *Our Town* (NBC)

62. Outstanding Special or Series Choreography: Ron Field for *The Sentry Collection Presents Ben Vereen—His Roots* (ABC)

63. Outstanding Special or Series Graphic Design and Title Sequence: Bill Davis, Bob Fletcher and Bill Melendez for *NBC The First 50 Years—A Closer Look* (NBC)

64. Outstanding Drama Special Costume Design: Noel Taylor for "Actor" on *Hollywood Television Theatre* (PBS)

E   Emmy Awards 1977

65. **Outstanding Music/Variety Series or Special Costume Design**: Bob Mackie and Ret Turner for *Mitzi ... Zings Into Spring* (CBS)

66. **Outstanding Drama or Comedy Series Costume Design**: Edith Almoslino and Peggy Farrell for *Holocaust* (NBC)

67. **Outstanding Individual Achievement in Costume Design**: William Pitkin for *Romeo and Juliet* (PBS)

68. **Outstanding Series or Special Makeup**: Richard Cobos and Walter Schenck for *How the West Was Won, Part Two* (ABC)

69. **Outstanding Individual Achievement in Children's Programming**: Robert Checchi (Set Design), Bill Hargate (Costume Design) and Ken Johnson (Art Direction) for *Once Upon a Brothers Grimm* (CBS)

70. **Outstanding Comedy Series Art Direction**: Robert Checchi and Edward Stephenson for *Soap, Episode One* (ABC)

71. **Outstanding Drama Series Art Direction**: Tim Harvey for "I, Claudius, Episode One" on *Masterpiece Theatre* (PBS), Derek Rodd for "Anna Karenina" on *Masterpiece Theatre* (PBS), Wilfred J. Shingleton, Theo Harish, Jurgen Kiebach and Max Hareiter for *Holocaust* (NBC)

72. **Outstanding Comedy/Variety or Music Series Art Direction**: Roy Christopher for *The Richard Pryor Show* (NBC)

73. **Outstanding Dramatic Special Art Direction**: John de Cuir and Richard C. Goddard for *Ziegfeld: The Man and His Women* (NBC)

74. **Outstanding Comedy/Variety or Music Special Art Direction**: Romain Johnston for *The Sentry Collection Presents Ben Vereen—His Roots* (ABC)

75. **Outstanding Series Film Sound Editing**: H. Lee Chaney, Mark Dennis, Douglas H. Grinderstaff, Don V. Isaacs, Dick Raderman, Hank Salerno, Christopher Chulack, Don Crosby, Donald V. Isaacs and Larry Singer for "River of Promises" on *Police Story* (NBC)

76. **Outstanding Achievement in Broadcast Journalism**: Charles Kuralt, Bill Moyers, *The Fire Next Door, Exploding Gas Tanks*

77. **Outstanding Achievement in Engineering Development**: Vlahos-Gottschalk Research Corporation for invention and development of Ultimatte video matting device

78. **Governor's Medallion to Frederick Wolcott for 30 years of service on the ATAS Engineering Awards Panel**

79. **Outstanding Daytime Drama Series**: *Days of Our Lives* (NBC)

80. **Outstanding Children's Entertainment Series**: *Captain Kangaroo* (CBS)

81. **Outstanding Children's Informational Series**: *Animals, Animals, Animals* (ABC)

82. **Outstanding Children's Instructional Series**: *Schoolhouse Rock* (ABC)

83. **Outstanding Children's Entertainment Special**: "Hewitt's Just Different" on *ABC Afterschool Special* (ABC)

84. **Outstanding Children's Information Special**: "Very Good Friends" on *ABC Afterschool Special* (ABC)

85. **Outstanding Daytime Talk, Service or Variety Series**: *Donahue* (syndicated)

86. **Outstanding Game or Audience Participation Series**: *The Hollywood Squares* (NBC)

87. **Outstanding Daytime Dramatic Actor**: James Pritchett in *The Doctors* (NBC)

88. **Outstanding Daytime Dramatic Actress**: Laurie Heineman for *Another World* (NBC)

89. **Outstanding Host or Hostess in a Talk, Service or Variety Series**: Phil Donahue in *Donahue* (syndicated)

90. **Outstanding Host or Hostess in a Game or Audience Participation Show**: Richard Dawson in *The Family Feud* (ABC)

91. **Outstanding Single Program Directing of a Daytime Drama Series**: Richard Dunlap for March 3 program of *The Young and the Restless* (CBS)

92. **Outstanding Single Program Directing of a Daytime Variety Series**: Martin Haig Mackey for March 20 program of *Over Easy* (PBS)

93. **Outstanding Single Program Directing of a Daytime Game or Audience Participation Show**: Mike Gargiulo for June 20 program of *The $20,000 Pyramid* (ABC)

Emmy Awards 1978 E

94. **Outstanding Writing in a Daytime Drama Series**: Claire Labine, Paul Avila Mayer, Mary Munisteri, Allan Leicht and Judith Pinsker for *Ryan's Hope* (ABC)
95. **Outstanding Special Event Coverage**: *The Great English Garden Party—Peter Ustinov Looks at 100 Years of Wimbledon* (NBC)
96. **Outstanding Individual Achievement in Children's Programming**: Tony Di Girolamo and Tom Aldredge in "Henry Winkler Meets William Shakespeare" on *CBS Festival of Lively Arts for Young People* (CBS), Jan Hartman for "Hewitt's Just Different" on *ABC Afterschool Special* (ABC), David Wolf for "The Magic Hat" on *Unicorn Tales* (syndicated), Bonnie Karrin for "Big Apple Birthday" on *Unicorn Tales* (syndicated), and Brianne Murphy for "Five Finger Discount" on *Special Treat* (NBC)
97. **Outstanding Daytime Programming Individual Achievement**: Connie Wexler for *Search for Tomorrow* (CBS), Steve Cunningham, Hector Ramirez, Sheldon Mooney, Martin Wagner and David Finch for *After Hours: Singin', Swingin' & All That Jazz* (CBS), Steve Cunningham, Fred Gough, Mike Stitch and Joe Vicens for *The Young and the Restless* (CBS), David M. Clark for "The New York Remotes" on *The Mike Douglas Show* (syndicated), and Joyce Tamara Grossman for "Valentine's Day Special" on *The Family Feud* (ABC)
98. **Outstanding Religious Programming Individual Achievement**: Carolee Campbell for *This Is My Son* (NBC), and Douglas Watson and Joseph Vadala for *Continuing Creations* (NBC)
99. **Outstanding Live Sports Special**: *World Championship Boxing (Ali/Spinks)* (CBS)
100. **Outstanding Live Sports Series**: *The NFL Today/NFL Football on CBS* (CBS)
101. **Outstanding Edited Sports Special**: *The Impossible Dream: Ballooning Across the Atlantic* (CBS)
102. **Outstanding Edited Sports Series**: *The Way It Was* (syndicated)
103. **Outstanding Sports Personality**: Jack Whitaker
104. **Outstanding Sports Directing**: Ted Nathanson for *AFC Championship Football* (NBC)
105. **Outstanding Individual Achievement in Sports**: Steve Sabol for "Joe and the Magic Bean: The Story of Superbowl III" on *NFL Today* (CBS), Steve Sabol for "Skateboard Fever" on *Sportsworld* (NBC), Arthur Tinn for *Superbowl Today/Superbowl XII* (CBS), Bob Levy, Jerome Haggert, Richard Leible, Charles Liotta, John Olszewski, Mathew F. McCarthy and Peter Caesar for *Sportsworld* (NBC)
106. **Outstanding Achievement in Religious Programming**: Doc Siegel for "The Healer" on *This Is the Life* (syndicated), and *Marshall Efron's Illustrated, Simplified and Painless Sunday School* (CBS)
107. **National Award for Community Service**: KOOL-TV, Phoenix Arizona for *Water*
108. **International Fiction Award**: Granada Television Ltd., London for *The Collection*
109. **International Non-Fiction Award**: Canadian Broadcasting Corporation for *Henry Ford's America*, and Yorkshire Television Ltd., England for *The Good, Bad and Indifferent*

1978 Emmy Awards

1. **Outstanding Comedy Series**: *Taxi* (ABC)
2. **Outstanding Drama Series**: *Lou Grant* (CBS)
3. **Outstanding Limited Series**: *Roots: The Next Generation* (ABC)
4. **Outstanding Comedy/Variety or Music Program**: *Steve and Eydie Celebrate Irving Berlin* (NBC)
5. **Outstanding Animated Program**: *The Lion, the Witch and the Wardrobe* (CBS)
6. **Outstanding Children's Program**: *Christmas Eve on Sesame Street* (PBS)
7. **Outstanding Comedy or Drama Special**: *Friendly Fire*
8. **Outstanding Information Program**: *Scared Straight* (syndication)
9. **Outstanding Program in the Performing Arts**: "Balanchine IV—Dance in America" on *Great Performances* (PBS)

E Emmy Awards 1978

10. **Outstanding Special Classification Program Achievement:** *Lifeline* (NBC) and *The Tonight Show Starring Johnny Carson* (NBC)
11. **Outstanding Special Events Program Achievement:** *51st Annual Academy Awards Ceremonies* (ABC)
12. **Outstanding Comedy Series Lead Actress, Episode:** Ruth Gordon in "Sugar Mama" on *Taxi* (ABC)
13. **Outstanding Comedy Series Lead Actor:** Carroll O'Connor in *All in the Family* (CBS)
14. **Outstanding Comedy/Variety or Music Series Supporting Actress:** Sally Struthers in "California Here We Come" on *All in the Family* (CBS)
15. **Outstanding Comedy/Variety or Music Series Supporting Actor:** Robert Guillaume in *Soap* (ABC)
16. **Outstanding Limited Series or Special Lead Actress:** Bette Davis in *Strangers: The Story of a Mother & Daughter* (CBS)
17. **Outstanding Limited Series or Special Lead Actor:** Peter Strauss in *The Jericho Mile* (ABC)
18. **Outstanding Limited Series or Special Supporting Actress:** Esther Rolle in *Summer of My German Soldier* (NBC)
19. **Outstanding Limited Series or Special Supporting Actor:** Marlon Brando in *Roots: The Next Generation* episode (ABC)
20. **Outstanding Drama Series Lead Actress:** Mariette Hartley in "Married" on *The Incredible Hulk* (CBS)
21. **Outstanding Drama Series Lead Actor:** Ron Liebman in *Kaz* (CBS)
22. **Outstanding Drama Series Supporting Actress:** Kristy McNichol in *Family* (ABC)
23. **Outstanding Drama Series Supporting Actor:** Stuart Margolin in *The Rockford Files* (NBC)
24. **Outstanding Comedy, Comedy/Variety or Music Series Director:** Noam Pitlik for "The Harris Incident" on *Barney Miller* (ABC)
25. **Outstanding Limited Series or Special Director:** David Greene for *Friendly Fire* (ABC)
26. **Outstanding Drama Series Director:** Jackie Cooper for *White Shadow* pilot (CBS)
27. **Outstanding Information Program Individual Achievement Director:** John Korty for *Who Are the DeBolts & Where Did They Get 19 Kids?* (ABC)
28. **Outstanding Comedy, Comedy/Variety or Music Series Writer:** Alan Alda for "Inga" on *M*A*S*H* (CBS)
29. **Outstanding Limited Series or Special Writer:** Patrick Nolan & Michael Mann for *The Jericho Mile* (ABC)
30. **Outstanding Drama Series Writer:** Michele Gallery for "Dying" on *Lou Grant* (CBS)
31. **Outstanding Special Events Individual Achievement:** Mikhail Baryshnikov in *Baryshnikov at the White House* (PBS)
32. **Outstanding Single Episode Film Editing of a Series:** M. Pam Blumenthal for "Paper Marriage" on *Taxi* (ABC)
33. **Outstanding Limited Series or Special Film Editing:** Arthur Schmidt for *The Jericho Mile* (ABC)
34. **Outstanding Film Sound Editing:** William H. Wistrom for *Friendly Fire* (ABC)
35. **Outstanding Film Sound Mixing:** Bill Teague, George R. Porter, Eddie J. Nelson and Ray West for *The Winds of Kitty Hawk* (NBC)
36. **Outstanding Single Episode Cinematography of a Series:** Ted Voigtlander for "The Craftsman" on *Little House on the Prairie* (NBC)
37. **Outstanding Limited Series or Special Cinematography:** Howard Schwartz for *Rainbow* (NBC)
38. **Outstanding Limited Series or Special Videotape Editing:** Ken Denisoff, Tucker Wiard and Janet McFadden for *The Scarlet Letter, Part Two* (PBS)
39. **Outstanding Technical Direction and Electronic Camerawork:** Jerry Weiss, Don Barker, Peggy Mahoney, Reed Howard, Kurt Tonnesson, Bill Landers, Lou Cywinski, George Loomis and Brian Sherriffe for *Dick Clark's Live Wednesday, Program One* (NBC)
40. **Outstanding Series Art Direction:** Richard C. Goddard and Howard E. Johnson for *Little Women, Part One* (NBC)
41. **Outstanding Limited Series or Special Art Direction:** Jan Scott and Bill Harp for *Studs Lonigan, Part Three* (NBC)
42. **Outstanding Choreography:**

Kevin Carlisle for *The Third Barry Manilow Special* (ABC)

43. **Outstanding Series Costume Design**: Jean-Pierre Dorleac for "Furlon" on *Battlestar Gallactica* (ABC)

44. **Outstanding Limited Series or Special Costume Design**: Ann Hollowood, Sue Le Cash and Christine Wilson for "King at Last" on *Edward the King* (syndicated)

45. **Outstanding Series Music Composition**: David Rose for "The Craftsman" on *Little House on the Prairie* (NBC)

46. **Outstanding Limited Series or Special Music Composition**: Leonard Rosenman for *Friendly Fire* (ABC)

47. **Outstanding Graphic Design and Title Sequence**: Etyan Keller and Stu Bernstein for *Cinderella at the Palace* (CBS)

48. **Outstanding Lighting Direction**: Roy A. Barnett and George Riesenberger for *You Can't Take It With You* (CBS)

49. **Outstanding Tape Sound Mixing**: Ed Greene, Phillip J. Seretti, Dennis S. Sands and Gary Ulmer for *Steve and Eydie Celebrate Irving Berlin* (NBC)

50. **Outstanding Makeup**: Tommy Cole, Mark Bussan and Ron Walters for *Backstage at the White House, Book Four* (NBC)

51. **Outstanding Hairstyling**: Janice D. Brandow for *The Triangle Factory Fire Scandal* (NBC)

52. **Outstanding Informational Program Individual Achievement**: Robert Niemack for *Scared Straight* (syndicated)

53. **Outstanding Creative Technical Crafts Individual Achievement**: John Dykstra, Richard Edlund and Joseph Gross for "Saga of a Star World" on *Battlestar Gallactica* (ABC), and Tom Ancell for *Giulini's Beethoven's Ninth Live: A Gift from Los Angeles* (PBS)

54. **ATAS Governor's Award**: Walter Cronkite

55. **Special Presentation**: Milton Berle

56. **Outstanding Series Videotape Editing**: Andy Zall for "Stockard Channing in Just Friends" (Pilot) (CBS)

57. **Outstanding Engineering Development**: SONY Video Products Company, the Society of Motion Picture and Television Engineers, and Ampex Corporation for development of Automatic Scan Tracking System for helical videotape equipment

58. **Outstanding Children's Entertainment Series**: *Kids Are People Too* (ABC)

59. **Outstanding Children's Informational Series**: *Big Blue Marble* (syndicated)

60. **Outstanding Children's Instructional Series**: "Science Rock" on *Schoolhouse Rock* (ABC)

61. **Outstanding Children's Entertainment Special**: "The Tap Dance Kid" on *Special Treat* (NBC)

62. **Outstanding Children's Informational Special**: February 1 program of *Razzmatazz* (CBS)

63. **Outstanding Daytime Drama Series**: *Ryan's Hope* (ABC)

64. **Outstanding Talk, Service or Variety Program**: *Donahue* (syndicated)

65. **Outstanding Game or Audience Participation Show**: *The Hollywood Squares* (NBC)

66. **Outstanding Achievement Daytime Drama Technical Excellence**: William Edwards, Joanne Goodhart, Paul York, Edward R. Atchison, William Hughes, Arie Hefter, Jay Millard, Barbara Miller, Robert Saxon and Roman Spinner for *The Edge of Night* (CBS)

67. **Outstanding Program Coverage of Special Events**: *Horowitz: Live!* (NBC), and *Leontyne Price at the White House* (PBS)

68. **Outstanding Special Classification Program Achievement**: *Camera* (CBS)

69. **Outstanding Daytime Dramatic Actor**: Al Freeman, Jr. in *One Life to Live* (ABC)

70. **Outstanding Daytime Dramatic Actress**: Irene Dailey in *Another World* (NBC)

71. **Outstanding Daytime Supporting Dramatic Actor**: Peter Hansen in *General Hospital* (ABC)

72. **Outstanding Daytime Supporting Dramatic Actress**: Suzanne Rogers in *Days of Our Lives* (NBC)

73. **Outstanding Host or Hostess in a Talk, Service or Variety Series**: Phil Donahue in *Donahue* (syndicated)

74. **Outstanding Host or Hostess in a Game or Audience Participation**

E Emmy Awards 1978

Show: Dick Clark in *The $20,000 Pyramid* (ABC)

75. **Outstanding Direction of a Daytime Drama Series**: Jerry Evans and Lela Swift for *Ryan's Hope* (ABC)

76. **Outstanding Direction for a Variety Program**: Ron Wiener for "Nazis and the Klan" on *Donahue* (syndicated)

77. **Outstanding Single Program Direction for Game or Audience Participation Show**: Jerome Shaw for June 20 program of *The Hollywood Squares* (NBC)

78. **Outstanding Director for Children's Programming**: Larry Elikann for "Mom and Dad Can't Hear Me" on *ABC Afterschool Special* (ABC)

79. **Outstanding Daytime Drama Series Writing**: Claire Labine, Paul Avila Mayer, Mary Munisteri, Judith Pinsker and Jeffrey Lane for *Ryan's Hope* (ABC)

80. **Outstanding Children's Program Performers**: Jack Gilford in "Hello in There" on *Big Blue Marble* (syndicated), Geraldine Fitzgerald in "Rodeo Red and the Runaway" on *NBC Special Treat* (NBC), and Frank Oz, Jim Henson, Carroll Spinney, Jerry Nelson and Richard Hunt in "The Muppets of Sesame Street" on *Sesame Street* (PBS)

81. **Outstanding Performers in Special Event Coverage**: Vladimir Horowitz in *Horowitz: Live!* (NBC), and Leontyne Price in *Leontyne Price at the White House* (PBS)

82. **Outstanding Individual Achievement in Religious Programming**: Martin Hoade, director, and Rolanda Mendels, performer, for *Interrogation at Budapest* (NBC), and Joseph J. Vadala for *This Other Eden* (NBC)

83. **Outstanding Special Classification of Individual Achievement**: Paul Lynde, panelist on May 18 *The Hollywood Squares* (NBC), and Bill Walker, Jay Burton, Tom Perew, Mark Davidson and Fred Tatashore, writers for *Dinah!* (syndicated)

84. **Outstanding Achievement in Daytime Drama Design Excellence**: Lloyd R. Evans, Wesley Laws, Dean Nelson, Bob Anton, Lee Halls, Phyllis Sagnelli and Lou Dorfsman for *Love of Life* (CBS)

85. **Outstanding Live Sports Special**: *Superbowl XIII* (NBC)

86. **Outstanding Edited Sports Special**: *Spirit of '78 – The Flight of the Double Eagle II* (ABC)

87. **Outstanding Live Sports Series**: *ABC's Monday Night Football* (ABC)

88. **Outstanding Edited Sports Series**: *The American Sportsman* (ABC)

89. **Outstanding Sports Directing**: Harry Coyle for *1978 World Series* (NBC)

90. **Outstanding Individual Achievement in Sports**: Bob Angelo, Ernie Ernst, Jay Gerber, Stan Leshner, Hank McElwee, Howard Neef, Jack Newman, Steve Sabol, Bob Smith, Art Spieller and Phil Tuckett for *NFL Game of the Week* (syndicated), Horace Ruiz, Dick Roecker, Ray Figelski, Robert McKearnin, Jack Bennett, Ernest Thiel, Jerry Ireland, Bob Brown, Leonard G. Basile, Mario J. Ciarlo, Roy Ratliff, George Loomis, Bernard Joseph, Louis Gerard, Steve Cimino, Mike Stramsky, Rodger Harbaugh, Al Rice, Jr., William M. Goetz, Jim Johnson, Brian Cherriffe, Phil Cantrell, Steven H. Gonzales, Russ K. Ross, Art Parker, Bill Landers, Jim Bragg, James Culley, Corey Liebele and Len Stucker for *1978 World Series* (NBC), Horace Ruiz, Joe Commare, Bob McKearnin, Jack Bennett, George Loomis, Rodger Harbaugh, William W. Landers, Michael C. Stramsky, Roy V. Ratliff, Leonard Basile, Mario J. Ciarlo, Tom C. Dezondorf, Steve Cimino, William M. Goetz, Louis Gerard, Len Stucker, Steven H. Gonzales, Jim Johnson, Cory Leible, Don Mulvaney, Al Rice, Jr. and Russ K. Ross for *Super Bowl XIII* (NBC), Sandy Bell, Bob Brown, Ralph Savignano, Art Tinn, Barry Drago, Jim McCarthy, Joe Sakota, George Rothweiler, George Naeder, John Lincoln, Tom McCarthy, Hans Singer, Keeth Lawrence, Jim Murphy, Neil McCaffrey, Herman Lang, Sig Meyers, Frank McSpedon, Anthony Hlavaty, Wayne Wright, Johnny Morris, Ed Ambrosini, Frank Florio and Tom Spalding for *Daytona 500* (CBS), and James M. Grau for "Closing Logo" for *CBS Sports Programs* (CBS)

91. **Outstanding Sports Personality**: Jim McKay

92. **Outstanding Individual Achievement in Children's Programming**: Charles Gross, Dorothy Weaver and Ian Maitland for "Rodeo Red and the Runaway" on *Special Treat* (NBC), John Morris and Norman Gay for "The Tap

Dance Kid" on *Special Treat* (NBC), Jack Regas, Harvey Berger and Ron Hays for *Krofft Superstar Hour Starring the Bay City Rollers* (NBC), Michael Baugh for "Todos Los Ninos Del Mundo" on *Villa Alegre* (PBS), Dick Maitland and Roy Carch for *Sesame Street* (PBS), Gene Piatrowsky for "A Special Day in the Year of the Child" on *CBS Festival of Lively Arts for Young People* (CBS), Rene Verxier for *Big Blue Marble* (syndicated), Dick Young for "Day of the Jouster" on *Big Blue Marble* (syndicated), Vince Humphrey for *Gaucho* (ABC), Ken Gutstein for "The Secret of Charles Dickens" on *CBS Festival of Lively Arts for Young People* (CBS), and Roy Stewart for "Flat" on *Freestyle!* (PBS)
93. **National Community Service Award**: WBBM-TV, Chicago for *Agent Orange: The Human Harvest*
94. **International Fiction Award**: Televise Radio Omroep Stichting, the Netherlands for *The Fly*
95. **International Non-Fiction Award**: Canadian Broadcasting Corporation for *Four Women*

1979 Emmy Awards

1. **Outstanding Comedy Series**: *Taxi* (ABC)
2. **Outstanding Drama Series**: *Lou Grant* (CBS)
3. **Outstanding Drama or Comedy Special**: *The Miracle Worker* (NBC)
4. **Outstanding Variety/Music Program**: *IBM Presents Baryshnikov on Broadway* (ABC)
5. **Outstanding Informational Program**: *The Body Human: The Magic Sense* (CBS)
6. **Outstanding Limited Series**: *Edward and Mrs. Simpson* (syndicated)
7. **Outstanding Animated Program**: *Carlton Your Doorman* (CBS)
8. **Outstanding Children's Program**: *The Halloween That Almost Wasn't* (ABC)
9. **Outstanding Classical Program in the Performing Arts**: *Live from Studio 8H: A Tribute to Toscanini* (NBC)
10. **Outstanding Special Classification Program Achievement**: *Fred Astaire: Change Partners and Dance* (PBS)
11. **Outstanding Special Events Program Achievement**: *The 34th Annual Tony Awards* (CBS)
12. **Outstanding Comedy Series Lead Actress**: Cathryn Damon in *Soap* (ABC)
13. **Outstanding Comedy Series Lead Actor**: Richard Mulligan in *Soap* (ABC)
14. **Outstanding Drama Series Lead Actress**: Barbara Bel Geddes in *Dallas* (CBS)
15. **Outstanding Drama Series Lead Actor**: Ed Asner in *Lou Grant* (CBS)
16. **Outstanding Drama Series Supporting Actress**: Nancy Marchand in *Lou Grant* (CBS)
17. **Outstanding Drama Series Supporting Actor**: Stuart Margolin in *The Rockford Files* (NBC)
18. **Outstanding Comedy Series Supporting Actor**: Harry Morgan in *M*A*S*H* (CBS)
19. **Outstanding Comedy Series Supporting Actress**: Loretta Swit in *M*A*S*H* (CBS)
20. **Outstanding Limited Series or Special Supporting Actor**: George Grizzard in *The Oldest Living Graduate* (NBC)
21. **Outstanding Limited Series or Special Supporting Actress**: Mare Winningham in *Amber Waves* (ABC)
22. **Outstanding Limited Series or Special Lead Actress**: Patty Duke Astin in *The Miracle Worker* (NBC)
23. **Outstanding Limited Series or Special Lead Actor**: Powers Boothe in *Guyana Tragedy: The Story of Jim Jones* (CBS)
24. **Outstanding Comedy Series Director**: James Burrows for "Louie and the Nice Girl" on *Taxi* (ABC)
25. **Outstanding Drama Series Director**: Roger Young for "Cop" on *Lou Grant* (CBS)
26. **Outstanding Limited Series or Special Director**: Marvin J. Chomsky for *Attica* (ABC)
27. **Outstanding Variety or Music Program Director**: Dwight Hemion for *IBM Presents Baryshnikov on Broadway* (ABC)
28. **Outstanding Comedy Series Writing**: Bob Colleary for "Photographer" on *Barney Miller* (ABC)
29. **Outstanding Drama Series**

E Emmy Awards 1979

Writing: Seth Freeman for "Cop" on *Lou Grant* (CBS)

30. **Outstanding Variety or Music Program Writing**: Buz Kohan for *Shirley MacLaine ... Every Little Movement* (CBS)

31. **Outstanding Limited Series or Special Writing**: David Chase for *Off the Minnesota Strip* (ABC)

32. **Outstanding Series Videotape Editing**: John Hawkins for *The Muppet Show with Liza Minnelli* (syndicated)

33. **Outstanding Limited Series or Special Videotape Editing**: Danny White for *Olivia Newton-John—Hollywood Nights* (ABC)

34. **Outstanding Informational Program Film Editing**: Robert Eisenhardt, Hank O'Karma and Jane Kurson for *The Body Human: The Body Beautiful* (CBS)

35. **Outstanding Tape Sound Mixing**: Bruce Burns and Jerry Clemans for *Sinatra: The First 40 Years* (NBC)

36. **Outstanding Film Sound Mixing**: Ray Barons, David Campbell, Bob Pettis and John Reitz for *The Ordeal of Dr. Mudd* (CBS)

37. **Outstanding Informational Program Film Sound Mixers**: David Clark, Joel Fein, Robert L. Harman and George E. Porter for "Dive to the Edge of Creation" on *National Geographic Special* (PBS)

38. **Outstanding Series Cinematography**: Enzo A. Martinelli for "Breakthrough" on *The Contender* (CBS)

39. **Outstanding Informational Program Cinematography**: Bryan Anderson, Bob Elfstrom and Al Giddings for *Mysteries of the Sea* (ABC)

40. **Outstanding Series Music Composition**: Patrick Williams for "Hollywood" on *Lou Grant* (CBS)

41. **Outstanding Limited Series or Special Music Composition**: Jerry Fielding for *High Midnight* (CBS)

42. **Outstanding Graphic Design and Title Sequence**: Phil Norman for *The French Atlantic Affair, Part One* (ABC)

43. **Outstanding Children's Program Individual Achievement**: Bob O'Bradovich for makeup for *The Halloween That Almost Wasn't* (ABC)

44. **Outstanding Individual Achievement in Creative Technical Crafts**: Scott Schachter for Live Audio Mixing for *Live from Studio 8H: A Tribute to Toscanini* (NBC)

45. **Outstanding Individual Achievement in Creative Technical Crafts**: Mark Schubin for Live Stereo Simulcast for *Luciano Pavarotti and the New York Philharmonic* (PBS)

46. **Outstanding Individual Achievement in Special Classification**: Geof Bartz for film editing for "Dr. James 'Red' Duke, Trauma Surgeon" on *Operation Lifeline* (NBC)

47. **Outstanding Music Direction**: Ian Fraser, Ralph Burns and Billy Byers for *IBM Presents Baryshnikov on Broadway* (ABC)

48. **Outstanding Lighting Direction**: Peter S. Edwards, William Knight and Peter S. Passas for *FDR the Last Year* (NBC)

49. **Outstanding Limited Series Cinematography**: Gayne Rescher for "The Silent Lovers" on *Moviola* (NBC)

50. **Outstanding Limited Series or Special Film Editing**: Bill Blunden and Alan Pattillo for *All Quiet on the Western Front* (CBS)

51. **Outstanding Variety/Music Program Art Direction**: Charles Lisanby and Dwight Jackson for *IBM Presents Baryshnikov on Broadway* (ABC)

52. **Outstanding Choreography**: Alan Johnson for *Shirley MacLaine ... Every Little Movement* (CBS)

53. **Outstanding Technical Direction and Electronic Camerawork**: Wayne Parsons, Tom Geren, Dean Hall, Bob Highton, William Landers and Ron Sheldon for *The Oldest Living Graduate* (NBC)

54. **Outstanding Series Art Direction**: James D. Bissell and William Webb for "The Old Sister" on *Palmerstown, U.S.A.* (CBS)

55. **Outstanding Limited Series or Special Art Direction**: Willfred Shingleton, Juliann Sacks, Jean Taillander, Robert Christides and Cheryal Kearney for *Gauguin the Savage* (CBS)

56. **Outstanding Limited Series or Special Costume Design**: Travilla for "The Scarlet O'Hara War" on *Moviola* (NBC)

57. **Outstanding Makeup**: Richard Blair for "The Scarlet O'Hara War" on *Moviola* (NBC)

Emmy Awards 1979 E

58. **Outstanding Hairstyling**: Larry Germain and Donna Gilbert for *The Miracle Worker* (NBC)
59. **Outstanding Series Film Editing**: M. Pam Blumenthal for "Louie and the Nice Girl" on *Taxi* (ABC)
60. **Outstanding Film Sound Editing**: Don Crosby, Mark Dennis, Tony Garber, Doug Grindstaff, Don V. Isaacs, Hank Salerno and Larry Singer for *Power, Part One* (NBC)
61. **Governor's Award**: Johnny Carson
62. **Outstanding Series Costume Design**: Pete Menefee for *The Big Show with Tony Randall and Herve Villechaize* (NBC)
63. **Outstanding Achievement in Engineering Development**: National Bureau of Standards, Public Broadcasting Service and American Broadcasting Company for their development of Closed Captioning for the deaf
64. **Outstanding Daytime Drama Series**: *Guiding Light* (CBS)
65. **Outstanding Talk, Service or Variety Series**: *Donahue* (syndicated)
66. **Outstanding Game or Audience Participation Show**: *The Hollywood Squares* (NBC), and *The $20,000 Pyramid* (ABC)
67. **Outstanding Children's Entertainment Special**: "The Late, Great Me: Story of a Teenage Alcoholic" on *ABC Afterschool Special* (ABC)
68. **Outstanding Children's Informational/Instructional Short Format Programming**: *ABC Schoolhouse Rock* (ABC), *Ask NBC News* (NBC), *H.E.L.P.!!! (Dr. Henry's Emergency Lessons for People)* (ABC), and *In the News* (CBS)
69. **Outstanding Children's Entertainment Series**: *Hot Hero Sandwich* (NBC)
70. **Outstanding Children's Informational/Instructional Series or Special**: *Sesame Street* (PBS), *30 Minutes* (CBS), and "Why a Conductor" on *CBS Festival of Lively Arts for Young People* (CBS)
71. **Outstanding Children's Anthology/Dramatic Programming**: "Animal Talk" on *CBS Library* (CBS), "The Gold Bug" on *ABC Weekend Special* (ABC), "Leatherstocking Tales" on *Once Upon a Classic* (PBS), and "Once Upon a Midnight Dreary" on *CBS Library* (CBS)
72. **Outstanding Series or Special Religious Programming**: *Directions* (ABC), and *For Our Times* (CBS)
73. **Outstanding Special Events Coverage**: *La Gioconda* (PBS), and *Macy's 53rd Annual Thanksgiving Parade* (NBC)
74. **Outstanding Special Classification of Program Achievement**: *FYI* (ABC)
75. **Outstanding Daytime Dramatic Actor**: Douglass Watson in *Another World* (NBC)
76. **Outstanding Daytime Dramatic Actress**: Judith Light in *One Life to Live* (ABC)
77. **Outstanding Daytime Supporting Dramatic Actor**: Warren Burton in *All My Children* (ABC)
78. **Outstanding Daytime Supporting Dramatic Actress**: Francesca James in *All My Children* (ABC)
79. **Outstanding Daytime Drama Guest or Cameo Appearance**: Hugh McPhillips in *Days of Our Lives* (NBC)
80. **Outstanding Host or Hostess in a Talk, Service or Variety Series**: Phil Donahue in *Donahue* (syndicated)
81. **Outstanding Host or Hostess in a Game or Audience Participation Show**: Peter Marshall in *The Hollywood Squares* (NBC)
82. **Outstanding Daytime Drama Series Direction**: Lela Swift and Jerry Evans for *Ryan's Hope* (ABC)
83. **Outstanding Talk, Service or Variety Series Direction**: Duke Struck for "Henry Fonda Tribute" on *Good Morning America* (ABC)
84. **Outstanding Individual Game or Audience Participation Show Direction**: Jerome Shaw for the June 14 Program *The Hollywood Squares* (NBC)
85. **Outstanding Daytime Drama Series Writing**: Claire Labine, Paul Avila Mayer, Mary Munisteri, Judith Pinsker and Jeffrey Lane for *Ryan's Hope* (ABC)
86. **Outstanding Individual Achievement in Religious Programming**: Dean Jagger in "Independence and 76" on *This Is the Life* (syndicated), Richard F. Morean, writer of "If No Birds Sang" on *This Is the Life* (syndicated), Justus Taylor for "Seeds of Revolution" on

E Emmy Awards 1979

Directions (ABC), John Duffy for *A Talent for Life: Jews of the Italian Renaissance* (NBC), and Thomas E. Azzari for "Stable Boy's Christmas" on *This Is the Life* (syndicated)

87. Outstanding Individual Achievement in Special Event Coverage: Kirk Browning, director, and Luciano Pavarotti and Renata Scotto, performers, in *La Gioconda* (PBS)

88. Outstanding Individual Achievement in Children's Programming: Arthur Allen Seidelman, director, and Melissa Sue Anderson, performer for "Which Mother Is Mine" on *ABC Afterschool Special* (ABC), Jan Hartman, writer, Anthony Lover, director, Vincent Sklena, film editor and Maia Danziger, performer in "The Late Great Me: Story of a Teenage Alcoholic" on *ABC Afterschool Special* (ABC), Butterfly McQueen, performer in "The Seven Wishes of a Rich Kid" on *ABC Afterschool Special* (ABC), Fred Rogers, performer on "Mister Rogers Goes to School" on *Mister Rogers' Neighborhood* (PBS), David Axlerod, Joseph A. Bailey, Andy Breckman, Bruce Hart, Richard Camp, Sherry Coben, Carole Hart and Marianne Mayer, writers for December 8 program of *Hot Hero Sandwich* (NBC), Alex Thompson and Steven Atha for "The Gold Bug" on *ABC Weekend Special* (ABC), Steven Zink for *Sesame Street* (PBS), John Gonzales, Charles Liotta, John A. Servidio and George A. Magda for *Time Out* (NBC), George Alch for "A Special Gift" on *ABC Afterschool Special* (ABC), Lee Dichter for *Big Blue Marble* (syndicated), John Beymer and Mike Fash for "Movie Star's Daughter" on *ABC Afterschool Special* (ABC), Robert Collins for "Heartbreak Winner" on *ABC Afterschool Special* (ABC), David Sanderson for "Once Upon a Midnight Dreary" on *CBS Library* (CBS), Jack Sholder for "Noisy/Quiet Hearing" on *3-2-1 Contact* (PBS), Merle Worth for "Fast/Slow – Speed Up/Slow Down" on *3-2-1 Contact* (PBS), Ronald Baldwin for "Growth/Decay" on *3-2-1 Contact* (PBS), Nat Mongoli for "Hot/Cold" on *3-2-1 Contact* (PBS), and Michael Baugh for "I Can Sing a Rainbow" on *Villa Alegre* (PBS)

89. Outstanding Daytime Drama Technical Achievement: Joseph Solomito, Howard Zweig, Lawrence Hammond, Robert Ambrico, Dianne Cates-Cantrell, Christopher N. Mauro, Larry Strack, Vincent Senatore, Albin S. Lemanski, Len Walas, Diana Wenman, Jean Dadario, Roger Haenelt, John L. Grella, Irving Robbin, Jim Reichert and Teri Smith for *All My Children* (ABC)

90. Outstanding Daytime Drama Design Excellence: William Mickley, William Itkin, Donna Larson, Mel Handelsman, Carol Luiken, Sylvia Lawrence, Michael Huddle and Hy Bley for *All My Children* (ABC)

91. Outstanding Achievement for Special Classification: Danny Seagren for "The Annual Thanksgiving Turkey Day Raffle" on *Miss Peach and the Kelly School* (syndicated)

92. Outstanding Special Event Individual Achievement: Ron Craft, Kenneth Patterson, Gary Emrick, Luis A. Fuerte, Daniel J. Webb, Jack Reader, Thomas Tucker, William Kelsey, Greg Harms, Tom Ancell, Val Riolo, Roy Stewart, Zack Brown, Ken Dettling and Luciano Pavarotti for *La Gioconda* (PBS)

93. Outstanding News Program Achievement: *Showdown in Iran-CBS Reports* (CBS), and *The Boat People-CBS Reports* (CBS)

94. Outstanding Individual Achievement in News Film Editing: Maurice Murad for *The Boston Goes to China-CBS Reports* (CBS), Joseph Murania for "Baryshnikov" on *60 Minutes* (CBS), and Mili Bonsignori for *But What About the Children-CBS Reports* (CBS)

95. Outstanding Individual Achievement in News Videotape Editing: Susan Raymond for *The Police Tapes-ABC News Close-Up* (ABC)

96. Outstanding Individual Achievement in News Writing: George Crile, III and Bill Moyers for *Battle for South Africa-CBS Reports* (CBS), Andrew A. Rooney for "Who Won What in America, a Few Minutes with Andy Rooney" on *60 Minutes* (CBS), Tom Spain for *Anyplace but Here-CBS Reports* (CBS), and Perry Wolff for *1968-CBS News Special* (CBS)

97. Outstanding Individual Achievement in News Directing: Tom Priestly for *The Killing Ground-ABC News Close-Up* (ABC), Howard Stringer for *The Boston Goes to China-CBS Reports* (CBS),

Emmy Awards 1979 E

Andrew Lack for *The Boat People-CBS Reports* (CBS), and Maurice Murad for *Anyplace but Here-CBS Reports* (CBS)

98. **Outstanding Individual Achievement in News Camerawork**: Tom Spain for *Anyplace but Here-CBS Reports* (CBS)

99. **Outstanding Individual Achievement in News Audio**: James R. Camery and Phillip Gleason for *The Boston Goes to China-CBS Reports* (CBS)

100. **Outstanding Achievement in News Writing**: *Anyplace but Here-CBS Reports* (CBS), *The Police Tapes-ABC News Close-Up* (ABC), *Is Anyone Out There Learning-CBS Report Card on American Education* (CBS), and "The Rating Game" on *60 Minutes* (CBS)

101. **Outstanding Achievement in News Film Editing**: *The Killing Ground* (ABC), *Migrants-NBC Nightly News* (NBC), *Children of Hope-NBC Weekend* (NBC), *Erasing Vietnam-NBC Nightly News* (NBC), *Mission Mind Control* (ABC), and *Paul Jacobs and the Nuclear Gang* (PBS)

102. **Outstanding Achievement in News Music**: "Misha" on *60 Minutes* (CBS), "Teddy Kolleck's Jerusalem" on *60 Minutes* (CBS), "Pops" on *60 Minutes* (CBS), "Noah" on *60 Minutes* (CBS), *1968-CBS News Special* (CBS), *Incest: The Best Kept Secret* (CBS), *The Boston Goes to China-CBS Reports* (CBS), *A Very, Very Special Place-NBC Weekend* (NBC), and *Palestine* (PBS, Thames Television, London)

103. **Outstanding Live Sports Special**: *1980 Winter Olympic Games* (ABC)

104. **Outstanding Edited Sports Special**: *Gossamer Albatross—Flight of Imagination* (CBS)

105. **Outstanding Live Sports Series**: *NCAA College Football* (ABC)

106. **Outstanding Edited Sports Series**: *NFL Game of the Week* (syndicated)

107. **Outstanding Sports Directing**: Sandy Grossman for *Superbowl XIV* (CBS)

108. **Outstanding Sports Film Editing**: Jon Day, Sam Fine, Angelo Bernarducci, John Petersen, Vincent Reda, Anthony Scandiffio, Wayne Weiss and Ted Winterburn for "Up Close and Personals" on *1980 Winter Olympic Games* (ABC)

109. **Outstanding Sports Audio**: Trevor Carless, George Hause, Jim Lynch, Dennis Fierman and Jan Schulte for "Up Close and Personals" on *1980 Winter Olympic Games* (ABC)

110. **Outstanding Sports Cinematography**: Bob Angelo, Ernie Ernst, Jay Gerber, Stan Leshner, Don Marx, Hank McElwee, Howard Neef, Jack Newman, Steve Sabol, Bob Smith, Art Spieller and Phil Tuckett for *NFL Game of the Week* (syndicated), and Harvey Harrison, Harry Hart and Don Shapiro for "Up Close and Personals" on *1980 Winter Olympic Games* (ABC)

111. **Outstanding Sports Music Composition**: Chuck Mangione for *1980 Winter Olympic Games* (ABC)

112. **Outstanding Sports Associate Direction/Videotape Editing**: Barbara Bowman, Paul Fanelli, Charles Gardner, Marvin Gench, Roger Haenelt, Conrad Kraus, Ann Stone, Alex Moscovic, Lou Rende, Nathan Rogers, Erskine Roberts, Mario Schencman, Arthur Volk, Francis Guigliano, Ronald Ackerman, Michael Altieri, Tom Capace, John Croak, Jakob Hierl, Tony Jutchenko, Hector Kicelian, Ken Klingbeil, Pete Murphy, Hiorshi Nakamoto, Carl Pollack, Merrit Roesser, Winston Sadoo, Fausto Sanchez, Leo Stephan, Richard Velasco and Ed Zlotnik for *1980 Winter Olympic Games* (ABC)

113. **Outstanding Sports Engineering Supervision/Technical Direction/Electronic Camerawork**: Julius Barnathan, Bill Stone, Joseph De Bonis, Joseph A. Maltz, Charles Baldour, David E. Eschelbacher, David Linick, Eric Rosenthal, Abdelnour Tadros, Tony Uttendaele, Dick Horan, Robert Armbruster, Bill Blummel, Loren Coltran, Geoffrey Felger, Mike Jochim, Jacques Lesgards, Bill Maier, Gary Larkins, Joseph Polito, Elliott R. Reed, Martin Sandberg, Tony Versley, Mike Fisher, Joseph Kresnicka, Bud Untiedt, Les Weiss, Werner Gunther, Chester Mazurek, William Morris, Joseph Schiavo, Joe Nesi, Ernie Buttleman, J. Allen, Gerry Bucci, H. Falk, David Smith, Dianne Cates-Cantrell, Gary Donatelli, Danny La Mothe, Charles Mitchell, Steve Nikifor, William Sullivan, Don Farnham, Rick Knipe, Morton Lipow and Joseph Montesano for *1980 Winter Olympic Games* (ABC)

114. **Outstanding Sports Personality**: Jim McKay

115. **Outstanding Sports Individual Achievement**: Jerry P. Caruso and Harry Smith, creators and developers of the Radio Frequency Golf Cup Mike

1980 Emmy Awards

1. **Outstanding Comedy Series**: *Taxi* (ABC)
2. **Outstanding Drama Series**: *Hill Street Blues* (NBC)
3. **Outstanding Limited Series**: *Shogun* (NBC)
4. **Outstanding Variety/Music Comedy Program**: *Lily: Sold Out* (CBS)
5. **Outstanding Drama Special**: *Playing for Time* (CBS)
6. **Outstanding Classical Program**: "Jerome Robbins Ballets" on *Live from Studio 8H* (NBC)
7. **Outstanding Informational Special**: *The Body Human: The Bionic Breakthrough* (CBS)
8. **Outstanding Informational Series**: *Steve Allen's Meeting of the Minds* (PBS)
9. **Outstanding Animated Program**: *Life Is a Circus, Charlie Brown* (CBS)
10. **Outstanding Children's Program**: "Donahue and Kids" on *Project Peacock* (NBC)
11. **Outstanding Limited Series or Special Lead Actress**: Vanessa Redgrave in *Playing for Time* (CBS)
12. **Outstanding Limited Series or Special Lead Actor**: Anthony Hopkins in *The Bunker* (CBS)
13. **Outstanding Limited Series or Special Supporting Actress**: Jane Alexander in *Playing for Time* (CBS)
14. **Outstanding Comedy Series Lead Actress**: Isabel Sanford in *The Jeffersons* (CBS)
15. **Outstanding Comedy Series Lead Actor**: Judd Hirsch in *Taxi* (ABC)
16. **Outstanding Comedy Series Supporting Actress**: Eileen Brennan in *Private Benjamin* (CBS)
17. **Outstanding Comedy Series Supporting Actor**: Danny Devito in *Taxi* (ABC)
18. **Outstanding Drama Series Lead Actor**: Daniel J. Travanti in *Hill Street Blues* (NBC)
19. **Outstanding Drama Series Lead Actress**: Barbara Babcock for "Fecund Hand Rose" on *Hill Street Blues* (NBc)
20. **Outstanding Drama Series Supporting Actress**: Nancy Marchand in *Lou Grant* (CBS)
21. **Outstanding Variety/Music or Comedy Special Director**: Don Mischer for *The Kennedy Center Honors* (CBS)
22. **Outstanding Comedy Series Directing**: James Burrows for "Elaine's Strange Triangle" on *Taxi* (ABC)
23. **Outstanding Drama Series Direction**: Robert Butler for "Hill Street Station" on *Hill Street Blues* (NBC)
24. **Outstanding Limited Series or Special Direction**: James Goldstone for *Kent State* (NBC)
25. **Outstanding Drama Series Writers**: Steven Bochco and Michael Kozoll for *Hill Street Blues* (NBC)
26. **Outstanding Comedy Series Writing**: Michael Leeson for "Tony's Sister and Jim" on *Taxi* (ABC)
27. **Outstanding Variety/Music or Comedy Program Writers**: Jerry Juhl, David Odell and Chris Langham for *The Muppet Show*, episode with Carol Burnett (syndicated)
28. **Outstanding Limited Series or Special Writing**: Arthur Miller for *Playing for Time* (CBS)
29. **Outstanding Music and Lyrics**: Ken Welch and Mitzi Welch for "This Is My Night" on *Linda in Wonderland* (CBS)
30. **Outstanding Comedy Series Film Editing**: M. Pam Blumenthal and Jack Michon for "Elaine's Strange Triangle" on *Taxi* (ABC)
31. **Outstanding Drama Series Film Sound Editing**: Samuel Horta, Robert Cornett, Denise Horta and Eileen Horta for "Hill Street Station" on *Hill Street Blues* (NBC)
32. **Outstanding Series Videotape Editing**: Andy Ackerman for "Bah, Humbug" on *WKRP in Cincinnatti* (CBS)
33. **Outstanding Drama Series Cinematography**: William H. Cronjager for "Hill Street Station" on *Hill Street Blues* (NBC)
34. **Outstanding Limited Series or Special Cinematography**: Arthur F. Ibbetson for *Little Lord Fauntleroy* (CBS)
35. **Outstanding Choreography**: Walter Painter for "Lynda Carter's

Celebration" on *Linda in Wonderland* (CBS)
36. **Outstanding Makeup:** Albert Paul Jeyte and James Kail for *Peter and Paul* (CBS)
37. **Outstanding Music Direction:** Ian Fraser, Billy Byers, Chris Boardman and Bob Florence for "Linda Carter's Celebration" on *Linda in Wonderland* (CBS)
38. **Special Award:** Lawrence Welk
39. **Special Award:** Max Liebman, producer
40. **Special Award:** Lucille Ball
41. **Special Award:** Sarah Vaughn
42. **Outstanding Technical Achievement:** Rank Precision Industries, Ltd. for development of Mark III Flying Spot Telecine
43. **Governor's Award:** Elton H. Rule, ABC Network president
44. **Outstanding Drama Series Supporting Actor:** Michael Conrad in *Hill Street Blues* (NBC)
45. **Outstanding Supporting Actor in a Limited Series or Special:** David Warner in *Masada* (ABC)
46. **Outstanding Series Art Direction:** Howard E. Johnson, John M. Dwyer and Robert C. Freer for *The Gangster Chronicles* (NBC)
47. **Outstanding Limited Series or Special Videotape Editing:** Marco Zappia and Branda S. Miller for *Perry Como's Christmas in the Holy Land* (ABC)
48. **Outstanding Film Sound Mixing:** William R. Teague, Robert L. Harman, William L. McCaughey and Howard Wollman for *Evita Peron, Part One* (NBC)
49. **Outstanding Tape Sound Mixing:** Jerry Clemans, Doug Nelson and Donald Worsham for *John Denver with His Special Guest George Burns: Two of a Kind* (ABC)
50. **Outstanding Technical Direction and Electronic Camerawork:** Heino Ripp, Peter Basil, Al Camoin, Tom Dezendorf, Vince Di Pietro and Gene Martin for "An Evening with Jerome Robbins" on *Live from Studio 8H* (NBC)
51. **Outstanding Lighting Direction:** Ralph Holmes for "Nureyev and the Joffrey Ballet/In Tribute to Nijinsky" on *Dance in America* (PBS)
52. **Outstanding Special Classification of Individual Achievement:** Sarah Vaughn for *Rhapsody and Song—A Tribute to George Gershwin* (PBS)
53. **Outstanding Creative Technical Crafts Individual Achievement:** John Allison, Adolf Schaller, Don Davis, Rick Sternbach, Jon Lomberg, Anne Norica and Ernie Norcia for "The Shores of the Cosmic Ocean" on *Cosmos* (PBS), and Carey Melcher, Bob Bruckner, Steve Burum, Jim Dow, John Gale, Larry Heider, Mike Johnson, Robert C. King, Cleve Landsberg, Joseph Matza, George C. Reilly and Joe Wolcott for "The Shores of the Cosmic Ocean" on *Cosmos* (PBS)
54. **Outstanding Limited Series or Special Art Direction:** Ray Storey, Dennis Peeples and David Love for *John Steinbeck's East of Eden, Episode Three* (ABC)
55. **Outstanding Music or Variety Art Direction:** Roy Christopher for *53rd Annual Academy Awards* (ABC)
56. **Outstanding Drama Series Music Composition:** Bruce Broughton for "The Satyr" on *Buck Rogers* (NBC)
57. **Outstanding Limited Series or Special Music Composition:** Jerry Goldsmith for *Masada, Episode 2* (ABC)
58. **Outstanding Series Costume Design:** Shin Nishida for *Shogun* (NBC)
59. **Outstanding Special Costume Design:** Willa Kim for "The Tempest Live with the San Francisco Ballet" on *Dance in America* (PBS)
60. **Outstanding Hairstyling:** Shirley Padgett for *Madame X* (NBC)
61. **Outstanding Graphic Design and Title Sequences:** Phil Norman for *Shogun, Episode One* (NBC)
62. **Outstanding Limited Series or Special Film Editing:** John A. Martinelli for *Murder in Texas* (NBC)
63. **Outstanding Informational Programming Individual Achievement:** Kent Gibson and Gerald Zelinger for "Blues for a Red Planet" on *Cosmos* (PBS), and Chuck White, Gary Bourgeois, Dave Dockendorf and John Mack for "Gorilla" on *National Geographic Special* (PBS)
64. **Outstanding Daytime Drama:** *General Hospital* (ABC)
65. **Outstanding Children's Entertainment Series:** *Captain Kangaroo* (CBS), and "A Tale of Two Cities" on *Once Upon a Classic* (PBS)
66. **Outstanding Children's Enter-

tainment Special: "A Matter of Time" on *ABC Afterschool Special* (ABC)

67. **Outstanding Children's Informational/Instructional Series**: *30 Minutes* (CBS)

68. **Outstanding Children's Informational/Instructional Special**: "Julie Andrews' Invitation to the Dance with Rudolf Nureyev" on *CBS Festival of Lively Arts for Young People* (CBS)

69. **Outstanding Short Form Children's Instructional/Informational Programming**: *In the News* (CBS)

70. **Outstanding Achievement in Religious Programming**: *Directions* (ABC), and *Insight* (syndicated)

71. **Outstanding Achievement in Special Classification**: *FYI* (ABC)

72. **Outstanding Talk or Service Series**: *Donahue* (syndicated)

73. **Outstanding Variety Series**: *The Merv Griffin Show* (syndicated)

74. **Outstanding Game or Audience Participation Series**: *The $20,000 Pyramid* (ABC)

75. **Outstanding Daytime Dramatic Actor**: Douglass Watson in *Another World* (NBC)

76. **Outstanding Daytime Dramatic Actress**: Judith Light in *One Life to Live* (ABC)

77. **Outstanding Daytime Supporting Dramatic Actor**: Larry Haines in *Search for Tomorrow* (CBS)

78. **Outstanding Daytime Supporting Dramatic Actress**: Jane Elliot in *General Hospital* (ABC)

79. **Outstanding Host or Hostess in a Talk or Service Series**: Hugh Downs for *Over Easy* (PBS)

80. **Outstanding Host or Hostess in a Variety Series**: David Letterman for *The David Letterman Series* (NBC)

81. **Outstanding Host or Hostess in a Game or Audience Participation Series**: Peter Marshall in *The Hollywood Squares* (NBC)

82. **Outstanding Daytime Drama Series Direction**: Marlena Laird, Alan Pultz and Philip Sogard for *General Hospital* (ABC)

83. **Outstanding Individual Direction for a Talk or Service Series**: Jerry Kupcinet for the March 13 program of *The Richard Simmons Show* (syndicated)

84. **Outstanding Variety Series Direction**: Sterling Johnson for *Dinah & Friends in Israel* (syndicated)

85. **Outstanding Individual Direction for a Game or Audience Participation Show**: Mike Gargiulo for the May 15 program *The $20,000 Pyramid* (ABC)

86. **Outstanding Special Classification of Outstanding Individual Achievement**: Merrill Markoe, Rich Hall, David Letterman, Gerard Mulligan, Paul Raley and Ron Richards, writers for *The David Letterman Show* (NBC), Caroly Wilcox, Cheryl Blalock and Edward G. Christie for *Sesame Street* (PBS)

87. **Outstanding Daytime Drama Series Writing**: Douglas Marland, Robert Dwyer, Nancy Franklin and Harding Lemay for *The Guiding Light* (CBS)

88. **Outstanding Individual Achievement in Children's Programming**: Robert E. Fuisz, M.D., writer and Marlo Thomas, performer in *The Body Human: Facts of Life for Girls* (CBS), Robert Elfstrom and Ken Howard in *The Body Human: Facts of Life for Boys* (CBS), Bill Cosby in "The Secret" on *The New Fat Albert Show* (CBS), Danny Aiello in "Family of Strangers" on *ABC Afterschool Special* (ABC), John Herzfeld, director for "Stoned" on *ABC Afterschool Special* (ABC), Blossom Elfman, writer for "I Think I'm Having a Baby" on *The CBS Afternoon Playhouse* (CBS), and Mary Munisteri, writer for *Mandy's Grandmother* (syndicated), Eric Van Haren Noman for "Egyptian Weavers" on *Big, Blue Marble* (syndicated), Joe Consentino for "Globetrotter" on *Big, Blue Marble* (syndicated), Peter Hammer for "Do Me a Favor ... Don't Vote for My Mom" on *Big, Blue Marble* (syndicated), Allen Kirkpatrick for "Bike Racing" on *Big, Blue Marble* (syndicated), Dick Maitland for "Tuning the Engine" on *Sesame Street* (PBS), Dick Hyman and Steven Atha for "Sunshine's on the Way" on *Special Treat* (NBC), Dorothy Weaver for "Family of Strangers" on *ABC Afterschool Special* (ABC), and Lewis Gifford, Paul Kim and Tom Yohe for *Drawing Power* (NBC)

89. **Outstanding Individual Achievement in Religious Programming**: Dahl Delu, C. Murawski, Scott Heineman and Martin Sheen in "Long Road Home" on *Insight* (syndicated)

90. **Outstanding Daytime Creative**

Technical Craft Individual Achievement: Donald Spangolia, Thomas Burton and Claudio Zeitlin Burtin for *The John Davidson Show* (syndicated), Michael Gass for *Good Morning America* (ABC), Dayton Anderson for *The Mike Douglas Show* (syndicated), and Robert Hoffman, Anthony Gambino and Lawrence Hammond for *All My Children* (ABC)

91. Outstanding Daytime Drama Technical Excellence: *All My Children* (ABC)

92. Outstanding Daytime Drama Design Excellence: *Ryan's Hope* (ABC)

93. Outstanding News Programs and Program Segments: *Pope John Paul II in Poland* (NBC), *Fishing Boat Sinks* (NBC), *CBS Reports: Miami—The Trial That Sparked the Riots* (CBS), *CBS Reports: On the Road* (CBS), *Too Little, Too Late?* (CBS), "Bette Davis" on *60 Minutes* (CBS), *Post Election Special Edition* (ABC), "Onward Christian Voters" on *60 Minutes* (CBS), "Here's Johnny!" on *60 Minutes* (CBS), "George Burns: An Update" on *20/20* (ABC), "VW Beetle: The Hidden Danger" on *20/20* (ABC), "The Invisible World" on *National Geographic Special* (PBS), "Heart Transplant" on *Prime Time Sunday* (NBC), *Murder of a Correspondent* (ABC), "Arson for Profit—Parts I and II" on *20/20* (ABC), "Mysteries of the Mind" on *National Geographic Special* (PBS), *CBS Reports: Teddy* (CBS), *Lights, Camera ... Politics* (ABC), "Who Killed Georgi Markov?" on *World* (PBS), "Urethane" on *Prime Time Saturday* (NBC), and "Nicaragua" on *20/20* (ABC)

94. Outstanding News Individual Achievement: Morton Silverstein and Chris Wallace for *NBC Reports: The Migrants* (NBC), Mike Edwards and Steve Sheppard for "Inside Afghanistan" on *60 Minutes* (CBS), Jack Clark and Jim Cefalo for *Shooting of Bill Stewart* (ABC), John Godfrey, Jon Alpert and Keiko Tsuno for *Third Avenue: Only the Strong Survive* (PBS), Nils Rassmussen, Kenneth E. Werner and Patrick M. Cook for *Death in a Southwest Prison* (ABC), Marlene Sanders and Judy Towers Reemtsma for *CBS Reports: What Shall We Do About Mother?* (CBS), Bill Moyers for "Our Times" on *Bill Moyers Journal* (PBS), Irwin Rosten for "Mysteries of the Mind" on *National Geographic Special* (PBS), Perry Wolff for *American Dream, American Nightmare* (CBS), Ray Lockart for *NBC White Paper: If Japan Can, Why Can't We?* (NBC), Roger Phenix for *NBC Reports: To Be a Doctor* (NBC), Alan Raymond for *To Die for Ireland* (ABC), Ruth Neuwald for *CBS Reports: The Trial That Sparked the Riots* (CBS), Maurice Murad for *CBS Reports: The Saudis* (CBS), Robert Rogow and Joel Dulberg for "Pavarotti" on *60 Minutes* (CBS), and Lionel Hampton for *No Maps on My Taps* (PBS)

95. Outstanding Live Sports Special: *Kentucky Derby* (ABC)

96. Outstanding Edited Sports Special: *ABC's Wide World of Sports 20th Anniversary Show* (ABC)

97. Outstanding Live Sports Series: *PGA Tour on CBS* (CBS)

98. Outstanding Edited Sports Series: *American Sportsman* (ABC)

99. Outstanding Sports Program Individual Achievement: Ray Savignano, Jesse Rineer, Sandy Bell, Robert Brown, Edward Ambrosini, Robert Squittieri, Donald Resch, James Murphy, Neil McCaffrey, Herman Lang, Frank McSpedon, Thomas McCarthy, Barry Drago, Joseph Sokota, Stephen Gorsuch, George Rothweiler, George Naeder, David Graham, Jeffrey Pollack, James McCarthy, Hans Singer and Sigmund Meyers for *Daytona 500* (CBS), Louis Scannapieco, Arthur Tinn, Charles D'Onofrio, Sandy Bell, Edward Ambrosini, Robert Hanford, Robert Pieringer, Frank Florio, George Klimcsak, George Naeder, James McCarthy, George Rothweiler, Al Loreto, Herman Lang, Hans Singer, Nicholas Lauria, James Murphy, Harry Haigood, Michael English, John Lincoln, Frank McSpedon, Dennis McBride, Stan Gould, Joseph Sokota, Barry Drago, Neil McCaffrey, David Graham, Walter Soucy, Robert Welch, David Finch, Richard E. Kearney, Joseph Sidlo and W. Haigood for *The Masters* (CBS), Tony Tocci, Ken Brown and Gary Bradley for *The Baseball Bunch* (syndicated), Rob Beiner, Dick Buffington, Jeff Cohan, Vince Dedario, Kathy Cook, John Delisa, Joel Feld, Ben Harvey, Bob Hersh, Jack Graham, Bob Lanning, Peter Lasser, Carol Lehti, Brian McCullough, Dennis Mazzocco, Bob Rosburg, Norm Samet, Ned Simon, Toni Slotkin, Larry Carolina and Bob Dekas for *ABC's Wide*

E Emmy Awards 1981

World of Sports (ABC), Jim McQueen, Jeff U'Ren, Matthew McCarthy, Mark Jankeloff and Richard Lieble for *NBC Sportsworld* (NBC), Mike Adams, Bob Ryan and Phil Tuckett for *NFL Symfunny* (syndicated), Cathy Barreto, Joel Arnowitz, Jack Black, Bob Coffey, Joe D'Ornellas, Stanley Faer, Bob Halper, Beth Hermelin, Howard N. Miller, Gady Reinhold, Roni Scherman, Steve Dellapietra, Barry Hicks, George Palmisano, John Wells, Jim Alkins, Curtis Campbell, Bob Clark, Ted Demers, Joe Drake, Tom Durkin, Bob Foster, Harve Gilman, Al Golly, Sigismund Gordon, Elliott Greenblatt, Bob Hickson, Frank Hodnett, George Joanitis, Andy Klein, Gary Kozak, Ed Knudholt, Pete La Corte, Marvin Lee, George Magee, Mario Marino, John Mayer, Walter Matwichuk, Henry Menusan, Jeff Ringel, Jesse Michnick, Charlotte Robinson, Allan Segal, Bill Vandenort, Irv Villafana, Hank Wolf and Bill Zizza for *NFL Today* (CBS), Angelo Bernarducci, Vincent Reda, Richard Rossi, Anthony Scandiffo, Norman Smith, Chris Riger, Ted Winterburn and Anthony Zaccaro for *The American Sportsman* (ABC), Robert Brown, Frank Florio, Edward Kushner, Robert Hanford, Rick Blane, Stan Gould, Steven Gorsuch, John Lincoln, George Klimcsak, Robert Jamieson, David Graham, James Murphy, Frank McSpedon, Jeffrey Pollack, Joseph Vincens and David Finch for *NFC Championship Game* (CBS), Joe Schavio, Joseph Lee, Drew Derosa, Jim Heneghan, Andrew Armentani, Jessel Kohn, Gary Donatelli, Jack Dorfman, Jack Savoy, Steve Nikifor, Tom O'Connell, Joe Cotugno and Roy Hitchings for *NFL Football* (ABC), Gilbert A. Miller, Donald Resch, Emanuel Kaufman, John Curtin, Thomas McCarthy, James McCarthy, Neil McCaffrey, Steven Gorsuch and Michael English for *NFL Today* (CBS), and James M. Grau for NFL and U.S. Open closing logos (CBS).

100. **Outstanding Special Sports Program**: *The Baseball Bunch* (syndicated), and "The Arlberg Kandahar Downhill from St. Anton" on *NBC Sportsworld* (NBC)

101. **Outstanding Special Sports Individual**: Steve Gonzalez for *Superbowl XV* (NBC), and Don Ohlmeyer and Ted Nathanson for *Friday Night Fights* (NBC)

102. **Outstanding Sports Host**: Dick Enberg

103. **Outstanding Sports Analyst**: Dick Button

104. **International Documentary**: Canadian Broadcasting Corporation for *Fighting Back*

105. **International Popular Arts**: British Broadcasting Corporation for *Not the Last of the Nine O'Clock News*

106. **International Drama**: Yorkshire Television Limited, England for *A Rod of Iron*

107. **International Performing Arts**: Societe Radio, Canada for *L'Oiseau de Feu (The Firebird)*

1981 Emmy Awards

1. **Outstanding Drama Special**: "A Woman Named Golda" on *Operation Prime Time* (syndicated)

2. **Outstanding Drama Series**: *Hill Street Blues* (NBC)

3. **Outstanding Comedy Series**: *Barney Miller* (ABC)

4. **Outstanding Music/Variety or Comedy Program**: *Night of 100 Stars* (ABC)

5. **Outstanding Lead Actress in a Limited Series or a Special**: Ingrid Bergman for "A Woman Named Golda" on *Operation Prime Time* (syndicated)

6. **Outstanding Lead Actor in a Limited Series or a Special**: Laurence Olivier in *Brideshead Revisited* (PBS)

7. **Outstanding Series Comedy Lead Actor**: Alan Alda in *M*A*S*H* (CBS)

8. **Outstanding Series Comedy Supporting Actress**: Loretta Swit in *M*A*S*H* (CBS)

9. **Outstanding Drama Series Lead Actor**: Daniel J. Travanti in *Hill Street Blues* (NBC)

10. **Outstanding Drama Series Supporting Actor**: Michael Conrad in *Hill Street Blues* (NBC)

11. **Outstanding Drama Series Lead Actress**: Michael Learned in *Nurse* (CBS)

12. **Outstanding Drama Series Supporting Actress**: Nancy Marchand in *Lou Grant* (CBS)

13. **Outstanding Comedy Lead

Actress: Carol Kane in "Simka Returns" on *Taxi* (ABC)

14. **Outstanding Comedy Supporting Actor**: Christopher Lloyd in *Taxi* (ABC)

15. **Outstanding Comedy Series Director**: Alan Rafkin for "Barbara's Crisis" on *One Day at a Time* (CBS)

16. **Outstanding Drama Series Director**: Harry Harris for "To Soar and Never Falter" on *Fame* (NBC)

17. **Outstanding Drama Special Director**: Marvin J. Chomsky for *Inside the Third Reich* (ABC)

18. **Outstanding Children's Program Director**: Dwight Hemion for *Goldie & Kids ... Listen to Us* (ABC)

19. **Outstanding Limited Series or Special Film Editing**: Robert F. Shugrue for "A Woman Named Golda" on *Operation Prime Time* (syndicated)

20. **Outstanding Limited Series**: *Marco Polo* (NBC)

21. **Outstanding Informational Special**: *Making of "Raiders of the Lost Ark"* (PBS)

22. **Outstanding Children's Program**: *The Wave* (ABC)

23. **Outstanding Classical Program in the Performing Arts**: *La Boheme, Live from the Met* (PBS)

24. **Outstanding Information Series**: *Creativity with Bill Moyers* (PBS)

25. **Outstanding Animated Program**: *The Grinch Grinches the Cat in the Hat* (ABC)

26. **Outstanding Limited Series or Special Lead Actor**: Mickey Rooney in *Bill* (CBS)

27. **Outstanding Limited Series or Special Supporting Actress**: Penny Fuller in *The Elephant Man* (ABC)

28. **Outstanding Series Film Editing**: Andrew Chulack for "Of Mouse and Man" on *Hill Street Blues* (NBC)

29. **Outstanding Videotape Series Editing**: Ken Denisoff for *Barbara Mandrell and the Mandrell Sisters* (NBC)

30. **Outstanding Limited Series or Special Videotape Editing**: William H. Breshears, Sr., Pam Marshall and Tucker Wiard for *American Bandstand's 30th Anniversary Special* (ABC)

31. **Outstanding Comedy Series Writing**: Ken Estin for "Elegant Iggy" on *Taxi* (ABC)

32. **Outstanding Drama Series Writing**: Steven Bochco, Anthony Yerkovich, Jeffrey Lewis, Michael Wagner and Michael Kozoll for "Freedom's Last Stand" on *Hill Street Blues* (NBC)

33. **Outstanding Limited Series or Special Writing**: Corey Blechman and Barry Morrow for *Bill* (CBS)

34. **Outstanding Variety or Music Writing**: John Candy, Joe Flaherty, Eugene Levy, Andrea Martin, Catherine O'Hara, Rick Moranis, Dave Thomas, Dick Blasucci, Paul Flaherty, Bob Dolman, John McAndrew, Doug Steckler, Mert Rich, Jeffrey Barron, Michael Short, Chris Cluess, Stuart Kreisman and Brian McConnachie for "Moral Majority Show" on *SCTV Network* (NBC)

35. **Outstanding Series Cinematography**: William W. Spencer for "Alone in a Crowd" on *Fame* (NBC)

36. **Outstanding Limited Series or Special Cinematography**: James Crabe for *The Letter* (ABC)

37. **Outstanding Special Creative Individual Achievement**: Andy Zall, videotape editor for *Shirley MacLaine ... Illusions* (CBS)

38. **Outstanding Film Sound Editing**: William H. Wistrom, Russ Tinsley, Peter Bond, Tom Cornwell, David Elliott, Tony Garber, Peter Harrison, Charles W. McCann, Joseph Mayer, Joseph Melody, R. William, and A. Thiederman for *Inside the Third Reich* (ABC)

39. **Outstanding Drama Series Music Composition**: David Rose for "He Was Only Twelve–Part 2" on *Little House on the Prairie* (NBC)

40. **Outstanding Limited Series or Drama Special Music Composition**: Patrick Williams for *The Princess and the Cabbie* (CBS)

41. **Outstanding Music Direction**: Elliot Lawrence, Bill Elton, Tommy Newsom, Torrie Zito, Johnathan Tunick and Lanny Meyers for *Night of 100 Stars* (ABC)

42. **Outstanding Music and Lyrics**: Larry Grossman and Alan Buz Kohan for "On the Outside Looking In" on *Shirley MacLaine ... Illusions* (CBS)

43. **Outstanding Film Sound Mixing**: Robert W. Glass, Jr., William Marky, William M. Nicholson and Howard

E Emmy Awards 1981

Wilmarth for "Personal Foul" on *Hill Street Blues* (NBC)

44. **Outstanding Tape Sound Mixing**: Christopher L. Haire, Richard J. Masci and Doug Nelson for *Perry Como's Easter in Guadalajara* (ABC)

45. **Outstanding Series Art Direction**: Ira Diamond and Joseph Stone for "Tomorrow's Farewell" on *Fame* (NBC)

46. **Outstanding Limited Series or Special Art Direction**: James Hulsey and Jerry Adams for *The Letter* (ABC)

47. **Outstanding Variety or Music Art Direction**: Ray Klausen for *The Fifty-Fourth Annual Academy Awards* (ABC)

48. **Outstanding Technical Direction and Electronic Camerawork**: Jerry Weiss, Bruce Bottone, Dean Hall, Ken Dahlquist, James Herring, Royden Holm, Wayne Nostaja, David Nowell and Tom Munshower for *The Magic of David Copperfield* (CBS)

49. **Outstanding Regular or Limited Series Costume Design**: Enrico Sabbatini for *Marco Polo, Part 3* (NBC)

50. **Outstanding Special Costume Design**: Donald Brooks for *The Letter* (ABC)

51. **Outstanding Make-Up**: Paul Stanhope for *World War III* (NBC)

52. **Outstanding Hairstyling**: Hazel Catmull for *Eleanor, First Lady of the World* (CBS)

53. **Outstanding Electronic Lighting Direction**: Ken Dettling and George W. Reisenberger for "Working" on *American Playhouse* (PBS)

54. **Outstanding Choreography**: Debbie Allen for "Come One, Come All" on *Fame* (NBC)

55. **Outstanding Individual Achievement in Children's Programming**: Ralph Holmes for "Alice at the Palace" on *Project Peacock* (NBC)

56. **Outstanding Individual Achievement in Animated Programming**: Bill Perez for *The Grinch Grinches the Cat in the Hat* (ABC)

57. **Outstanding Special Classification of Individual Achievement**: Nell Carter and Andre DeShields, performers for *Ain't Misbehavin'* (NBC), and Marilyn Matthews, costume supervisor for "The Strike" on *Fame* (NBC)

58. **Outstanding Engineering Development**: American Broadcasting Company and Dubner Computer Systems, Inc. for the Dubner CBG-2 electronic and background character generator and Hal Collins for his contributions to the art and development of videotape editing

59. **ATAS Governor's Award**: Hallmark Cards, Inc. for *Hallmark Hall of Fame*

60. **Outstanding Daytime Drama Series**: *Guiding Light* (CBS)

61. **Outstanding Children's Entertainment Series**: *Captain Kangaroo* (CBS)

62. **Outstanding Children's Entertainment Special**: "Starstruck" on *ABC Afterschool Special* (ABC)

63. **Outstanding Children's Informational/Instructional Series**: *30 Minutes* (CBS)

64. **Outstanding Short Format Informational/Instructional Programming**: *In the News* (CBS)

65. **Outstanding Children's Informational/Instructional Special**: *Kathy* (PBS)

66. **Outstanding Achievement in Religious Programming**: *Insight* (syndicated)

67. **Outstanding Special Classification of Program Achievement**: *FYI*

68. **Outstanding Talk or Service Series**: *The Richard Simmons Show* (syndicated)

69. **Outstanding Variety Series**: *The Regis Philbin Show* (NBC)

70. **Outstanding Game or Audience Participation Show**: *Password Plus* (NBC)

71. **Outstanding Daytime Dramatic Actor**: Anthony Geary on *General Hospital* (ABC)

72. **Outstanding Daytime Dramatic Actress**: Robin Strasser in *One Life to Live* (ABC)

73. **Outstanding Daytime Supporting Dramatic Actor**: David Lewis in *General Hospital* (ABC)

74. **Outstanding Daytime Supporting Dramatic Actress**: Dorothy Lyman in *All My Children* (ABC)

75. **Outstanding Host or Hostess in a Talk or Service Series**: Phil Donahue in *Donahue* (syndicated)

76. **Outstanding Host or Hostess in a Game or Audience Participation

Emmy Awards 1981

Show: Bob Barker in *The Price Is Right* (CBS)

77. **Outstanding Host or Hostess in a Variety Series:** Merv Griffin in *The Merv Griffin Show* (syndicated)

78. **Outstanding Performer in Children's Programming:** Bob Keeshan in *Captain Kangaroo* (CBS)

79. **Outstanding Daytime Drama Series Direction:** Marlena Laird, Alan Pultz and Phillip Sogard for *General Hospital* (ABC)

80. **Outstanding Variety Series Direction:** Ron Wiener for the January 21 program of *Donahue* (syndicated)

81. **Outstanding Individual Direction of a Variety Series:** Barry Glazer for the April 18 program of *American Bandstand* (ABC)

82. **Outstanding Individual Direction of a Game Show:** Paul Alter for the May 29 program of *Family Feud* (ABC)

83. **Outstanding Individual Direction of a Children's Program:** Arthur Allan Seidelman for "She Drinks a Little" on *ABC Afterschool Special* (ABC)

84. **Outstanding Individual Achievement in Direction for Special Classification:** Alfred R. Kelman for *The Body Human: The Loving Process — Women* (CBS)

85. **Outstanding Daytime Drama Series Writing:** Douglas Marland, Nancy Franklin, Patrick Mulcahey, Gene Palumbo and Frank Salisbury for *Guiding Light* (CBS)

86. **Outstanding Children's Writing:** Paul W. Cooper for "She Drinks a Little" on *ABC Afterschool Special* (ABC)

87. **Outstanding Individual Achievement Writing for Special Classification:** Elaine Meryl Brown, Betty Cornfeld, Mary Ann Donahue, Joe Gustaitis and Robin Westin for *FYI* (ABC)

88. **Outstanding Children's Cinematography:** Tom Hurwitz for "Horseman of Inner Mongolia" on *Big, Blue Marble* (syndicated)

89. **Outstanding Children's Film Editing:** Peter Hammer and Allen Kirkpatrick for "Horsemen of Inner Mongolia" on *Big, Blue Marble* (syndicated)

90. **Outstanding Daytime Drama Design Excellence:** James Ellingwood, Mercer Barrows, Grant Velie, Thomas Markle, John Zak, Jim O'Daniel, P.K. Cole, Vikki McCarter, Diane Lewis, Katherine Kotarakos, Debbie Holmes, Jill Farren Phelps, Dominic Messinger and Charles Paul for *General Hospital* (ABC)

91. **Outstanding Children's Music Composition:** Elliott Lawrence for "The Unforgivable Secret" on *ABC Afterschool Special* (ABC)

92. **Outstanding Daytime Drama Technical Excellence:** Joseph Solomito, Howard Zweig, Diana Wenman, Jean Dadario, Barbara Martin Simmons, Lawrence Hammond, Robert Ambrico, Larry Strack, Vincent Senatore, Jay Kenn, Trevor Thompson, Len Walas, Al Lemanski, Charles Eisen, Roger Haenelt and Barbara Wood for *All My Children* (ABC)

93. **Outstanding Daytime Technical Directing/Electronic Camerawork:** Sanford Bell and Hal Classon for *The Guiding Light* (CBS)

94. **Outstanding Daytime Art Direction/Scenic Design/Set Decoration:** Bob Keene and Griff Lambert for *The Richard Simmons Show* (syndicated)

95. **Outstanding Daytime Lighting Direction:** Everett Melosh for *One Life to Live* (ABC)

96. **Outstanding Daytime Costume Design:** Nancy Simmons for *The Richard Simmons Show* (syndicated)

97. **Outstanding Children's Art Direction/Scenic Design/Set Decoration:** Claude Bonniere for "My Mother Was Never a Kid" on *ABC Afterschool Special* (ABC)

98. **Outstanding Children's Audio:** Steven J. Palecek for "An Orchestra Is a Team, Too!" on *CBS Festival of the Lively Arts for Young People* (CBS)

99. **Outstanding Children's Make-Up and Hair Design:** Judy Cooper Sealy for "My Mother Was Never a Kid" on *ABC Afterschool Special* (ABC)

100. **Outstanding Children's Graphic Design:** Ray Favita and Michael J. Smollin for *The Great Space Coaster* (syndicated)

101. **National Community Service:** WTHR-TV, Indianapolis, Indiana for *Klan*

102. **International Documentary:** Societe Nationale de Television Francaise—1, France for *Charters Pour L'Enfer (Charters to Hell)*

103. **International Drama:** Mariner

Films and Channel 7, Australia for *A Town Like Alice*
104. **International Performing Arts**: London Weekend Television, Ltd., United Kingdom for *Sweeney Todd: Scenes from the Making of a Musical*
105. **International Popular Arts**: Treve Globo, Ltda., Brazil for *Vincius Para Criancas or Arca De Noe (Noah's Ark)*
106. **Founders Award**: Roone Arledge and Shaun Sutton
107. **Directorate Award**: Sir Huw Wheldon
108. **Trustee Award**: Agnes E. Nixon

1982 Emmy Awards

1. **Outstanding Drama Series**: *Hill Street Blues* (NBC)
2. **Outstanding Drama Special**: *Special Bulletin* (NBC)
3. **Outstanding Comedy Series**: *Cheers* (NBC)
4. **Outstanding Limited Series**: *Nicholas Nickelby* (syndicated)
5. **Outstanding Children's Program**: *Big Bird in China* (NBC)
6. **Outstanding Variety/Music or Comedy Special**: *Motown 25: Yesterday, Today, Forever* (NBC)
7. **Outstanding Animated Program**: *Ziggy's Gift* (ABC)
8. **Outstanding Informational Series**: *The Barbara Walters Specials* (ABC)
9. **Outstanding Classical Pogram in the Performing Arts**: *Pavarotti in Philadelphia: La Boheme* (PBS)
10. **Outstanding Informational Special**: *The Body Human: The Living Code* (CBS)
11. **Outstanding Lead Actress in a Comedy Series**: Shelly Long in *Cheers* (NBC)
12. **Outstanding Lead Actor in a Comedy Series**: Judd Hirsch in *Taxi* (NBC)
13. **Outstanding Lead Actress in a Drama Series**: Tyne Daly in *Cagney & Lacey* (CBS)
14. **Outstanding Lead Actor in a Drama Series**: Ed Flanders in *St. Elsewhere* (NBC)
15. **Outstanding Lead Actress in a Limited Series or Special**: Barbara Stanwyck in *The Thorn Birds, Part One* (ABC)
16. **Outstanding Lead Actor in a Limited Series or Special**: Tommy Lee Jones in *The Executioner's Song* (NBC)
17. **Outstanding Dramatic Series Supporting Actress**: Doris Roberts in "Cora and Arnie" on *St. Elsewhere* (NBC)
18. **Outstanding Dramatic Series Supporting Actor**: James Coco in "Cora and Arnie" on *St. Elsewhere* (NBC)
19. **Outstanding Comedy Series Supporting Actress**: Carol Kane in *Taxi* (NBC)
20. **Outstanding Comedy Series Supporting Actor**: Christopher Lloyd in *Taxi* (NBC)
21. **Outstanding Limited Series or Special Supporting Actress**: Jean Simmons in *The Thorn Birds* (ABC)
22. **Outstanding Limited Series or Special Supporting Actor**: Richard Kiley in *The Thorn Birds* (ABC)
23. **Outstanding Individual Performance in Variety or Music Program**: Leontyne Price in *Live from Lincoln Center: Leontyne Price, Zubin Mehta and the New York Philharmonic* (PBS)
24. **Outstanding Drama Series Directing**: Jeff Bleckner for "Life in the Minors" on *Hill Street Blues* (NBC)
25. **Outstanding Comedy Series Directing**: James Burrows for "Sundown—Part 2" on *Cheers* (NBC)
26. **Outstanding Variety or Music Program Directing**: Dwight Hemion for *Sheena Easton ... Act 1* (NBC)
27. **Outstanding Limited Series or Special Directing**: John Erman for *Who Will Love My Children?* (ABC)
28. **Outstanding Informational Program Individual Achievement**: Alfred R. Kelman and Charles Bangert, directors and Louis H. Gorfain and Robert E. Fuisz, writers for *The Body Human: The Living Code* (CBS)
29. **Outstanding Series Film Editing**: Ray Daniels for "Phantom of the Hill" on *Hill Street Blues* (NBC)
30. **Outstanding Limited Series or Special Film Editing**: C. Timothy O'Meara for *The Thorn Birds* (ABC)
31. **Outstanding Series Videotape Editing**: Larry M. Harris for "Change of a Dollar" on *The Jeffersons* (CBS)
32. **Outstanding Limited Series or**

Special Videotape Editing: Arden Rynew for *Special Bulletin* (NBC)

33. **Outstanding Series Cinematography**: Joseph Biroc for "The Masterbuilder's Woman" on *Casablanca* (NBC)

34. **Outstanding Limited Series or Special Cinematography**: Charles Correll and Steven Larner for "Into the Maelstrom" on *The Winds of War* (ABC)

35. **Outstanding Comedy Series Writing**: Glen Charles and Les Charles for "Give Me a Ring Sometime" on *Cheers* (NBC)

36. **Outstanding Drama Series Writing**: David Milch for "Trial by Fury" on *Hill Street Blues* (NBC)

37. **Outstanding Limited Series or Special Writing**: Marshall Herskovitz and Edward Zwick for *Special Bulletin* (NBC)

38. **Outstanding Variety or Music Writing**: John Candy, Joe Flaherty, Eugene Levy, Andrea Martin, Martin Short, Paul Flaherty, Dick Blasucci, John McAndrew, Doug Steckler, Bob Dolman, Michael Short and Mary Charlotte Wilcox for "The Energy Ball/Sweeps Week" on *SCTV Network* (NBC)

39. **Outstanding Individual Achievement in Informational Programming Writing**: Louis H. Gorfain and Robert E. Fulaz for *The Body Human: The Living Code* (CBS)

40. **Outstanding Limited Series or Special Art Direction**: Robert MacKichan and Jerry Adams for *The Thorn Birds, Part One* (ABC)

41. **Outstanding Series Art Direction**: John W. Corso, Frank Grieco, Jr. and Robert G. Freer for *Tales of the Gold Monkey* (ABC)

42. **Outstanding Variety or Music Program Art Direction**: Ray Klausen and Michael Corenblith for *55th Annual Academy Awards Presentation* (ABC)

43. **Outstanding Series Technical Direction and Electronic Camerawork**: Heino Ripp, Mike Bennett, Al Camoin, Jan Kasoff, John Pinto and Maurey Verschore for *Saturday Night Live* (NBC)

44. **Outstanding Limited Series or Special Technical Direction and Electronic Camerawork**: Hank Geving for *Special Bulletin* (NBC)

45. **Outstanding Series Costume Design**: Theodora Van Runkle for "Dungeon of Death" on *Wizards and Warriors* (CBS)

46. **Outstanding Limited Series or Special Costume Design**: Phyllis Dalton for *The Scarlet Pimpernel* (CBS)

47. **Outstanding Individual Costumers Achievement**: Tommy Welsh, Paul Vachon, Johannes Nilmark and John Napolitana for "The Storm Breaks" on *The Winds of War* (ABC)

48. **Outstanding Makeup**: Del Acevedo for *The Thorn Birds* (ABC)

49. **Outstanding Hairstyling**: Eddie Panda for *Rosie: The Rosemary Clooney Story* (CBS)

50. **Outstanding Series Electronic Lighting Direction**: Robert A. Dickinson and C. Frank Olivas for *Solid Gold* (syndicated)

51. **Outstanding Limited Series or Special Electronic Lighting Direction**: John Rook, Ken Wilcox and Bob Pohle for *Sheena Easton ... Act 1* (NBC)

52. **Outstanding Series Music Composition**: Bruce Broughton for "The Ewing Blues" on *Dallas* (CBS)

53. **Outstanding Limited Series or Special Music Composition**: Billy Goldenberg for *Rage of Angels* (NBC)

54. **Outstanding Musical Direction**: Dick Hyman for *Eubie Blake: A Century of Music* (PBS)

55. **Outstanding Music and Lyrics**: James Di Pasquale and Dory Previn for "We'll Win This World" on *Two of a Kind* (CBS)

56. **Outstanding Graphic Design and Title Sequences**: James Castle and Bruce Bryant for "Showdown" on *Cheers* (NBC)

57. **Outstanding Series Film Sound Editing**: Sam Horta, Don Ernst, Avram Gold, Eileen Horta, Constance A. Kazmer and Gary Krivacek for "Stan the Man" on *Hill Street Blues* (NBC)

58. **Outstanding Limited Series or Special Film Sound Editing**: James Troutman, Dave Caldwell, Paul Clay, Paul Laune, Tony Magro, Richard Raderman, Karen Rasch, Jeff Sandler, William Shenberg, Dan Thomas and Ascher Yates for *The Executioner's Song* (NBC)

59. **Outstanding Series Film Sound Mixing**: William B. Marky, John B. Asman, William Nicholson and Ken S.

E Emmy Awards 1982

Polk for "Trial by Fury" on *Hill Street Blues* (NBC)

60. **Outstanding Limited Series or Special Film Sound Mixing**: John Mitchell, Gordon L. Day, Stanley A. Wetzel and Howard Wilmarth for *The Scarlet and the Black* (CBS)

61. **Outstanding Series Tape Sound Mixing**: Frank Kulaga and Ken Hahn for "The Magic Flute" on *Dance in America* (PBS)

62. **Outstanding Limited Series or Special Tape Sound Mixing**: Edward J. Greene, Ron Estes and Carroll Pratt for *Sheena Easton ... Act 1* (NBC)

63. **Outstanding Choreography**: Debbie Allen for "Class Act" on *Fame* (NBC)

64. **Outstanding Special Visual Effects**: Gene Warren, Jr., Michael Milner, Jackson De Govia, Peter Kleinow and Leslie Huntley for "Defiance" on *The Winds of War* (ABC)

65. **Citation**: Ampex Corporation for development of ADO Digital Effects Unit

66. **Citation**: Ikegami Electronics and CBS for the engineering and development of the EC-35 Electronic Camera

67. **Emmy**: Eastman Kodak Company for engineering development for high speed color film 5294/7294

68. **Governor's Award**: Sylvester L. (Pat) Weaver former NBC president who revolutionized network programming in the late 1940's and early 1950's

69. **Citation**: Ampex Corporation for development of the ADO, a digital effects unit displaying unique capabilities with improved picture quality

70. **Outstanding Daytime Drama Series**: *The Young and the Restless* (CBS)

71. **Outstanding Children's Entertainment Series**: *Captain Kangaroo* (CBS), and *Smurfs* (NBC)

72. **Outstanding Children's Informational/Instructional Series**: *Sesame Street* (PBS)

73. **Outstanding Children's Entertainment Special**: "The Woman Who Willed a Miracle" on *ABC Afterschool Special* (ABC)

74. **Outstanding Children's Informational/Instructional Special**: *Winners* (syndicated)

75. **Outstanding Achievement in Series Religious Programming**: *Insight* (syndicated)

76. **Outstanding Achievement in Special Religious Programming**: *The Juggler of Notre Dame* (syndicated), and *The Land of Fear, The Land of Courage* (NBC)

77. **Outstanding Program Achievement in the Performing Arts**: *Hansel and Gretel: Live from the Met* (PBS), and *Zubin and the I.P.O.* (NBC)

78. **Outstanding Achievement in Coverage of a Special Event**: *Macy's Thanksgiving Day Parade* (NBC)

79. **Outstanding Short Form Instructional/Informational Program**: *In the News* (CBS)

80. **Outstanding Program Achievement in a Special Classification**: *American Bandstand* (ABC)

81. **Outstanding Talk/Service Series**: *This Old House* (PBS)

82. **Outstanding Variety Series**: *The Merv Griffin Show* (syndicated)

83. **Outstanding Game or Audience Participation Show**: *The $25,000 Pyramid* (CBS)

84. **Outstanding Daytime Dramatic Actor**: Robert Woods in *One Life to Live* (ABC)

85. **Outstanding Daytime Dramatic Actress**: Dorothy Lyman in *All My Children* (ABC)

86. **Outstanding Daytime Supporting Dramatic Actor**: Darnell Williams in *All My Children* (ABC)

87. **Outstanding Daytime Supporting Dramatic Actress**: Louise Shaffer in *Ryan's Hope* (ABC)

88. **Outstanding Performer in Children's Programming**: Cloris Leachman in "The Woman Who Willed a Miracle" on *ABC Afterschool Special* (ABC)

90. **Outstanding Individual Achievement in Religious Programming**: Lois Nettleton in "A Gun for Mandy" on *Insight* (syndicated), and Edwin Newman, moderator in *Kids, Drugs and Alcohol* (NBC)

91. **Outstanding Host or Hostess in a Variety Series**: Leslie Uggams in *Fantasy* (NBC)

92. **Outstanding Host or Hostess in a Talk or Service Program**: Phil Donahue in *Donahue* (syndicated)

93. **Outstanding Host or Hostess in

a Game or Audience Participation Show: Betty White in *Just Men!* (NBC)
94. **Outstanding Individual Achievement in Performing Arts**: Zubin Mehta, conductor in *Zubin and the I.P.O.* (NBC)
95. **Outstanding Individual Achievement in a Special Classification**: Hal Linden, host in *FYI* (ABC)
96. **Outstanding Daytime Drama Direction**: Allen Fristoe, Norman Hall, Peter Miner and David Pressman for *One Life to Live* (ABC)
97. **Outstanding Children's Programming Directing**: Sharon Miller for "The Woman Who Willed a Miracle" on *ABC Afterschool Special* (ABC)
98. **Outstanding Episode Direction for a Variety Series**: Dick Carson for the September 17 program of *The Merv Griffin Show* (syndicated)
99. **Outstanding Episode Direction for a Talk/Service Series**: Glen Swanson for November 10 program of *Hour Magazine* (syndicated)
100. **Outstanding Episode Direction for a Game or Audience Participation Show**: Mark Breslow for the December 30 program of *The Price Is Right* (CBS)
101. **Outstanding Daytime Drama Series Writing**: Claire Labine, Paul Avila Mayer, Mary Ryan Munisteri, Eugene Price, Judith Pinsker, Nancy Ford, B.K. Perlman, Rory Metcalf and Trent Jones for *Ryan's Hope* (ABC)
102. **Outstanding Writing for Children's Programming**: Arthur Heinemann for "The Woman Who Willed a Miracle" on *ABC Afterschool Special* (ABC)
103. **Trustees' Award**: Robert E. Short, daytime programmer for Proctor and Gamble
104. **Outstanding Daytime Drama Design Excellence**: Sid Ramin, Teri Smith, Robert Chui, Richard Greene, Scott Hersh, Sylvia Lawrence, Carol Luiken, Robert Griffin, Donald Gavitt, Donna Larson, William Itkin and William Mickley for *All My Children* (ABC)
105. **Outstanding Daytime Drama Technical Excellence**: Howard Zweig, Henry Enrico Ferro, Diana Wenman, Jean Dadario, Lawrence Hammond, Robert Ambrico, Trevor Thompson, Vincent Senatore, Robert Bellairs, Thomas French and Richard Westlein for *All My Children* (ABC)
106. **Outstanding Children's Music**: Elliott Lawrence for "Sometimes I Don't Like My Mother" on *ABC Afterschool Special* (ABC)
107. **Outstanding Children's Cinematography**: Terry Meade for "The Shooting" on *CBS Afternoon Playhouse* (CBS)
108. **Outstanding Children's Film Editing**: Scott McKinsey for "The Shooting" on *CBS Afternoon Playhouse* (CBS)
109. **Outstanding Daytime Special Event Technical Direction/Electronic Camerawork**: Eric Eisenstein, Terry Rohnke, Carl Eckert, Mike Bennett, Barry Frischer, Bill Boetz, Steve Gonzalez, Dave Hagen, John Hillyer, Gene Martin, Don Mulvaney and John Pinto for *Macy's Thanksgiving Day Parade* (NBC)
110. **Outstanding Children's Associate Director/Videotape Editing**: Ilie Agopian for *Young People's Specials* (syndicated)
111. **Outstanding Achievement in a Daytime Technical Craft**: Robert Ryan, Les Brown and Jack Urbont for *Lorne Greene's New Wilderness* (syndicated), Victor Dinapoli and Gerri Brioso for *Sesame Street* (PBS), Jay David Saks for *Hansel and Gretel: Live from the Met* (PBS), John N. Castaldo for *Donahue* (syndicated), and Nicholas Hutak for "Franconia Notch" on *The Guiding Light* (CBS)
112. **Outstanding Religious Film Editing**: Scott McKinsey for *Insight* (syndicated), and Ed Williams for *Land of Fear, Land of Courage* (NBC)
113. **Outstanding Live Sports Series**: *NFL Football* (CBS)
114. **Outstanding Edited Sports Series**: *The American Sportsman* (ABC)
115. **Outstanding Live Sports Special**: *NCAA Basketball Championship Final* (CBS)
116. **Outstanding Edited Sports Special**: *Indianapolis 500* (ABC)
117. **Outstanding Sports Personality/Analyst**: John Madden
118. **Outstanding Sports Personality/Host**: Jim McKay
119. **Outstanding Breaking News

Program: "Disaster on the Potomac" on *ABC World News Tonight* (ABC)

120. **Outstanding Breaking News Segment**: "Personal Note/Beirut" on *ABC World News Tonight* (ABC), "New Mexico's Yates Oil Company" on *CBS Evening News with Dan Rather* (CBS), and "Linda Down's Marathon" on *World News This Morning* (ABC)

121. **Outstanding Current News Analysis Program**: *Chrysler: Once Upon a Time ... And Now* (PBS), *From the Ashes ... Nicaragua Today* (PBS), and "Guatemala" on *CBS Reports* (CBS)

122. **Outstanding Current News Analysis Segment**: "Tanks" on *A Few Minutes with Andy Rooney* (CBS), and "Welcome to Palermo" on *60 Minutes* (CBS)

123. **Outstanding Investigative Program**: *Frank Terpil: Confessions of a Dangerous Man* (PBS)

124. **Outstanding Investigative Segments**: "Air Force Surgeon" and "The Nazi Connection" on *60 Minutes* (CBS)

125. **Outstanding Interview/Interviewers Program**: Ted Koppel and Bob Jordan for "The Palestinian Viewpoint" on *Nightline* (ABC), and Barbara Walters and Beth Polson for *The Barbara Walters Special* (ABC)

126. **Outstanding Interview/Interviewers Segment**: Ed Bradley and Monika Jensen for "In the Belly of the Beast" on *60 Minutes* (CBS)

127. **Outstanding Continuing News Story Program**: Howard Husock and Scott Simon for *The Petterson Project* (PBS)

128. **Outstanding Continuing News Story Segment**: Rita Braver, David Browning, Quentin Neufeld, Terry Martin, David Gelber, Bruce Morton, Jerry Bowen, Ed Rabel, Terry Drinkwater and Ray Brady for "Coverage of American Unemployment" on *CBS Evening News with Dan Rather* (CBS)

129. **Outstanding Informational, Cultural or Historical Program**: James M. Messenger and Stuart Sillery for *The Taj Mahal* (PBS), and Andrew McGuire for *Here's Looking at You, Kid* (PBS)

130. **Outstanding Informational, Cultural or Historical Segment**: Dick Schaap and Betsy Osha for "Sid Caesar" on *20/20* (ABC), Brett Alexander and Billy Taylor for "Eclectic: A Profile of Quincy" on *Sunday Morning* (CBS), and Jeanne Solomon and Ed Bradley for "Lena" on *60 Minutes* (CBS)

131. **Outstanding Special Classification Program Achievement**: *Vietnam Requiem* (ABC)

132. **Outstanding Special Classification Segment Achievement**: "It Didn't Have to Happen" on *60 Minutes* (CBS)

133. **Outstanding News Writing Individual Achievement**: Sharon Blair Brysac and Perry Wolff for *Juilliard and Beyond: A Life in Music* (CBS), Charles Kuralt for "Cicada Invasion" on *CBS Evening News with Dan Rather* (CBS)

134. **Outstanding News Direction Individual Achievement**: Jonas McCord and William Couturie for *Vietnam Requiem* (ABC), and Bill Jersey for *Children of Violence* (PBS)

135. **Outstanding News Camerawork Individual Achievement**: James Deckard and James Lipscomb for "Polar Bear Alert" on *National Geographic* (PBS), Norris Brock for "Egypt: Quest for Eternity" on *National Geographic Special* (PBS), Arnie Serlin for *The Taj Mahal* (PBS), and Bill Bacon for *Alaska: Story of a Dream* (syndicated)

136. **Outstanding News Electronic Videographers**: David Green for "Guerillas in Usulatan" on *CBS Evening News with Dan Rather* (CBS), and George Fridrick for *Along Route 30* (NBC)

137. **Outstanding News Sound Individual Achievement**: Larry Loewinger, Francis Daniel, Michael Lonsdale, Peter Miller and David Moshlak for *Juilliard and Beyond: A Life in Music* (CBS), Tim Cohen for *The Campaign* (PBS), and Simon Jones, Mike Lonsdale, Kim Ornitz and David Moshlak for *FDR* (ABC)

138. **Outstanding News Associate Directors Individual Achievement**: Consuelo Gonzalez and Neill Phillipson for *FDR* (ABC)

139. **Outstanding News Videotape Editors Individual Achievement**: Cathy Black, Catherine Isabella, Dean Irwin, Carla Morgenstern, Edward Bude, Ruth Iwano, Chris Von Benge and Mike Seigal for *FDR* (ABC), Anthony Ciccimarro, Kathy Hardigan, Don Orrico and Matty Powers for *The Man Who Shot the Pope: A Study in Terrorism* (NBC), and Thomas

Micklas for "Ice Sculptor" on *CBS Evening News with Dan Rather* (CBS)

140. **Outstanding News Film Editors Individual Achievement**: James Flanagan, Nils Rasmussen, William Longo and Walter Essenfeld for *FDR* (ABC), Nobuko Oganesoff for *Juilliard and Beyond: A Life in Music* (CBS), and Bob Brady for *The Campaign* (PBS)

141. **Outstanding News Graphic Designers Individual Achievement**: Rebecca Allen for *Walter Cronkite's Universe* (CBS), and David Millman for "The Cuban Missile Crisis" on *Nightline* (ABC)

142. **Outstanding News Music Composition Individual Achievement**: James G. Pirie for *Alaska: Story of a Dream* (syndicated)

143. **Community Service Award**: WCCO-TV, Minneapolis, Minnesota for *Sexual Abuse of Children*

144. **International Documentary**: Radio Telefis Eireann, Ireland for *Is There One Who Understands Me?—The World of James Joyce*

145. **International Drama**: Thames Television, United Kingdom for *A Voyage Round My Father*

146. **International Performing Arts**: Grenada Television, United Kingdom for *A Lot of Happiness*

147. **International Popular Arts**: TV Globo, Brazil for *Death and Life Severinian*

1983 Emmy Awards

1. **Outstanding Drama Series**: *Hill Street Blues* (NBC)
2. **Outstanding Drama/Comedy Special**: "Something About Amelia" on *An ABC Theatre Presentation* (ABC)
3. **Outstanding Comedy Series**: *Cheers* (NBC)
4. **Outstanding Limited Series**: "Concealed Enemies" on *American Playhouse* (PBS)
5. **Outstanding Animated Program**: *Garfield on the Town* (CBS)
6. **Outstanding Variety/Music or Comedy Program**: *The 6th Annual Kennedy Center Honors: A Celebration of the Performing Arts* (CBS)
7. **Outstanding Children's Program**: *He Makes Me Feel Like Dancin'* (NBC)
8. **Outstanding Classical Program in the Performing Arts**: "Placido Domingo Celebrates Seville" on *Great Performances* (PBS)
9. **Outstanding Informational Special**: *America Remembers John F. Kennedy* (syndicated)
10. **Outstanding Informational Series**: *A Walk Through the 20th Century with Bill Moyers* (PBS)
11. **Outstanding Lead Actress in a Limited Series or a Special**: Jane Fonda in "The Dollmaker" on *An ABC Theatre Presentation* (ABC)
12. **Outstanding Lead Actor in a Limited Series or a Special**: Laurence Olivier in *King Lear* (syndicated)
13. **Outstanding Lead Actress in a Dramatic Series**: Tyne Daly in *Cagney and Lacey* (CBS)
14. **Outstanding Lead Actor in a Dramatic Series**: Tom Selleck in *Magnum, P.I.* (CBS)
15. **Outstanding Lead Actress in a Comedy Series**: Jane Curtin in *Kate & Allie* (CBS)
16. **Outstanding Lead Actor in a Comedy Series**: John Ritter in *Three's Company* (ABC)
17. **Outstanding Supporting Actor in a Comedy Series**: Pat Harrington, Jr. in *One Day at a Time* (CBS)
18. **Outstanding Supporting Actor in a Limited Series or Special**: Art Carney in "Terrible Joe Moran" on *An ITT Theatre Special* (CBS)
19. **Outstanding Supporting Actress in a Limited Series or Special**: Roxana Zal in "Something About Amelia" on *An ABC Theatre Presentation* (ABC)
20. **Outstanding Supporting Dramatic Actress**: Alfre Woodard in "Doris in Wonderland" on *Hill Street Blues* (NBC)
21. **Outstanding Supporting Dramatic Actor**: Bruce Weitz in *Hill Street Blues* (NBC)
22. **Outstanding Supporting Actress in a Comedy Series**: Rhea Perlman in *Cheers* (NBC)
23. **Outstanding Individual Performance in a Variety or Music Program**: Cloris Leachman in *Screen Actors Guild 50th Anniversary Celebration* (CBS)
24. **Outstanding Limited Series or**

Special Direction: Jeff Bleckner for "Concealed Enemies" on *American Playhouse* (PBS)

25. **Outstanding Drama Series Directing**: Corey Allen for "Goodbye, Mr. Scripps" on *Hill Street Blues* (NBC)

26. **Outstanding Comedy Series Directing**: Bill Persky for "A Very Loud Family" on *Kate & Allie* (CBS)

27. **Outstanding Variety or Music Program Directing**: Dwight Hemion for *Here's Television Entertainment* (NBC)

28. **Outstanding Series Film Editing**: Andrew Chulack for "Old Flames" on *Cheers* (NBC)

29. **Outstanding Limited Series or Special Film Editing**: Jerrold L. Ludwig for "A Streetcar Named Desire" on *An ABC Theatre Presentation* (ABC)

30. **Outstanding Series Videotape Editing**: Howard Brock for "Gonna Learn How to Fly" on *Fame* (syndicated)

31. **Outstanding Limited Series or Special Videotape Editing**: Jim McQueen and Catherine Shields for *American Film Institute Salute to Lillian Gish* (CBS)

32. **Outstanding Series Film Sound Editing**: Sam Shaw, Michael Ford, Donlee Jorgensen, Mark Roberts, Breck Warwick, Bob Weatherford, Michael Wilhoit, Nicholas Korda and Gene Gillette for *Airwolf* (CBS)

33. **Outstanding Limited Series or Special Film Sound Editing**: Christopher T. Welch, Brian Courcier, Greg Dillon, David R. Elliott, Michael Hilkene, Fred Judkins, Carl Mahakian, Joseph Mayer, Joseph Melody, Catherine Shorr, Richard Shorr, Jill Taggart and Roy Prendergast for "The Day After" on *An ABC Theatre Presentation* (ABC)

34. **Outstanding Series Film Sound Mixing**: John B. Asman, David Schneiderman, William M. Nicholson and Ken S. Polk for "Parting Is Such Sweep Sorrow" on *Hill Street Blues* (NBC)

35. **Outstanding Limited Series or Special Film Sound Mixing**: Richard Raguse, William L. McCaughey, Mel Metcalfe and Terry Porter for "A Streetcar Named Desire" on *An ABC Theatre Presentation* (ABC)

36. **Outstanding Limited Series or Special Writing**: William Hanley for "Something About Amelia" on *An ABC Theatre Presentation* (ABC)

37. **Outstanding Drama Series Writing**: Tom Fontana, John Masius and John Ford Noonan for "The Women" on *St. Elsewhere* (NBC)

38. **Outstanding Comedy Series Writing**: David Angell for "Old Flames" on *Cheers* (NBC)

39. **Outstanding Variety or Music Program Writing**: Steve O'Donnell, Gerard Mulligan, Sanford Frank, Joseph E. Toplyn, Christopher Elliott, Matt Wickline, Heff Martin, Ted Greenberg, David Yazbek, Merrill Markoe and David Letterman for "Show Number 312" on *Late Night with David Letterman* (NBC)

40. **Outstanding Limited Series or Special Cinematography**: Bill Butler for "A Streetcar Named Desire" on *An ABC Theatre Presentation* (ABC)

41. **Outstanding Series Cinematography**: James Crabe for "More Than Murder" on *Mickey Spillane's Mike Hammer* (CBS)

42. **Outstanding Series Technical Direction/Camerawork**: Gene Crowe, Sam Drummy, Larry Heider, Dave Levisohn, Wayne Orr, Ron Sheldon and Mark Sanford for *On Stage America, Number Five* (syndicated)

43. **Outstanding Limited Series or Special Technical Direction/Camerawork**: Lou Fusari, Les Atkinson, Bruce Bottone, George Falardeau, Dean Hall, Dave Hilmer, Roy Holm, David Nowell and Jerry R. Smith for *The Magic of David Copperfield VI* (CBS)

44. **Outstanding Special Visual Effects**: William M. Klages for *The 26th Annual Grammy Awards* (CBS), and Robert Blalack, Nancy Rushlow, Dan Pinkham, Chris Regan, Larry Stevens, Dan Nosenchuck and Chris Dierdorff for *The Day After* (ABC)

45. **Outstanding Graphic Design and Title Sequence**: Ted Woolery and Gerry Woolery for "Filling Buddy's Shoes" on *The Duck Factory* (NBC)

46. **Outstanding Individual Achievement in Animated Programming**: R.O. Blechman for *The Solder's Tale* (PBS)

47. **Outstanding Individual Achievement in Informational Programming**: Emile Ardolino for *He Makes*

Me Feel Like Dancin' (NBC), and Bill Moyers for *Marshall, Texas* (PBS)
48. **Outstanding Series Art Direction**: James Hulsey and Bruce Kay for *The Duck Factory* (NBC)
49. **Outstanding Limited Series or Special Art Direction**: James Hulsey and George R. Nelson for "A Streetcar Named Desire" on *An ABC Theatre Presentation* (ABC)
50. **Outstanding Variety or Music Program Art Direction**: Roy Christopher for *56th Annual Academy Awards* (ABC)
51. **Outstanding Series Lighting Direction**: Robert A. Dickinson and C. Frank Olivas for *Solid Gold* (syndicated)
52. **Outstanding Limited Series or Special Art Direction**: William M. Klages for *The 6th Annual Kennedy Center Honors: A Celebration of the Performing Arts* (CBS)
53. **Outstanding Choreography**: Michael Smuin for "A Song for Dead Warriors" on *Dance in America* (PBS)
54. **Outstanding Music Direction**: Ian Fraser, Billy Byers, Chris Boardman, J. Hill and Lenny Stack for *The Screen Actors Guild 50th Anniversary Celebration* (CBS)
55. **Outstanding Series Music Composition**: Bruce Broughton for "The Letter" on *Dallas* (CBS)
56. **Outstanding Limited Series or Special Music Composition**: Bruce Broughton for *The First Olympics—Athens 1896, Part One* (NBC)
57. **Outstanding Music and Lyrics**: Larry Grossman and Buz Kohan for "Gone Too Soon" from *Here's Television Entertainment* (NBC)
58. **Outstanding Limited Series or Special Live and Tape Sound Mixing**: Edward J. Greene and Carroll Pratt for *Anne Murray's Winter Carnival ... From Quebec* (CBS)
59. **Outstanding Series Live and Tape Sound Mixing**: Mark Hanes, Stu Fox, Dean Okrand and Ed Suski for "The Hawaii Show—Sarah's Wedding" on *Real People* (NBC)
60. **Outstanding Series Costume Design**: Bob Mackie and Ret Turner for "Mama's Birthday" on *Mama's Family* (NBC)
61. **Outstanding Limited Series or Special Costume Design**: Julie Weiss for "The Dollmaker" on *An ABC Theatre Presentation* (ABC)
62. **Outstanding Makeup**: Michael Westmore for *Why Me?* (ABC)
63. **Outstanding Hairstyling**: Dino Ganziano for *The Mystic Warrior* (ABC)
64. **Outstanding Individual Achievement in Classical Music/Dance Programming**: Merrill Brockway for "A Song for Dead Warriors" on *Dance in America* (PBS), James Levine for "Centennial Gala, Part Two" on *Live from the Met* (PBS), and Leontyne Price for *In Performance at the White House—An Evening of Spirituals and Gospel Music* (PBS)
65. **Governor's Award**: Bob Hope
66. **Special Award**: David L. Wolper for the ceremonies at the Olympics
67. **Outstanding Achievement in Engineering Development**: Corporate Communications Consultants, Inc. for the 60XL Color Correction System
68. **Outstanding Edited Sports Special**: *Wimbledon '83* (NBC)
69. **Outstanding Sports Associate Directing**: Angelo Bernarducci and Jean MacLean for "Triumph on Mt. Everest" on *The American Sportsman* (ABC)
70. **Outstanding Sports Graphic Designers**: Douglas E. Towey and Bill Feigenbaum for *NBA World Championship Series* (CBS)
71. **Outstanding Sports Special Classification, Journalism**: Michael Marley, Ed Silverman, Howard Cosell, Maury Rubin, Noubar Stone and Rob Beiner for *ABC Sportsbeat* (ABC)
72. **Outstanding Sports Special Classification, Music**: John Tresh for *World University Games* (CBS)
73. **Outstanding Edited Sports Series**: *The American Sportsman* (ABC)
74. **Outstanding Sports Special Classification, Film Editor**: Yale Nelson for *The 79th World Series* (NBC)
75. **Outstanding Sports Special Classification, Writing**: Steve Sabol and Phil Tuckett for *Wake Up the Echoes: The History of Notre Dame Football* (Independent), and George Bell, Jr., for "A Retrospective of William Holden's Africa" on *The American Sportsman* (ABC)
76. **Outstanding Sports Personality, Analyst**: John Madden
77. **Outstanding Sports Engineer-

E Emmy Awards 1983

ing/Technical Supervisors: Walter Pile and John Pumo for *Daytona 500* (CBS)

78. **Outstanding Live Sports Series**: *CBS Sports Presents the National Football League* (CBS)

79. **Outstanding Sports Lighting Director**: Joe Crookham for *NCAA Football on CBS* (CBS)

80. **Outstanding Sports Cinematographers**: Peter Henning and Bill Philbin for *The Iditarod Dog Sled Race* (CBS), and Kurt Diemburger and David Breshears for "The Mt. Everest East Face" on *The American Sportsman* (ABC)

81. **Outstanding Sports Program Special Achievement**: Roone Arledge, Dennis Lewin, Larry Kamm and Peter Lasser for "Great American Bike Race" on *ABC's Wide World of Sports* (ABC), John Wilcox for "Triumph on Mt. Everest" on *The American Sportsman* (ABC), and Robert Carmichael for *Football in America* (PBS)

82. **Outstanding Sports Videotape Editors**: Mike Kostel, Rick Reed, Rich Domich and John Servideo for *NBC Baseball Pre-Game/Major League Baseball: An Inside Look* (NBC), Bob Hickson, George Joanitis and Lito Magpayo for Closing Segment—*NCAA Basketball Championship Game* (CBS), and Sandy Bell, Bob Brown, Anthony Filippi, Bob Siderman, Tom Jimenez, Robert Pieringer, Tom Delilla, Bill Berridge, Donald S. Resch, Jim Murphy, Neil McCaffrey, Tom McCarthy, Herman Lang, Barry Drago, Joe Sokota, Jim McCarthy, Jeff Pollack, Frank McSpedon, George Rothweiler, Ray Christe, George Naeder, George Graffeo, Hans Singer, Sig Meyers and Walt Soucy for *Daytona 500* (CBS)

83. **Outstanding Live Sports Special**: *The 79th World Series* (NBC)

84. **Outstanding Sports Personality, Host**: Dick Enberg

85. **Outstanding International Drama**: Granada Television Limited, United Kingdom for *King Lear*

86. **Outstanding International Documentary**: Swedish Television, Sweden for *The Miracle of Life*

87. **Outstanding International Popular Arts**: British Broadcasting System, United Kingdom for *The Black Adder: The Archbishop*

88. **International Children's Programming**: Canadian Broadcasting Corporation, Canada for *Fraggle Rock*

Index

The awards listed in this book are cross-referenced so the reader can check which artists have won awards from different organizations. A sample listing is:

Streisand, Barbra G64-2, -6, E64-8, G65-6, G66-6, T70-17, G78-3, -5, G81-6

The entry # codes following the artist's name are actually quite simple. "G" indicates a Grammy Award; "T" stands for a Tony Award; "E" refers to an Emmy Award; and "C" indicates an award from the Country Music Association.

The two digits following the letter indicate the year in which the award was made.

Since the numbers following the hyphen indicate the category in which the award was made, simply check the text to find the name of the award category.

In the example shown, Barbra Streisand won Grammy Awards in 1964 for "Album of the Year" (category 2) and "Best Female Solo Vocal" (category 6); also in 1964 she received an Emmy for "Outstanding Achievement of an Actor or Performer in Entertainment" (category 8); in 1965 she received a Grammy for "Best Female Solo Vocal" (category 6); she won a Grammy in 1966 for "Best Female Solo vocal" (category 6); in 1970 she received a Special Tony Award (category 17); in 1978 she received Grammy Awards as both writer of one of the two best songs of the year (category 3) and "Best Contemporary/Pop Female Solo Vocal" (category 5); and, finally, in 1981 she received a Grammy as member of the "Best Contemporary/Pop Vocal Duo" (category 6).

The typeface in the index helps distinguish among entries. Personal names, organizations, and the like appear in regular type; song titles are in quotation marks; titles of television shows appear in italics, and the titles of plays appears in small caps.

A

ABC E58-40, E61-28, E69-65, E70-69, E72-66, E74-89, E76-73, E79-63, E81-58
ABC Afternoon Playbreak E73-88, -91, -98, E74-42, -43, -70
ABC Afterschool Special E72-12, E73-12, E76-83, E77-83, -84, -96, E78-78, E79-67, -88, E80-66, -88, E81-62, -83, -86, -91, -97, -99, E82-73, -88, -97, -102, -106
ABC Friday Night Movie, The E76-27,
ABC Matinee Today E73-42, -43, -44, -107, -109
ABC Monday Night Movie E74-58, -82, E78-87
ABC Movie of the Week E70-38
ABC Movie Special E74-33, -36, -61, -76, -81
ABC News E73-117

Index

ABC News Closeup E73-114, -118
ABC Schoolhouse Rock E79-68
ABC Sportsbeat E83-71
ABC Stage 67 E66-14, -41
ABC Sunday Night Movie, The E71-43
ABC Television Limited (Middlesex, Great Britain) E67-56
ABC Theatre E73-25, -29, -63, -68, -69, E74-26, -27, -51, -67, -73, -79, -82, E75-6, -39, -53, -61, -66, -77, E76-7, -29, -38, -59, -65, -68, -71, E83-2, -11, -19, -29, -33, -35, -36, -40, -49, -61
ABC Weekend Special E79-71, -88
ABC Wide World of Entertainment E73-76
ABC Wide World of Sports E65-33, E66-12, E67-15, -27, E69-19, E70-20, E71-21, E72-13, E73-17, -78, E75-22, -48, E80-99, E83-81
ABC Wide World of Sports 20th Anniversary Show E80-96
ABC World News Tonight E82-119
ADO Digital Effects Unit E82-65
AFC Championship, The E71-57
AFC Championship Football E77-104
APA – Phoenix Theatre T68-19
A. T. & T. Science Series E56-23
"Abbey Road" G70-42
Abbott, George T55-14, T56-14, T60-14, -15, T63-17
Abbott, L.B. E64-29, E65-40, E66-35, E70-60
A-Bomb Coverage E55-12
Abrahams, Doris Cole T75-1
Abravanel, Maurice T50-14
Abroms, Edward R. E69-36, E71-36
A.C. Philips Gloelampenfabrieken E66-40
Academy of St. Martin-in-the-Fields G82-52
Aceti, Joe E75-64
Acevedo, Del E82-48
Ackerman, Andy E80-32
Ackerman, Ron E75-64, E79-112
Acona, Edward E64-31
ACT, THE T78-10
Actor E77-64
Actors' Equity Association T74-19
Actors' Equity Library Theatre, New York T77-20
Actors' Fund of America T73-19, T82-20
Actors Theatre of Louisville T80-20
Acts of Love and Other Comedies E72-62
Adams, Don E66-17, E67-23, E68-6
Adams, Edith T57-12
Adams, Jerry E81-46, E82-40
Adams, Lee T61-9, T70-7
Adams, Mike E80-99

Adams Chronicles, The E75-31, -62, -72, -73
Adderley, Cannonball, Quintet G68-7
Addie and the King of Hearts E75-98
Addison, John G64-22
Adelman, Jerry E75-81
Adler, Richard T55-15, T56-15
Adrian, Louis T54-17
"Adventures in Jazz" G63-8
Adversaries, The E73-112
Advocates, The E72-16
Affair to Forget, An E74-56
Africa E67-6
"African Waltz" G62-9, -10
After Hours: Singin', Swingin' & All That Jazz E77-97
AFTER THE FALL T64-5
"After the Fire Is Gone" G72-16
"After the Love Has Gone" G80-25, -28
"Afternoon Delight" G77-9
"Against the Wind" G81-13, -54
"Age to Age" G83-38
"Ageless Medley" G84-37
Agent Orange: The Human Harvest E78-93
Ages of Man E65-7
"Ages of Man" (Readings from Shakespeare) G80-32
Aghayan, Ray E66-31
AGNES OF GOD T82-5
Agnew Resignation, The E73-111
Agopian, Ilie E82-110
Agutter, Jenny E71-15
Ahern, Lloyd E71-45
Aiello, Danny E80-88
AIN'T MISBEHAVIN' T78-7, -11, -15, G79-35, E81-57
"Ain't No Sunshine" G72-18
"Ain't Nobody" G84-31
"Ain't Nothing Like the Real Thing" G75-20
"Ain't That Beautiful Singing?" G70-27
Air Force Surgeon E82-124
Air War, The E71-29
"Airport Love Theme" G71-30
Airwolf E83-32
"AJA" G78-47
"Al No Corrida" G82-9
Alabama C81-7, -9, C82-1, -7, -9, C83-1, -3, -7, G83-26, G84-26
"Alabama" G84-26
"Alabama Jubilee" G83-27
Alan Young Show, The E50-13
Alaska: Story of a Dream E82-135, -142
Albee, Edward T63-1, G64-17
"Albeniz" G75-37
Alberghetti, Anna Maria T62-12

Index

Albertson, Chris G71-42
Albertson, Jack T65-3, E74-32, E75-24
Alch, George E79-88
Alcoa-Goodyear Theatre E58-2, -26, -30
Alda, Alan E73-19, -27, E76-28, E78-28, E81-7
Alda, Robert T51-10
Aldredge, Theoni V. T77-18, T80-18, T84-18
Aldredge, Tom E77-96
Alexander, Brett E82-130
Alexander, James G66-44
Alexander, Jane T69-5, E80-13
Alexander, Larry G76-43
"Alfie" G68-27
Alfred Hitchcock Presents E55-30, E56-19, E57-22
Alice at the Palace E81-55
Alice Cooper—The Nightmare E75-63
Alice Through the Looking Glass E66-31
Alkins, Jim E80-99
"All Fly Home" G79-14
"All I Need Is You" G82-32
"All in Good Time" G84-17
All in the Family E70-1, -6, -10, E71-1, -9, -10, -18, -33, -42, -61, E72-1, -61, E73-31, E76-8, E77-1, -13, -14, -16, -33, -38, E78-13, -14
All My Children E72-29, E79-77, -78, -89, -90, E80-90, -91, E81-74, -92, E82-85, -86, -104, -105
ALL MY SONS T47-4
"All 'n All" G79-24
All Quiet on the Western Front E79-50
ALL THE WAY HOME T61-5
Allardice, James E54-23
Allen, Corey E83-25
Allen, Debbie E81-54, E82-63
Allen, J. E79-113
Allen, Johnny G72-7
Allen, Lewis T77-7
Allen, Rae T71-5
Allen, Rebecca E82-141
Allen, Steve G64-9
Allen, Vera T48-12
Allers, Franz T57-15, T61-16
"Alley Cat" G63-18
Allison, John E80-53
Almeida, Laurindo G61-29, -34, G62-33, -34, G65-8
Almoslino, Edith E77-65
"Almost Persuaded" G67-10, -11, -13
"Alone" G71-11
"Alone at Last" G73-13
Alone in a Crowd E81-35
Along Route 30 E82-136

Alpert, Herb G66-1, -10, -24, G67-9, -25, G80-8
Alpert, Jon E80-94
Alphabet Conspiracy E58-33
"Alright Again" G83-33
"Also Sprach Zarathustra" G74-8
Alter, Paul E81-82
Altieri, Michael E79-112
Altman, Herb E74-59
Alton, Robert T52-13
Altschuler, Ernest G61-40
"Alvin's Harmonica" G60-29
"Always on My Mind" C82-2, -3, -4, G83-3, -23, -25, C83-4
AMADEUS T81-1, -2, -6, -16, -17
"Amazing Grace" G73-28, G82-35
Amazing Howard Hughes, The E77-48
Amazing Rhythm Aces G77-19
Ambassador, The E74-63, -80, -85
Amber Waves E79-21
Ambrico, Robert E79-89, E81-92, E82-105
Ambrosian Opera Chorus G69-34
Ambrosini, Ed E78-90, E80-99
America G73-47
America E72-5, -64, -71
America Remembers John F. Kennedy E83-9
America Salutes Richard Rodgers: The Sound of His Music E76-31, -55, -60, -63, -69
"America the Beautiful" G70-43
American Ballet Theatre E77-9
American Ballet Theatre: Swan Lake E76-35
American Bandstand E81-81, E82-80
American Bandstand's 30th Anniversary Special E81-30
American Bandstand's 25th Anniversary E76-41
American Conservatory Theatre T79-19
American Dream, American Nightmare E80-94
American Film Institute Salute to James Cagney, The E74-62, -87
American Film Institute Salute to Lillian Gish E83-31
American Playhouse E81-53, E83-4, -24
American Shakespeare Festival T57-22
American Sportsman E78-88, E80-98, -99, E82-114, E83-69, -73, -75, -80, -81
American Symphony Orchestra G66-32
American Telephone and Telegraph Company E62-30
American White Paper: United States

Index

Foreign Policy E65-27
American Woman: Portraits of Courage, The E76-84
America's Nerve Gas Arsenal E73-112
Among the Paths to Eden E67-18
Ampex E56-29, E59-24, E66-39, E69-64, E78-57, E82-65
Amy Prentiss E74-25
"Anatomy of a Murder" G60-13, -19, -20
Ancell, Tom E70-55, E78-53, E79-92
And David Wept E71-69
"And His Mother Called Him Bill" G69-12
"And I Am Telling You I'm Not Going" G83-29
AND MISS REARDON DRINKS A LITTLE T71-5
Anderson, Barbara E67-22
Anderson, Bryan E79-39
Anderson, Dayton E80-90
Anderson, Gary E73-64, -65, E74-60, E76-41
Anderson, John C83-2, -11
Anderson, Judith T48-3, E54-18, E60-11
Anderson, Lynn C71-5, G71-14
Anderson, Melissa Sue E79-88
Anderson, Sheri E75-79
Andersonville Trial, The E70-8, -48, -55
Anderton, Piers E62-9
"Andre Previn Plays Harold Arlen" G62-7
Andrews, Julie G65-17
Andrews, William E74-61, E75-65
Andy Griffith Show, The E60-13, E61-13, E62-16, E65-16, E66-19, -20
Andy Williams Show, The E62-2, E65-2, E66-2
Angel, James E72-48, E74-73
ANGEL IN THE WINGS T48-6, -7
Angell, David E83-38
Angelo, Bob E78-90, E79-110
Angelos, Bill E72-63
Animal Talk E79-71
Animals, Animals, Animals E77-81
Anna Karenina E77-71
Anne Murray's Winter Carnival ... From Quebec E83-58
ANNE OF THE THOUSAND DAYS T49-2, -15
ANNIE T77-7, -10, -12, -13, -14, -16, -18, G78-35
Annie, the Women in the Life of a Man E69-3, -51
Annual Thanksgiving Turkey Day Raffle, The E79-91
ANOTHER PART OF THE FOREST T47-3, -7
Another World E74-69, E75-9, E77-88,
E78-70, E79-75, E80-75
Anouilh, Jean T61-6
"Anselma" G84-47
Anton, Bob E78-84
Antonini, Alfredo E71-69
ANTONY AND CLEOPATRA T48-3
Antoon, A.J. T73-6
Any Old Port in a Storm E73-73
ANY WEDNESDAY T64-4
Anyplace But Here—CBS Reports E79-96, -97, -98, -100
Apollo: A Journey to the Moon E69-27
Apollo Color Television E69-63
Apollo VII, VIII, IX and X Astronauts E68-44
Apollo X, XI and XII E69-27
Appalachian Autumn E69-60
APPLAUSE T70-7, -10, -12, -13
APPLE TREE, THE T67-10
Aquarius: Hello Dali! E74-18
"Aquarius/Let the Sunshine In" G70-1, -6
Archers, The G81-36
Ardolino, Emile E83-47
ARENA STAGE, THE T76-19
"Aren't You Glad You're You?" G78-37
Arkin, Alan T63-3
Arlberg Kandahar Downhill from St. Anton, The E80-100
Arledge, Roone E81-106, E83-81
Armbruster, Robert E79-113
Armchair Theatre E67-56
Armentani, Andrew E80-99
Armistead, Horace T48-10
Armstrong, Charles E74-83
Armstrong, Del E72-51, E75-92
Armstrong, Louis G65-5
Armstrong, Will Steven T62-20
Arnold, Eddy C67-1
Arnold, Robert G62-37
Arnowitz, Joel E80-99
Aronson, Boris T51-19, T67-15, T69-15, T71-16, T72-16, T76-16
Arson for Profit—Parts I and II E80-93
Art Carney Special E59-3
Art Linkletter's House Party E54-14
"Art of Courtly Love, The" G77-38
"Art of the Prima Donna" G62-29
Arthur, Beatrice T66-11, E76-9
Arthur, Brooks G76-43
Arthur Rubinstein E69-31
"Arturo Toscanini, The Greatest Recordings of" G84-62
AS THE GIRLS DO T49-18
Ash, Ingram T71-21
Ashcroft, Ronald E74-61
Asher, Peter G78-50

Index

Asher, William E65-19
Ashkenazy, Vladimir G74-36, G79-40, G82-47
Ashley, Elizabeth T62-5
Ask NBC News E79-68
Asleep at the Wheel G79-20
Asman, John B. E82-59, E83-34
Asner, Edward E70-17, E71-16, E74-28, E75-32, E76-16, E77-18, E79-15
Assignment: The Young Greats E68-45
Astaire, Fred E58-22, E60-12, E77-32
Astaire Time E60-2, -12
Astin, Patty Duke (Also see Patty Duke) E76-25, E79-22
"Astonishing, Outrageous, Amazing, Incredible, Unbelievable, Different World of Gary S. Paxton, The" G77-28
"At Fargo, 1940 Live" G80-16
"At Seventeen" G76-5
"At the Vanguard" G84-16
Atchison, Edward R. E78-66
Atha, Steven E80-88
Atkins, Chet C67-9, C68-9, G68-28, C69-9, G71-17, G72-17, G75-18, G76-18, G77-20, C81-10, C82-10, G82-27, C83-10, C84-10
"Atkins–Travis Travelling Show, The" G75-18
Atkinson, Brooks T62-23
Atkinson, Les E83-43
Attica E79-26
Auberjonois, Rene T70-9
Aubort, Marc J. G84-64
AUNTIE MAME T57-5, -19
Aurbach, Arnold E55-22
Australia Show, The E73-49
Autobiography of Miss Jane Pittman, The E73-6, -26, -30, -52, -81, -94, -106, -108, -110
Automatic Scan Tracking E78-57
AUTUMN GARDEN, THE T51-21
Avakian, George G61-40
Avian, Bob T76-14, T79-14
Axelrod, David E79-88
Ayers, Lemuel T49-14, -16
Aykroyd, Dan E76-52
Azenberg, Emanuel T78-7, T84-1
Azzari, Thomas E. E76-56, E79-86

B

BBC Symphony G73-39
"BBC Tribute to John Kennedy" G65-19
Babboons of Gombe, The E73-67, -70

Babcock, Barbara E80-19
Babe E75-29, -85
"Baby Elephant Walk" G63-22
Bacall, Lauren T70-10, T81-10
"Bach" G62-32, G63-31, G64-26, G70-37, -41, G76-38, G78-44, G83-46, -50
Bach Choir G64-33
Bachrach, Burt G68-27, G70-30, -31
"Back Home Again" C75-4
Backer, Brian T81-3
Backstage at the White House E78-50
Bacon, Bill E82-135
BAD SEED, THE T55-4
Baer, Art E71-62
Bagdasarian, Ross (David Seville) G59-9, -10, G61-14
Bah, Humbug E80-32
Bailey, Anne Howard E71-63
Bailey, Frank E75-68
Bailey, Joseph A. E73-125, E79-88
Bailey, Pearl T68-19
Bain, Barbara E66-16, E67-20, E68-9
Bain, Bill E74-47
Baird, Gordon E70-55
Baker, Blanche E77-25
Baker, Herbert E70-50
Baker, Janet G76-40, G78-44
Baker, Lenny T77-9
Baker, Rick E73-108
BAKER STREET T65-19
Balanchine IV – Dance in America E78-9
Balatsch, Norbert G81-51
Balden, James E72-48, E73-76, E74-73
Balderson, Walter E76-39
Baldour, Charles E79-113
Baldwin, Ronald E73-126, E79-88
Balet, Jan G65-43
Ball, Lucille E52-2, E55-5, E66-18, E67-24, E80-40
Ballard, Lucinda T47-7, T62-21
Ballas, James E74-61
Ballerina E73-119
Ballet Shoes, Parts I and II E76-34
BALLROOM T79-14
Balsam, Martin T68-2
Balzer, George E58-31, E59-15
Bamattre, Alex E69-42
Bancroft, Anne T58-5, T60-4
"Band on the Run" G75-6, -42
Bandy, Moe C80-8
Bangert, Charles E82-28
Banner, Bob E57-21
"Baptism of Jesse Taylor, The" G75-27
Baranski, Christine T84-5
Barbara's Crisis E81-15

Index 138

Barbara Mandrell and the Mandrell Sisters E81-29
Barbara Stanwyck Show, The E60-9
Barbara Walters Specials, The E82-8, -125
Barber, Samuel G65-37
"Barber" G70-40
Barber of Seville, The E64-33, E76-66
Barbieri, Gato G74-9
Barbra Streisand: A Happening in Central Park E68-39
Barbra Streisand Album, The G64-2, -6, -38
Barbra Streisand ... and Other Musical Instruments E73-50, -59, -96, -97, -103
Bare, Bobby G64-11
Barefoot in Athens E66-13
BAREFOOT IN THE PARK T64-7
Barenboim, Daniel G77-36, -39, G83-49
Baretta E74-22, E75-70
Barker, Bob E81-76
Barker, Don E78-39
Barnathan, Julius E79-113
Barnes, Billy E71-57
Barnes, Paul E56-27, E57-27
Barnett, Roy A. E78-48
Barney Miller E78-24, E79-28, E81-3
BARNUM T80-8, -16, -18
Barons, Ray E79-36
"Baroque Guitar" G67-34
Barr, Richard T63-7, T79-7
Barrault, Jean-Louis T57-22
Barreto, Cathy E80-99
Barron, Jeffrey E81-34
Barrows, Mercer E81-90
Barry, John G70-32
Barry Manilow Special, The E76-6
Bart, Lionel T63-14
Bartholomew, Brian E72-60, E73-103, E76-72
Bartlett, Des E72-46
Bartlett, Jen E72-46
"Bartok" G61-27, G62-31, G64-27, G66-33, -44, G74-33, -34, -41, G80-46
Bartz, Geof E79-46
Baryshnikov, Mikhail E78-31
Baryshnikov E79-94
Baryshnikov at the White House E78-31
Baseball Bunch, The E80-99, -100
Baseball World of Joe Garagiola, The E74-59
Basehart, Richard E64-12
BASIC TRAINING OF PAVLO HUMMEL, THE T77-2
Basie, Count G59-13, -14, G61-17, G64-15, G77-14, G78-13, G81-17, G83-17

"Basie" G59-13, -14
"Basie and Zoot" G77-14
Basil, Peter E80-50
Basile, Ben E74-83
Basile, Leonard G. E78-90
Bassman, Don E75-66
Bates, Alan T73-2
"Batman" G67-24
Battle, Hinton T81-9, T84-8
Battle for South Africa – CBS Reports E79-96
"Battle Hymn of the Republic" G60-21
"Battle of Kookamonga" G60-12
"Battle of New Orleans, The" G60-3, -8
Battlestar Gallactica E78-43, -53
Baugh, Michael E78-92, E79-88
Bavier, Frances E66-20
Bay, Howard T60-20, T66-15
Bay of Pigs E63-9
Bayreuth Festival Orchestra G83-52
"Be Bop Medley" G84-14
Beacon Hill E75-88
Beals, Carleton G65-42
Bear, Jack E72-50
Beard, Chris E67-35
"Beat It" G84-1, -12
Beatles, The (also individual names: Lennon, McCartney, Harrison, Starr) G65-27, -45, G68-2, -36
Beaton, Cecil T55-20, T57-20, T60-22, T70-16
Beatts, Anne E75-75, E76-52
Beatty, John Lee T80-16
Beatty, Robert E71-62, E72-63, E73-83, E74-65, E77-40
"Beautiful Isle of Somewhere" G69-24
Beck, Mrs. Martin T58-22
BECKET T61-1, -6, -8, -20, -21, -23
Bedford, Brian T71-2
BEDROOM FARCE T79-3, -5
Bee Gees G78-6, -51, G79-2, -6, -9, -50
Beecham, Sir Thomas G61-33
"Beethoven" G59-25, G60-23, -25, G62-28, G65-30, -33, G66-34, G71-34, G74-36, G76-34, G77-36, -39, G78-42, G79-39, -40, -45, G84-54
Beethoven's Birthday: A Celebration in Vienna with Leonard Bernstein E71-5
Beetley, Samuel E. E73-60, E75-60
"Before the Next Teardrop Falls" C75-2
Begley, Ed T56-3
"Behind Closed Doors" C73-2, -3, -4, G74-14, -16
"Behind My Camel" G82-10
Behind the Lines E73-112
Beiner, Rob E80-99, E83-71

Index

"Being With You" G84-8
Beisman, Paul T48-12
Bel Geddes, Barbara E79-14
Belafonte, Harry T54-11, E59-11, G61-20, G66-20
"Belafonte at Carnegie Hall" G60-30
Belafonte Folk Singers G62-19
"Belafonte Folk Singers at Home and Abroad" G62-19
Belkin, Gary E69-51, E73-83, E74-65
Bell, George, Jr. E83-75
Bell, Sandy E78-90, E80-99
Bell, Sanford E81-93
Bell, Thom G75-46
Bell, William E73-120
Bell, William J. E75-79
Bell System Family Theatre E71-4, -44, -52, -66, E72-41, -56
Bell Telephone Hour E60-22, E63-10, E67-40, E68-26
Bell Telephone Jubilee E76-64
Bell Telephone Science Series, The E57-24
Bell Telephone Special E58-33
Bellairs, Robert E82-105
Bellamy, Ralph T58-2
"Bellavia" G77-10
BELLE OF AMHERST T77-4, G78-27
BELLS ARE RINGING T57-10, -11
Bellwood, Peter E69-51
Belushi, John E76-52
Ben Casey E62-14, -17
Benatar, Pat G81-11, G82-11, G83-11, G84-11
Beneath the Frozen World E73-122, -124
Benjamin Franklin E74-63, -75, -80, -85
Bennett, Alan T63-22
Bennett, Jack E71-57, E74-83, E78-90
Bennett, Michael T72-14, -15, T74-14, T76-14, T76-14, -15, T79-14, T82-14
Bennett, Mike E82-43, -109
Bennett, Robert Russell T57-22, G60-28, E62-23
Bennett, Tony G63-1, -5
Bennewitz, Rick E70-55
Bennington, Bill E68-17
Benny, Jack E57-15, E58-13
Benson, George G77-1, -8, -25, G79-23, G81-19, -29, -31, -43, G84-8
Bent Fabric G68-18
Bentley, Larry E70-55
Berg, Gertrude E50-3, T59-4
Berg, John G64-38, G68-44, G69-38, G77-46
"Berg" G65-29, G66-36, G68-4, -41, G81-44, -47, -50, -52
Bergen, Polly E57-12

Berger, Fred W. E75-59
Berger, Harvey E78-92
Berger, Ralph E54-29, E59-20
Bergman, Alan G75-3, -30, E76-62
Bergman, Ingrid T47-2, E59-10, E81-5
Bergman, Marilyn G75-3, -30, E76-62
Berio, Luciano G70-38
"Berio" G70-38
Benjamin Franklin E74-4
Berle, Milton E49-2, E78-55
Berlin, Irving T63-22
Berlin Philharmonic G70-39, G79-39
Berlin Wall E65-45
Berlind, Roger S. T81-1, T82-7, T84-1
"Berlioz" G65-35, G71-32, -37, G72-39, -40, G73-39, G75-33, -34, -40, -41, G83-53
Berman, Henry E64-23
Berman, Shelly G60-11
Bernadette E58-35
Bernard, Alan E76-44
Bernarducci, Angelo E79-108, E80-99, E83-69
Bernhardt, Melvin T78-6
Bernstein, Aline T50-18
Bernstein, Elmer E63-24
Bernstein, Leonard T53-15, -16, E56-28, E57-28, E59-21, G62-13, -17, G63-13, -28, E64-5, G64-13, G65-4, G68-4, -40, T69-16, G74-38, G76-40, G78-38
Bernstein, Stu E76-64, E78-47
"Bernstein: Symphony #3" G65-4
Bernstein and the New York Philharmonic E75-5
"Bernstein Conducts for Young People" G64-13
Berridge, Bill E83-82
Berry, Loren E72-38
"Best Is Yet to Come, The" G84-18
BEST LITTLE WHOREHOUSE IN TEXAS T79-9, -11
BEST MAN, THE T60-2
"Best of My Love" G78-24
"Best of the Stan Freberg Show, The" G59-17
BetMar T83-1
Bette Davis E80-93
"Bette Davis Eyes" G82-1, -3
Bette Midler—Ole Red Hair Is Back E77-6, -58
Betts, Harry G78-7
"Between the Lines" G76-43
Betz, Carl E68-8
Beverly, Trazana T77-5
Bewitched E65-17, -19, E67-26
Beymer, John E79-88

Index

BEYOND THE FRINGE T63-21
Bhargava, Grish E75-62
Bialek, Robert G61-21
Bicentennial Minutes E75-8
"Bicentennial Nigger" G77-26
Big Apple Birthday E77-96
"Big Bad John" G62-11
Big Bird in China E82-5
Big Blue Marble E75-12, E78-59, -80, -92, E79-88, E80-88, E81-88, -89
Big Deal at Gothenburg E66-44
Big Event, The E76-23, -26, -39, -43, -47, -53, -54, -62
BIG FISH, LITTLE FISH T61-3, -7
Big Henry and the Polka Dot Kid E76-82
"Big Sandy/Little Britches" G80-24
Big Show with Tony Randall and Herve Villechaize, The E79-62
Big Valley E65-11
Biggs, E. Power G69-31, -33
Bigley, Isabel T51-13
Bike Racing E80-88
Bill E81-26, -33
Bill Cosby Special E68-3
"Bill Cosby Talks to Kids About Drugs" G72-31
"Bill Evans Album, The" G72-10, -12
"Bill Evans at the Montreux Jazz Festival" G69-11
Bill Moyers Journal E73-112, -116, -117, E80-94
"Billie Holliday (Giants of Jazz)" G80-55
"Billie Jean" G84-28, -30
Billson, Bruce E67-37
"Billy May's Big Fat Brass" G59-11
"Bing Crosby: A Legendary Performer" G78-49
"Bing Crosby Collection: Vols. I and II, A" G79-49
Bionic Woman, The E76-13
Bird, Henry E70-44
"Bird" G74-11
"Birdland" G81-9, -21
Biroc, Joseph E71-46, E82-33
BIRTHDAY PARTY, THE T68-3
Bishop, Carole T76-11
Bissell, James D. E79-54
Bissell, Richard T55-14
"Bitches Brew" G71-12
"Bizet" G65-34, G74-38
Bjoerling, Jussi G60-26
"Bjoerling in Opera" G60-26
Black, Cathy E82-139
Black, Jack E80-99
Black Adder: The Archbishop, The E83-87
Black Friday E55-31

Black History: Lost, Stolen or Strayed E68-23
Black Journal E69-23
"Black Moses" G73-8
Black View of South Africa, A E70-28
Blacklist E63-13, -19
Blackmer, Sidney T50-2
Blackwood Brothers G67-12, G68-23, G70-28, G73-27, G74-27, G80-34, G81-35, G83-37
Blackwood, James G82-36
Blair, Richard E79-57
Blake, Peter G68-43
Blake, Robert E74-22
Blalack, Robert E83-44
Blalock, Cheryl E80-86
Blane, Rick E80-99
Blasucci, Dick E81-34, E82-38
Blechman, Corey E81-33
Blechman, R.O. E83-46
Bleckner, Jeff E82-24, E83-24
BLESS YOU ALL T51-20
Blewitt, David E65-24
Bley, Hy E79-90
Blinn, William E71-60, E76-51
Blister, Barry E55-22
Block, Ivan T84-1
Blocker, Joel E72-70
"Blood on the Tracks" G76-45
Blood, Sweat & Tears G70-2, -9
"Blood, Sweat & Tears" G70-2
Bloomgarden, Kermit T49-7, T53-8, T56-8, T58-18, T75-1
"Blowin' in the Wind" G64-19, -25
Blue Collar Trap, The E72-65
"Blue Eyes Crying in the Rain" G76-16
"Blue Kentucky Girl" G80-21
Blue Knight, The E73-23, -51, -58, -60
Blue Print for Murder E71-45
"Blue Rondo a la Turk" G82-19
"Blues and Jazz" G84-33
"Blues and the Beat" G61-9
Blues for a Red Planet E80-63
"Blues in the Street" G67-20
Blumenthal, M. Pam E78-32, E79-59, E80-30
Blummel, Bill E79-113
Blunden, Bill E79-50
Blyden, Larry T72-9
Blye, Allan E68-34
Boardman, Chris E80-37, E83-54
Boat People—CBS Reports, The E79-93, -97
Bob Cummings Show, The E57-14, E58-18
"Bob Dylan's Greatest Hits" G68-44

Bob Hope Presents the Chrysler Theatre E63-14, -16, -18, E65-8, -9, -18
Bob Newhart Show E61-3
Bochco, Steven E80-25, E81-32
Bock, Jerry T60-16, G64-21, T65-15
Boddicker, Michael G84-43
Body Human, The E77-8, E79-5, -34, E80-7, -88, E81-84, E82-10, -28, -39
Boettscher, George E72-40, E75-64
Boetz, Bill E82-109
Bogert, Paul E64-20, E67-38, E69-33, E77-33
Bogert, Vincent E55-22
Boheme, La, Live from the Met E81-23
Bohm, Karl G66-36
Bold Ones—The Lawyers, The E71-31, -65
Bold Ones—The Senator, The E70-34, -37, -46
Bolger, Ray T49-10
Bologna, Joseph E72-62
Bolt, Robert T62-6
Bonanza E64-31, E65-25, E70-65
Bond, Peter E81-38
Bond, Sheila T53-13
Bondi, Beulah E76-19
Bonfils, Helen T71-7
Boni, John E72-11
Bonifazio, Michael E75-64
Bonniere, Claude E81-97
Bonsignori, Mili E79-94
"Boogie on Reggae Woman" G75-22
"Boogie Wonderland" G80-29
Boone, Debby G78-51, G81-34
Booth, Shirley T49-5, T50-3, T53-4, E61-9, E62-12
Boothe, Powers E79-23
Borodin, Alexander T54-15
Borrowers, The E73-101
BORSTAL BOY T70-1
Bosley, Tom T60-11
Boston Goes to China—CBS Reports, The E79-94, -97, -99, -102
Boston Symphony Chamber Players G67-33
Boston Symphony Orchestra G60-22, G62-27, -35, G64-27, -31, G65-29, G66-34, G67-32, G81-47
Bostwick, Barry T77-8
"Both Sides Now" G69-23
Botkin, Perry, Jr. G78-7
Botnick, Bruce G73-25
Bottone, Bruce E81-48, E83-43
Boulez, Pierre G68-4, -41, G69-30, G70-35, G71-33, -39, G74-33, -34, G76-35, G79-46, G81-44, -50, G83-52
Bourgeois, Gary E80-63

Bowen, Jerry E82-128
Bowling, Roger C77-4
Bowman, Barbara E75-64, E79-112
Bowman, Don C67-10
"Boy from New York City" G82-6
Boy in the Plastic Bubble, The E76-27
"Boy Named Sue, A" C69-2, G70-14, -16
Boyajian, Aram E64-14
Boyer, Charles T52-17
"Boys in the Trees" G79-48
Bracken's World E69-35
Brackett, Eddie G67-42
Braddock, Bobby C80-4, C81-4
Bradford, John E74-66
Bradley, Ed E82-126, -130
Bradley, Gary E80-99
Brady, Bob E82-140
Brady, Phil E71-29
Brady, Ray E82-128
Bragg, George G69-33
Bragg, Jim E78-90
"Brahms" G61-28, G71-35, G73-37, -40, G75-35, G79-38, G80-43, -44, -50, G81-47, G83-48, G84-52
Bramble, Mark T81-7
Brand, Curt E75-64
Brand New Life, A E72-21
Brando, Marlon E78-19
Brandow, Janice D. E78-51
Brantley, Al E74-83
Braver, Rita E82-128
"Break It Gently" G83-24
Breakdown E55-30
"Breakfast at Tiffany's" G62-16, -22
"Breakfast in America" G80-52, -53
"Breakin' Away" G82-4
Breakout E65-46
Breakthrough E79-38
Bream, Julian G64-28, G67-34, G72-35, G73-36
Breckman, Andy E79-88
Breese, Gerry E72-38
"Breezin'" G77-8, -45
Brennan, Eileen E80-16
Brenner, Alfred E58-30
Breshears, David E83-80
Breshears, William H., Sr. E81-30
Breslow, Mark E82-100
Brewster, Allen E76-39
Brian's Song E71-8, -14, -37, -46, -60, G73-32
Bricusse, Leslie G63-3
Brideshead Revisited E81-6
"Bridge Over Troubled Water" G71-1, -2, -3, -9, -10, -40, G72-19
Bridgewater, Dee Dee T75-11

Index 142

BRIGADOON T47-6, E66-5, -25, -33, -37, -38
BRIGHTON BEACH MEMORIES T83-3, -6
"Brimstone & Treacle" G84-10
Brioso, Gerri E82-111
Brisson, Frederick T55-18, T56-18
British Broadcasting Corporation E67-50, E73-130, -132, E74-18, -19, E80-105, E83-87
Brittan, Robert T74-7, G75-31
Britten, Benjamin G64-4, -33, -34
"Britten" G63-13, G64-4, -33, -34, G65-36, -38, -43, G80-49
Brock, Howard E83-30
Brock, Norris E82-135
Brockway, Merrill E83-64
Broderick, Matthew T83-3
"Broken Lady" G77-16
Brolin, James E69-14
Bronstein, Don G65-41
Brook, Peter T66-6, T71-6
Brooks, Donald E81-50
Brooks, James L. E70-49, E76-50
Brooks, Joe G78-3
Brooks, Mel E66-28
Brooks, Michael G79-49, G80-55, G82-57
Brooks, Ron E73-76, E74-73
Brosten, Harve E77-38
Brothers Johnson G78-25
Broughton, Brock E73-105
Broughton, Bruce E80-56, E82-52, E83-55, -56
Brown, Barry T84-7
Brown, Bob E78-90, E80-99
Brown, Clarence Gatemouth G83-33
Brown, Edward R. E75-71
Brown, Elaine Meryl E81-87
Brown, Fred E72-41
Brown, Gregory E75-81
Brown, James G66-16
Brown, Jim Ed C77-8
Brown, Joe E. T48-12
Brown, L. Slade T61-18
Brown, Les E82-111
Brown, Pamela E61-14
Brown, Ray G64-9
Brown, Robert E80-99
Brown, Russ T56-11
Brown, William F. T75-7
Brownell, Gene G72-42
Brownell, William F. E77-61
Browning, David E82-128
Browning, Kirk E79-87
Bruckner, Bob E80-53
"Bruckner" G81-45
Brunton, Greg E77-59

Bryan, Ron E77-58
Bryant, Bruce E82-56
Brynner, Yul T52-9
Brysac, Sharon Blair E82-133
"Bubbling Brown Sugar" G77-33
Bucci, Gerry E73-76, E79-113
Buck Rogers E80-56
Buckaroos, The C67-8, C68-8
Buckley, Betty T83-11
Bude, Edward E82-139
Buffington, Dick E80-99
Bunin, Elinor E74-84
Bunker, The E68-37, E80-12
Bunkers and the Swingers, The E72-61
"Bunny Berrigan (Giants of Jazz)" G83-57
Burgess, Russell G72-39
Burghoff, Gary E76-10
Burling, Jerry E76-39
Burman, Tom E73-122
Burmen, Ellis E72-51
Burnett, Carol T69-16, E61-12, E62-15
Burnham, Charlie E75-64
Burns, Allan E67-34, E70-49, E76-50
Burns, Bruce E79-35
Burns, David T58-11, T63-10, E70-15
Burns, Michael T62-22
Burns, Ralph E79-47
Burns, Stan E71-62
Burr, Raymond E58-15, E60-8
Burrow, Milton C. E74-61, E76-43
Burrow, Richard E74-61
Burrows, Abe T51-14, T62-14, -15
Burrows, James E79-24, E82-25
Burstyn, Ellen T75-4
Burtin, Claudio Zeitlin E80-90
Burton, Gary G73-13, G80-15, G82-16
Burton, Jay E78-83
Burton, Richard T61-10, G76-33
Burton, Thomas E80-90
Burton, Warren E79-77
Burum, Steve E80-53
Bury, John T81-16, -17
Bush, Henry G72-41
Bussan, Mark E78-50
"Busted" G64-12
"But Not for Me" G60-5
But What About the Children—CBS Reports E79-94
"Butch Cassidy and the Sundance Kid" G70-30
Butler, Larry G76-14, G80-56
Butler, Robert E73-51, -58, E80-23
Butler, William E76-47, E83-40
BUTLEY T73-2
Buttelman, Ernie E72-48, E74-73, E79-113

Index

BUTTERFLIES ARE FREE T70-5
Button, Dick E80-103
"Button Down Mind" G61-2, -40
"Button Down Mind Strikes Back" G61-15
By the Dawn's Early Light E74-34
"By the Time I Get to Phoenix" G68-5, -33, G69-2
BYE, BYE BIRDIE T61-9, -11, -14, -15, -17, -18
"Bye Bye Blackbird" G82-20
Byers, Billy E79-47, E80-37, E83-54
Byers, Harold E72-40
Bynum, Hal C77-4

C

CBS E56-29, E58-40, E61-28, E65-44, E68-45, E69-65, E70-29, -69, E72-73, E74-86, E82-66
CBS Afternoon Playhouse E80-88, E82-107, -108
CBS Evening News with Dan Rather E82-120, -128, -133, -136, -139
CBS Evening News with Walter Cronkite E67-31, E68-21, E69-26, E70-31, -58, E71-29, E72-47, -69, -70, E73-111, -121, -122
CBS Festival of Lively Arts for Young People E74-13, E75-14, E77-96, E78-92, E79-70, E80-68, E81-98
CBS Friday Night Movies E69-54, E71-32
CBS Golf Classic E65-32
CBS Library E79-71, -88
CBS News Hour E68-23, -24, -25, -27, -28, -29, E69-24, -25, -31
CBS News Special Report: The Senate and the Watergate Affair E73-114
CBS News Special: Solzhenitsyn E73-116
CBS Playhouse E67-17, -33, -38, -44, E68-32, -33, -36, E69-33, -57, -60, E73-99, -102, -104
CBS Reports E67-30, E68-18, E72-65, E73-115, E82-121
CBS Sports Programs, Closing Logo E78-90
CBS Thursday Night Movies, The E72-31, -52
CBS Video Enterprises T82-19
CBW: The Secrets of Secrecy E68-30
Caballe, Montserrat G69-35
CABARET T67-7, -9, -11, -12, -13, -14, -15, -16, G68-25
Cabina, La E73-131
Cabot, Sebastian G75-32
Caesar, Peter E77-105

Caesar, Shirley G72-26, G81-37
Caesar, Sid E51-4, E56-9
Caesar's Hour E55-7, E56-1, -9, -10, -11, -12, E57-13
CAGE AUX FOLLES, LA T84-7, -9, -12, -13, -15, -18
Cagney & Lacey E82-13, E83-13
Caine Mutiny Court Martial E55-8, -24, -25
Caird, John T82-6
Calder–Marshall, Anna E68-13
Caldwell, Dave E82-58
Caldwell, John C. E70-60
Caldwell, Zoe T66-5, T68-4, T82-4
California Here We Come E78-14
Call Me Daddy E67-56
CALL ME MADAM T51-11, -12, T52-16
CAMELOT T61-10, -16, -19, -22
Camera E78-68
Camera Three E65-30
Camery, James R. E79-99
Camoin, Al E69-49, E71-44, E80-50, E82-43
Camp, Richard E79-88
Campaign, The E82-137, -140
Campbell, Archie C69-10
Campbell, Carolee E77-98
Campbell, Charles L. E73-70
Campbell, Curtis E80-99
Campbell, David E79-36
Campbell, Glen C68-1, G68-5, C68-6, G68-9, -12, -33, G69-2, G82-44
Campus Chorus and Orchestra E50-9
Can the World Be Saved? E69-26
CAN-CAN T54-13, -16, G61-24
Canadian Broadcasting Company E64-33, E68-48, E77-109, E78-95, E83-88
CANDIDE T57-19, T74-12, -15, -16, -18, -19
Candy, John E81-34, E82-38
CANTERBURY TALES T69-14
Cantrell, Phil E78-90
Capace, Tom E79-112
Capers, Virginia T74-10
Capone, Ron G72-41
Capote, Truman E66-41
Captain and Tenille (also see Daryl Dragon) G76-1
Captain Kangaroo E77-80, E80-65, E81-61, -78, E82-71
Captains and the Kings E76-25
Car 54, Where Are You? E61-16
"Car Wash" G77-32
Cara, Irene G84-5, -43
Carch, Roy E78-92
Cardinal Act of Mercy E62-14, -17

Carey, MacDonald E73-39, E74-40
Cariou, Len T79-8
Carless, Trevor E79-109
Carlin, George G73-24
Carlisle, Kevin E78-42
Carlos, Walter G70-34, -37, -41
Carlson, Earl E69-57
Carlton, Larry G82-8
Carlton Your Doorman E79-7
Carmichael, Robert E83-81
Carnes, Kim G82-1, G84-43
Carney, Art E53-6, E54-6, E55-6, E66-43, E67-29, E83-18
CARNIVAL T62-12, -20
CARNIVAL IN FLANDERS T54-12
Carol Burnett Show, The E68-42, E70-45, E71-2, -19, -62, E72-28, -57, -63, E73-2, -35, -49, -83, E74-2, -49, -65, E75-37, -87, E76-20, -32, E77-24, -35, -40, -50, -60
Carolina, Larry E80-99
Caron, Larry E73-70
Carow, Larry E76-42
Carpenter, Pete (Clarence) G76-7
Carpenters, The G71-6, -43, G72-6
Carr, Allan T84-7
Carr, Lawrence T59-18
Carroll, Diahann T62-12
Carroll, Pat E56-12, G81-33
Carroll, Sidney E64-13
"Carroll County Accident" C69-4
Carry On, Hawkeye E73-48
Carson, Dick E73-56, E82-98
Carson, Johnny E79-61
Carson, Wayne C82-4, G83-3, C83-4, G83-23
Carter, Ellis W. E58-33
Carter, June G68-13, C69-7, G71-16
Carter, Nell T78-11, E81-57
Cartwright, William T. E63-25, E65-24
Caruso, Jerry P. E79-115
Casablanca E82-33
Casagrande, John E72-49
Casey, Harry Wayne (also see K.C. & the Sunshine Band) G76-19
Cash, Johnny C68-3, G68-13, C69-1, -2, -3, -6, -7, G69-15, -39, G70-16, -44, G71-16
Cass, Peggy T57-5
Cassidy, Jack T64-11
"Cast Your Fate to the Winds" G63-9
Castaldo, John N. E82-111
Castle, James E82-56
"Cat, The" G65-9
Catafalque E70-63
"Catch a Falling Star" G59-4

Cates–Cantrell, Dianne E79-89, -113
Catherina Howard E71-13
Catlin, Stanton G65-42
Catmull, Hazel E81-52
Cato, Robert G65-41, G68-44
CATS T83-7, -11, -12, -13, -15, -17, -18, G84-44
Cavanaugh, Dave G60-34
Cavanaugh, James P. E56-19
Caylor, Sam E71-41
Cecil, Malcom G74-42
Cefalo, Jim E80-94
Central Park in the Dark/A Hero's Life E75-86
Cerf, Christopher G73-G78-37
"Chain of Fools" G69-18
"Chaka Kahn" G84-29
Challengers, The E69-54
Chaloupka, Hugh E61-20
Chamberlain, Dora T47-8
Chamberlin, Lee G73-33
Chambers, John E73-122
Champion, Gower T49-17, T61-15, -17, T64-15, -18, T68-14, -15, T81-14
Champion, Marge E74-74
Champlin, Bill G80-25, G83-28
Champs, The G59-8
Chaney, Edward E67-44
Chaney, H. Lee E77-75
Change of a Dollar E82-31
"Changing Face of Harlem, the Savoy Sessions, The" G77-47
CHANGING ROOM, THE T73-3
"Changing Times" G80-37
Channel 7, Australia E81-103
Channing, Carol T64-12, T68-19
Chaplin, Saul G62-23
Chaplin, Sidney T57-10
Chapman, Edward G64-33
CHAPTER TWO T78-5
"Charade" G64-36
Charbonneau, Ron E71-57
"'Chariots of Fire,' Theme from" G83-8
Charles, Glen E82-35
Charles, Les E82-35
Charles, Ray G61-4, -5, -11, -13, G62-12, G63-12, G64-12, G67-14, -15, E70-68, E71-68, G76-21
"Charley McCoy/The Real McCoy" G73-18
"Charley Pride Sings Heart Songs" G73-16
Charlie Brown Christmas, A E65-4
Charlie Brown Thanksgiving, A E73-101
Charlie Noon E69-40
"Charlie Parker: The Complete Savoy Decision" G80-54

Charmoli, Tony E55-35, E73-92, E75-83
Charnin, Martin E71-35, T77-13, G78-35
Charters pour l'Enfer E81-102
Charters to Hell E81-102
Chase, Chevy E75-38, -75, E77-41
Chase, David E79-31
Chase, Ken E76-68
Checci, Robert E74-78, -80, E75-89, E77-69, -70
Checker, Chubby G62-18
Checkmate E60-23
Cheech and Chong G74-24
Cheers E82-3, -11, -25, -35, -56, E83-3, -22, -28, -38
Chegwidden, Ann E73-67
Chenier, Clifton & His Red Hot Louisiana Band G84-48
Cher C74-32, -35, -78, E75-89, E77-59
Cherin, Milt G76-42, G77-44
Cherriffe, Brian E78-90
CHERRY ORCHARD, THE T77-17, -18
"Chester and Lester" G77-20
Chevalier, Maurice T68-19
Chicago G77-6
Chicago Brass Ensemble G70-36
Chicago Symphony Chorus G78-45, G79-45, G80-50, G83-53, G84-57
Chicago Symphony Orchestra G61-27, G63-34, G65-35, G67-4, G72-33, G73-34, -35, G74-36, G75-34, -35, G76-34, G77-37, G78-39, -45, G79-38, -45, G80-43, -44, -50, G82-45, -46, G83-47, -49, -53, G84-50, -51, -57
"Chicago X" G77-46
Chico and the Man E75-24
Child, Julia E65-35
CHILDREN OF A LESSER GOD T80-1, -2, -4
Children of Hope—NBC Weekend E79-101
"Children of Sanchez" G79-8
Children of Violence E82-134
CHILD'S PLAY T70-2, -3, -6, -14, -15
Chilton, John G83-57
China: The Roots of Madness E66-9, -36
China Trip, The E71-25
Chipmunks, The (see Ross Bagdasarian)
"Chipmunks Sing the Beatles, The" G65-40
"Chipmunk Song, The" G59-9, -10, -26
CHOCOLATE SOLDIER, THE T47-7
Chodorov, Jerome T53-14
"Chokin' Kind, The" G70-21
Chomsky, Marvin J. E77-34, E79-26, E81-17
"Chopin" G65-33, G73-38

CHORUS LINE, A T76-7, -9, -10, -11, -12, -13, -14, -15, -17, T84-20
Chorus of the Covent Garden G73-39
Choul, Lim Youn E71-47
Christian, Jerry E71-41
Christides, Robert E79-55
Christie, Edward G. E80-86
Christie, Ray E83-82
Christmas Carol, A E54-29
Christmas Eve on Sesame Street E78-6
Christmas Memory, A E66-14, -41
Christofer, Michael T77-1
Christopher, Johnny C82-4, G83-3, C83-4, G83-23
Christopher, Roy E77-72, E80-55, E83-50
Chronolog E71-26
Chrysler: Once Upon a Time ... And Now E82-121
Chrysler Presents the Bob Hope Christmas Special E65-6
Chui, Robert E82-104
Chulack, Andrew E81-28, E83-28
Chumbley, Leonard E75-72
Ciarlo, Mario E71-57, E78-90
Cicada Invasion E82-133
Ciccimarro, Anthony E82-139
Cillario G69-35
Cimino, Steve E78-90
Cinderella E69-4
Cinderella at the Palace E78-47
CIRCLE IN THE SQUARE T76-19
"Citizen Kane Soundtrack" G79-27
City at Night E50-4
City Beneath the Sea E70-60
City of the King, A E71-69
"Civil War, Volume 1, The" G63-35
"Civil War, Volume 2, The" G64-37
Clair, Dick E73-83, E74-65, E77-40
Clanking Savannah Blacksmith E73-121
Clapton, Eric G73-2
Clark, Bob E80-99
Clark, Carroll E62-27
Clark, Cortelia G67-20
Clark, David E77-97, E79-37
Clark, Dick E78-74
Clark, Jack E80-94
Clark, Petula G65-20, G66-30
Clark, Roy C73-1, C75-9, C76-9, C77-10, C78-10, C80-10, G83-27
Clark, Susan E75-29
Clarke, Willie G76-19
Class Act E82-63
"Class of '57" G73-17
"Classic Eric Wolfgang Korngold, The" G75-45

Index

"Classical Gas" G69-8, -9, -29
Classon, Hal E81-93
Clawson, Cynthia G81-36
Clay, Paul E82-58
CLEARING IN THE WOODS, A T57-19
Clemans, Jerry E79-35, E80-49
Clemens, George E60-21
Clements, Richard E73-98
Cleveland, James G75-28, G78-32, G81-38
Cleveland Brass Ensemble G70-36
Cleveland Orchestra G70-35, G71-33, -39, G76-41, G77-41
Cleveland Orchestra Chorus G76-41, G77-41
Cliburn, Van G59-20, G60-24
Close, Glenn T84-4
"Close Encounters of the Third Kind" G79-10, -34
"Close to You" G71-6
Closed Captioning for the Deaf E79-63
"Closer You Get, The" C83-3
"Cloud Nine" G69-20
"Clouds" G70-26
Cluess, Chris E81-34
Clymer, Warren E63-28, E64-26
"Coal Miner's Daughter" C80-3
Coast to Coast Big Mouth E65-22
Coben, Sherry E79-88
Cobos, Richard E77-68
Cocker, Joe G83-6
COCKTAIL PARTY, THE T50-1, -5, -6
Coca, Imogene E51-5
Coco, James E82-18
COCO T70-9, -16
Codron, Michael T84-1
Coe, Fred E55-28, T60-8, -11
Coffey, Bob E80-99
Cohan, Jeff E75-64, E80-99
Cohen, Alexander H. T67-1
Cohen, Randy E72-40
Cohen, Tim E82-137
Coil, Marvin E65-25
Colder, Ben (see Sheb Wooley)
Cole, Bill E66-34, E69-44
Cole, Nat "King" G60-33
Cole, Natalie G76-20, -48, G77-22
Cole, Olivia E76-17
Cole, P.K. E81-90
Cole, Tommy E78-50
Coleman, Cy E74-66, T78-12
Coleman, Shepard T64-17
Coleman, Wanda E75-79
Coles, Charles 'Honi' T83-9
Colgan, Michael E69-42
Colgate Comedy Hour E53-4

Colleary, Bob E79-28
Collection, The E77-108
Collins, Bob E70-57
Collins, Hal E81-58
Collins, Judy G69-23
Collins, Robert E79-88
"Color Him Father" G70-19
"Colorful Peter Nero, The" G63-16
Colt, Alvin T56-20
Colter, Jessi C76-3
Coltran, Loren E79-113
Coltrane, John G82-20
Columbia Chamber Ensemble G71-36
Columbia Records Presents Vladimir Horowitz G63-4, -32
Columbia Symphony Orchestra G62-4, G63-26, -30, G68-37
Columbo E71-11, -36, -45, -58, E73-4, -73, E74-24, -34, -71, E75-26
Comden, Betty T53-9, T68-13, T70-7, T78-12, -13
"Come and Gone" G75-43
COME BACK, LITTLE SHEBA T50-2, -3
"Come Dance with Me" G60-2, -4, -31, -34
Come One, Come All E81-54
Comedian, The E57-3, -18
COMEDIANS, THE T77-3
Coming Out Party, The E67-34
COMMAND DECISION T48-2
Commare, Joe E78-90
Communications Satellite Corporation E65-43
Como, Perry E54-15, E55-18, -19, E56-15, E58-20, E59-4
COMPANY T71-8, -13, -14, -16, -19, -20, G71-29
Computer Video Tape Editing System E72-73
Con Thien, 1st Cavalry E67-31
Concealed Enemies E83-4, -24
"Concert for Bangla Desh, The" G73-2
"Concert of the Century" G78-38
Concertgebouw Orchestra G81-47
"Conchinos, Los" G74-24
Condie, Norman (see Mormon Tabernacle Choir)
"Confessions of a Broken Man" G67-39
Connell, Dave E69-62
Connell, Leigh T57-7
Conniff, Ray, Singers G67-28
Connors, Jimmy E74-16
Conrad, Michael E80-44, E81-10
Conroy, Frank T57-3
Consentino, Joe E80-88
Consolidated Video Systems E73-129

Index

Constantine, Michael E69-19
CONSUL, THE T51-18
Contender, The E79-38
Conti, Tom T79-2
Continual Roar of Musketry, A E70-37
Continuing Creations E77-98
"Conversations with Myself" G64-7
"Conversations with the Guitar" G61-29
Convy, Bert E76-88
Conway, Tim E72-28, E76-20, E77-24, -40
Cook, Barbara T58-13
Cook, Fielder E66-25, E70-35
Cook, Kathy E80-99
Cook, Patrick M. E80-94
Cook, Peter T63-22, T74-19, G75-25
Cooke, Alistair E72-71, E74-46
Cookman, Jim E75-69
Coolidge, Rita G74-17, G76-17
Cooney, Joan G71-31
Cooper, Jackie E73-48, E78-26
Cooper, Marilyn T81-11
Cooper, Paul W. E81-86
Cop E79-25, -29
"Copacabana (At the Copa)" G79-4
Copeland, Alan, Singers G69-7
Copland, Aaron G61-32
"Copland" G80-45, G84-35
Cora and Arnie E82-17, -18
Corby, Ellen E72-27, E74-31, E75-35
Corea, Chick G76-11, G77-7, -12, G79-12, G80-15, G82-16
Corenblith, Michael E82-42
Cornelius, Helen C77-8
Cornell, Katherine T48-3
Cornett, Robert E73-70, E80-31
Cornfeld, Betty E81-87
Cornwell, Tom E81-38
Cornyn, Stan G66-43, G67-40
Corporate Communications Consultants, Inc. E83-67
Correll, Charles E82-34
Corrigan, Michael E77-48
Corriston, Peter G82-55
Corso, John W. E82-41
Cosby, Bill E65-10, G65-18, G66-15, G66-18, G67-18, E67-19, G68-19, G69-21, G70-24, G72-31, G73-33, E80-88
Cosell, Howard E83-71
Cosmos E80-53, -63
Costigan, James E58-29, E74-67, E75-77
Coswick, Harry E60-20
Cotler, Douglas G84-43
Cotter, Ed E77-45

Cotugno, Joe E80-99
Cougar, John G83-12
"Could I Have This Dance" G81-23
"Country — After All These Years" G82-27
"Country Bumpkin" C74-2, -4
COUNTRY GIRL, THE T51-4, -19
Courcier, Brian E83-33
Cousteau, Philippe E73-122
Couterie, William E82-134
Coverage of American Unemployment E82-128
Coward, Noel T70-17
Coyle, Harry E78-89
Crabe, James E81-36, E83-41
Craft, Ron E79-92
Craftsman, The E78-36, -45
Crane, Les G72-23
Crawford, Cheryl T51-8
Creativity with Bill Moyers E81-24
Creatore, Luigi (see Hugo & Luigi)
Crile, George, III E79-96
"Crimes of Passion" G81-11
Crinkley, Richmond T79-1
Crisis in the Cities E67-7
Croak, John E72-40, E75-64, E79-112
Cromwell, John T52-3
Cronjager, William H. E80-33
Cronkite, Walter E69-28, E70-29, E72-70, E78-54
Cronyn, Hume T64-3
Crookham, Joe E83-79
Cropper, Steve G69-17
Crosby, Don E79-60
Crosby, Stills & Nash G70-45
Cross, Christopher G81-1, -2, -3, -15, -59
"Cross Country Suite" G59-18
Crouch, Andrae G76-28, G79-31, G80-36, G81-36, G82-38
Crouch, Sandra G84-40
Crouse, Russell T59-22, T60-14
Crowe, Gene E77-54, E83-42
Crowe, J.D. (see The New South)
CRUCIBLE, THE T53-1, -5, -6, -8
CRUCIFER OF BLOOD, THE T79-17
Crusade in Europe E49-9
Cry Help! An NBC White Paper on Mentally Disturbed Youth E70-40
"Crying Time" G67-14, -15
Cuban Missile Crisis, The E82-141
Cuban Revolution E58-39
Cukor, George E74-51
Culley, Jim E71-57, E78-90
Cullum, John T75-8, T78-8
Culture Club G84-65
Cummings, Constance T79-4
Cummings, Robert E54-17

Index   148

Cunningham, A.J. E66-37, E67-44, E68-36
Cunningham, Steve E77-97
Curran, Charles E73-132
Curtin, Jane E83-15
Curtin, John E80-99
Curtis, Craig E65-26
Curtis, Keene T71-10
Curtis, King G70-23
Cynthia Is Alive and Living in Avalon E70-56
CYRANO T74-8
CYRANO DE BERGERAC T47-1
Cywinski, Lou E78-39

D

"D.N.A." G83-10
DA T78-1, -2, -3, -6
Dadario, Jean E79-89, E81-92, E82-105
Dahlquist, Ken E81-48
Dailey, Irene E78-70
Dale, Jim T80-8
d'Alisera, Silvio E58-32
"Dallas" E79-14, E82-52, E83-55
Dalton, Phyllis E82-46
Daly, James E65-12
Daly, John E54-19
Daly, Tyne E82-13, E83-13
DAMN YANKEES T56-9, -10, -11, -12, -14, -15, -16, -17, -18, -21
Damon, Cathryn E79-12
Dana, Leora T73-5
Dance, Stanley G64-39
Dance in America E80-51, -59, E82-61, E83-53, -64
"Dance with Basie" G61-17
DANCIN' T78-14, -17
"Dang Me" G65-11, -14, -15
"Dang Me/Chug-a-Lug" G65-12
Dangerfield, Rodney G81-32
Daniel, Francis E82-137
Daniels, Charlie C79-10
Daniels, Danny T84-14
Daniels, Ray E82-29
Daniels, Stan E74-64, E76-50
Daniels, Charlie, Band C79-2, -9, C80-9, G80-23
Danner, Blythe T70-5
Danny Kaye Show E63-2, -15, -23, -27
Danny Kaye's Look at the Metropolitan Opera E75-14
Danny Thomas Show, The E56-22, E60-16

Danny's Comeback E56-22
Dante, Nicholas T76-12
Dante, Ron T78-7
Danziger, Maia E79-88
Darin, Bobby G60-1, -34, -35
Darion, Joe T66-12
DARKNESS AT NOON T51-2
DARLING OF THE DAY T68-11
Da Silva, Howard E77-30
David, Hal G70-31
David Brinkley's Journal E61-5, E62-5, E63-5
David Frost Program, The E69-2, E70-3
David Letterman Show, The E80-80, -86
Davids, S. Spencer T76-1
Davidson, Gordon T77-6
Davidson, Mark E78-83
Davies, Dennis Russell G80-45
Davies, Hugh G61-35, G69-37
Davis, Ann B. E57-14, E58-18
Davis, Bette E78-16
Davis, Bill E72-33, E74-50, E77-63
Davis, Billy, Jr. (also see Fifth Dimension) G77-24
Davis, Colin G71-32, -37, G72-39, G73-39, G75-40, G76-39, G80-49
Davis, Danny C69-8, C70-9, G70-18, C71-9, C72-9
Davis, Don E80-53
Davis, Elias E77-40
Davis, John T54-21
Davis, Leard E66-33, E69-60
Davis, Luther T54-14
Davis, Marvin Aubrey E62-27
Davis, Miles G61-10, G71-12, G83-20
Davis, Tess E74-79
Davis, Tom E75-75, E76-52, E77-41
"Dawn" G78-36
Dawson, Richard E77-90
Day, Gordon L. E69-41, E82-60
Day, Jon E79-108
Day After, The E83-33, -44
DAY IN HOLLYWOOD/A NIGHT IN THE UKRAINE, A T80-11, -14
Day of the Jouster E78-92
Day the Lion Died, The E70-34
Days of Our Lives E73-39, -53, -72, E74-40, -41, E75-79, E77-79, E78-72, E79-79
"Days of Wine and Roses" G64-1, -3, -24
Daytona 500 E78-90, E80-99, E83-77, -82
Dazz Band G83-31
"Dead End Street" G68-16
Dean, Jimmie G62-11

Dear Friends E67-38
DEAR WORLD T69-10
Death and Life Severinian E82-147
Death in a Southwest Prison E80-94
Death Lends a Hand E71-36, -58
DEATH OF A SALESMAN T49-1, -3, -6, -7, -8, -15, E66-23, -42, T84-19
De Bonis, Joseph E79-113
De Burgos & Foster G76-37
"Debussy" G60-22, G65-33, G69-30, G70-35, G72-34
Deckard, James E82-135
de Cuir, John E77-73
Dedario, Vince E80-99
"Deep Purple" G64-18
Defeat at Dacca E71-28, -29, -47
Defection of Simas Kudirka, The E77-37, -47
Defenders, The E61-1, -8, -15, -17, E62-1, -11, -18, -20, -24, E63-1, -13, -19, E64-20, -21
Defiance E82-64
De Govia, Jackson E82-64
de Hartog, Jan T52-1
"Deja Vu" G80-26
de Joux, Jean E76-49
Dekas, Bob E80-99
de Larrocha, Alicia G75-38, G76-37
Delerue, George E67-48
Delfonics, The G71-21
de Liagre, Alfred, Jr. T59-8, T83-19
DELICATE BALANCE, A T67-5
Delilla, Tom E83-82
de Lisa, John E72-40, E75-64
Delisa, John E80-99
Dell, Alan G83-58
Dellapietra, Steve E80-99
Dell'Isola, Salvatore T59-16
Dellutri, Ernest E73-72
Deloire, Michael E71-70
Delu, Dahl E80-89
de Luca, Rudy E73-83, E74-65
de Main, John G78-43
Demers, Ted E80-99
de Mille, Agnes T47-6, T62-17
Demos, Nick E66-38, E68-36
Deniear, Walt E74-83
Denisoff, Ken E78-38, E81-29
Dennis, Mark E77-75, E79-60
Dennis, Sandy T63-5, T64-4
Denoff, Sam E63-20, E65-22, E66-28
Denver, John C75-1, -4
Deodato, Eumir G74-8
Departure of Marines for Korea E50-10
DEPUTY, THE T64-8
Derosa, Drew E80-99

Derricks, Cleavant T82-9
Dervin, Joseph E64-23
"Desafinado" G63-7
Desert Whales, The E69-38
De Shannon, Jackie G82-3
De Shields, Andre E81-57
"Desiderata" G72-23
DESPERATE HOURS, THE T55-1, -6, -7, -8
DESTRY RIDES AGAIN T60-18
Determining Force, A E75-100
"Detroit City" G64-11
Dettling, Ken E79-92, E81-53
"Devil Made Me Buy This Dress, The" G71-22
"Devil Went Down to Georgia, The" C79-2, G80-23
Devito, Danny E80-17
de Vorzan, Barry G78-7
Dewes, Norman H. E71-42
Dewhurst, Coleen T61-5, T74-4
Dews, Peter T69-6
Dexter, John T75-6
Dezendorf, Tom E78-90, E80-50
DIAL M FOR MURDER T53-3
Diamond, Al E74-83
Diamond, Ira E81-45
Diamond, Neil G74-30
Diamond Jubilee of Lights E54-32
Diana E71-53
Diana Ross and the Supremes and the Temptations on Broadway E69-59
DIARY OF ANNE FRANK, THE T56-1, -6, -8
DiBella, Joe E76-68
Dichter, Lee E79-88
Dick, David E72-70
Dick Cavett Show, The E68-15, E71-3, E73-18
Dick Clark's Live Wednesday E78-39
Dick Powell Show, The E61-10
Dick Van Dyke and Company E76-2
Dick Van Dyke Show E61-18, E62-3, -19, -21, E63-3, -11, -12, -20, -22, E64-1, -9, E65-1, -14, -15, -22
Dickinson, Robert A. E82-50, E83-51
"Didn't I (Blow Your Mind This Time)" G71-21
Diehl, Walter F. T79-19
Diemburger, Kurt E83-80
Dierdorff, Chris E83-44
Dietrich, Marlene T68-19
Di Girolamo, Tony E77-96
"Digital III at Montreux" G82-18
Dillman, Bradford E74-42
Dillon, Carmen E74-79
Dillon, Greg E83-33

Index 150

Dinah! E74-11, -54, E75-17, -47, -54, -91, E78-83
Dinah & Friends in Israel E80-84
Dinah Salutes Broadway E74-54
Dinah Shore Chevy Show E57-7, -21, E58-9
Dinah's Place E72-10, E73-46
Dinapoli, Victor E82-111
Dinnerstein, Harvey G73-44
"Dinorah, Dinorah" G81-7
Dinsdale, Shirley E48-1
Directions E79-72, -86, E80-70
Dirksen, Sen. Everett M. G68-20
Disaster on the Potomac E82-119
"Discantus" G62-34
Discovery '63–'64 E63-6
DISENCHANTED, THE T59-2
Disney, Walt E55-29
Disneyland E54-3, -21, -27, E55-29
Dive to the Edge of Creation E79-37
Dixie Hummingbirds G74-28
Do Me a Favor ... Don't Vote for My Mom E80-88
Do Not Go Gentle into that Good Night E67-17, -33, -44
"Do You Know the Way to San Jose?" G69-5
Dockendorf, Dave E80-63
Dr. John G81-43, G83-45
Dr. James "Red" Duke, Trauma Surgeon E79-46
"Dr. Seuss" G66-17, G67-17, G68-18
"Dr. Zhivago" G67-22
Doctors, The E71-20, E73-7, -40, E77-87
Dodge, Jim E76-48
Dodsworth E56-14
DOES A TIGER WEAR A NECKTIE? T69-3
Dollmaker, The E83-11, -61
Dolman, Bob E81-34, E82-38
Dombrow, Walter E68-28
Domich, Rich E83-82
"Dominique" G64-20
Don Adams Special: Hooray for Hollywood, The E69-61
Donahue, Mary Ann E81-87
Donahue, Phil E76-87, E77-89, E78-73, E79-80, E81-75, E82-92
Donahue E76-87, E77-85, -89, E78-64, -73, -76, E79-65, -80, E80-72, E81-75, -80, E82-92, -111
Donahue and Kids E80-10
Donatelli, Gary E79-113, E80-99
Donehue, Vincent J. T58-7
D'Onofrio, Charles E74-83, E80-99
"Donovan's Brain" G82-34
"Don't Bother Me, I Can't Cope" G73-31

Don't Count the Candles E68-24, -29
"Don't Give Up" G82-38
"Don't It Make My Brown Eyes Blue?" C78-4, G78-16, -17
"Don't Leave Me This Way" G78-22
"Don't Play that Song" G71-19
"Don't Stand So Close to Me" G82-13
"Don't Stop Till You Get Enough" G80-27
"Don't Touch Me" G67-12
Doobie Brothers, The G80-1, -6, G81-43
Dorfman, Jack E80-99
Dorfsman, Lou E78-84
Doris in Wonderland E83-20
Dorleac, Jean-Pierre E78-43
D'Ornellas, Joe E80-99
Dorothy Hammill Special, The E76-70
Dorsey, Tommy G83-58
Dorsky, Nathaniel E67-46
"Double Fantasy" G82-2
Doud, Mike G80-53
Doug Henning's World of Magic E76-48
Douglas, Jack E54-23
Douglas, Jerry (see The New South)
Douglas, Melvyn T60-2, E67-17
Douglass, Everett E65-25
Dow, Jim E80-53
Dowd, Gerald M. E73-77
Dowling, Robert T48-12
Down, Robert E70-63
"Down to You" G75-10
Downey, James E76-52
Downs, Hugh E80-79
"Downtown" G65-20
DRACULA T78-18, -19
Dragnet E52-11, E53-11, E54-12, -26, -31
Drago, Barry E78-90, E80-99, E83-82
Drago, George E74-83
Dragon, Daryl (see Captain & Tennille)
Drake, Alfred T54-10
Drake, Joe E80-99
Drawing Power E80-88
DREAMGIRLS T82-8, -9, -10, -12, -14, -17, G83-43
Drexler, Rosalyn E73-84
Driftwood, Jimmy G60-3
Drinkwater, Terry E82-128
Droege, Chuck E76-39
Drummy, Sam E73-127, E83-42
Dubner Computer Systems E81-58
du Bois, Raoul Pene T53-19
Duck Factory, The E83-45, -48
"Dude, The" G82-31
Duel E71-41
"Dueling Banjos" G74-18
"Duet" G80-15
"Duets with a Spanish Guitar" G59-27

Duffy, John E79-86
Dufor, Val E76-85
Duke, Daryl E70-34
Duke, Patty (Also see Patty Duke Astin) E69-13
Dulberg, Joel E80-94
Dumbrow, Walter E73-119
Dunbar, Ronald G71-18
Dungeon of Death E82-45
Dunlap, Richard E74-52, E77-91
Dunn, Robert E66-38
Dunphy, Thomas E72-38
Dunsmuir, Tom E72-11
Duquette, Tony & Adrian T61-22
Duran Duran G84-66, -67
Durante, Jimmy E52-1
Durkin, Tom E80-99
Duty Bound E72-15
Dvonch, Frederick T60-17
Dwyer, John M. E80-46
Dwyer, Robert E80-87
Dying E78-30
Dykstra, John E78-53
Dylan, Bob G73-2, G80-12
DYLAN T64-2
Dylan Thomas: The World I Breathe E67-12

E

"E.T. the Extra-Terrestrial" G83-42, G84-49
Eagle in a Cage E65-12, -21
Eagles G76-6, G78-1, -9, G80-9
Early Bird Satellite E65-43
Early Music Consort of London G77-38
Earth, Wind & Fire G76-22, G79-24, -25, G80-28, -29, G83-31
East Side/West Side E63-21
Eastman Ektachrome Video News Film E75-102
Eastman Kodak Company E82-67
Easton, Sheena G82-60
"Easy Loving" C71-4, C72-4
Ebb, Fred T67-12, G68-25, E72-58, T81-13
Eckert, Carl E82-109
Eclectic: A Profile of Quincy E82-130
Economou, Michael E70-37
Ed Sullivan Show, The E55-3
Eddie E58-26, -30
"Eddie Murphy: Comedian" G84-34
Edel, Walter E75-72, E76-72
Edgar, David T82-1

Edge of Night, The E72-9, E73-87, E78-66
Edith's 50th Birthday E77-33
Edith's Problem E71-61
Edlund, Richard E78-53
Edward and Mrs. Simpson E79-6
Edward the King E78-44
Edwards, Jonathan and Darlene (see Paul Weston and Jo Stafford)
Edwards, Mike E80-94
Edwards, Peter E76-70, E79-48
Edwards, Sherman T69-7
Edwards, William E78-66
Egypt: Quest for Eternity E82-135
Egyptian Weavers E80-88
"8:30" G80-19
Einarsen, Edwin E72-38
Einstein, Bob E68-34
Eisen, Charles E81-92
Eisenhardt, Robert E79-34
Eisenhower, President Dwight D. E55-38
Eisenstein, Eric E82-109
"El Paso" G61-12
Elaine's Strange Triangle E80-22, -30
Elder, Ann E75-78
Eleanor and Franklin E75-6, -39, -53, -61, -66, -71, -77, -90, -92, -95, -99, E76-7, -29, -38, -59, -65, -68, -71
Eleanor, First Lady of the World E81-52
"Eleanor Rigby" G67-30
Electric Company, The E72-11, G73-33, E73-126, E76-80
Electronic Engineering Company of California E71-73
Elegant Iggy E81-31
Elephant in a Cigar Box, An E68-31
ELEPHANT MAN, THE T79-1, -4, -6, E81-27
Elevator Story, The E71-42
Elfman, Blossom E80-88
Elfstrom, Bob E79-39, E80-88
"Elgar" G83-49
Elikann, Larry E78-78
Eliot, Gene E76-43
Eliot, T.S. T50-5, T83-12, -13
"Elite Hotel" G77-17
Elizabeth R E71-6, -7, -12, -55
Elizabeth the Queen E67-5
"Ella Fitzgerald Sings the Duke Ellington Songbook" G59-6
"Ella Fitzgerald Sings the George and Ira Gershwin Songbook" G61-37
"Ella Fitzgerald Sings the Irving Berlin Songbook" G59-5
"Ella Swings Brightly with Nelson Riddle" G63-6

Index 152

"Ella Swings Lightly" G60-6
Elliman, Yvonne G79-2
Ellington, Duke G60-13, -19, -20, G66-8, G68-8, G69-12, G72-11, G73-12, G77-13, G80-16
"Ellington Era, The" G64-39
"Ellington '66" G66-8
"Ellington Suites, The" G77-13
Ellingwood, James E81-90
Elliot, Jane E80-78
Elliot, Patricia T73-11
Elliott, Christopher E83-39
Elliott, David E81-38, E83-33
Ellis, Don G73-7
Ellison, Bob E70-51, E76-50
Elton, Bill E81-41
"Elvira" C81-2, G82-26
Emerick, G.E. G68-47, G70-42, G75-42
Emotions G78-24
"Empire Strikes Back, The" G81-14, -40
Emrick, Gary E79-92
Enberg, Dick E80-102, E83-84
"Encore: Woody Herman, 1963" G64-8
"End Is Not in Sight" G77-19
Energy Ball/Sweeps Week, The E82-38
Engel, Lehman T51-18, T53-17
English, Michael E80-99
ENTER LAUGHING T63-3
"Entertainer, The" G75-8, G76-18
Epstein, Dasha T78-7
Equitable's American Heritage E60-14
Equity Community Theatre T53-22
Equity Library Theatre T77-20
EQUUS T75-1, -6
Erasing Vietnam—NBC Nightly News E79-101
Eric Hoffer: The Passionate State of Mind E67-9
Erickson, Gorm E66-38
Erman, John E82-27
Ernst, Don E76-43, E82-57
Ernst, Ernie E78-90, E79-110
"Errol Garner: Master of the Keyboard" G82-56
Erskine, Howard T55-8
Ertegun, Ahmet G60-34
Eschelbacher, David E. E79-113
Eskimo: Fight for Life, The E70-28
Essay on Watergate E73-117
Essenfeld, Walter E82-140
Estes, George G66-44
Estes, Ron E82-62
Estin, Ken E81-31
Eubie Blake: A Century of Music E82-54
Eugene O'Neill Memorial Theatre Center T79-19

EUGENIA T57-19
European Broadcasting Union E73-132
Evacuees, The E74-19
Evans, Bill G64-7, G69-11, G71-11, G72-10, -12, G81-16, -20
Evans, Gil G61-10
Evans, Jerry E78-75
Evans, Lloyd R. E78-84
Evans, Maurice T50-20, T54-8, E60-10
Evening at the Symphony E75-86
"Evening of Elizabethan Music" G64-28
"Evening with Belafonte/Makeba, An" G66-20
Evening with Carol Channing E65-23
Evening with Fred Astaire, An E58-3, -22, -27, -34, -36, -37, -38
"Evening with George Shearing and Mel Torme, An" G83-19
Evening with Jerome Robbins, An E80-50
Evening with John Denver, An E74-3, -50
"Evening with Mike Nichols and Elaine May, An" G62-14
Everglades, The E70-27
"Evergreen" G78-3
"Every Breath You Take" G84-3, -6
"Every Man Wants to Be Free" G71-26
"Everybody's Talkin'" G70-4
"Everything Is Beautiful" G71-4, -24
"Everytime I Feel the Spirit" G62-20
EVITA T80-7, -9, -10, -12, -13, -15, -17, G81-41
Evita Peron E80-48
Ewell, Tom T53-2
Ewing Blues, The E82-52
Execution of Private Slovak, The E73-61, -62
Executioner's Song, The E82-16, -58
"Exodus, Theme from" G61-3, -22
Experimental Theatre, Inc. T48-12
Eye for an Eye, An E72-30, -44
"Eye of the Tiger" G83-13
Eyen, Tom T82-12, G83-43

F

FDR E82-137, -138, -139, -140
"FDR Speaks" G61-21
FDR the Last Year E79-48
"FM (No Static at All)" G79-47
"FM & AM" G73-24
FYI E79-74, E80-71, E81-67, -87, E82-95
Fabray, Nanette T49-11, E55-7, -11, E56-10

Index

Fabulous Fifties E59-2
Face of Red China, The E58-7
Faer, Stanley E80-99
"Fairytale" G75-17
Faison, George T75-13
Faith, Percy G61-1, G70-7
Falardeau, George E83-43
Falk, H. E79-113
Falk, Peter E61-10, E71-11, E74-24, E75-26
"Falla" G65-35
Fame E81-16, -35, -45, -54, -57, E82-63, E83-30
Family E76-14, -15, E77-17, E78-22
Family Feud E76-78, E77-90, -97, E81-82
Family of Strangers E80-88
Family Upside Down, A E77-32
Fanelli, Paul E79-112
FANNY T55-10
Fantasy E82-91
"Far East Suite" G68-8
Fargo, Donna C72-2, G73-15
Farrell, Eileen G63-28
Farrell, Glenda E62-17
Farrell, Marty E70-51
Farrell, Peggy E77-66
Fash, Mike E79-88
Fast, Howard E74-63
Fast/Slow – Speed Up/Slow Down E79-88
Father Knows Best E56-7, E57-9, -10, E58-12, -28, E59-8
Fathers and Sons E69-24
"Faure" G76-37
Favita, Ray E81-100
Fear on Trial E75-76
Feather, Leonard G64-39
Fecund Hand Rose E80-19
Fehler, John E75-72, E76-72
Feigenbaum, Bill E83-70
Fein, Joel E79-37
Feld, Joel E80-99
Feldstein, Donald E72-72
Felger, Geoffrey E79-113
Feliciano, Jose G69-4, -40, G84-45
Feller, Peter T52-16
Fender, Freddy C75-2
Ferguson, Bob C69-4
Ferrari, William E55-34
Ferrer, Jose T47-1, T52-2, -6
Ferro, Henry Enrico E82-105
Feuer, Cy T51-17, T62-19
Few Minutes with Andy Rooney, A E82-122
Ffolkes, David T47-7
Fickett, Mary E72-29
FIDDLER ON THE ROOF T65-9, -10, -13, -14, -15, -16, -17, -18, -20, T72-19
Field, Ronald T67-13, T70-12, -13, E76-69, E77-62
Field, Sally E76-23
Fielding, Jerry E79-41
Fields, Dorothy T59-9, -14
Fields, Herbert T59-14
Fields, Joseph T53-14
Fierman, Dennis E79-109
Fierstein, Harvey T83-1, -2, T84-12
Fifth Dimension G68-1, -30, -32, -35, G70-1, -6
FIFTH OF JULY T81-5
55th Annual Academy Award Presentation E82-42
51st Annual Academy Award Ceremonies E78-11
Fifty-Fourth Annual Academy Awards, The E81-47
"52nd Street" G80-2, -4
56th Annual Academy Awards E83-50
53rd Annual Academy Awards E80-55
Figelski, Ray E74-83, E78-90
Fighter, The E77-52
Fighting Back E80-104
FIGHTING COCK, THE T60-3
Filippi, Anthony E83-82
Filling Buddy's Shoes E83-45
Finch, David E77-97, E80-99
Finch, Richard (also see K.C. & the Sunshine Band) G76-19
FIND YOUR WAY HOME T74-2
Fine, Robert G63-35, G64-37
Fine, Sam E79-108
"Fine and Mellow" G80-17
FINIAN'S RAINBOW T47-5, -6
Finnerman, Gerald Perry E77-53
FIORELLO! T60-9, -11, -14, -15, -16, -19
Fire! E73-114, -118
"Fire and Ice" G82-11
"Fireball" G84-27
Fireball Forward E71-43
Fireball in the Night, A E72-71
Firebird E80-107
Firing Line with William F. Buckley, Jr. E68-40
1st Calvary E67-31
First Churchills, The E70-12
"First Family, The" G63-2, -14
First Fifty Years, The E76-39
"First Flight" G73-11
FIRST GENTLEMAN, THE T58-20
First Ladies' Diaries: Edith Wilson E75-10, -45, -57, -80
First Ladies' Diaries: Martha Washington E75-44, E75-45

Index 154

First Months Are the Hardest, The E70-68
First Olympics—Athens 1896 E83-56
"First Recordings" G75-13
"First Time Ever I Saw Your Face, The" G73-1, -3
First Tuesday E68-30, E69-32, E73-112
Fischer, Clare G82-43
Fischer–Dieskau, Dietrich G71-38, G73-40, G78-38
Fish E76-56
Fisher, Art E71-34
Fisher, Gail E69-15
Fisher, Jules T73-17, T74-17, T78-17
Fisher, Mike E79-113
Fishing Boat Sinks E80-93
Fitzgerald, Ella G59-5, -6, G60-5, -6, G61-6, -7, G63-6, G77-15, G80-17, G81-18, G82-18, G84-18
Fitzgerald, Geraldine E78-80
Fitzgerald, Thomas H. T76-19
"Fitzgerald & Pass ... Again" G77-15
Five Finger Discount E77-96
Five Part Investigation of Welfare E70-30
Flack, Roberta G73-1, -6, G74-1, -5
Flaherty, Joe E81-34, E82-38
Flaherty, Paul E81-34, E82-38
Flanagan, James E82-140
Flanders, Ed T74-3, E75-40, E76-22, E82-14
Flannery, Susan E74-41
Flannigan, Fionnuala E75-41
"Flashdance" G84-5, -15, -43
Flat E78-92
Flatt, Ernest O. E70-45
Flatt & Scruggs G69-16
Fleetwood Mac G78-2
Fletcher, Bob E77-62
Fleury, Ron E76-39
Flip Wilson Show, The E70-2, -50
FLOATING LIGHT BULB, THE T81-3
Flock of Seagulls, A G83-10
"Flood, The" G63-33
FLORA, THE RED MENACE T65-12
Florence, Bob E80-37
Florio, Frank E74-83, E78-90, E80-99
FLOWER DRUM SONG T59-16
"Flowers on the Wall" G66-31
Fly, The E78-94
"Fly Me to the Moon Bossa Nova" G63-15
"Fly, Robin Fly" G76-23
"Flying" G83-7, -15
Fog Closing In E56-19
"Foggy Mountain Breakdown" G69-16
Fold, Charles, Singers G81-38
FOLLIES T72-10, -13, -14, -15, -16, -17, -18

Folsey, George E68-35
"Folsom Prison Blues" G69-15
Fonda, Henry T48-2, G77-27, T79-19
Fonda, Jane E83-11
Fonorow, Robert E67-44, E68-36, E74-83
Fontana, Robert E72-72
Fontana, Tom E83-37
Fontanne, Lynn E64-6, T70-17
Football in America E83-81
"Footlifters" G76-46
FOR COLORED GIRLS WHO HAVE CONSIDERED SUICIDE/WHEN THE RAINBOW IS ENUF T77-5
For Our Times E79-72
"For the Good Times" G71-15
"For the Last Time" G75-44
Ford, Michael E83-32
Ford, Nancy E82-101
Ford, Tennessee Ernie G65-22
Ford Motor Company E55-36
Ford Star Jubilee E55-8, -24, -25
Ford Startime E59-10
Forgotten Children E75-101
Forrest, George T54-9
Forsey, Keith G84-43
Forsythe, Henderson T79-9
Forsythe Saga, The E69-11
Forte, Robert R. E69-39
FORTY CARATS T69-4
44th Oscar Awards, The E72-49
42ND STREET T81-7, -14
Fosse, Bob T55-16, T56-17, T59-17, T63-16, T66-13, E72-34, -54, T73-14, -15, T78-14
Foster, Bob E80-99
Foster, David G80-25
Four Women E78-95
Fournier, Pierre G75-35, G76-36
FOURPOSTER, THE T52-1, -6
Fowler, Gene, Jr. E72-35, E73-60
Fowler, Marjorie E72-35, E73-60
Fox, Charles E69-52, E72-55, G74-3
Fox, Mahlon E72-43
Fox, Stu E83-59
FOXFIRE T83-4
FOXY T64-10
Fraggle Rock E83-88
Francis, Allan T77-1
Franconia Notch E82-111
Frank, Gary E76-14
Frank, Sanford E83-39
Frank Productions T58-18
Frank Sinatra: A Man and His Music E65-5, -38
Frank Sinatra: A Man and His Music, Part II E66-34

Index

Frank Terpil: Confessions of a Dangerous Man E82-123
Franken, Al E75-75, E76-52, E77-41
Franklin, Aretha G68-14, -15, G69-18, G70-20, G71-19, G72-19, G73-20, -28, G74-20, G75-20, G82-29
Franklin, Nancy E80-87, E81-85
Fraser, Ian E76-63, E77-57, E79-47, E80-37, E83-54
Frawley, James E66-24
Frazier, Dallas C67-4
Freberg, Stan G59-17, G61-36
Fred Astaire: Change Partners and Dance E79-10
Fred Astaire Show E67-49
Frederick, Lou E75-64
Frederick, Barry T76-1
Frederick, George E76-42
Freebairn–Smith, Ian G78-11
Freed, Fred E70-23
Freeda, William J. E72-38, E73-66
Freedman, Mike E68-17
Feeedman, Robert G79-7
Freedom's Last Stand E81-32
Freeman, Al, Jr. E78-69
Freeman, Charles L. E61-20
Freeman, Ernie G67-26, G71-10
Freeman, Seth E79-29
Freeman, Stan E77-60
Freer, Robert C. E80-46, E82-41
Freestyle! E78-92
Freid, Gerald E76-61
Frelich, Phyllis T80-4
French, Thomas E82-105
French Atlantic Affair, The E79-42
French Chef, The E65-35
French Repertory T57-22
Freschi, John E71-49, E72-49, E74-77, E75-82
Fricke, Janie C82-5, -6
Friday Night Fights E80-101
Fridrick, George E82-136
Fried, Walter T49-7
Friedberg, Billy E56-20, E57-20
Friedlander, Harold T74-19
Friedman, Dick E75-65
Friedman, Harry E73-89
Friedman, Steven R. T77-7
Friendly Fire E78-7, -25, -34, -46
"Friends" G79-12
Frischer, Barry E82-109
Fristoe, Allen E82-96
Fritz, Howard E75-64
Fritz, Peter E72-40
Frizzell, David C81-8, C82-8
From the Ashes ... Nicaragua Today E82-121
"From the Bottle to the Bottom" G74-17
Frontiere, Dominick E70-67
Fryer, Robert T53-18, T59-18, T79-7
Fuerte, Luis A. E79-92
Fugitive, The E65-3
Fuisz, Robert E., M.D. E80-88
Fulaz, Robert E. E82-39
Fuller, Penny E81-27
"Fullfillingness' First Finale" G75-2, -5
Funk, Robert E68-21
"Funny Girl" G65-24
Funny Side of Marriage, The E71-68
FUNNY THING HAPPENED ON THE WAY TO THE FORUM, A T63-8, -9, -10, -13, -17, -18, T72-8, -9
"Funny Way of Laughin'" G63-11
Funshine Saturday and Sunday E74-84
Furlon E78-43
Furse, Margaret E74-82
Furth, George T71-13
Fusari, Lou E83-43

G

G.E. College Bowl E62-10
G.E. Theatre E73-74, -75, -80, -86, E77-31, E77-56
Gabel, Martin T61-3
Gabriel, Ethel G83-58
"Gabrieli" G69-31, G70-36
Gabrieli Consort G69-31
Gaeta, Frank E71-44
Gaffney, Dominick E69-41
Gaines, George E70-62
"Gaite Parisienne" G59-22
Gaither, Bill, Trio G74-26, G76-26
Gale, John E80-53
Gallagher, Helen T52-11, T71-11, E75-43, E76-86
"Gallant Men" G68-20
Gallery, Michele E78-30
Gallivan, Jack E75-64
Galuten, Albhy G79-50
Gambino, Anthony E80-90
"Gambler, The" C79-3, -4, G79-16, G80-22
Game, The E65-8, -18
"Games People Play" G70-3, -10, -23
Gangster Chronicles, The E80-46
Ganziano, Dino E83-63
Garber, Tony E74-61, E76-43, E79-60, E81-38
Gardenia, Vincent T72-3

Index 156

Gardner, Charles E72-40, E75-64, E79-112
Garfield on the Town E83-5
Garfunkel, Art (Also see Simon & Garfunkel) G71-10
Gargiulo, Michael E59-24, E73-54, E75-55, E76-91, E77-93, E80-85
Garland, Judy T52-17, G62-2, -6
Garner, James E76-12
Garnett, Gale G65-21
Garrett, Lila E73-88, -91
Garszva, Jerry G82-54
Gary Moore Show, The E61-2, -12
Gass, Michael E80-90
Gathering, The E77-11
Gatlin, Larry G77-16
Gaucho E78-92, G82-54
Gauguin in Tahiti: The Search for Paradise E67-11, -46
Gauguin the Savage E79-55
Gavitt, Donald E82-104
Gay, Norman E78-92
GAY LIFE, THE T62-21
Gaye, Marvin E83-30, -32
Gayle, Crystal C77-5, C78-5, G78-17, G82-44, G83-45
Gaynor, Gloria G80-30
Gaynor, Jane T78-7
Geary, Anthony E81-71
Gebhardt, George T48-11
Geer, Will E74-30
Geffen, David T83-7
Gelbart, Larry T63-13
Gelber, David E82-128
Geld, Karyl E73-84
Geller, Bruce E66-26
Gench, Marvin E75-64, E79-112
General Electric E59-22, E70-71
General Hospital E78-71, E80-64, -78, -82, E81-71, -73, -79, -90
"Genius of Ray Charles" G61-5
Gennaro, Peter T77-14
"Gentle on My Mind" G68-9, -10, -12, -21
Gentry, Bobbie G68-6, -34, -48
George Burns: An Update E80-93
George Gobel Show, The E54-23
GEORGE M! T69-12
"Georgia on My Mind" G61-4, -11, G79-18
Geraldi, Vito E72-40
Gerard, Lou E74-83
Gerber, Jay E78-90, E79-110
Geren, Tom E79-53
Germain, Larry E79-58
"Gershwin" G77-41, -44, G78-43
"Gershwin Live!" G83-18

"Gertrude Stein, Gertrude Stein, Gertrude Stein" G81-33
"Get Closer" G83-56
Get Smart E66-17, -27, E67-1, -23, E68-1, -6
Getz, Stan G63-7, G65-1, -2, -7
"Getz/Gilberto" G65-2, -7, -39
Geving, Hank E82-44
Ghost and Mrs. Muir, The E68-7, E69-9
Ghostley, Alice T65-5
"Giant Steps" G74-12
"Giants, The" G78-15
Gibb, Barry (Also see The Bee Gees) G81-6
Gibbs, Terri C81-11
Gibson, Kent E80-63
Gibson, William T60-6
Giddings, Al E79-39
Gideon E71-49
Gielgud, Sir John T59-22, T61-7, G80-32
Gifford, Lewis E80-88
Gift of Tears E73-127
"Gigi" G59-19, T74-13
Gilbert, Donna E79-58
Gilbert, Richard G84-43
Gilbert, Stan E75-65
Gilbert, Willie T62-14
Gilberto, Astrud G65-1
Gilberto, Joao G65-2
Gilder, Rosamond T48-12
Gilford, Jack E78-80
Gillaspy, Richard E59-24
Gillespie, Dizzy G76-13
Gillette, Gene E83-32
Gillette Cavalcade of Sports E54-10
Gilley's 'Urban Cowboy' Band G81-26
Gilman, Harve E80-99
Gilroy, Frank T65-1
Gimbel, Norman G74-3
Gimble, Johnny C75-10
GIN GAME, THE T78-4
GINGERBREAD LADY T71-4
Gingold, Hermione G77-35
Gioconda, La E79-73, -87, -92
Giordano, Nick E72-37, E75-63
"Girl from Ipanema, The" G65-1
GIRL WHO CAME TO SUPPER, THE T64-13
Girl Who Couldn't Lose, The E74-9, -53
"Girls on Film/Hungry Like a Wolf" G84-66
Giselle E77-9
Giulini, Carlo Maria G72-33, G78-39, G79-38, G81-51
Giulini's Beethoven's Ninth Live: A Gift from Los Angeles E78-53

Index

"Give 'Em Hell, Harry" G76-25
Give Me a Ring Sometime E82-35
"Give Me the Night" G81-29
Glaser Brothers, The C70-7
Glass, Robert W., Jr. E81-43
Glass Eye, The E57-22
Glass House, The E71-32
"Glass Houses" G81-12
Glass Menagerie, The E73-33, -34, -37, -38
Glazer, Barry E81-81
Gleason, Jackie T60-10
Gleason, Phillip E79-99
GLENGARRY GLEN ROSS T84-3
Glines, John T83-1
Globetrobber E80-88
Glock, Will E64-23
"Glorious Sound of Brass, The" G68-46
"Glory of Gabrieli" G69-33
Glouner, Richard E74-71
Glynn, Carlin T79-11
Go E75-13
Gobel, George E54-8
"God Is in the House" G74-13, -44
Goddard, Richard C. E77-73, E78-40
"Godfather, The" G73-30
Godfrey, John E80-94
Godspeed Opera House T80-20
"Godspell" G72-29
Goetz, William M. E78-90
"Goin' Out of My Head" G67-7
Gold, Avram E82-57
Gold, Ernest G61-3, -22
Gold Bug, The E79-71, -88
Goldenberg, Billy E74-75, E77-55, E82-53
Goldie & Kids ... Listen to Us E81-18
GOLDILOCKS T59-11, -13
Goldman, Byron T84-1
Goldman, Hal E59-15
Goldman, Sherwin M. T77-19, G78-43
Goldmark, Peter E74-89
Goldmark Laboratories E74-89
Goldsmith, Jerry E72-56, E74-76, E75-85, E80-57
Goldstone, James E80-24
Golly, Al E80-99
Gone Too Soon E83-57
Gonna Learn How to Fly E83-30
Gonzales, Conseulo E82-138
Gonzales, John E79-88
Gonzales, Steven H. E78-90, E80-101, E82-109
Gonzales, Victor E75-64
GOOD DOCTOR, THE T74-5
"Good Evening" G75-25

GOOD EVENING T74-19
"Good Feelin'" G71-27
"Good King Bad, Theme from" G77-25
"Good Hearted Woman" C76-2
Good Morning America E79-83, E80-90
GOODBYE, MY FANCY T49-5
Goodbye, Mr. Scripps E83-25
Goode, Richard G83-48
Goodman, Hal E58-31, E65-23, E70-50
Goodman, Paul G83-54
Goodman, Roger E75-58
Goodrich, Francis T56-6
Gordon, Al E58-31, E59-15, E65-23
Gordon, Gerald E75-44
Gordon, Ruth E78-12
Gordon, Sigismund E80-99
Goren, Rowby E73-89
Gorey, Edward T78-18
Gorfain, Louis H. E82-39
Gorilla E80-63
Gorman, Cliff T72-2
Gorme, Eydie G61-25, G67-6
Gorsuch, Stephen E80-99
Gossamer Albatross—Flight of Imagination E79-104
Gossett, Louis, Jr. E76-18
"Got to Get You into My Life" G79-11
"Gotta Serve Somebody" G80-12
Gottleib, Carl E68-34
Gottlieb, Morton T71-7
Gough, Fred E68-36, E77-97
Gough, Michael T79-3
Gould, Glenn G74-45, G83-46, -50, G84-54
Gould, Morton G67-4
Gould, Stan E74-83, E80-99
Goulet, Robert G63-39, T68-9
Goupil, Pierre E71-70
"Graduate, The" G69-27
Graf, Irwin E72-38
Grafalo, Tony E73-90
Graffeo, George E83-82
Graham, David E80-99
Graham, Edward T. (Bud) G68-46, G74-41, G76-42, G77-44, G79-46, G82-53
Graham, Jack E80-99
Gramaglia, Al E72-43, E73-69
Grammar Rock E75-16
Granada Television Ltd., London E77-108, E83-85
"Grand Old Gospel" G67-21
Grant, Amy G83-38, G84-37
Grant, Anne E76-84
Grant, Lee E65-13, E70-14
Grant, Micki G73-31

Index

Granville, Fred Leroy E72-42
Grau, James M. E78-90, E80-99
"Gravy Waltz" G64-9
Gray, Bruce E76-48
Gray, Dolores T54-12
Graydon, Jay G80-25, G83-28
Great American Bike Race E83-81
"Great American Documents" G77-27
Great American Dream Machine, The E70-24, E7126
Great American Novel, The E68-25, -28
"Great Band with Great Voices" G62-26
Great English Garden Party—Peter Ustinov Looks at 100 Years of Wimbleon E77-95
"Great Gospel Songs" G65-22
Great Performances E75-93, E77-30, E78-9, E83-8
"Great Scenes from Gershwin's *Porgy and Bess*" G64-29
"Great Songs of Love and Faith" G63-20
Great Space Coaster, The E81-100
Great Whales, The E77-10
GREAT WHITE HOPE, THE T69-1, -2, -5
Green, Adolph T53-9, T68-13, T70-7, T78-12, -13
Green, Al G82-39, G83-39, -40, G84-41
Green, David E68-32, E82-136
Green, Gerald E77-39
Green, Harry T56-21
Green, Johnny G62-23
Green, Ruth T51-22
Greenberg, Noah G65-31
Greenberg, Ted E83-39
Greenblatt, Elliott E80-99
Greenblatt, Kenneth D. T82-7, T84-7
Greene, David E75-49, E76-30, E78-25
Greene, Edward J. E77-58, E78-49, E82-62, E83-58
Greene, Herbert T58-18
Greene, Jack C67-2, -3, -6
Greene, Jerry E76-49
Greene, Richard E82-104
Greenwood, Lee C83-6, G84-25
Gregory, Paul E55-24
Grella, John L. E79-89
Grenada Network (England) E62-28, E82-146
Grennon, Henry J. E70-40
Grey, Joel T67-9
Grieco, Frank, Jr. E82-41
Gries, Tom E63-21, E71-32
Griffin, Merv E73-90, E81-77
Griffin, Robert E82-104
Griffith, Robert T55-18, T56-18, T60-19
Grimes, Tammy T61-13, T70-4
Grinch Grinches the Cat in the Hat, The E81-25, -56
Grindstaff, Douglas H. E69-42, E75-65, E77-75, E79-60
Grizzard, George E79-20
Grodin, Charles E77-41
Gross, Charles E78-92
Gross, Joseph E78-53
Gross, Winfield E72-40
Grossman, Joyce Tamara E77-97
Grossman, Larry E81-42, E83-57
Grossman, Sandy E79-107
Growth/Decay E79-88
Grusin, Dave G69-27, G84-7
"Guajira Pa' la Jeva" G82-43
Guaraldi, Vince G63-9
Guare, John T72-12
Guatemala E82-121
Guenette, Robert E70-28
Guerico, James William (Also see Blood, Sweat & Tears) G77-11
Guerillas in Usulatan E82-136
Guest, Christopher E75-78
Guiding Light E79-64, E80-87, E81-60, -85, -93, E82-111
Guigliano, Francis E79-112
Guillaume, Robert E78-15
"Guilty" G81-6
Guinness, Alec T64-2
"Guitar from Ipanema" G65-8
Guiterrez, John E76-48
Gulf of Tonkin Segment E70-25
Gun for Mandy, A E82-90
Gunsmoke E57-2, -23, E58-17, E67-21, E69-40
Gunther, Werner E79-113
Gurasich, Lynda E73-110
Gustaitis, Joe E81-87
Guthrie, James G81-53
Guthrie, Tyrone T56-7
Guthrie Theatre T82-20
Gutstein, Ken E78-92
Guy, Rory G75-45
Guyana Tragedy: The Story of Jim Jones E79-23
GUYS AND DOLLS T51-7, -9, -10, -13, -14, -15, -16, -17
Guzman, Claudio E58-35
"Gypsy" G60-18, T75-10
Gypsy in My Soul E75-7, -83

H

H.E.L.P.!! (Dr. Henry's Emergency Lessons for People) E79-68

Index

Hackett, Albert T56-6
HADRIAN VII T69-6
Haenelt, Roger E75-64, E79-89, -112, E81-92
Hafley, Lou E68-37
Hagen, Dave E82-109
Hagen, Earl E67-47
Hagen, Uta T51-4, T63-4
Haggard, Merle C70-1, -2, -3, -6, C72-3, C83-8
Haggert, Jerome E77-105
Haggerty, Mick G80-53
Hague, Albert T59-15
Hahn, Ken E82-61
Hahn, Phil E67-35
Haigood, Harry E80-99
Haines, Larry E75-42, E80-77
"Hair" G69-28
Haire, Christopher L. E81-44
Haitink G81-47
Hale, Barbara E58-16
Halee, Roy G71-40
Haley, Jack, Jr. E67-39
Hall, Dean E79-53, E81-48, E83-43
Hall, Delores T77-11
Hall, Delos E73-121
Hall, Don E66-30, E70-41
Hall, Joyce C. E60-26
Hall, Juanita T50-11
Hall, Norman E82-96
Hall, Peter T67-6, T81-6
Hall, Rich E80-86
Hall, Sherwood, III G59-27
Hall, Tom T. G73-45
Hall of Kings E66-7
HALLELUJAH, BABY! T68-8, -11, -12, -13, -16
Halliday, Richard T60-19
Hallmark Cards, Inc. E81-59
Hallmark Hall of Fame E54-18, E57-26, E58-11, -23, -25, -29, E60-1, -7, -10, -11, -15, E61-7, -11, -14, E62-13, -26, E63-17, -28, E64-2, -6, -7, -22, -24, -26, -28, E65-12, -21, -37, E66-13, E67-5, E68-5, E69-6, -12, E70-13, -15, -16, -35, -44, -54, -61, -64, E71-15, -49, E73-101, E76-49
Halloween is Grinch Night E77-4
Halloween That Almost Wasn't, The E79-8, -43
Halls, Lee E78-84
Halper, Bob E80-99
Hamill, Pete G76-45
HAMLET T64-3, E70-16, -44, -54, -61, -64
Hamlisch, Marvin G75-3, -8, -30, -47, T76-13

Hammer, Peter E80-88, E81-89
Hammerstein, Oscar, II T50-12, -15, T52-7, T60-9, -19, G61-23
Hammerstein, William T57-22
Hammond, Lawrence E79-89, E81-92, E82-105
Hampshire, Susan E69-11, E70-12, E72-23
Hampton, Lionel E80-94
Hancock, Herbie G84-32
"Handel" G61-33, G67-35
Handelsman, Mel E79-90
Handley, Alan E65-20
"Handy Man" G78-4
Hanes, Mark E83-59
Haney, Carol T55-13
Hanford, Robert E80-99
"Hang on Sloopy" G74-23
Hanley, William E83-36
Hanrahan, Jack E67-35
Hansel and Gretel: Live from the Met E82-77, -111
Hansen, Peter E78-71
"Happiest Girl in the Whole USA, The" C72-2, G73-15
Happy Anniversary, Charlie Brown E75-15
HAPPY BIRTHDAY T47-2, -7
Happy Days E77-45
Happy Goodman Family, The G69-25, G79-29
"Happy Gospel of the Happy Goodman Family, The" G69-25
"Happy Man" G79-28
HAPPY TIME, THE T68-9, -14, -15
Harbaugh, Rodger E78-90
"Hard Again" G78-33
"Hard Day's Night, A" G65-27
Hardigan, Kathy E82-139
Hardwick, Keith G81-56
Hardy, Joseph T70-6
Hareiter, Max E77-71
Hargate, Bill E76-49, E77-68
Harish, Theo E77-71
Harlequin E74-13
Harman, Robert L. E73-71, E76-44, E77-49, E79-37, E80-48
Harmon, Barry E73-83, E77-38
Harms, Greg E79-92
Harnell, Joe G63-15
Harney, Ben T82-8
Harnick, Sheldon T60-9, G64-21, T65-15
Harp, Bill E64-27, E78-41
Harper, Ken T75-7
Harper, Valerie E70-18, E71-17, E72-24, E74-21

"Harper Valley P.T.A." C68-2, G69-14
Harrell, Lynn G82-47
Harrington, Pat, Jr. E83-17
Harris, Barbara T67-10
Harris, Emmylou G77-17, C80-5, G80-21, G81-25
Harris, Harry E81-16
Harris, Julie T52-4, T56-4, E58-23, E61-11, T69-4, T73-4, T77-4, G78-27
Harris, Larnelle G84-39
Harris, Larry M. E82-31
Harris, Richard G74-25
Harris, Rosemary T66-4, E75-27
Harris Incident, The E78-24
Harrison, George (Also see The Beatles) G71-28, G73-2
Harrison, Harvey E79-110
Harrison, Lee E71-72
Harrison, Lynn E54-27
Harrison, Peter E81-38
Harrison, Rex T49-2, T57-9, T69-16
Harry O E75-36
Harry S Truman: Plain Speaking E76-22
Hart, Bruce E69-62, E79-88
Hart, Carole E69-62, E79-88
Hart, Freddy C71-4, C72-4
Hart, Harry E79-110
Hart, Larry G79-30
Hart, Moss T57-17
Hart, Stan E71-62, E72-63
Hartford, John G68-10, -21, G77-31
Hartley, Mariette E78-20
Hartman, Grace T48-7
Hartman, Jan E77-96, E79-88
Hartman, Paul T48-6
Harvey, Ben E80-99
Harvey, Richard E75-91
Harvey, Tim E76-57, E77-71
Haskell, Jimmie G68-29, G71-10, G77-11, E77-56
Hassinger, Dave G65-40
"Hasten Down the Wind" G77-5
Hastings, Hal T56-16
Hastings, Michael E71-64
"Hatari!" G63-36
Hatfield, Robert E73-127
Hathaway, Donny G73-6
Hathaway, William E74-83
Hause, George E79-109
Havinga, Nicholas E75-57
Hawaii Five-O E69-55, E73-93
Hawaii Show—Sarah's Wedding, The E83-59
"Hawk Flies, The" G75-44
Hawkins, Edwin, Singers G70-29, G71-26, G78-31

Hawkins, John E79-32
Hawkins, Rick E77-40
Hawkins, Ronnie E75-58
Hawkins, Tremaine G81-36
Hawkins, Walter G81-36
Haworth, Jann G68-43
"Haydn" G82-52, G84-53, -57
Hayes, Dermot T82-16
Hayes, Helen T47-2, E52-6, T58-4, G77-27
Hayes, Isaac G72-7, -28, G73-8
Hayes, Joseph T55-8
Hayman, Lillian G68-12
Hays, Ron E78-92
Hayward, Chris E67-34
Hayward, Leland T48-4, T50-15, T60-19
Hazam, Lou E61-19, E71-30
Hazel E61-9, E62-12
HAZEL FLAGG T53-10, -20
He and She E67-34
He Is Risen E62-23
He Makes Me Feel Like Dancin' E83-7, -47,
"He Set My Life to Music" G83-36
"He Stopped Loving Her Today" C80-2, -4, C81-4, G81-24
"He Touched Me" G73-26
He Was Only Twelve E81-39
Healer, The E77-106
Hearn, George T84-9
Heart in Hiding E74-43, -70
Heart Transplant E80-93
"Heartbreak Tonight" G80-9
Heartbreak Winner E79-88
"Heaven's Just a Sin Away" C78-2, G78-19
Hee Haw E70-42
"Heed the Call" G80-35
Heeley, Desmond T68-17, -18
Hefter, Arie E78-66
Hefti, Neal G67-24
Heggen, Thomas T48-1, -5
Heider, Larry E77-54, E80-53, E83-42
Heidi E68-38
Heifetz, Jascha G62-28, G63-27, G65-30
"Heifetz/Piatigorsky Concerts" G63-27
Heim, Alan E77-46
Heineman, Laurie E77-88
Heineman, Scott E80-89
Heinemann, Arthur E82-102
HEIRESS, THE T48-2, -9
Helburn, Theresa T58-8
Helen Morgan Story, The E57-12
Helias, Albert J. E72-38
HELLO, DOLLY! T64-9, -12, -14, -15, -16, -17, -18, -19, -20, -21, G65-3, -5

Index

Hello, Goodbye, Hello E69-45
Hello in There E78-80
"Hello Muddah, Hello Faddah" G64-14
"Help Me Make It Through the Night" C71-2, G72-13, -14
Hemion, Dwight A. E69-34, E73-50, -59, E75-51, E76-31, E77-36, E79-27, E81-18, E82-26, E83-27
Hemo the Magnificent E57-24
Henderson, Peter G80-52
Heneghan, Jim E80-99
Henning, Peter E83-80
Henry, Buck E66-27
HENRY VIII T47-7
Henry Fonda Tribute E79-83
Henry Ford's America E77-109
Henry Steele Commager E73-116
Henry Winkler Meets William Shakespeare E77-96
Henson, Jim E75-97, E78-80, G79-37, G80-42, G82-44
Hepburn, Audrey T54-4, T68-19
Hepburn, Katherine E74-27
"Herbert: The Music of Victor Herbert" G77-42
"Here Comes My Baby" G65-13
"Here You Come Again" G79-17
Here's Johnny! E80-93
Here's Looking at You, Kid E82-129
Here's Peggy Flemming E68-35
Here's Television Entertainment E83-27, -57
Herman, Jerry T64-16, G65-3, G67-23, T84-13
Herman, Woody G64-8, G74-12, G75-12
Hermelin, Beth E80-99
Herring, James E81-48
Herrmann, Edward T76-3
Herschberg, Lee G67-42
Hersey, David T80-17, T83-17
Hersh, Bob E80-99
Hersh, Scott E82-104
Hershong, Albert E56-26
Herskovitz, Marshall E82-37
Herzfeld, John E80-88
"He's a Rebel" G84-36
Hess, Jake G69-24, G70-27, G71-24, G82-36
Hessel, Rick E72-38
Hewitt's Just Different E77-83, -96
Hey, Jerry G81-7, G82-9, G83-14, G84-43
"(Hey Won't You Play) Another Somebody Done Somebody Wrong Song" G76-14
Hicks, Barry E80-99
Hickson, Bob E80-99, E83-82
Hickson, Joan T79-5

Hierl, Jakob E72-40, E75-64, E79-112
Higgins, Donald E77-48
High Band Videotape Recorder E66-39
HIGH BUTTON SHOES T48-8
High Midnight E79-41
"High Flying" G62-25
High Hat E77-60
High School Profile, The E69-37
"Higher Plane" G83-39
Highgate School Choir" G64-33
Hight of the Vicious Valentine E66-22
Highton, Bob E79-53
Hiken, Nat E55-22, -26, E56-20, E57-20, E61-16
Hilkene, Michael E83-33
Hill, Arthur T63-2
Hill, Ed E69-60
Hill, J. E83-54
Hill, Lucienne T61-1
Hill, Pamela E73-118
Hill, Richard E. E71-73
Hill Street Blues E80-2, -18, -19, -23, -25, -31, -33, -44, E81-2, -9, -10, -28, -32, -43, E82-1, -24, -29, -36, -57, -59, E83-1, -20, -21, -25, -34
"Hill Street Blues, Theme from" G82-8, -14
Hill Street Station E80-23, -31, -33
Hilliard, Robert E72-63
Hillis, Margaret G78-45, G79-45, G80-50, G83-53, G84-57
Hillyer, John E82-109
Hilmer, David E72-48, E73-76, E77-54, E83-43
"Hindemith" G74-45
Hines, Douglas E74-56, E76-36
Hinkley, Don E71-62
Hirsch, Judd E80-15, E82-12
Hirschfield, Al T75-18, T84-20
Hirt, Al G64-16
"Hit the Road Jack" G62-12
Hitchings, Duane G84-43
Hitchings, Roy E80-99
Hlavaty, Anthony E78-90
Hoade, Martin E78-82
Hoagland, Ellsworth E65-25
"Hoagy Carmichael" G82-57
Hoch, Winston C. E65-41
Hodnett, Frank E80-99
Hoenack, Jeremy E74-61
Hoffman, Harold E74-83
Hofsiss, Jack T79-6
Hogan's Goat E71-40
Hogan's Heroes E67-25, E68-12
Holbrook, Hal T66-2, E70-11, E73-25, -29, E75-28

Index 162

Holbrook, Richard E73-100
"Hold It Right There" G67-16
"Hold On I'm Comin'" G82-29
Holden, William E73-23
Holder, Geoffrey T75-14, -17
Holgate, Ronald T69-9
Holiday, Jennifer T82-10, G83-29
Holiday, Judy T57-11
Holloway, Sterling G75-32
Hollowood, Ann E78-44
Hollywood E79-40
Hollywood Bowl Symphony G59-22
"Hollywood Palace, The" E65-39
Hollywood Squares, The E73-45, -47, -89, E74-10, -45, -55, E77-86, E78-65, -77, -83, E79-66, -81, -84, E80-81
Hollywood String Quartet G59-25
Hollywood Television Theatre E70-48, -55, E71-54, E77-64
Hollywood: The Dream Factory E71-23
Holm, Ian T67-3
Holm, Roy E81-48, E83-43
Holmes, Debbie E81-90
Holmes, Ralph E80-51, E81-55
Holocaust E77-7, -21, -22, -25, -34, -39, -46, -66, -71
Holt, Fritz T84-7
Holy Terror, The E64-26
"Home Where I Belong" G78-28
HOMECOMING, THE T67-1, -2, -3, -6
"Homenaje a Beny More" G79-36
Homer & Jethro G60-12
"Honey" C68-4, G76-44
Hookman E73-93
Hope, Bob E58-41, E83-65
Hopkins, Anthony E75-30, E80-12
Hopkins, Linda T72-11
Horan, Dick E79-113
Horizon: The Making of a Natural History Film E73-130
Horne, Lena T81-20, G82-5
Horne, Marilyn G65-47, G82-51, G84-55
Horowitz, Vladimir G63-4, -32, G64-32, G65-33, G66-4, -35, G68-39, G69-32, G72-32, -36, G73-38, G74-37, G77-40, G78-38, E78-81, G79-41, -42, G80-47, G82-49
"Horowitz at Carnegie Hall" G66-4, -35, -40, G68-39
"Horowitz Concerts" G77-40, G82-49
"Horowitz Concerts 1978–79, The" G80-47
Horowitz: Live! E78-67, -81
"Horowitz on Television" G69-32

"Horowitz Plays Chopin" G73-38
"Horowitz Plays Scriabin" G74-37
Horsemen of Inner Mongolia E81-88, -89
Horta, Denise E80-31
Horta, Eileen E80-31, E82-57
Horta, Sam E80-31, E82-57
Horton, David E74-61
Horton, Johnny G60-8
Hospital E69-22, -29
Hot/Cold E79-88
Hot Hero Sandwich E79-69, -88
"Hot Stuff" G80-11
"Hotel California" G78-1
Hour Magazine E82-99
HOUSE OF FLOWERS T55-19
House Without a Christmas Tree, The E72-53
Houston, David G67-10, -13
Houston, Thelma G78-22
Houston Grand Opera, The T77-19
Houston Grand Orchestra G78-43
"How Deep Is Your Love?" G78-6
"How Glad I Am" G65-16
"How Great Thou Art" G68-22, G75-26
"How I Got Over" G77-30
HOW, NOW, DOW JONES T68-10
How the West Was Won E77-26, -68
How to Kill a Woman E57-23
HOW TO SUCCEED IN BUSINESS WITHOUT REALLY TRYING T62-9, -10, -11, -14, -15, -18, -19, G62-21
Howard, Cy E68-34
Howard, Ken T70-3, E80-88
Howard, Marc T78-1
Howard, Reed E78-39
Howard, Trevor E62-13
Hubbard, Elizabeth E73-40, E75-45
Hubbard, Freddie G73-11
Huckleberry Hound E59-6
Huddle, Michael E79-90
Hughes, Barnard E77-28, T78-2
Hughes, Ken E58-30
Hughes, Raymond E76-67
Hughes, William E78-66
Hughes Aircraft Corporation E65-43
Hugo & Luigi (Also see Hugo Peretti and Luigi Creatore) G77-33
Hulsey, James E81-46, E83-48, -49
"Hummel" G84-53
"Humor in Music" G62-17
Humphrey, Vince E78-92
Hunger in America E68-18, -22
Hunt, Martita T49-4
Hunt, Peter T69-13
Hunt, Richard E75-97, E78-80
Huntley, Leslie E82-64

Huntley–Brinkley Report E58-6, E59-4, E60-4, E61-4, E62-4, E63-4, E68-22, E69-26, -37, -47, E70-60
Hupp, Debbie G80-20
"Hurts So Good" G83-12
Hurwitz, Tom E81-88
Husock, Howard E82-127
"Hustle, The" G76-8
Hutak, Nicholas E82-111
Huth, Thomas J. E77-58
Huynh, Vo E67-45
Hyland, Diana E76-27
Hyman, Dick E80-88, E82-54
Hymes, Phil E6424

I

IBM Presents Baryshnikov on Broadway E79-4, -27, -47, -51
IBM Presents Clarence Darrow E74-68
"I.O.U." G84-25
ITT Theatre Special, An E83-18
I AM A CAMERA T52-4, -5
"I Am Woman" G73-5
"I Believe in You" C81-3
I Can Sing a Rainbow E79-88
"I Can't Help It (If I'm Still in Love with You)" G76-15
"I Can't Stop Loving You" G63-12, G64-23
I, Claudius E77-71
I Climb the Stairs E54-25
"I Dig Chicks" G60-7
I DO! I DO! T67-8
"I Don't Wanna Play House" G68-11
"I Honestly Love You" G75-1, -5
"I Know a Place" G66-30
"I Left My Heart in San Francisco" G63-1, -5, -23
I, Leonardo E64-10
I Love Lucy E52-3, E53-2, E55-5
I LOVE MY WIFE T77-9, -15
I OUGHT TO BE IN PICTURES T80-5
I See Chicago E65-47
I Spy E65-10, E66-15, E67-19, -47
"I Started Out as a Child" G65-18
I Think I'm Having a Baby E80-88
"I Will Say Goodbye" G81-20
"I Will Survive" G80-30
"I Wish" G77-23
"I Won't Mention It Again" C71-3
"I Write the Songs" G77-3
Ian, Janis G76-5, G83-45
Ibbetson, Arthur F. E80-34

Icarus Productions T84-1
Ice Sculptor E82-139
Iditarod Dog Sled Race, The E83-80
"If He Walked Into My Life" G67-6
"If I Had a Hammer" G63-19, -24
"If I Were a Carpenter" G71-16
If No Birds Sang E79-86
"If You Leave Me Now" G77-6, -11
If You Turn On E70-72
Ikegami Electronics E82-66
"I'll Be Thinking of You" G80-36
"I'll Never Fall in Love Again" G71-5
"I'll Never Love This Way Again" G80-5
"I'll Rise Again" G84-41
"(I'm a) Stand by My Woman Man" G77-18
"I'm Following You" G83-37
"I'm Here" G84-48
"I'm Ready" G79-33
"I'm So Glad I'm Standing Here Today" G84-42
"Images" G76-9, -12
Imamichi, Junzo E74-88
Immortal, The E69-42
Imperials G76-27, G78-30, G80-35, G82-37
Impossible Dream: Ballooning Across the Atlantic, The E77-101
In Concert with Cat Stevens E73-76
"'In' Crowd, The" G66-7
In Defense of Ellen McKay E71-65
"In Gospel Country" G70-28
"In Harmony" G83-45
"In Harmony/A Sesame Street Record" G81-43
"In the Beginning God" G67-8
In the Belly of the Beast E82-126
"In the Ghetto" G75-28
In the News E79-68, E80-69, E81-64, E82-79
Incest: The Best Kept Secret E79-102
Incredible Flight of the Snow Geese, The E72-39, -46
Incredible Hulk, The E78-20
Independence and '76 E79-86
Indianapolis 500 E82-116
"Indianola Mississippi Seeds" G71-41
Inga E78-28
Ingram, James G82-30
INHERIT THE WIND T56-2, -3, -19, E65-37
INNER CITY T72-11
"Innervisions" G74-2, -42
INNOCENTS, THE T50-17
Inside Afghanistan E80-94
"Inside Shelly Berman" G60-11

Index 164

Inside Story: Marek E74-18
Inside the Third Reich E81-17, -38
Inside/Out E73-15
Insight E80-70, -89, E81-66, E82-75, -90, -112
"'Interplay' Sessions, The" G84-61
Interrogation at Budapest E78-82
"Intimate Bach, The" G63-38
Into the Maelstrom E82-34
Invasion of Kevin Ireland, The E71-31
Investigation of Teenage Drug Addition, An: Odyssey House E69-26
Invincible Mr. Disraeli, The E62-13, -26
Invisible World E80-93
Irakere G80-41
Ireland, Jerry E78-90
IRENE T73-9
IRMA LA DOUCE T61-12
Irons, Jeremy T84-2
Ironside E67-22
Irving, George S. T73-9
Irwin, Dean E82-139
Is Anyone Out There Learning—CBS Report Card on American Education E79-100
"Is It Something I Said?" G76-24
"Is That All There Is?" G70-5
Is There One Who Understands Me?—The World of James Joyce E82-144
"Isaac Stern 60th Anniversary Celebration" G82-48, -53
Isaacs, Don V. E76-43, E77-75, E79-60
Isabella, Catherine E82-138
ISLAND, THE T75-2
Isley Brothers G70-22
Israel Philharmonic G76-40, G83-51
Israel's Northern Front E73-111
Istomin, Eugene G71-34
It Didn't Have to Happen E82-132
It Takes a Thief E67-43
"It Was a Lover and His Lass (Morley, Byrd and Others)" G65-31
"It Was a Very Good Year" G66-5, -25
"It Was Almost Like a Song" C78-3
Italians, The E66-8
Ithica College Concert Choir G67-35
Itkin, William E79-90, E82-104
It's Good to Be Alive E73-74, -75
It's Mental Work E63-18
"It's Too Late" G72-1
It's Whether You Win or Lose E72-32
"It's Your Thing" G70-22
Iwano, Ruth E82-139
Ives, Burl G63-11
Ives, Charles G66-39
"Ives" G66-32, G67-4, -35, G71-36
Ivey, Judith T83-5

J

J.B. T59-1, -6, -7, -8
Jabara, Paul G79-21
Jack and the Beanstalk E66-4
Jack Benny Show, The E58-4, -13, -31, E59-13, -15, E60-3
Jackie Gleason Show, The E53-6, E54-6, -7, -30, E55-6, E66-43, E67-29
Jackpot! E73-54
Jackson, Dwight E79-51
Jackson, Glenda E71-12
Jackson, Mahalia G62-20, G63-20, G77-30
Jackson, Michael G80-27, G84-1, -2, -4, -12, -28, -30, -49, -63
Jackson, William E77-48
"Jackson" G68-13
Jacoby, Coleman E55-22, E56-20, E57-20
Jacoby, Scott E72-26
Jagger, Dean E79-86
James, Bob G81-8
James, Francesca E79-78
James, Hal T66-7, T68-16
James, Mark C82-4, G83-3, C83-4, G83-23
Jamieson, Robert E80-99
Jampolis, Neil Patrick T75-16
"Janacek" G82-50
Jane Eyre E71-66
Jane Goodall and the World of Animal Behavior E72-64, -71, E73-67, -70
Jankeloff, Mark E80-99
Japanese, The E69-25
Jarre, Maurice G67-22
Jarreau, Al G78-14, G79-14, G81-43, G82-4, -19
"Java" G64-16
"Jaws" G76-30
"Jazz Suite on the Mass Texts" G66-9, -42
Jeffersons, The E80-14, E82-31
Jenkins, Gordon G66-25
Jennett, Jim E75-64
Jennings, Jack E68-36
Jennings, Waylon G70-17, C75-6, C76-2, -3, -8, G79-19
Jenny E75-93
Jensen, Dick E70-41
Jensen, Monika E82-126
Jericho Mile, The E78-17, -29, -33
Jerome Robbins Ballets E80-6
Jersey, Bill E82-134
Jessel, Patricia T55-5
"Jessie's Girl" G82-12

Index

"Jesus, We Just Want to Thank You" G76-26
Jeyte, Albert Paul E80-36
Jimenez, Tom E83-82
JOAN OF LORRAINE T47-2
Joanitis, George E80-99, E83-82
Jobe, Bill E73-107
Jochim, Mike E79-113
Joe and the Magic Bean: The Story of Superbowl III E77-105
JOE EGG T68-5
Joel, Billy G79-1, -3, G80-2, -4, G81-12, G83-45
Joelson, Ben E71-62
John, Tom E64-27, E72-59, E75-88
John Adams, Lawyer E75-31
John Davidson Show, The E80-90
John Denver and Friend E76-45
John Denver with His Special Guest George Burns Two of a Kind E80-49
"John F. Kennedy—As We Remember Him" G66-19
JOHN LOVES MARY T47-7
JOHN MURRAY ANDERSON'S ALMANAC T54-11
John Steinbeck's America and Americans E67-10, -42
John Steinbeck's East of Eden E80-54
"Johnathan and Darlene Edwards in Paris" G61-16
"Johnny Cash at Folsom Prison" C68-3, G69-39
"Johnny Cash at San Quentin Prison" C69-3
Johns, Glynis T73-10
Johnson, Alan E79-52
Johnson, Arte E68-43
Johnson, Coslough E67-35
Johnson, Don E75-66
Johnson, Gary E73-89
Johnson, General G71-18
Johnson, George E70-39, E72-38
Johnson, Howard E. E80-46
Johnson, Jack E70-41
Johnson, Jim E78-90
Johnson, Ken E77-69
Johnson, Mary Lea T79-7
Johnson, Mike E80-53
Johnson, Peter E67-40, E72-36
Johnson, Sterling E70-33, E80-84
Johnston, Bruce G77-3
Johnston, Dale E71-41
Johnston, Romain E76-58, E77-74
Joio, Norman Fello E64-17
"Jonathan Livingston Seagull" G74-25, -30

Jones, Bobby, & New Life G84-42
Jones, George C80-2, -6, C81-6, G81-24
Jones, Henry T58-3
Jones, Jack G62-5, G64-5
Jones, James Earl T69-2, G77-27
Jones, Jonah G60-7
Jones, Phil E71-29
Jones, Quincy G64-23, G70-13, G72-8, G74-7, E76-61, G79-7, G81-7, G82-7, -9, -31, -42, -58, G84-49, -63
Jones, Rickie Lee G80-58
Jones, Robert M. G60-32, G63-37, G64-40, G65-43, G66-42, G67-39
Jones, Simon E82-137
Jones, Thad G79-13
Jones, Tom G66-47
Jones, Tommy Lee E82-16
Jones, Trent E82-101
"Joplin" G74-35
Jordan, Bob E82-125
Jorgensen, Donlee E83-32
Joseph, Bernard E78-90
Joseph, Buddy E71-57
Joseph, Eddie C. E75-64
Journey to the Outer Limits E73-71, -115
"Jousts" G80-18
Judd for the Defense E68-8, -31
Judge E77-28
Judgment: The Court-Martial of Lt. William Calley E74-60
Judkins, Fred E83-33
"Judy at Carnegie Hall" G62-2, -6, -37, -38
Juggler of Notre Dame, The E82-76
Juhl, Jerry E69-62, E73-125, E80-27
Juilliard and Beyond: A Life in Music E82-133, 137, 140
Juilliard Quartet G66-33, G72-34, G78-40
Jujamcyn Theatre T78-19
"Julian & John" G73-36
Julie and Carol at Carnegie Hall E62-15, -22
Julie Andrews Hour, The E72-2, -33, -37, -48, -49, -50, -60
Julie Andrews' Invitation to the Dance with Rudolf Nureyev E80-68
June 30, 1971, A Day in History: The Supreme Court and the Pentagon Papers E71-25
Jury, Harold W. E49-11
"Just a Little Talk with Jesus" G78-29
Just Men! E82-93
"Just the Two of Us" G82-28
"Just the Way You Are" G79-1, -3

Index 166

Justice Black and the Bill of Rights E68-27
Jutchenko, Tony E79-112

K

K.C. & the Sunshine Band G79-2
KDIN (Des Moines, Iowa) E72-74
KFI University E50-12
KKK—The Invisible Empire E65-28
KLZ (Denver) E66-45
KNBC (Los Angeles) E69-66
KNBH/NBC E50-15
KNXT (Los Angeles) E70-72
KOOL-TV (Phoenix) E77-107
KPIX (San Francisco) E63-30
KTLA E48-4, E49-8, E50-8
KTLA Newsreel E50-11
K2 T83-16
Kahn, Michael E75-61
Kail, James E80-36
Kaiser, Burton C. T70-1
Kajita, Alvin E74-61, E75-65
Kalcheim, Lee E72-61
Kamm, Larry E75-58, E83-81
Kander, John T67-12, G68-25, E72-58, T81-13
Kane, Carol E81-13, E82-19
Kani, John T75-2
Kania, Robert E74-83
Kanin, Fay E73-80, -86
Kanter, Hal E54-23
Kantrowe, John H. E77-61
Karlin, Fred E73-94
Karlin, Norman E69-40
Karloff, Boris G68-18
Karnilova, Maria T65-13
Karp, David E64-21
Karrin, Bonnie E77-96
Kasha, Lawrence T70-7
Kasoff, Jan E82-43
Kate & Allie E83-15, -26
Kathy E81-65
Katz, Sid E62-24
Katzenberg, Mr. & Mrs. Ira T47-8
Kaufman, Emanuel E80-99
Kaufman, George S. T51-7
Kaufman, Larry E73-70, E76-43
Kavigan, Joe E69-42
Kavner, Julie E77-15
Kay, Bruce E83-48
Kay, Keith E67-31
Kaye, Danny T53-22, E63-15
Kaz E78-21

Kazan, Elia T47-4, T49-6, T59-7
Kazdan, Andrew G82-53
Kazmer, Constance A. E82-57
Kearney, Cheryal E79-55
Kearney, Richard E. E80-99
Kedrova, Lila T84-10
Keene, Bob E81-94
Keep, Ted G59-26, G60-29
Keep Your Eye on the Sparrow E75-70
Keepnews, Orin G84-61
Keeshan, Bob E81-78
Kefauver, U.S. Senator Estes E51-7
Kelbish, Evelyn G70-43
Kellard, Rick E73-89
Keller, Eytan E76-64, E78-47
Keller, Frank E56-23
Keller, Sheldon E65-23
Kelley, William P. E71-57
Kelly, Douglas C. E73-109
Kelly, Jack E75-68
Kelly, James E72-40
Kelly, Nancy T55-4
Kelly, Patsy T71-12
Kelly, Paul T48-2
Kelly, Robert E74-78, E76-60
Kelman, Alfred R. E81-84, E82-28
Kelsey, William E79-92
Kemp, Robert A. E72-48
Kendalls, The C78-2, G78-19
Kendy, Arthur G71-39, G79-46
Kenn, Jay E81-92
Kennedy, Arthur T49-3
Kennedy, Jacqueline E61-28
Kennedy, John F. E62-30
Kennedy Center Honors, The E80-21, E83-52
KENNEDY'S CHILDREN T76-5
Kenney, H. Wesley E73-53, -55, -57
Kenny, Sean T63-19
Kent State E80-24
Kenton, Stan G62-8, G63-8
Kentucky Derby E80-95
Kerr, John T54-3
Kerr, Anita, Singers G66-21, -26, G67-27
Kestenbaum, Jack E75-68
Key Biscayne Bank Charter Struggle, The E73-111
Keyes, Paul E67-35
Keys, Bob E77-54
Khan, Chaka G84-14, -29, -31
Kicelian, Hector E79-112
Kidd, Michael T47-6, T51-16, T54-16, T57-16, T60-18
Kids Are People Too E78-58
Kids, Drugs and Alcohol E82-90
Kiebach, Jurgen E77-71

Index

Kiley, Richard T59-10, T66-8, E82-22
Killing Ground, The—ABC News Close-Up E79-97, -101
"Killing Me Softly with His Song" G74-1, -3, -5
KILLING OF SISTER GEORGE, THE T67-4
Kim, Paul E80-88
Kim, Willa E80-59, T81-18
Kimberleys, The G70-17
King, B.B. G71-20, G82-40, G84-33
King, Carole G72-1, -2, -3, -5
King, Donald R. E76-90
King, Marshall E74-62
King, Dr. Martin Luther, Jr. G71-23
King, Robert C. E80-53
King, Tom E74-69
King E77-55
KING & I, THE T52-7, -9, -10, -14, -15
King at Last E78-44
King Lear E83-12, -85
"King of the Road" G66-11, -14, -15, -28, -29
Kingston Trio, The G59-7, G60-15
"Kingston Trio at Large" G60-15
Kinoy, Ernest E63-19, E76-51
Kipness, Joseph T70-7
Kirkpatrick, Allen E80-88, E81-89
Kirkwood, James T76-12
Kirschner, Jack E71-41
KISMET T54-9, -10, -14, -15, -17, -18
"Kiss an Angel Good Mornin'" G73-14
KISS ME KATE T49-9, -12, -13, -14
Klages, William M. E73-99, E76-70, E83-44, -52
Klan E81-101
Klaris, Harvey J. T82-7
Klausen, Raymond E75-89, E81-47, E82-42
Kleban, Edward T76-13
Klein, Andy E80-99
Klein, Larry E70-50
Kleinow, Peter E82-64
Klemperer, Otto G63-31
Klemperer, Werner E67-25, E68-12
Klimcsak, George E74-83, E80-99
Kline, Kevin T78-9, T81-8
Kling, Woody E71-62, E72-63
Klingbeil, Ken E75-64, E79-112
Klotz, Florence T72-18, T73-18, T76-18
Klugh, Earl G81-8
Klugman, Jack E63-13, E70-9, E72-14
Knapp, Sam T59-21
Knechtel, Larry G71-10
Knight, Gladys, & the Pips G74-6, -22
Knight, Shirley T76-5
Knight, Ted E72-25, E75-34

Knight, William E79-48
Knotts, Don E60-13, E61-13, E62-16, E65-16, E66-19
Knox, Tom G83-55
Knudholt, Ed E80-99
Kogen, Arnie E72-63, E73-83, E74-65
Kohan, Buz E72-63, E76-55, E79-30, E81-42, E83-57
Kohara, Roy G81-54
Kohn, Jessel E80-99
Kojak E73-21, E74-38
Kondrashin, Kiril G59-20, G60-24
Konrad Adenauer's Funeral E67-32
Kook, Edward T52-17
Kool & the Gang G79-2
Koppel, Ted E82-125
Korda, Nicholas E83-32
Korman, Harvey E68-42, E71-19, E73-35
Korn, Jerry G80-55
Korty, John E73-52, E78-27
Kosberg, Marvin I. E74-61, E75-65
Kosh G78-48, G83-56
Kostal, Irwin G62-23
Kostel, Mike E83-82
Kotarakos, Katherine E81-90
Kovacs, Ernie E61-22
Kozak, Gary E80-99
Kozloff, Charles E74-69
Kozoll, Michael E80-25, E81-32
Kraft Music Hall E69-34, -43, -49, -53
Kraft Television Theatre E55-27, E56-25
Krages, William E75-82
Krampf, Craig G84-43
Krasny, Paul E66-29
Kraus, Conrad E72-40, E79-112
Kraus, John G61-36, G62-36
Kraus, Marvin A. T84-7
Krause, E. Jay E69-58, E71-53
Kreiner, Charles E73-102, -104
Kreisman, Stuart E81-34
Kremlin, The E63-26
Kresnicka, Joseph E79-113
Krewson, Rollie E75-96
Krieger, Henry G83-43
Krinski, Sandy E73-88, -91
Kristofferson, Kris C70-4, G72-13, G74-17, G76-17
Krivacek, Gary E82-57
Krofft Superstar Hour Starring the Bay City Rollers E78-92
Krone, Truck E72-49
Ku Klux Klan E64-34
Kudelski, Stefan E70-71
Kukla, Fran and Ollie E53-9, E70-52

Index 168

Kulaga, Frank E82-61
Kulukundis, Eddie T76-1
Kung Fu E71-56, E72-30, -44
Kupcinet, Jerry E80-83
Kuralt, Charles E68-21, E82-133
Kurnit, Abe T53-21
Kurson, Jane E79-34
Kurtz, Swoosie T81-5
Kushner, Edward E80-99
KWAMINA T62-17

L

Labine, Claire E76-92, E77-94, E78-79, E79-85, E82-101
Lacey, Franklin T58-14
Lachman, Mort E74-53
Lack, Andrew E79-97
Lacombe, Art E74-73
La Corte, Pete E80-99
Ladanyi, Greg G83-55
Ladwig, Jim G76-44
Lady Randolph Churchill E75-93
Lagler, Rene E75-91
Lahr, Bert T64-10
Laird, Marlena E80-82, E81-79
Lambert, Griff E81-94
Lambert, Hendricks & Ross G62-25
La Mothe, Danny E79-113
Lampell, Millard E65-21
Lampert, Zohra E74-38
Land of Fear, The Land of Courage, The E82-76, -112
Landers, Bill E78-39, -90, E79-53
Landsberg, Cleve E80-53
Lane, Burton G66-23
Lane, Jeffrey E78-79, E79-85
Lane, Lawrence T83-1
Lane, Stewart F. T84-7
Lane, Tony G79-48
Lang, Herman E74-83, E78-90, E80-99, E83-82
Lange, Hope E68-7, E69-9
Langella, Frank T75-3
Langer, Lawrence T58-8
Langham, Chris E80-27
Lanning, Bob E80-99
Lansbury, Angela T66-10, T69-10, T75-10, T79-10
Lansbury, Edgar T65-1
Lapotaire, Jane T81-4
LARK, THE T56-4, -20
Larkin, Peter T54-19, T56-19
Larkins, Gary E79-113

Larner, Steven E82-34
Lars Affair, The E73-32
Larson, Donna E79-90, E82-104
Larson, Ron G83-56
Larter, Douglas G65-38
Lasser, Peter E80-99, E83-81
Lassie E54-13, E55-17
Last Bride of Salem, The E74-42
Last Campaign of Robert Kennedy, The E68-47
"Last Dance" G79-21, -22
LAST OF MRS. LINCOLN, THE T73-4, -5
Last of the Curlews E72-12
"Last Tango in Paris" G74-9
Last Tenant, The E77-43
Late, Great Me: Story of a Teenage Alcoholic, The E79-67, -88
Late Night with David Letterman E83-39
Lateiner, Jacob G65-30
"Latin Ala Lee" G61-38
Laughridge, Billy E75-95
Laughton, Charles G63-17
Laune, Paul E82-58
Laurence, John E67-31, E70-22
Laurents, Arthur T68-8, T84-15
Lauria, Nicholas E80-99
Laver, Rod E74-16
LaVine, Ronald E71-41
Law, The E74-6
Law and Order E68-19
Lawrence, Bill E71-71
Lawrence, Elliot T62-18, E71-67, E81-41, -91, E82-106
Lawrence, Gertrude T52-10
Lawrence, Keeth E78-90
Lawrence, Steve G61-25
Lawrence, Sylvia E79-90, E82-104
Lawrence, Vicki E75-37
Laws, Wes E75-88, E78-84
Laya E67-47
Layton, Joe T62-17, E64-25, T69-12
Layton, Lewis G60-28, G62-35, G63-34, G64-35
L.B.J. the Man and the President E72-70
Leach, Wilford T81-15
Leachman, Cloris E72-21, E73-32, E74-35, -37, E82-88, E83-23
Learned, Michael E72-19, E73-22, E75-25, E81-11
Leatherstocking Tales E79-71
Le Cash, Sue E78-44
Lederer, Charles T54-14, -18
Ledner, Caryl E77-42
Lee, Bill E69-42

Index

Lee, Eugene T74-16, T79-16
Lee, Franne T74-16, -18, T79-18
Lee, Joanna E73-79
Lee, Johnny G79-48
Lee, Joseph E80-99
Lee, Marvin E80-99
Lee, Ming Cho T83-16
Lee, Peggy G70-5
Leeson, Michael E80-26
LeFrak, Francine T82-7
Le Gallienne, Eve T64-22, E77-29
"Legend in My Time, A" C75-3
Legend of Lizzie Borden, The E74-58, -82
Legrand, Dick E66-30, E77-48
Legrand, Michel G72-30, G73-10, -32, G76-9, -12
"Lehar" G79-43
Lehman, Acy G73-44
Lehti, Carol E75-64, E80-99
Leible, Corey E71-57, E74-83, E78-90
Leible, Richard E77-105
Leicht, Allan E77-94
Leigh, Mitch T66-12
Leigh, Richard G78-16, C78-4
Leigh, Vivien T63-11
Leighton, Margaret T57-4, T62-4, E70-16
Leinsdorf, Erich G60-27, G61-31, G64-27, -30, -31, G65-29, G66-34, G67-32, G69-34, G72-37
Lemanski, Albin S. E79-89, E81-92
Lemay, Harding E74-69, E80-87
Lemmon, Jack E71-4
Lena E82-130
"Lena Horne: the Lady and Her Music Live on Broadway" G82-42
"Lena ... Lovely and Alive" G63-37
Lenard, Kay E75-79
LEND AN EAR T49-17
Lennon, John (Also see The Beatles) G67-3, G71-28, G82-2
LENNY T72-2, G73-25
Lenya, Lotte T56-13
Lenz, Kay E74-43
Leonard, David G83-55
Leonard, Hugh T78-1
Leonard, Sheldon E56-22, E60-16
Leonard Bernstein and the New York Philharmonic in Japan E61-24
Leonard Bernstein and the Philharmonic E60-24
Leonardo: To Know How to See E72-72
"Leontyne Price and Marilyn Horne in Concert at the Met" G84-55
Leontyne Price at the White House E78-67, -81

Leopold Stokowski E70-5
"Leprechaun, The" G77-12
"Leprechaun's Dream" G77-7
Lerner, Alan Jay T57-13, G66-23, T74-13
Lesgards, Jacques E79-113
Leshner, Stan E78-90, E79-110
"Let It Be" G71-28
"Let It Whip" G83-31
"Let Me Be There" G74-15
"Let Me Live" G72-25
"Let Me Tell You About a Song" C72-3
Let My People Go E64-12
"Let the Good Times Roll" G61-13
"Let's All Sing with the Chipmunks" G61-14
"Let's Get Small" G78-26
"Let's Just Praise the Lord" G74-26
"Let's Twist Again" G62-18
Letter, The E81-36, -46, -50, E83-55
Letterman, David E80-80, -86, E83-39
Leventhal, Jules T47-8
Leverette, Les G67-39
Levin, Audrey Davis E74-70, E75-80
Levin, Herman T57-18, T69-1
Levine, James G83-47, E83-64, G84-56
Levine, Larry G66-41
Levinson, Barry E73-83, E74-65
Levinson, Richard E69-50, E71-58
Levisohn, Dave E83-42
Levitch, Steve E73-89
Levitt, Saul E70-48
Levy, Bob E77-105
Levy, Eugene E81-34, E82-38
Levy, Ralph E59-13
Lewin, Dennis E83-81
Lewis, David E81-73
Lewis, Diane E81-90
Lewis, Henry G81-49
Lewis, Jeffrey E81-32
Lewis, Mel G79-13
Lewis, Ramsey G66-7, G67-16, G74-23
Lewis, Shari E72-12
Lie, The E73-99, -102, -104
Lieberson, Goddard G66-19
Lieble, Richard E80-99
Liebman, Max E80-39
Liebman, Ron E78-21
LIFE AND ADVENTURES OF NICHOLAS NICKLEBY T82-1, -2, -6, -16
Life in the Minors E82-24
Life Is a Circus, Charlie Brown E80-9
Life of Riley E49-6
Life of Samuel Johnson, The E57-11
Lifeline E78-10
"Lift Up the Name of Jesus" G80-34

Index

Light, Judith E79-76, E80-76
"Light My Fire" G69-4
Light the Way E73-95
Lights, Camera ... Politics E80-93
"Like Young" G60-14
LIL' ABNER T57-12, -16
Lillie, Beatrice T53-22
Lily E73-3, -84
Lily: Sold Out E80-4
Lily Tomlin E75-78
Lincoln, John E78-90, E80-99
"Lincoln Portrait, A" G60-16
Linda Carter's Celebration E80-35, -37
Linda Down's Marathon E82-120
Linda in Wonderland E80-35, -37
Lindbergh Kidnapping Case, The E75-30
Linden, Hal T71-9, E82-95
Lindon, Lionel E69-46, E70-57
Lindsay, Howard T59-22, T60-14
Lindsay, John T73-19
Lindsey, Mort E68-39
Linick, David E79-113
Link, William E69-50, E71-58
Linkletter, Art, and Diane G70-25
LION IN WINTER, THE T66-4
Lion, The Witch and The Wardrobe, The E78-5
Lion's Club E71-55
Liotta, Charles E77-105, E79-88
Lipow, Morton E79-113
Lipscomb, James E82-135
Lipsius, Fred (Also see Blood, Sweat & Tears) G70-11
Lisanby, Charles E74-80, E79-51
Lister, Hovie G82-36
Literary Man, The E72-35
Lithgow, John T73-3
Little, Cleavon T70-8
LITTLE GLASS CLOCK T57-20
"Little Good News, A" G84-24
"Little Green Apples" G69-3, -13
Little House on the Prairie E77-52, E78-36, -45, E81-39
Little Lord Fauntleroy E80-34
LITTLE ME T63-16
Little Moon of Alban E58-11, -23, -25, -29, E63-17
LITTLE NIGHT MUSIC, A T73-7, -10, -11, -12, -13, -18, G74-31
"Little Prince, The" G76-33
Little Women E78-40
"Live and Direct" G79-32
"Live and Let Die" G74-10
Live from Lincoln Center/Great Performances E76-35, -66, E77-9
Live from Lincoln Center: Leontyne Price,

Zubin Mehta and the New York Philharmonic E82-23
"Live from Lincoln Center—Sutherland—Horne—Pavarotti" G82-51
Live from Studio 8H E80-6, -50
Live from Studio 8H: A Tribute to Toscanini E79-9 -44
Live from the Met E83-64
"Live in London" G79-31
"Live on Sunset Strip" G83-34
"Living for the City" G75-19, G76-21
Lloyd, Christopher E81-14, E82-20
Lloyd, David E75-74, E76-50
Lloyd, John J. E60-23
Lobos, Los G84-47
Lock, James G84-58
Lockart, Ray E80-94
Lockart, Robert G71-41
Lockhart, June T48-12
Loden, Barbara T64-5
Loesser, Frank T51-15, T62-9, G62-21
Loewe, Frederick T57-14, T74-13
Loewinger, Larry E82-137
Logan, Joshua T48-5, T50-4, -12, -15, T53-7
Loggins, Kenny G80-3, G81-4, G83-45
Lohmann, Paul E75-71
"Lollipops and Roses" G62-5
Lomberg, Jon E80-53
London, Marc E67-35
"London Muddy Waters Show, The" G73-29
London Philharmonic Orchestra G76-37, G77-36, -39, G78-41
London Symphony Chorus E64-4, G72-39, G74-40, G77-43
London Symphony Orchestra G64-4, -33, G68-4, -40, G72-35, -37, -39, G74-40, G77-43, G78-8
London Weekend Television E74-18, E81-104
Lonely Wizard, The E57-19
Long, Shelly E82-11
Long, William Ivey T82-18
LONG DAY'S JOURNEY INTO NIGHT T57-1, -2, -6, -7, E72-20
Long Road Home E80-89
Long Wharf Theatre, The T78-20
Longo, William E82-140
Longstreet E70-38
"Lonesome Cities" G69-22
Lonsdale, Michael E82-137
"Look to the Rainbow" G78-14
Loomis, George E78-39, -90
Lopez, Priscilla T80-11

Index

Loquasto, Santo T77-18
"Lord, Let Me Be an Instrument" G81-38
"Lord Will Make a Way, The" G82-39
"Lord's Prayer, The" G81-36
Lorenz, William E76-39
Loreto, Al E80-99
Loretta Young Show, The E54-5, E56-8, -24, E58-14
Lorne, Marion E67-26
Lorne Greene's New Wilderness E82-111
Los Angeles—Earthquake E70-58
Lot of Happiness, A E82-146
Lou and Edie Story, The E73-82
Lou Grant E77-18, -19, -28, E78-2, -30, E79-2, -15, -16, -25, -29, -40, E80-20, E81-12
Loudermilk, John D. G68-45
Loudon, Dorothy T77-10
Louie and the Nice Girl E79-24, -59
Louvre, The E64-11, -13, -14, -15, -16, -17
Love, David E80-54
Love, Kermit E75-96
"Love" G73-27
Love, American Style E69-52, E72-55
Love Among the Ruins E74-26, -27, -51, -67, -79, -82
Love and Marriage E55-23
Love Child, The E70-65
"Love Is a Battlefield" G84-11
LOVE LIFE T49-11
Love of Life E78-84
"Love Song, A" G75-15
"Love Theme from 'A Star Is Born'" G78-5, -11
"Love Theme from Romeo and Juliet" G70-7, -8
"Love Will Keep Us Together" G76-1
Lovelady, John E75-96
Lover, Anthony E79-88
"Lover Please" G76-17
"Loves Me Like a Rock" G74-28
"Lowdown" G77-21
Lower, Elmer E74-89
Loweree, Robert E67-42, E70-40
Lowry, W. McNeil T63-22
Luboff, Norman, Choir G61-26
Lubow, Sidney E71-41
Lucas, Reggie G81-27
Lucinao Pavarotti and the New York Philharmonic E79-45
"Luciano Pavarotti: Hits from Lincoln Center" G79-44
"Lucille" C77-2, -4, G78-18
Lucky Strike Commercial E49-10
Lucy Show, The E66-18, E67-24
Ludden, Allen E75-46

Ludwig, Jerrold L. E83-29
Luiken, Carol E79-90, E82-104
Luisi, James E75-44
Lukather, Steve G83-28
Lunt, Alfred T54-7, T55-2, E64-7, T70-17
Lupone, Patti T80-10
Lurie, Victor T78-19
LUTHER T64-1, -6
LUV T65-7, -8, -19
Lydecker, Howard E65-40
"Lyin' Eyes" G76-6
Lyman, Dorothy E81-74, E82-85
Lynch, Jim E79-109
Lynde, Paul E78-83
Lynn, Joe T50-19
Lynn, Loretta C67-5, C72-1, -5, -8, G72-16, C73-5, -8, C74-8, C75-8, G82-44
Lyons, James G73-46

M

*M*A*S*H* E73-1, -19, -27, -48, E74-48, E75-50, -59, E76-10, -28, E78-28, E79-18, -19, E81-7, -8
MFSB G75-23, G79-2
MVR Corporation E65-44
Maazel, Lorin G77-41
McAloney, Michael T70-1
McAndrew, John E81-34, E82-38
McAndrew, William R. E68-44
"MacArthur Park" G69-10, G70-17
McBeath, Gerber E72-40
Macbeth E54-18, E60-1, -7, -10, -11, -15
McBride, Dennis E80-99
McCaffrey, Neil E78-90, E80-99, E83-82
McCann, Charles W. E81-38
McCann, Elizabeth I. T78-19, T79-1, T81-1, T82-1
McCarter, Vikki E81-90
McCarthy, Edward E72-40, E75-64
McCarthy, Jim E78-90, E80-99, E83-82
McCarthy, Mathew F. E77-105, E80-99
McCarthy, Tom E78-90, E80-99, E83-82
McCartney, Paul (Also see The Beatles & Wings) G67-3, -30, G71-28, G72-9, G75-6
McCaughey, William L. E80-48, E83-35
McClintock, David G81-55
MacColl, Ewan G73-3

Index 172

McConnachie, Brian E81-34
McConnell, Bob, and Boss Brass G84-17
McCoo, Marilyn (Also see Fifth Dimension) G77-24
McCord, Jonas E82-134
McCormick, Myron T50-9
McCoy, Charlie C72-10, C73-10, G73-18
McCoy, Clair E64-32
McCoy, Van G76-8
McCullough, Brian E80-99
McCully, Anne D. E76-59
Mac Davis Show, The E76-58
MacDermott, Galt G62-9, -10, G69-28
McDonald, Howard T57-21
McDonald, Michael (Also see The Doobie Brothers) G80-3, -14
MacDonald, P.A. T47-8
McDonald, Phillip G70-42
MacDonald, Ralph G79-2, G82-28
McDonald, Wayne E76-48
McDowall, Roddy T60-3, E60-14
McElroy, Jim E74-60
McElwee, Hank E78-90, E79-110
McFadden, Janet E78-38
McGannon, Donald E67-51
McGee, Frank E67-32
McGoohan, Patrick E74-34
McGuire, Andrew E82-129
McGuire, Dony G81-36
Machito G83-44
McIntyre, Peter E71-47
Mack, John E80-63
"Mack the Knife" G60-1, -34, G61-6
"Mack the Knife—Ella in Berlin" G61-7
McKay, Graig E77-46
McKay, Jim E67-27, E70-53, E72-66, E73-78, E74-39, E75-48, E78-91, E79-114, E82-118
McKearnin, Robert E78-90
McKechnie, Donna T76-10
McKellen, Ian T81-2
McKenna, Pat E71-40
Mackerras, Sir Charles G82-50
Mackey, Martin Haig E77-92
MacKichan, Robert E82-40
Mackie, Bob E69-59, E75-94, E77-65, E83-60
McKinsey, Scott E82-108, -112
MacKintosh, Cameron T83-7
McKuen, Rod G69-22
MacLean, Jean E83-69
McLean, Michael S. E76-38
MacLeish, Archibald T59-6
McMahon, Frank T70-1
McMahon, Jenna E73-83, E74-65, E77-40

McManus, Louis E48-6
McNichol, Kristy E76-15, E78-22
McPhillips, Hugh E79-79
McQueen, Butterfly E79-88
McQueen, Jim E80-99, E83-31
McSpedon, Frank E74-83, E78-90, E80-99, E83-82
Macy's 53rd Annual Thanksgiving Parade E79-73
Macy's Thanksgiving Day Parade E82-78, -109
Madame X E80-60
Madden, John E82-117, E83-76
Madman, The E62-18, -20
MADWOMAN OF CHAILLOT, THE T49-4
Maen, Norman E69-56
Magda, George A. E79-88
Magee, George E80-99
Magee, Patrick T66-3
Magic Flute, The E82-61
Magic Hat, The E77-96
Magic of David Copperfield, The E81-48
Magic of David Copperfield VI, The E83-43
Magness, Ronald G84-43
Magnificent Yankee, The E64-2, -6, -7, -22, -24, -28
Magnum, P.I. E83-14
Magpayo, Lito E83-82
Magro, Tony E82-58
Mahakian, Carl E83-33
"Mahler" G65-29, G67-32, G68-4, -40, G69-36, G72-33, G73-34, -35, -41, -42, G76-40, G78-39, G82-45, -46, G83-47, -54, G84-50, -51, -58
Mahomo, Nana E70-28
Mahoney, Peggy E78-39
Maier, Bill E79-113
Maitland, Dick E78-92, E80-88
Maitland, Ian E78-92
MAJOR BARBARA T57-21
MAJORITY OF ONE, A T59-4, -19
Makarova, Natalia T83-10
Make a Wish E73-13
Make Room for Daddy E53-13, E54-2, -4
Makeba, Miriam G66-20
Making of "Butch Cassidy and the Sundance Kid," The E70-27
Making of "Raiders of the Lost Ark," The E81-21
Making of the President 1960, The E63-7, -8, -24, -25
Making of the President 1964, The E65-24
Malang, Albert E61-27
Male of the Species E68-10, -13
Mallinson, James G80-57, G82-59
Mallory's Tragedy on Mt. Everest E54-24

Malloy, James G64-36
Maltby, Richard, Jr. T78-15
Maltz, Joseph A. E79-113
Malvin, Artie E75-87, E77-60
Mamas & the Papas G67-31
Mama's Birthday E83-60
"Mamas Don't Let Your Babies Grow Up to Be Cowboys" G79-19
Mama's Family E83-60
MAME T66-9, -10, -11, G67-23
"Man and a Woman, A" G67-27
MAN FOR ALL SEASONS, A T62-1, -2, -6, -7, -8, -22
Man from U.N.C.L.E., The E64-23, -30
MAN OF LA MANCHA T66-7, -8, -12, -14, -15
Man on the Moon: The Epic Journey of Apollo XI E69-28
Man Who Dances: Edward Villella E68-26
Man Who Shot the Pope: A Study in Terrorism, The E82-139
Manchester, Melissa G83-5
Mancini, Henry G59-2, -12, G61-9, -18, -19, G62-1, -3, -16, -22, -24, G63-22, G64-1, -3, -24, G65-10, -25, -44, G70-8, G71-7, -8
Mandel, Johnny G66-3, -22, G82-7
Mandell, Daniel E66-30
Mandell, Loring E67-33
Mandell, Steve G74-18
Mandrell, Barbara C79-5, C80-1, C81-1, -5, G83-36, G84-42
Mandy's Grandmother E80-88
Manfredi, Frank E71-57
Manger, William L. E76-43
Mangione, Chuck G77-10, G79-8, E79-111
Manhattan Transfer, The G81-21, G82-6, -21, G83-21, G84-21
Manhattans G81-30
Manilow, Barry T77-20, G79-4
Mann, Abby E72-52
Mann, Johnny, Singers G62-26, G68-31
Mann, Michael E78-29
Mann, Theodore T57-7
Manning, Marty G63-23
Mannings, Allan E67-35
Mannix E69-15
Manoff, Dinah T80-5
Mantegna, Joe T84-3
Mantel, Richard G69-38
Mantle, Burns T47-8
MARAT/SADE T66-1, -3, -6, -16
Marceau, Marcel E55-21
March, Fredric T47-1, T57-2
Marchand, Lou E73-77

Marchand, Nancy E77-19, E79-16, E80-20, E81-12
Marco Polo E81-20, -49
Marconi's Wireless Telegraph Co. E60-25
Marcus, Ann E75-81
Marcus–Nelson Murders, The E72-31, -52
Marcus Welby, M.D. E69-5, -10, -14, -45
Mardin, Arif G76-47, G84-14
Margolin, Arnold E69-52
Margolin, Stuart E78-23, E79-17
Margouleff, Robert G74-42
Mariner Films E81-103
Marino, Mario E80-99
Mark Taper Forum Theatre, Los Angeles T77-20
Mark III Flying Spot Telecine E80-42
MARK TWAIN TONIGHT! T66-2, E66-32
"Mark Twang" G77-31
Markel, Bob E54-24
Markinson, Martin T83-1
Markle, Thomas E81-90
Markoe, Merrill E80-86, E83-39
Marky, William E81-43, E82-59
Marland, Douglas E74-69, E80-87, E81-85
Marley, Michael E83-71
Marlo Thomas and Friends in Free to Be ... You and Me E73-16
Marlow, Derek E71-64
Marlow, Ric G63-10
Marmer, Mike E71-62
Marre, Albert T66-14
MARRIAGE-GO-ROUND, THE T59-5
Married E78-20
Marriner, Neville G82-52
Marsalis, Wynton G84-20, -53
Marsh, Jean E74-23
Marshall, Armina T58-8
Marshall, David E72-41, E76-43
Marshall, E.G. E61-8, E62-11
Marshall, Pam E77-51, E81-30
Marshall, Peter E73-45, -47, E74-45, E79-81, E80-81
Marshall Efton's Illustrated, Simplified and Painless Sunday School E77-106
Marshall, Texas E83-47
Marsolais, Ken T77-1
Marta, Jack E70-56
Martin, Andrea E81-34, E82-38
Martin, Ernest H. T51-17, T62-19
Martin, Gene E69-49, E71-44, -57, E80-50, E82-109
Martin, George G74-10
Martin, Heff E83-39
Martin, Mary T48-12, T50-10, E55-9, T55-12, T60-12, G61-23

Martin, Steve E68-34, G78-26, G79-26
Martin, Terry E82-128
Martin Luther King's Assassination and Aftermath E68-20
Martinelli, Enzo A. E79-38
Martinelli, John A. E74-58, E77-47, E80-62
Martinez, Manuel E76-39
Marx, Don E79-110
Marx, Groucho E50-1
Mary Hartman, Mary Hartman E75-81, E76-11
"Mary Poppins" G65-17, -23
Mary Richards Goes to Jail E74-64
Mary Tyler Moore Show, The E70-17, -18, -32, -49, E71-16, -17, E72-17, -24, -25, -32, E73-20, -28, -32, -82, -85, E74-1, -28, -29, -37, -56, -64, E75-1, -23, -33, -34, -74, E76-1, -36, -50
Mary White E77-42
Masada E80-45, -57
Masci, Richard J. E81-44
Masius, John E83-37
Mask of Love, The E73-42, -44, -107, -109
"MASTER HAROLD" ... AND THE BOYS T82-3
"Master of Eyes" G74-20
Masteroff, Joe T67-7
Masterpiece Theatre E70-12, E71-12, E72-23, E73-5, E74-23, -46, E75-4, -27, E76-3, E77-71
Masters, The E80-99
"Masters V, The" (see J.D. Sumner, James Blackwood, Hovie Lister, Rosie Rozell and Jake Hess) G82-36
Masters Tournament E74-83
Matalon, Vivian T80-6
MATCHMAKER, THE T56-7
Matinee Theatre E55-14
Matosky, Dennis G84-43
Matter of Time, A E80-66
Matthau, Walter T62-3, T65-2
Matthews, Marilyn E81-57
Matwichuk, Walter E80-99
Matz, Peter E64-19, G65-26, E69-53, E72-57
Matza, Joseph E80-53
Mauceri, John T83-19
Maude E76-9
Mauro, Christopher N. E79-89
Maverick E58-5
Maxwell Smart, Private Eye E67-37
Maxwell Street Jimmy G81-39
May, Billy G59-11, G60-31
May, Elaine G62-14

Mayer, John E80-99
Mayer, Joseph E81-38, E83-33
Mayer, Marianne E79-88
Mayer, Paul Avila E76-92, E77-94, E78-79, E79-85, E82-101
Mazur, Nick E72-40, E75-64
Mazurek, Chester E79-113
Mazzocco, Dennis E80-99
"Me & Jerry" G71-17
"Me & Mrs. Jones" G73-21
"Me Enamore" E84-45
Meade, Terry E82-107
Meader, Vaughn G63-2, -14
Meadows, Audrey E54-7
Medal for Margaret E58-28
MEDEA T48-3, T82-4
Medic E54-25, E55-31
Medical Story E75-60, -65
MEDIUM, THE T48-10
Medoff, Mark T80-1
Meehan, Thomas T77-12
Meet Mr. Lincoln E58-32
Mehta, Zubin G82-48, E82-94, G83-51
Melanby, Ralph E75-58
Melcher, Carey E80-53
Melchiorre, Frank E73-77
Melendez, Bill E77-63
Melody, Joseph E81-38, E83-33
Melosh, Everett E81-95
Memion, Mac E68-17
Men at Work G83-61
Mendels, Rolanda E78-82
Menefee, Pete E79-62
Menkin, Helen T66-17
Menuhin, Yehudi G68-38, G78-38
Menusan, Henry E80-99
Mercer, Johnny G62-3, G64-3
Mercer, Marian T69-11
"Mercy, Mercy, Mercy" G68-7
Meredith, Burgess T60-24, E76-26
Meredith, Don E70-53
Merkel, Una T56-5
Merlin, Jan E74-69
Merman, Ethel T51-12, G60-18, T72-19
Merrick, David T61-8, -24, T64-1, -19, T68-19, T76-1, T81-7
Merrick, David, Arts Foundation T68-7
Merrill, Robert G65-24
Merv Griffin Show, The E73-10, -56, -90, E76-77, E80-73, E81-77, E82-82, -98
Mesak, Charles E48-5
Messel, Oliver T55-19
Messenger, James M. E82-129
Messerschmidt, Karl E76-48
Messinger, Dominic E81-90

Index

Metcalf, Rory E82-101
Metcalfe, Mel E83-35
Meth, Max T49-18, T52-12
Metheny, Pat, Group G83-22, G84-22
Metropolitan Opera Chorus G74-38
Mewman, Hans E75-65
Mexican Connection, The E72-65
"Mexico (Legacy Collection)" G65-42
Meyer, Irwin T77-7
Meyers, Lanny E81-41
Meyers, Sig E74-83, E78-90, E80-99, E83-82
Miami — The Trial That Sparked the Riots: CBS Reports E80-93
"Michael Nesmith in Elephant Ears" G82-61
Michaels, Frankie T66-9
Michaels, Lorne E73-84, E75-75, -78, E76-52, E77-41
Michelangelo: The Last Giant E65-36
"Michelle" G67-3
Michnick, Jesse E80-99
Michon, Jack E80-30
Mickey Spillane's Mike Hammer E83-41
Micklas, Thomas E82-139
Mickley, William E79-90, E82-104
MIDDLE OF THE NIGHT T56-21
Midler, Bette G74-46, T74-19, G81-5, -43
"Midnight Cowboy" G70-32
"Midnight Flyer" G60-33
"Midnight Train to Georgia" G74-22
MIDSUMMER NIGHT'S DREAM T71-6
Mielziner, Jo T49-15, T50-17, T52-14, T70-14, -15
Mighty Clouds of Joy G79-32, G80-37
Migrants — NBC Nightly News E79-101
Migrants: NBC Reports, The E80-94
Mike Douglas Show, The E66-11, E76-90, E77-97, E80-90
Mike in Hollywood with Ray Charles and Michel Legrand E76-90
Milch, David E82-36
Miles, Joanna E73-34, -38
Millard, Jay E78-66
Miller, Arthur T47-8, T49-8, T53-6, E66-42, E80-28
Miller, Barbara E78-66
Miller, Branda S. E80-47
Miller, Gilbert T50-6, T65-21
Miller, Gilbert A. E80-99
Miller, Howard N. E80-99
Miller, J.P. E68-33
Miller, Jason T73-1
Miller, Jody G66-13
Miller, Johnathan T63-22

Miller, Marilyn Suzanne E75-75, E76-52
Miller, Marvin G66-17, G67-17
Miller, Peter E82-137
Miller, Roger G65-11, -12, -14, -15, G66-11, -12, -14, -15, -28, -29
Miller, Sharon E82-97
Miller, T. E55-32
Miller, Walter C. E71-35
Millman, David E82-141
Mills, Juliet E74-36
Mills, Stephanie G81-28
Milner, Jack E74-61
Milner, Michael E82-64
Milsap, Ronnie C74-6, C75-3, G75-16, C76-6, C77-1, -3, -6, G77-18, C78-3, G82-25
Milstein, Nathan G76-38
Miner, Peter E82-96
Minerva, Patrick E72-38
Minnelli, Liza T65-12, T74-19, T78-10
"Minute by Minute" G80-6
Miracle of Life, The E83-86
MIRACLE WORKER, THE T60-1, -4, -6, -7, -8, -23, E79-3, -22, -58
Mirror, Mirror on the Wall E74-57
Mischer, Don E80-21
Misha E79-102
Miss Kline, We Love You E73-55, -57, -65
MISS LIBERTY T50-19
Miss Peach and the Kelly School E79-91
Missile Crisis, The E63-9
Missiles of October, The E74-73
Mission: Impossible E66-3, -16, -26, -29, E67-4, -20, E68-9, G68-24, E68-26, -37, E69-41, E70-63
Mission Mind Control E79-101
Mr. Axelford's Angel E74-19
"Mr. Lucky" G61-18, -19
MR. PRESIDENT T63-21
MISTER ROBERTS T48-1, -2, -4, -5
Mister Rogers Goes to School E79-88
Mister Rogers Neighborhood E79-88
"Misty" G76-10
Mitchell, Charles E79-113
Mitchell, David T77-16, T80-16
Mitchell, John E82-60
Mitchell, Joni G70-26, G75-10
Mitchell, Keith E71-13
Mitchell, Ruth T67-7
Mitchell, Thomas E52-5, T53-10
Mitchell — Stans Trial E73-122
Mitzi ... A Tribute to the American Housewife E73-92
Mitzi and the Hundred Guys E75-82
Mitzi ... Roarin' in the 20's E75-82, -94

Mitzi ... Zings Into Spring E77-65
Mitzi's 2nd Special E69-58
Model Hippie E69-47
Modugno, Domenico G59-1, -3
Moffitt, John C. E76-33
Mokae, Zakes T82-3
Mole, Albert E72-38
Molinari–Pradelli G62-29, G68-42
Mollica, Phil E75-64
Mom and Dad Can't Hear Me E78-78
Moman, Chips G76-14
Monash, Paul E57-19
"Monday, Monday" G67-31
Monday Night Special, The E71-23
Mondello, Anthony E75-90
Monet, Gaby E76-84
Moneychangers, The E76-24
Mongioi, Nat E73-126, E79-88
Monkees, The E66-1, -24
Monkeys, Apes and Man E71-38
Montalban, Ricardo E77-26
Montesano, Joseph E79-113
Montevecchi, Liliane T82-11
Montgomery, Little Brother G81-39
Montgomery, Robert T55-7
Montgomery, Wes G67-7, G70-12
"Montreaux '77 – Oscar Peterson Jam" G79-15
"Moods" G73-43
"Moody's Mood" G81-19
Moon and Sixpence, The E59-9, -12
MOON FOR THE MISBEGOTTEN, A T74-3, -4, -6, -19, E75-40
"Moon River" G62-1, -3, -24
Mooney, Sheldon E77-97
Moore, Dudley T63-22, T74-19, G75-25
Moore, Mary Tyler E63-12, E65-15, E72-17, E73-20, -28, E75-23, T80-20
Moore, Melba T70-11
Moore, Ray G71-39, G74-41, G76-42, G77-44, G79-46, G82-53
Moore, Russell E72-38
Moral Majority Show E81-34
Moranis, Rick E81-34
"More" G64-10
"More Grand Old Gospel" G68-23
"'More' Live" G83-16
More Than Murder E83-41
"More Than Wonderful" G84-39
Morean, Richard F. E79-86
Morehead, Agnes E66-22
Moreno, Rita G73-33, T75-5, E76-21, E77-27
Morgan, Harry E67-36, E79-18
Morgan, Roger T79-17
Morgenstern, Carla E82-139

Morgerstern, Dan G74-44, G75-44, G77-47, G82-56
Moria, Colin E73-70
Moriarty, Michael E73-33, -37, T74-2, E77-22
Mormon Tabernacle Choir G60-21
MORNING'S AT SEVEN T80-3, -6, -19
Moroder, Giorgio G84-15, -43
Morris, Frank E73-61, -62
Morris, John E73-77, E78-92
Morris, Johnny E78-90
Morris, William E79-113
Morrison, Bob G80-20
Morrow, Barry E81-33
Morse, Robert T62-10
Morton, Bruce E70-31, E82-128
Mosher, Bill E68-31, E69-35
Moshlak, David E82-137
Moskovic, Alex E72-40, E75-64, E79-112
Moss, Jeffrey E69-62, E73-125
Mostel, Zero T61-2, T63-9, T65-10
"Moszkowski" G81-46
Mother of the Bride E73-88, -91
Motley T58-20, T61-21
Motown 25: Yesterday, Today, Forever E82-6
Mouat, Colin E76-42
Mt. Everest East Face, The E83-80
"Mountain Music" G83-26
"Movements for Piano and Orchestra" G62-34
Movie of the Week E69-42, E70-41, -43, -47, -57, E71-14, -37, -41, -46, -56, -60, E72-21
Movie Star's Daughter E79-88
Movin' with Nancy E67-39
Moviola E79-49, -56, -57
Moyers, Bill E73-117, E79-96, E80-94, E83-47
"Mozart" G60-27, G66-27, G69-34, G76-39, G81-51, G84-53, -56
"Mrs. Robinson" G69-1, -6
MRS. WARREN'S PROFESSION T76-3
Mtume, James G81-27
Much Ado About Nothing E72-43, -59
Mudd, Roger E72-70
"Muddy 'Mississippi' Waters Live" G80-38
"Muddy Waters Woodstock Album, The" G76-29
Mulcahey, Patrick E81-85
Muller, Alfred E73-63
Mulligan, Gerard E80-86

Mulligan, Gerry G82-17, E83-39
Mulligan, Richard E79-13
Mulligan, Robert E59-12
Mulvaney, Donald E69-49, E71-44, E78-90, E82-109
Mumford, Thad E72-11
Munch, Charles G60-22, G62-27, -35
Muni, Paul T56-2
Munich Olympic Tragedy E72-66
Munisteri, Mary E76-92, E77-94, E78-79, E79-85, E80-88, E82-101
Munrow, David G77-38
Munshower, Tom E81-48
"Muppet Movie, The" G80-42
Muppet Show, The E76-21, E77-3, E79-32, G79-37, E80-27
Muppets E73-125, E75-96, -97, G81-43, G82-44
Muppets of Sesame Street, The E78-80
Murad, Maurice E79-94, E80-94
Murawski, C. E80-89
Murder in Texas E80-62
Murder of a Correspondent E80-93
Muriania, Joseph E79-94
Murphy, Anthony E72-22
Murphy, Bob E73-90
Murphy, Brianne E77-96
Murphy, Eddie G84-34
Murphy, Jim E78-90, E80-99, E83-82
Murphy, Pete E79-112
Murphy, Rosemary E75-39
Murphy, Walter G79-2
Murray, Anne G75-15, G79-5, G81-23, G84-24
Murray, Bill E76-52
Murray, Darold E71-39
Murray, Peg T67-11
Murrow, Edward R. E53-7, E55-16, E56-6, -17, E57-17, E58-24, E65-48, G67-19
Music, Jerry E68-34
"Music from Peter Gunn, The" G59-2, -12
MUSIC MAN, THE T58-9, -10, -11, -13, -14, -15, -16, -18, G59-15, T59-21
Musser, Tharon T72-17, T76-17, T82-17
Mutual of Omaha's Wild Kingdom E65-31, E66-10, E68-41, E69-20
MY FAIR LADY T57-8, -9, -13, -14, -15, -17, -18, -19, -20, T76-8
My Mom's Having a Baby E76-83
My Mother Was Never a Kid E81-99
My Name Is Barbra E64-3, -8, -19, -25, -27, G66-6
MY ONE AND ONLY T83-8, -9, -14
My Sweet Charlie E69-13, -36, -50
My World and Welcome to It E69-1, -8

"My Woman, My Woman, My Wife" G71-13
Mysteries of the Mind E80-93, -94
Mysteries of the Sea E79-39
Mystic Warrior, The E83-63

N

NAGRA IV Recorder E70-71
NASA E69-63, -65
NBA World Championship E83-70
NBC E58-40, E61-28, E69-65, E71-73
NBC Baseball Pre-Game/Major League Baseball: An Inside Look E83-82
NBC Children's Theatre E72-12
NBC Monday Night Movies E69-46, E76-44
NBC Mystery Movie E71-11, E73-24
NBC Nightly News E70-30, -39, E71-28, -29, -39, -47, E72-38, E73-66
NBC Special Treat E78-80
NBC Sportsworld E80-99, -100
NBC Sunday Mystery Movie E74-25
NBC The First 50 Years—a Closer Look E77-63
NBC Wednesday Night at the Movies E73-61, -62
NBC White Paper E70-23, E72-65
NBC White Paper: If Japan Can, Why Can't We? E80-94
NBC World Premiere Movie E74-6, E75-30, E76-7
NBC World Premiere: The Big Event E76-24
NBC's Best Seller E76-25, -46
NBC's Saturday Night Live E75-2, -38, -52, -75, E76-52, E77-23, E82-43
NCAA Basketball Championship Final E82-115
NCAA Basketball Championship Game E83-82
NCAA College Football E79-105, E83-79
NET Opera Theatre E71-63
NET Playhouse E68-4
NFC Championship Game E80-99
NFL Football E80-99, E82-113, E83-78
NFL Game of the Week E78-90, E79-106, -110
NFL Games, The E69-19
NFL Monday Night Football E70-53, E75-20
NFL Symfunny E80-99
NFL Today E77-105, E80-99
NFL Today/NFL Football on CBS, The E77-100

Index 178

Nace, Arthur E75-64
"Nadia's Theme (The Young and the Restless)" G78-7
Naeder, George F. E74-83, E78-90, E80-99, E83-82
Naegler, Karl—August G81-52
Nagy, Ivan G71-41
Nakamoto, Hiorshi E79-112
Naked City E60-20, E61-20, -21, E62-25
Name of the Game E68-14, E70-56
Napolitana, John E82-47
Napier, John T82-16, T83-18
Nashville Brass with Danny Davis C69-8, C70-9, G70-18, C71-9, C72-9, C73-9, C74-9
"Nashville Skyline" G70-44
Nathanson, Ted E77-104, E80-101
National Bureau of Standards E79-63
National Geographic Special E71-38, E73-71, -115, E77-10, E79-37, E80-63, -93, -94, E82-135
National Theatre Company of Great Britain, The T69-16
National Theatre for the Deaf T77-20
"Natural Man, A" G72-20
Natwick, Mildred E73-24
Nazi Connection, The E82-124
Nazis and the Klan E78-76
Neal, Patricia T47-3
Necklace, The E48-3
Nederlander, James M. T82-1, -7, T84-7
Neef, Howard E78-90, E79-110
Negri, Vittorio G69-31, -33, G72-40
Negro Ensemble Company, The T69-16, T74-1
Neiman, Larry E76-42
"Neither One of Us (Wants to Be the First to Say Goodbye)" G74-6
"Nel Blu Dipinto di Blu (Volare)" G59-1, -3
Nelson, Dean E78-84
Nelson, Dick E68-36
Nelson, Doug E74-85, E76-45, E80-49, E81-44
Nelson, Eddie E72-42, E73-71, E76-44, E77-49, E78-35
Nelson, George R. E83-49
Nelson, Jerry E75-97, E78-80
Nelson, Ralph E56-21
Nelson, Richard T84-17
Nelson, Willie C76-2, -3, -8, G76-16, C79-1, G79-18, -19, G81-22, C82-2, -3, C83-8, G83-25
Nelson, Yale E83-74
Nemiroff, Robert T74-7
Neon Ceiling, The E70-14
Nero, Peter G62-40, G63-16

Nesbitt, Cathleen E73-42, -44
Nesi, Joe E79-113
Nesmith, Michael G82-61
Nettleton, Lois E76-84, E82-90
Neufeld, Quentin E82-128
Neuwald, Ruth E80-94
"Never Knew Love Like This Before" G81-27, -28
New CBS Tuesday Night Movies E72-51
New Christy Minstrels, The G63-25
New England Conservatory Ragtime Ensemble G74-35
New Fat Albert Show, The E80-88
NEW GIRL IN TOWN T58-12
"New Kid in Town" G78-9
New Mexico's Yates Oil Company E82-120
"New Orleans Suite" G72-11
New Philharmonic Orchestra G69-30, -34, -40, G70-40
New South, The (Also see Ricky Skaggs, Jerry Douglas, Tony Rice, J.D. Crowe, Todd Phillips) G84-27
New Vaudeville Band G67-29
New York City Opera Orchestra & Chorus G79-43
New York Library Theatre Collection T56-22
New York Philharmonic Orchestra E59-21, G62-13, -17, G63-13, -28, G64-13, G65-4, G70-38, G74-33, -34, G76-35, G82-48
New York Philharmonic with Leonard Bernstein E65-42
New York Philharmonic Young People's Concert with Leonard Bernstein E61-6, E64-4, -5
New York Pro Musica G65-31
New York Remotes, The E77-97
New York Shakespeare Festival T58-22, T70-17, T72-1, -7, T73-1, T76-7, T81-19
Neway, Patricia T60-13
Newhart, Bob G61-2, -15, -39
Newley, Anthony G63-3
Newman, Alfred G71-30
Newman, Edwin E82-90
Newman, Jack E78-90, E79-110
Newman, Phyllis T62-13
Newmar, Julie T59-5
Newsom, Tommy E81-41
Newton, Juice G83-24
Newton—John, Olivia C74-5, G74-15, G75-1, -5, G83-62
Nibley, Aaron E60-20, E61-20
Nicaragua E80-93
Nicholas Nickelby E82-4

Index

Nichols, Mike G62-14, T64-7, T65-7, T68-6, T72-6, T77-7, T84-6
Nichols, Roger G78-47, G79-47
Nicholson, George E54-26, E70-38
Nicholson, William E81-43, E82-59, E83-34
Nickrenz, Joanna G84-64
Nictern, Claire T65-8
Niemack, Robert E78-52
Night in Jail, A Day in Court, A E71-24
Night of 100 Stars E81-4, -41
Night of Terror E72-45
NIGHT OF THE IGUANA T62-4
Night to Remember, A E56-25
"Nightingale Sang in Berkeley, A" G82-15
Nightline E82-119, -125, -141
Nikifor, Steve E79-113, E80-99
Nilmark, Johannes E82-47
Nilsson, Harry G70-4, G73-4
NINE T82-7, -11, -13, -15, -18
"9 to 5" G82-23, -24
1980 Winter Olympic Games E79-103, -108, -109, -110, -111, -112, -113
1978 World Series E78-89, -90
1975 World Series E75-19
1974 Stanley Cup Playoffs, The E74-83
1974 World Series, The E74-83
1972 Summer Olympic Games E72-13, -40
1968—CBS News Special E79-96, -102
19th Summer Olympic Games E68-16, -17
Nippon Electronic Company E74-86
Nishida, Shin E80-58
Nixon, Agnes E. E81-108
Nixon–Khrushchev Debates in Moscow, The E59-24
No Maps on My Taps E80-94
"No Mystery" G76-11
NO, NO, NANNETTE T71-11, -12, -15, -18
"No Respect" G81-32
"No Shortage" G76-27
NO STRINGS T62-12, -16, -17, G63-21
NO TIME FOR SERGEANTS T56-19
Noah E79-102
Noah's Ark E81-105
Noisy/Quiet Hearing E79-88
Nolan, Bud E73-68, E75-69
Nolan, Lloyd E55-8
Nolan, Patrick E78-29
Noman, Eric Van Haren E80-88
Noonan, John Ford E83-37
Norica, Anne E80-53
Norica, Ernie E80-53
Norman, Phil E74-81, E79-42, E80-61
North, Alex E75-84
Northshield, Robert E71-30
Norton, Elliot T71-21

Nosenchuck, Dan E83-44
Nostaja, Wayne E81-48
Not the Last of the Nine O'Clock News E80-105
Not Without Honor E60-14
Notorious Woman E75-27
Now Is the Time E67-52
Nowell, David E81-48, E83-43
Ntshona, Winston T75-2
Nugent, Nelle T78-19, T79-1, T81-1, T82-1
Nunn, Trevor T82-6, T83-15
Nureyev and the Joffrey Ballet/In Tribute to Nijinsky E80-51
Nurse E81-11
Nusbaum, Jane C. T68-16
Nype, Russell T51-11, T59-11

O

O.R.T.F. (Office de Radiodiffusion Television Francais, Paris) E67-55
"O Sole Mio" G80-48
Oak Ridge Boys, The G71-25, G75-27, G77-29, C78-7, -9, G78-29, C81-2, G82-26
O'Bradovich, Robert E64-28
O'Brien, Dave E60-18
O'Brien, Pat E73-41, -43
O'Connell, Tom E80-99
O'Connor, Carroll E71-9, E76-8, E77-14
O'Connor, Donald E53-4
"October War, The" E73-111
O'Daniel, Jim E81-90
ODD COUPLE, THE T65-2, -6, -7, -19, E70-9, E72-14, E74-20
"Ode to Billie Joe" G68-6, -29, -34
Odell, David E80-27
O'Dell, Kenny C73-4, G74-14
O'Donnell, Steve E83-39
O'Donoghue, Michael E75-75, E76-52
Oenslager, Donald T59-19
"Of Man and Mouse" E81-28
"Off Broadway" G81-31
"Offramp" G83-22
Oganesoff, Nobuko E82-140
Ogerman, Claus G80-7
"Oh Happy Day" G70-29
OH, WHAT A LOVELY WAR T65-11
O'Hara, Catherine E81-34
Ohlandt, Herb E75-64
Ohlmeyer, Don E75-58, E80-101
'Oiseau de Feu, L E80-107
Oistrakh, David G71-35, G75-36

Index

"Okie from Muskogee" C70-2, -3
Okrand, Dean E83-59
Old Flames E83-28
"Old Payola Roll Blues, The" G61-36
Oldfield, Mike G75-9
Oldham, Arthur G72-39, G74-40, G77-43
Oliansky, Joel E70-46
Olivas, C. Frank E82-50, E83-51
OLIVER! T63-14, -15, -19
"Olivia Physical" G83-62
Olivier, Laurence E59-9, E72-20, E74-26
Oliviero, Nino G64-10
Olson, Jon E76-48
Olszewski, John E77-105
Omartian, Michael G81-15
Omer, Yves E71-70
Omnibus E53-3, E54-9, E55-13, E56-28, E57-8, -11, -28, E58-8
"On a Clear Day" G66-23
"On Broadway" G79-23, G84-46
On the Outside Looking In E81-42
"On the Road" G81-17
"On the Road Again" G81-22
On the Road: CBS Reports E80-93
ON THE TWENTIETH CENTURY T78-8, -9, -12, -13, -16
ON YOUR TOES T83-10, -19
Once Upon a Classic E79-71, E80-65
Once Upon a Midnight Dreary E79-71, -88
"Onda Va Bien, La" G81-42
ONDINE T54-5, -7, -19, -20
One Billion Dollar Weapon; And Now the War is Over, The American Military in the 70's E72-65
One Day in the Life of Ivan Denisovich E63-16
"One Hundred Ways" G82-30
One Life to Live E73-77, E75-56, E78-69, E79-76, E80-76, E81-72, -95, E82-84, -96
"One O'Clock Jump" G79-20
"One on One" G81-8
O'Neill, Eugene T57-6
"Only the Lonely" G59-28
Ono, Yoko G82-2
Onward Christian Voters E80-93
"Operatic Recital" G59-23
Operation Challenge—A Study in Hope E63-30
Operation Undersea E54-21, -27
"Orange Blossom Special/Hoedown" G81-26
Orbach, Jerry T69-8

Orbison, Roy G81-25
Orchestra Is a Team, Too!, An E81-98
Orchestra of the German Opera G66-36
"Orchestral Suite from Tender Land Suite" G61-32
Orchestre de l'Opera de Paris G81-44, -50
Oregon Shakespearean Festival Association T83-20
"Orff" G68-40, G76-41
Original Texas Playboys, The C77-9
Orkin, Harry E55-22
Ormandy, Eugene G62-31, G68-40, G79-41
Ornitz, Kim E82-137
Orr, Wayne E77-54, E83-42
Orrico, Don E82-139
Ortolani, Riz G64-10
Osborn, Paul T80-19
Osborne, John T64-6
Osborne Brothers, The C71-7
"Oscar Peterson and Dizzy Gillespie" G76-13
O'Shea, Tessie T64-13
Osterman, Lester T77-1
Ostrow, Stuart T69-7
Oswald, Richard E76-43
OTHELLO T82-19
Other Americans, The E69-67
Other Side of the Shadow E67-54
Other Washington, The E67-53
Other Woman, The E73-8, -41, -43
Our Mr. Sun E56-23
Our Times E80-94
Our Town E55-23, E77-61
Our World E67-48
"Out-a-Space" G73-9
Over Easy E77-92, E80-79
OVER HERE! T74-11
Overton, Richard E71-43
Oz, Frank E75-97, E78-80
Ozawa, Seiji E75-86, G81-47

P

PGA Tour on CBS E80-97
PACIFIC OVERTURES T76-16, -18
Pacino, Al T69-3, T77-2
Padgett, Shirley E80-60
Padula, Edward T61-18
Page, Geraldine E66-14, E68-11
Page, Robert G68-40, G76-41
Paich, David E73-95, G77-21, G83-9, -14

Paich, Marty E73-95
Painter, Walter E80-35
PAJAMA GAME, THE T55-9, -13, -14, -15, -16, -18
PAL JOEY T52-11, -12, -13
Palance, Jack E56-13
Palecek, Steven J. E81-98
Palestine E79-102
Palestinian Viewpoint, The E82-125
Paley, William S. E77-44
Pallisers, The E76-57, -67
Palmerstown, U.S.A. E79-54
Palmieri, Eddie G76-32, G77-34
Palmisano, George E80-99
Palmstierna–Weiss, Gunilla T66-16
Palumbo, Gene E81-85
Pan, Hermes E58-38
Panda, Eddie E74-85, E82-49
Panich, David E67-35
Pantomime Quiz Time E48-2
"Papa Was a Rolling Stone" G73-19, -22, -23
"Papas Got a Brand New Bag" G66-16
Paper Marriage E78-32
Paper Palace, The E77-27
Papp, Joseph T72-1, -7, T73-1, T76-7, T81-19, T84-20
Paramount Presents ... ABC Wide World of Entertainment E73-64
Parent, Gail E72-63
Paris, Jerry E63-22
Paris National Opera G68-4, -41
Parker, Art E78-90
Parker, Charlie G75-13
Parker, James E72-40
Parnell, Jack E73-96, -97
Parry, Gordon G69-36, G73-42
Parry, Les E72-39
Parsons, Wayne E79-53
Parting Is Such Sweep Sorrow E83-34
Parton, Dolly C68-7, C70-8, C71-8, C75-5, C76-5, C78-1, G79-17, G82-23, -24
Pass, Joe G75-11
Passas, Peter S. E79-48
Password E73-9, E75-46
Password Plus E81-69
Pastoria, Andre T83-19
"Patches" G71-18
Patchett, Tom E72-63
Patinkin, Mandy T80-9
Patrick, James G80-54
Patrick, John T54-6
Patterson, James T68-3
Patterson, Kenneth E79-92
Patti, Sandi G84-39

Pattillo, Alan E79-50
Paul, Billy G73-21
Paul, Charles E81-90
Paul, Les G77-20
Paul Jacobs and the Nuclear Gang E79-101
Paul Simon Special, The E77-41
Paulson, Albert E63-16
Paulson, Pat E67-28
Pavarotti, Luciano G79-44, E79-87, -92, G80-48, G82-51
Pavarotti E80-94
Pavarotti in Philadelphia: La Boheme E82-9
Paxton, Gary S. G77-28
Payne, Russ G76-43
Pearce, Alice E65-17
Pearl, The E56-24
Pedersen, Niels G75-11
Peeples, Dennis E80-54
Pendergrass, Teddy G83-45
Penn, Arthur T60-7
Pentagon Papers, The E71-51
"People" G65-6, -26, -41
People Next Door, The E68-32, -33, -36
Peretti, Hugo (see Hugo & Luigi)
Perew, Tom E78-83
Perez, Bill E81-56
"Perfect Match/Ella and Basie, A" G81-18
Performance at the White House—An Evening of Spirituals and Gospel Music E83-64
Perl, Emily E73-125
Perlman, B.K. E82-101
Perlman, Itzhak G78-41, G79-38, -40, G81-46, -47, -48, G82-47, -48, G83-49
Perlman, Rhea E83-22
Pernick, Solly T63-21
Perret, Gene E73-83, E74-65, E77-40
Perrin, Sam E58-31, E59-15
Perry, Eleanor E66-41, E72-53
Perry Como Christmas Show, The E74-77
Perry Como's Christmas in the Holy Land E80-47
Perry Como's Easter in Guadalajara E81-44
Perry Como's Kraft Music Hall E61-23
Perry Mason E58-15, -16, E60-8
Persky, Bill E63-20, E65-22, E66-28, E83-26
Personal Foul E81-43
Personal Note/Beirut E82-120
Pescalek, Gene E74-83
Peter and Paul E80-36
"Peter and the Wolf" G60-10

Index 182

PETER PAN E55-9, T55-11, -12, -21, E76-49
Peter, Paul & Mary G63-19, -24, G64-19, -25, G70-33
"Peter, Paul & Mommy" G70-33
Peters, Ben G73-14
Peters, J. Baxter E63-26
Peters, Michael T82-14
Petersen, John E79-108
Peterson, Oscar G75-11, G78-15, G79-15, G80-18
Petrie, Daniel E75-53, E76-29
Petrocelli E74-57
Pettersen Project, The E82-127
Pettijohn, Dave E76-42
Pettis, Bob E79-36
Pettit, Tom E68-30, E69-32
Peyton Place E65-13
Phantom of the Hill E82-29
Phelps, Jill Farren E81-90
Phenix, Roger E80-94
Phil Silvers Show, The E56-2, -20, E57-5, -20
"Phil Woods Six, Live from the Showboat, The" G78-12
Philadelphia Brass Ensemble G70-36
Philadelphia Orchestra G68-40, G79-41
Philbin, Bill E83-80
Philharmonia Choir G63-31
Philharmonia Orchestra G81-49, -51
Philharmonic Orchestra G62-31, G63-31
Phillippi, Louis A. E69-61
Phillips, Todd (see The New South)
Phillipson, Neill E82-138
PHOENIX '55 T56-20
Photographer E79-28
Phyllis Whips Inflation E74-37
PIAF T81-4
"Piano Concerto" G65-37
Piatigorsky, Gregor G62-28, G63-27, G65-30
Piatrowsky, Gene E78-92
Piccadilly Circus E76-34
PICNIC T53-7, T54-21
Picture of Us, A E72-12
Pierce, George T48-11
Pierce, Laurens E72-47
Pieringer, Robert E80-99, E83-82
Pilafian, Peter E73-71
Pile, Walter E83-77
Piltz, Wilhelm G63-31
Pincus, Bernard F. E76-43
Pincus, Mathilde T76-19
"Pink Panther" G65-10, -25, -44
Pinkham, Dan E83-44
Pinsker, Judith E77-94, E78-79, E82-101

Pinter, Harold T67-1
Pinto, John E82-43, -109
Pinza, Ezio T50-8
PIPE DREAM T56-20
Pippin, Donald T63-15
PIPPIN T73-8, -14, -15, -16, -17
PIRATES OF PENZANCE T81-8, -15, -19
Pirie, James G. E82-142
Pirozzi, Jerry E77-48
Pitkin, William E77-67
Pitlik, Noam E78-24
Pitz, Wilhelm G63-31
Place, Mary Kay E76-11
Placido Domingo Celebrates Seville E83-8
Plante, Bill E71-29
Plaut, Fred G66-40, G71-39
Playbill T71-21
Playhouse 90 E56-3, -4, -13, -18, -21, -26, E57-1, -3, -12, -18, -25, E58-1, E59-1
Playing for Time E80-5, -11, -13, -28
Playwright's '56 E55-33
PLAZA SUITE T68-6
"Please Don't Tell Me How the Story Ends" G75-16
PLEASURE OF HIS COMPANY, THE T59-3
Plowright, Joan T61-4
Plumbicon Tube E66-40
PLUME DE MA TANTE, LA T59-11, -13
Plummer, Amanda T82-5
Plummer, Christopher T74-8, E76-24
Pohle, Bob E82-51
Poindexter, H.R. T71-17
POINT OF NO RETURN T52-3
Pointer Sisters, The G75-17
Polar Bear Alert E82-135
Police, The G81-10, G82-10, -13, G84-6, -13
Police Story E75-3, E77-75
Police Tapes—ABC News Close-up, The E79-95, -100
Polito, Joe G69-37
Polito, Joseph E79-113
Polk, Ken S. E82-59, E83-34
Pollack, Carl E79-112
Pollack, Jeffrey E80-99, E83-82
Pollack, Sidney E65-18
Pollini, Maurizio G80-46
Pollock, David E77-40
"Pollution" G72-42
Pollution Is a Matter of Choice E70-23
Polson, Beth E82-125
Pomerance, Bernard T79-1
Pomerantz, Earl E75-78
Poncia, Vini G78-21
PONDER HEART, THE T56-5

Index

Pony Cart, The E76-19
Pope John Paul II in Poland E80-93
Poppy Fields in Turkey—The Heroin of Marseilles—The New York Connection E72-67
Poppy Is Also a Flower, The E66-21
Pops E79-102
Population Explosion, The E59-16
Porcaro, Jeff G83-14
"Porgy and Bess" G60-17, T77-19
Portable Earth Station Transmitter E70-71
Portable Video Tape Equipment E73-129
Porte, George E. E72-42, E77-48, E79-37
Porter, Bob G80-54
Porter, Cole T49-13, G61-24
Porter, George R. E73-71, E76-44, E78-35
Porter, Terry E83-35
Porterfield, Robert T48-12
Portillo, Miguel E. E72-38
Post, Mike G69-8, G76-7, G82-8, -14
Post Election Special Edition E80-93
Poston, Tom E58-19
POTTING SHED, THE T57-3
"Poulenc" G66-38
Powell, Anthony T63-20
Powell, Dick E62-30
Power E79-60
Powers, Dave E73-49, E74-49, E76-32, E77-35
Powers, Matty E82-139
Pratt, Carroll E82-62, E83-58
Pre Game Program E69-39
"Precious Lord" G83-40
Prendergast, Roy E83-33
"Presenting the New Christy Minstrels" G63-25
Presley, Elvis G68-22, G73-26, G75-26
Pressman, David E75-56, E82-96
Preston, Billy G73-2, -9
Preston, Robert T58-10, T67-8
Pretty Soon Runs Out E68-46
Previn, Andre G59-19, G60-14, G61-8, G62-7, G72-35, G74-40, G77-43
Previn, Dory E82-55
Price, Eugene E82-101
Price, Leontyne G61-30, G64-29, G65-35, G66-37, G67-37, G68-42, G70-40, G72-38, G74-39, G75-39, E78-81, G81-49, E82-23, G83-51, E83-64, G84-55
Price, Ray G71-15, C71-3
Price, The E70]-13, -15, -35
Price Is Right, The E81-76, E82-100
Price of Tomatoes, The E61-10
Pride, Charley C71-1, -6, C72-6, G72-24, -25, G73-16
Priestly, John S. E61-21, E62-25
Priestly, Tom E64-16, E67-42, E69-48, E71-48, E79-97
Prima, Louis G59-16
"Prima Donna" G67-37
"Prima Donna, Volume 5" G81-49
"Prima Donna, Volume 2" G68-42
PRIME OF MISS JEAN BRODIE, THE T68-4
"Prime Time" G78-13
Prime Time Saturday E80-93
Prime Time Sunday E80-93
Primrose, William G62-28, G63-27
Prince, Harold S. T55-18, T56-18, T60-19, T63-18, T65-18, T67-7, -14, T71-19, -20, T72-15, T73-7, T74-15, T79-15, T80-15
Princess and the Cabbie, The E81-40
"Priority" G82-37
PRISONER OF SECOND AVENUE, THE T72-3, -6
Prisons Parts I through IV E70-39
Private Benjamin E80-16
PRIVATE LIVES T70-4
Producer's Showcase E55-1, -9, -23, -28, -33, E56-14
Profile in Music: Beverly Sills E74-7
Profile of Poverty in Appalachia E73-66
"Program of Song, A" G61-30
Project Peacock E80-10, E81-55
Project 20 E58-32, E62-23
"Prokofiev" G62-13, G65-32, G77-35, G81-46
PROMISES, PROMISES T69-8, -11, G70-31
Proscenium Productions T55-22
"Proud Mary" G72-21
Prudential's On-Stage E68-10, -13
Pryce, Johnathon T77-3
Pryor, Richard E73-84, G75-24, G76-24, G77-26, G82-33, G83-34
Public Broadcasting Service E79-63
"Puccini" G62-30, -39, G64-30, -35, -40, G74-39, G75-38
Pueblo E73-25, -29, -63, -68, -69
Puente, Tito G79-36, G84-46
Puerling, Gene G82-15
Pulitzer Prize Playhouse E50-6
Pultz, Alan E80-82, E81-79
Pumo John E74-83, E83-77
Purex Specials for Women E61-26
PURLIE T70-8, -11
Purple, David G72-41
"Put Your Hand in the Hand of the Man from Galilee" G72-26
Putnam, Curly C80-4, C81-4
Pyke, Albert E54-29

Index 184

Q

"Q" G78-25
QB VII, Parts 1 and 2 E74-33, -36, -61, -76, -81
Quadraplex Video Tape Cartridge Equipment E73-129
QUADRILLE T55-2, -20
Quality of Mercy, The E75-60, -65
Quayle, Anna T63-12
Quayle, Anthony E74-33
Queen Ida G83-41
Queen of the Gypsies E74-38
"Queen of the House" G66-13
Queen of the Stardust Ballroom E74-72, -74
Question of Impeachment, A E73-112
Quintero, Jose T57-7, T74-6

R

RCA E55-37, E59-24, E60-25, E73-129
RCA Italiana Opera Orchestra G64-30, G68-42, G69-35
Rabb, Ellis T76-6
Rabe, David T72-1
Rabel, Ed E82-128
"Rachmaninoff" G60-24, G72-32, -36, G77-43, G79-41
Raderman, Richard E. E69-40, E71-41, E77-75, E82-58
Radio Telefis Eirann, Ireland E82-144
Radiodiffusion Television Francais E63-29
Radner, Gilda E77-23
Rado, James G69-28
Rafkin, Alan E81-15
Ragaway, Martin E60-18
Rage of Angels E82-53
Ragni, Jerome G69-28
Raguse, Richard E83-35
Raid on Entebbe E76-43, -47
"Raiders of the Lost Ark" G82-41
"Raiders of the Lost Ark: The Movie on Record" G83-35
Rainbow E78-37
Rains, Claude T51-2
RAISIN T74-7, -10, G75-31
Raisins Verts, Les E63-29
Raley, Paul E80-86
Rambo, Dottie G69-26
Rambo, Reba G81-36
Ramin, Sid G62-23, E82-104

Ramirez, Hector E77-97
Ramone, Phil G65-39, G81-57, G84-43
Rams Football E50-7
Randall, Tony E74-20
Rank Precision Industries, Ltd. E80-42
Raposo, Joe E69-62, G73-33, G74-32
"Rare Blues" G81-39
Rasch, Karen E82-58
Rassmussen, Nils E80-94, E82-140
Rathbone, Basil T48-2
Rather, Dan E72-70
Rating Game, The E79-100
Ratliff, Roy E78-90
Rauschenberg, Robert G84-60
"Ravel" G62-27, -35, G76-35, -37, -42, G78-46
Raven, Richard T51-21
Rawlins, Lester T78-3
Rawls, Lou G68-16, G72-20, G78-23, G83-45
Ray, Ben H. E59-17
Raymond, Alan E80-94
Raymond, Susan E79-95
Razmofski, Peter E73-101
Razzmatazz E78-62
Reach, Jay E73-89
Reader, Jack E70-55, E79-92
Real People E83-59
REAL THING T84-1, -2, -4, -5, -6
"Reality ... What a Concept" G80-31
Really Useful Company, Ltd. T83-7
Reasoner, Harry E67-30, E73-117
Rebel, The E74-75
Recover E75-93
Red Pony, The E72-41, -56
Red Skelton Show, The E51-2, E60-18
Reda, Vincent E79-108, E80-99
Redding, Otis G69-17, -19
Reddy, Helen G73-5
Redgrave, Vanessa E80-11
REDHEAD T59-9, -10, -12, -14, -15, -17, -18, -20, G60-18
Reed, Elliott R. E79-113
Reed, Jerry C70-10, C71-10, G71-17, G72-15
Reed, Rick E83-82
Reemtsma, Judy Towers E80-94
Rees, Roger T82-2
"Refreshing" G79-29
Rega, Bill E75-79
Regan, Chris E83-44
Regas, Jack E78-92
"Regatta de Blanc" G81-10
REGINA T50-14, -18
Regis Philbin Show, The E81-69
Reichert, Jim E79-89

Index

Reid, Beryl T67-4
Reid, Mike G84-23
Reilly, Charles Nelson T62-11
Reilly, George C. E80-53
Reilly, Jean Burt E75-95
Reiner, Carl E56-11, E57-13, E61-18, E62-21, E63-20, E66-28
Reiner, Fritz G61-27, G63-34, G65-35
Reiner, Rob E73-31, E77-16
Reinhold, Gady E80-99
Reischauer, Edwin O. E69-31
Reisenberger, George W. E81-53
Reitano, Robert M. E77-46
Reitz, John E79-36
"Rejoice" G81-37
"Release Me (from My Sin)" G74-27
Rende, Louis E72-40, E75-64, E79-112
Renoir, Jacques E70-59
Reports from the Lt. Calley Trial E70-31
Reports on World Hunger E73-111
Requiem for a Heavyweight E56-3, -13, -18, -21, -26
Resch, Donald E80-99, E83-82
Rescher, Gayne E79-49
"Respect" G68-14, -15
Retrospective of William Holden's Africa, A E83-75
"Return of Roger Miller, The" G66-12
Return to Forever (see Chick Corea)
"Revenge" G68-19
Revere, Anne T60-5
"Rev. Du Rite" G82-33
"Reverie for Spanish Guitars" G62-33
Revlon Revue E59-11
"Revolver" G67-38
Reynolds, Gene E74-48, E75-50
Rhapsody and Song—A Tribute to George Gershwin E80-52
"Rhinestone Cowboy" C76-4
RHINOCEROS T61-2
Rhoda E74-21, E77-15
Rice, Al, Jr. E78-90
Rice, Tim T80-7, G81-41
Rice, Tony (see The New South)
Rich, Charlie C73-2, -3, -6, C74-1, -3, G74-16
Rich, David Lowell E77-37
Rich, Don C74-10
Rich, John E62-19, E71-33
Rich, Mert E81-34
Rich Man, Poor Man E75-32, -41, -49, -84
Richard Pryor Show, The E77-72
Richard Simmons Show, The E80-83, E81-68, -94, -96
Richards, Martin T79-7, T84-7

Richards, Ron E80-86
Richardson, Karl G79-50
Richardson, Paul Bruce E76-42
Richie, Lionel G83-4
Richie Almost Dies E77-44
Richmond, Bill E73-83, E74-65, E77-40
Richter, Sviatoslav G61-28
Ride on the Moon: The Flight of Apollo 15, A E71-25
Riddle, Nelson G59-18, G84-9
Rigby, Harry T68-16
Riger, Chris E80-99
Riggs, Otis E55-33
Riker's Island Plane Crash E57-6
Riley, Jeannie C. C68-2, G69-14
Rineer, Jesse E80-99
Ringel, Jeff E80-99
Ringer, Robert E68-17
RINK, THE T84-11
Rintels, David W. E74-68, E75-76
Riolo, Val E79-92
Ripp, Heino E69-49, E71-44, E80-50, E82-43
"Rise" G80-8
Riser, Paul G73-23
Ritchard, Cyril T55-11
Ritter, John E83-16
Ritter, Thelma T58-12
Ritual of Evil E69-46
RITZ, THE T75-5
River of Promises E77-75
RIVER NIGER, THE T74-1
Rivera, Chita T84-11
Robards, Jason, Jr. T59-2
ROBBER BRIDEGROOM, THE T77-8
Robbin, Irving E79-89
Robbins, Hargus "Pig" C76-10, G78-20
Robbins, Jerome T48-8, T58-17, T65-16, -17
Robbins, Marty G61-12, G71-13
Robert Montgomery Presents E52-4
Robert Young the Family E70-62
Roberts, Doris E82-17
Roberts, Erskin E75-64, E79-112
Roberts, Mark E83-32
Robertson, Cliff E65-8
Robinson, Charlotte E80-99
Robinson, Jane E75-93
Rockefeller, John D., III T60-24
Rockford Files, The G76-7, E76-12, E77-2, -27, E78-23, E79-17
"Rockit" G84-32
"Rockstra Theme" G80-10
Rod of Iron, A E80-106
Rodd, Derek E77-71
Rodda, Richard T55-21

Index 186

Rode, Donald R. E74-57
Roden, Peter E70-61
Rodeo Red and the Runaway E78-80, -92
Rodgers, Richard T50-13, -15, T52-7, T60-16, -19, G61-23, E61-25, T62-16, -23, G63-21, T72-19
Roecker, Dick E78-90
Roes, Dick E75-68
Roesser, Merrit E72-40, E75-64, E79-112
Roethle, Bob E76-39
Rogers, Fred E79-88
Rogers, Kenny C77-2, C78-8, G78-18, C79-3, -6, -8, G80-22
Rogers, Nathan E79-112
Rogers, Paul T67-2
Rogers, Suzanne E78-72
Rogow, Robert E80-94
Rohnke, Terry E82-109
Roland, Rita E76-38
Rolle, Esther E78-18
Roman, Murray E68-34
Romar, Harry T58-21
Rome Opera House Chorus and Orchestra G62-30, G63-29
Romeo and Juliet E77-67
"Ronnie Milsap Live" C77-3
Ronstadt, Linda G76-15, G77-5, G81-43
Rook, John E70-54, E82-51
Rookie of the Year E73-12
Room 222 E69-7, -16, -17
Rooney, Andy E68-23, E79-96
Rooney, Mickey E81-26
Roots E76-4, -16, -17, -18, -30, -37, -42, -51, -61
Roots: The Next Generation E78-3, -19
"Rosanna" G83-1, -9, -14
Rosburg, Bob E80-99
Rose, David E58-37, E70-65, E78-45, E81-39
Rose, David, Orchestra G60-14
Rose, George T76-8
Rose, Leonard G71-34
Rose, Reginald E61-17, E62-20
"Rose, The" G81-5
"Rose Garden" G71-14
ROSE TATTOO, THE T51-1, -3, -5, -6, -8, -19
Roseman, Leonard E78-46
Rosen, Arnold E55-22, E56-20, E71-62
Rosenberg, Stuart E62-18
ROSENKRANTZ AND GUILDENSTERN ARE DEAD T68-1, -7, -17, -18
Rosenman, Leonard E76-62
Rosenthal, Eric E79-113
Rosenthal, Jerry E74-61, E77-48
Rosenthal, Laurence E65-36

Rosie: The Rosemary Clooney Story E82-49
Ross, Diana T77-20
Ross, Dr. Isiah G81-39
Ross, Jerry T55-15, T56-15
Ross, Michael E72-61
Ross, Russ K. E78-90
Ross, Ted T75-9
Ross, William P. E68-37
Rossi, Richard E80-99
"Rossini" G69-35
Rosten, Irwin E80-94
Rostropovich, Mstislav G71-35, G78-38, G81-47, G84-52
Rota, Nino G73-30
ROTHSCHILDS, THE T71-9, -10
Rothweiler, George E78-90, E80-99, E83-82
Rotter, Stephen A. E77-46
Rounds, David T80-3
"Route 66" G83-21
Routledge, Patricia T68-11
Rowan and Martin's Laugh-In E67-2, -35, E68-2, -43, E70-36
Rowan and Martin's Laugh-In Special E67-3, -41
ROYAL FAMILY, THE T76-6, E77-29
Royal Flush E66-24
Royal Opera House Chorus G71-32, -37, G80-49
Royal Opera House Orchestra G62-29, G71-32, -37, G76-39, G80-49
Royal Philharmonic Orchestra and Chorus G61-33
Rozell, Rosie G82-36
Rubin, Maury E83-71
Rubino, George E77-43
Rubinstein, Arthur E69-30, -31
Rubinstein, Artur G60-23, -25, G64-31, G66-34, G73-37, G75-35, G76-36, G77-36, -39, G78-42
Rubinstein, John T80-2
Rudel, Julius G79-43
Rufus G75-22, G84-31
Ruggles, Charlie T59-3
Rugolo, Pete E69-54, E71-65
Ruiz, Horace E78-90
Rule, Elton H. E80-43
"Rumours" G78-2
Runaways, The E73-14
Runkle, Theodora Van E82-45
"Runnin'" G79-25
Rushlow, Nancy E83-44
Rusk, Jim E73-84, E75-78
Russell, Bobby C68-4, G69-3, -13
Russell, Leon G73-2
Russell, Rosalind T53-12

Index

Ryan, Bob E80-99, E82-111
Ryan, Terry E55-22, E57-20
Ryan's Hope E75-43, E76-76, -86, -89, -92, E77-94, E78-63, -75, -79, E79-82, -85, E80-92, E82-87, -101
Rynew, Arden E82-32

S

SCTV Network E81-34, E82-38
'S Wonderful, 'S Marvelous, 'S Gershwin E71-4, -35, -44, -52, -67
Sabbatini, Enrico E81-49
Sabol, Steve E77-105, E78-90, E79-110, E83-75
Sackler, Howard T69-1
Sacks, Juliann E79-55
Saddler, Donald T53-16, T71-15
Sadoo, Winston E79-112
Saga of a Star World E78-53
Saga of Western Man E64-10
Sage, Liz E77-40
Sagnelli, Phyllis E78-84
Sahara: La Caravanne du Sel E69-48
Sahlin, Donald E75-96
"Sail On" G78-30
"Sailing" G81-1, -3, -15
St. Elsewhere E82-14, -17, -18, E83-37
St. James, Susan E68-14
SAINT OF BLEECKER STREET, THE T55-17
St. Paul Chamber Orchestra G80-45
"Saint-Saens" G63-13, G65-43
Saint-Subber T49-14
Sainthill, Louden T69-14
Sakota, Joe E78-90
Saks, Gene T77-15, T83-6
Saks, Jay David E82-111
Salerno, Hank E75-65, E77-75, E79-60
Salisbury, Frank E81-85
Sally Sees Sesame Street E69-62
Salter, William G82-28
Salvatore, Anthony G67-41, G80-51
Sam & Dave G68-17
"Sam, Hard and Heavy" G72-43
Same Mud, Same Blood E67-45
SAME TIME, NEXT YEAR T75-4
Samet, Norm E80-99
Sammy's Visit E71-33
Samudio, Sam G72-43
Sanborn, David G82-32
Sanchez, Fausto E79-112
Sand, Paul T71-3
Sandberg, Martin E79-113

Sanburg, Carl G60-16
Sandburg's Lincoln E75-28
Sanders, Marlene E80-94
Sanderson, David E79-88
Sandler, Jeff E82-58
Sandlin, Edward E74-61, E76-43
"Sandpiper, The" G66-22
Sandreuter, Bill E75-68
Sandrich, Jay E70-32, E72-32
Sands, Dennis S. E78-49
Sanford, Isabel E80-14
Sanford, Mark E83-42
Santamaria, Mongo G78-36
Santini, Gabriele G62-30
SARATOGA T60-22
Sardi, Vincent, Sr. T47-8
Sargent, Herb E69-51, E73-84, E75-75, E76-52
Sargent, Joseph E72-31
Sarnoff, General David E61-28
"Saturday Night Fever" G79-2, -6
Satyr, The E80-56
Saudis: CBS Reports, The E80-94
Savage Bees, The E76-44
Savalas, Telly E73-21
Savel, Elizabeth E76-49
Savignano, Ralph E78-90
Savignano, Ray E80-99
Savoy, Jack E80-99
Saxon, Robert E78-66
Saxon, Spenser David E71-38
Sayer, Leo G78-21
Scaggs, Boz G77-21
Scandiffio, Anthony E79-108, E80-99
Scanimate Electronic Animation E71-72
Scannapieco, Louis E80-99
Scarecrow E71-54
Scared Straight E78-8, -52
Scarlet and the Black, The E82-60
Scarlet Letter, The E78-38
Scarlet Pimpernel, The E82-46
Scarlet O'Hara War, The E79-56, -57
Scent of Flowers, A E68-48
Schaap, Dick E82-130
Schachter, Scott E79-44
Schaefer, George T54-8, E58-25, E60-15
Schaffer, Anthony T71-1
Schaffner, Franklin E54-28, E55-24, -25, E61-15
Schaller, Adolf E80-53
Scharf, Leo E72-40
Scharf, Walter E70-66, E73-124
Schary, Dore T58-6, -8
Schavio, Joe E80-99
Scheiner, Elliot G78-47

Index 188

Schenck, Mary Percy T48-9
Schenck, Walter E77-68
Schencman, Mario E79-112
Schenkler, Marv E68-17
Scherman, Roland G68-44
Scherman, Roni E80-99
Schiavo, Joseph E79-113
Schieffer, Bob E71-29
Schifman, Milton E60-20
Schifrin, Lalo G65-9, G66-9, G68-24, -26
Schiller, Bob E70-50, E77-38
Schiller, Tom E75-75, E76-52
Schindler, Michael E73-69
Schippers, Thomas T55-17, G70-40
Schlitz, Don C79-4, G79-16
Schlitz Playhouse of Stars E57-19
Schmidt, Arthur E78-33
Schmitt, Al G63-36, G77-45, G78-47, G79-47, G83-55
Schnee, Bill G78-47, G82-54
Schneider, Alan T63-6
Schneider, Art E65-26, E67-41, E72-37
Schneider, Harold E73-89
Schneider, Laurence E65-42
Schneiderman, David E83-34
"Schoenberg" G78-40
Schone, Virginia E69-62
SCHOOL FOR SCANDAL, THE T63-20
SCHOOL FOR WIVES, THE T71-2
Schoolhouse Rock E77-82, E78-60
Schorn, Manfred E75-62
Schorr, Daniel E72-70
Schorr, Lester E54-25
"Schubert" G71-38, G76-36
Schubin, Mark E79-45
Schuller, Gunther G74-35, G76-46
Schulman, Billy E68-45
Schulte, Jan E79-109
Schulz, Charles M. E73-101
Schumann, Walter E54-31
"Schumann" G72-38, G78-42
Schuster, Rosie E75-75, E76-52
Schutzman, Carl E73-120
Schwartz, Al E60-18
Schwartz, Howard E72-45, E78-37
Schwartz, Joseph E73-120
Schwartz, Marvin G61-38, G62-39, G63-38, E70-47
Schwartz, Norm E74-85
Schwartz, Sherwood E60-18
Schwartz, Stephen G72-29
Schwarz, Gene E74-83
Science and Religion: Who Will Play God? E67-14
Science Rock E78-60

Scikner, William E55-31
Scofield, Paul T62-2, E68-10
Scoskie, Paul E72-40
Scott, Bobby G63-10
Scott, George C. E70-13
Scott, Jan E69-57, E71-54, E73-102, -104, E75-90, E76-59
Scott, Tom G75-10
Scotto, Renata E79-87
Screen Actors Guild 50th Anniversary Celebration E83-23, -54
"Scriabin" G74-37
Seagren, Danny E79-91
Seal, Elizabeth T61-12
Sealy, Judy Cooper E81-99
Search for the Nile, The E71-50, -64
Search for Tomorrow E75-42, E76-85, E77-97, E80-77
SEASCAPE T75-3
SEASON IN THE SUN T51-19
Seawell, Donald R. T83-19
Sebastian, Ray E69-61
Secret, The E80-88
Secret of Charles Dickens, The E78-92
Secrets of the Sunken Caves E71-70
Section Anderson, La E67-55
Sedlitz, Leon E75-65
See How She Runs E77-31, -56
See It Now E52-8, E53-12, E56-5, E57-17
Seeds of Revolution E79-86
Seely, Jeannie G67-12
SEESAW T74-9, -14
Segal, Alex E66-23
Segal, Allan E80-99
Seger, Bob & the Silver Bullet Band G81-13
Segovia, Andres G59-21
"Segovia Golden Jubilee" G59-21
"Segovia—The EMI Recordings 1927–39" G81-56
Seidelman, Arthur Allen E79-88, E81-83
Seigal, Mike E82-139
Selden, Albert T66-7, T68-16
Seldes, Marian T67-5
Sell, Janie T74-11
Selleck, Tom E83-14
Selling of Colonel Herbert, The E72-67, -68
Selling of the Pentagon, The E70-22
Sembello, Michael G84-43
Senate Hearings on Vietnam E65-29
Senator—The Bold Ones, The E70-7, -11
Senatore, Vincent E79-89, E81-92, E82-105
"Send in the Clowns" G76-3

Index

Sentry Collection Presents Ben Vereen—His Roots, The E77-36, -51, -54, -57, -62, -74
SEPARATE TABLES T57-4
"September of My Years" G66-2, -43
Seretti, Phillip J. E78-49
"Sgt. Pepper's Lonely Hearts Club Band" G68-2, -36, -43, -47
Serkin, Peter G66-45
Serkin, Rudolf G84-52
Serlin, Arnie E82-135
Serling, Rod E55-27, E56-18, E57-18, E59-14, E60-17, E63-18
Servidio, John A. E79-88, E83-82
Sesame Street E69-21, -62, E70-21, E71-22, G71-31, E72-11, E73-125, E75-96, -97, E76-81, E78-80, -92, E79-70, -88, E80-86, -88, G82-44, E82-72, -111
"Sesame Street Live" G74-32
Sevaried, Eric E72-70
700 Year Old Gang, The E64-20, -21
Seven Lively Arts E57-4
Seven Wishes of a Rich Kid, The E79-88
SEVEN YEAR ITCH, THE T53-2
1776 T69-7, -9, -13
Seventh Annual Young Performer's Concert E65-42
79th World Series, The E83-74, -83
Seville, David (see Ross Bagdasarian)
Sexual Abuse of Children E82-143
"Sexual Healing" G83-30, -32
SHADOW BOX, THE T77-1, -6
Shadow Game E69-33, -57
"Shadow of Your Smile" G66-3
"Shadows of the Night" G83-11
Shadwell, Cal E69-49, E71-57
Shaffer, Louise E82-87
Shaffer, Peter T75-1, T81-1
"Shaft" G72-28
Shankar, Ravi G68-38, G73-2
Shape of Things, The E73-36
Shapiro, Don E79-110
Shapiro, Mel T72-12
Sharaff, Irene T52-15
"Share Your Love With Me" G70-20
Sharp, Phil E57-20
Shaw, David T59-14
Shaw, Jerome E74-55, E78-77, E79-84
Shaw, Robert, Chorale G62-32, G65-36, G66-38, G67-35
Shaw, Sam E83-32
She Drinks a Little E81-83, -86
SHE LOVES ME T64-11, G64-21
Shea, George Beverly G66-21
Sheen, Bishop Fulton J. E52-12

Sheen, Martin E80-89
Sheena Easton ... Act 1 E82-26, -51, -62
Sheerer, Robert E63-23
Shelby, Robert E54-33
Sheldon, Ron E79-53, E83-42
Sheldon, Sidney T59-14
Shell's Wonderful World of Golf E65-34
Shelly, Carole T79-4
SHENANDOAH T75-8
Shenberg, William E82-58
Shepard, Thomas Z. G79-35
Sheppard, Martin E72-38
Sheppard, Steve E80-94
SHERLOCK HOLMES T75-15, -16
Sherman, Allan G64-14
Sherman, Hiram T53-11, T68-10
Sherman, Richard M. G65-23
Sherman, Robert B. G65-23
Sherriffe, Brian E78-39
Sherrill, Billy G67-11, G75-14
Shevelove, Burt T63-13
Shields, Catherine E83-31
Shingleton, Willfred E77-71, E79-55
"Shining Star" G76-22, G81-30
Ship of Spies E66-27
Shire, David G79-2
Shirley MacLaine ... Every Little Movement E79-30, -52
Shirley MacLaine: If They Could See Me Now E74-66
Shirley MacLaine ... Illusions E81-37, -42
Shogun E80-3, -58, -61
Sholder, Jack E79-88
Shooting, The E82-107, -108
Shooting of Bill Stewart E80-94
Shore, Dinah E54-16, E55-20, E56-16, E57-16, E58-21, E73-46, E75-47
Shores of the Cosmic Ocean, The E80-53
Shorr, Catherine E83-33
Shorr, Richard E83-33
Short, Martin E82-38
Short, Michael E81-34, E82-38
Short, Robert E. E82-103
"Shostakovich" G60-32, G75-36, G81-46
SHOT IN THE DARK, A T62-3
Show Biz E55-35
Show Number 312 E83-39
Showdown E82-56
Showdown in Iran—CBS Reports E79-93
Shower of Stars E54-29
SHRIKE, THE T52-2, -6
Shubert Organization, The T73-19, T78-7, T81-1, T82-1, T83-7, T84-1
Shugrue, Michael C. E69-37, E72-38
Shugrue, Robert F. E81-19
Shultis, John E69-43

Index 190

Shumlin, Herman T64-8
Shyre, Paul T57-22
Sickle Cell Disease: Paradox of Neglect E71-74
Sid Caesar E82-130
Sid Caesar, Imogene Coca, Carl Reiner, Howard Morris Special, The E66-6, -28
Sidaris, Andy E68-17, E75-58
Siderman, Bob E83-82
Sidlo, Jo E74-83, E80-99
Siegel, Doc E77-106
Siegel, Janis (Also see Manhattan Transfer) G81-9
Siegel, Larry E71-62, E72-63
"Siegel Schwall Band, The" G73-44
SIGN IN SIDNEY BRUSTEIN'S WINDOW, THE T65-5
Signoret, Simone E65-9
Silent Lovers, The E79-49
Silke, Jim G62-38
Sillery, Stuart E82-129
Sills, Beverly G77-42
Silver Convention G76-23
Silverman, Ed E83-71
Silverman, Treva E73-82, -85
Silvers, Phil T52-8, E55-4, -10, T72-8
Silverside, Jill E75-93
Silverstein, Morton E80-94
Silverstein, Shel G70-14
Simka Returns E81-13
Simmons, Barbara Martin E81-92
Simmons, Ed E73-83, E74-65, E77-40
Simmons, Jean E82-21
Simmons, Nancy E81-96
Simon, Carly G72-44, G81-43, G83-45
Simon, George T. G78-49
Simon, Joe G70-21
Simon, Lucy G81-43, G83-45
Simon, Ned E80-99
Simon, Neil T65-6, T75-18
Simon, Paul G69-27, G71-3, -9, -10, G76-2, -4, E77-41
Simon, Scott E82-127
Simon & Garfulkel (Also see Paul Simon & Art Garfunkel) G69-1, -6, G71-1, -2
"Simple Dreams" G78-48
Simpson, Robert G60-30
Sims, Jerry E68-28
Sinatra, Frank G59-28, G60-2, -4, -34, G61-24, G66-2, -5, G67-1, -2, -5, G83-58
"Sinatra a Man and His Music" G67-2
"Sinatra at the Sands" G67-40
Sinatra: The First 40 Years E79-35
Singer, Alexander E71-31
Singer, Hans E78-90, E80-99, E83-82

Singer, Larry E75-65, E77-75, E79-60
Singer Presents Burt Bachrach E70-4, -51
Singer Presents Liza with a Z E72-3, -34, -54, -58
Singing Nun, The (Soeur Sourire) G64-20
Sinnamon, Shandi G84-43
Sipherd, Ray E69-62, E73-125
"(Sittin' on) The Dock of the Bay" G69-17, -19
SIX CHARACTERS IN SEARCH OF AN AUTHOR T56-7
Six Wives of Henry VIII, The E71-13
6th Annual Kennedy Center Honors: A Celebration of the Performing Arts E83-6
$64,000 Question E55-15
60 Minutes E70-25, -26, E71-27, E72-67, -68, E73-119, -120, -123, E79-94, -96, -100, -102, E80-93, -94, E82-122, -124, -126, -130, -132
SIZWE BANZI IS DEAD T75-2
Skaggs, Ricky (Also see The New South) C82-6, -11, C83-9
Skalicky, Jan E76-66
Skateboard Fever E77-105
Skelton, Geoffrey T66-1
Skelton, Red E51-1, E60-18
"Sketches of Spain" G61-10
Skipper, Ross E72-40
Sklena, Vincent E79-88
SLAPSTICK TRAGEDY T66-5
Slate, Lane E76-54
Slatkin, Felix G59-22
Sleeping Beauty, The E72-4
SLEEPY HOLLOW T49-15
Slesar, Henry E73-87
SLEUTH T71-1, -7
Slezak, Walter T55-10
Sloane, Allan E71-59
Slotkin, Toni E80-99
Slow Guillotine, The E69-66
"Smackwater Jack" G72-8
Small Rebellion, A E65-9
Smalls, Charlie T75-12, G76-31
Smedley–Aston, Brian E77-46
Smight, Jack E58-26
Smith, Alexis T72-10
Smith, Bob E78-90, E79-110
Smith, Cal C74-2
Smith, Dave E73-76, E79-113
Smith, Dick E66-32
Smith, Erik G73-39
Smith, Frank E59-20
Smith, Gary E61-23
Smith, Grant E54-27
Smith, Gregg, Singers G67-35, G69-33, G71-36

Smith, Harry E79-115
Smith, Howard K. E59-16
Smith, Jerry R. E83-43
Smith, Keely G59-16
Smith, Milton T63-21
Smith, Norman E80-99
Smith, Oliver T57-19, T58-19, T60-21, T61-19, -20, T64-20, T65-19
Smith, Pat Falken E75-79
Smith, Sammi C71-2, G72-14
Smith, Teri E79-89, E82-104
Smollin, Michael J. E81-100
Smothers Brothers Comedy Hour, The E67-28, E68-34
Smuin, Michael E83-53
Smurfs E82-71
Snoop Sisters, The E73-24
Snow Goose, The E71-15
"Snowbird" G72-17
Snowdon, Lord E68-29
Snyder, Tom T73-18
Soap E77-70, E78-15, E79-12, -13
Societe Nationale de Television Francaise E81-102
Societe Radio, Canada E80-107
Society of Motion Picture Engineers E78-57
Soderberg, Theodore E71-43
Soeur Sourire (see The Singing Nun)
Sogard, Philip E80-82, E81-79
Soh, John E69-38
Sokota, Joseph E80-99, E83-82
Solar Eclipse: A Darkness at Noon E69-27
Soldier's Tale, The E83-46
Solid Gold E82-50, E83-51
Solomito, Joseph E79-89, E81-92
Solomon, Jeanne E82-130
Soloway, Leonard T77-1
Solti, Georg G63-29, G67-36, G73-34, -35, -41, G74-36, G75-33, -34, -38, G76-34, G77-37, G78-45, G79-45, G80-43, -44, -50, G81-45, G82-45, -46, G83-53, G84-50, -51, -56, -57
Solzhenitsyn E73-116
Some Footnotes to 25 Nuclear Years E69-32
Something About Amelia E83-2, -19, -36
Sometimes I Don't Like My Mother E82-106
"Somewhere My Love" G67-28
Son House G81-39
Sonderberg, Theodore E70-43
Sondheim, Stephen T63-8, T71-14, G71-29, T72-13, T73-13, G74-31, G76-3, T79-13, G80-40, -51
Song for Dead Warriors, A E83-53, -64

"Songs in the Key of Life" G77-2, -4
"Songs of the Cowboy" G61-26
Sonny and Cher Comedy Hour, The E71-34
Sony E72-73, E75-102, E78-57
SOPHISTICATED LADIES T81-9, -18
"Sophisticated Lady" G77-22
Soucy, Walter E80-99, E83-82
"Soul Man" G68-17
"Soul of Me, The" G69-26
"Soulful Strut" G80-7
Sound of Burt Bachrach, The E69-34, -43, -49, -53
Sound of Dolphins, A E71-23
Sound of Freedom E75-69
"Sound of Horowitz, The" G64-32
SOUND OF MUSIC, THE T60-9, -13, -14, -16, -17, -19, -21, G61-23
Sounds of America E60-22
Sounds of Chicago, The E67-40
South, Joe G70-3, -10
SOUTH PACIFIC T49-15, T50-4, -7, -8, -9, -10, -11, -12, -13, -15
Southern California Community Choir G75-28
"Southland Favorites" G66-21
Spain, Tom E79-96, -98
Spalding, Tom E78-90
Spangolia, Donald E80-90
"Spanish Album, The" G81-48
"Spanish Guitars of Laurindo Almeida" G61-34, -35
"Speaking in Tongues" G84-60
Special Act of Love, A E73-98
Special Bulletin E82-2, -32, -37, -44
Special Day in the Year of the Child, A E78-92
Special Gift, A E79-88
Special of the Week E71-40
Special Treat E76-82, E77-96, E78-61, -92, E80-88
Spencer, Richard G70-19
Spencer, William E64-18, E81-35
Spewack, Bella and Samuel T49-12
Spiegel, Ed E72-36
Spieller, Art E78-90, E79-110
Spinetti, Victor T65-11
Spinner, Roman E78-66
Spinney, Carroll E75-97, E78-80
"Spinning Wheel" G70-11
Spirit of '78 — The Flight of the Double Eagle II E78-86
Spitzer, George G82-57
Splinters, Judy E48-1
Sportsworld E77-105
Springfield, Rick G82-12
Springsteen, Bruce G83-45

Squittieri, Robert E80-99
Stable Boy's Christmas E79-86
Stack, Lenny E83-54
Stack, Robert E59-7
Stacy, John E71-41
Stafford, Jo G61-16
Stahlberg, David G70-43
STALAG 17 T52-6
Stampley, Joe C80-8
"Stan Freberg Presents the United States of America" G62-36
"Stand by Your Man" G70-15
Stanhope, Paul E81-51
Stanley, Kim E62-14
Stanley, Pat T59-13
Stanton, Frank E59-23, E71-71
Stanton, Garry E73-127
Stanwyck, Barbara E60-9, E65-11, E82-15
Stapleton, Jean E70-10, E71-10, E77-13
Stapleton, Maureen T51-5, E67-18, T71-4
Star Trek E74-12
"Star Wars" G78-8, -10, -34
Starland Vocal Band G77-9, -49
Starr, Ringo (Also see The Beatles) G71-28, G73-2
Starstruck E81-62
Statler Brothers, The G66-31, -46, C72-7, C73-7, G73-17, C74-7, C75-7, C76-7, C77-7, C79-7, C80-7
"Stayin' Alive" G79-9
STEAMING T83-5
Steckler, Allan G84-62
Steckler, Doug E81-34, E82-38
Stein, James R. E73-84
Stein, Joseph T65-14
Steinbeck, Robert E72-40
Steinberg, Norman E70-50
Steiner, Armin G73-43
Stephan, Leo E72-40, E75-64, E79-112
Stephenson, Edward E58-36
Stern, Isaac G62-31, G63-30, G65-32, G71-34, G78-38, G82-48
Stern, Leonard E56-20, E66-27
Stern, Stewart E76-53
Sternbach, Rick E80-53
Sternhagen, Frances T74-5
Steve Allen Show, The E58-19
Steve Allen's Meeting of the Minds E80-8
Steve and Eydie Celebrate Irving Berlin E78-4, -49
Steve and Eydie: Our Love Is Here to Stay E75-51
Stevens, April G64-18
Stevens, Jeremy E72-11

Stevens, Larry E83-44
Stevens, Morton E69-55, E73-93
Stevens, Ray G71-4, G76-10
Stevens, Robert E57-22
Stevens, Roger L. T62-8, T71-21, T83-19, T84-19
Stewart, Margaret E75-79
Stewart, Michael T61-14, T64-14, T81-7, T82-7
Stewart, Roy E76-40, E78-92, E79-92
Stewart, Sandy E73-106
STICKS AND BONES T72-1, -5
Stiles, Norman E73-125
"Still Crazy After All These Years" G76-2, -4
Sting G84-3, -10
Stitch, Mike E77-97
Stockard Channing in Just Friends E78-56
Stokowski, Leopold G66-32
Stoltzman, Richard G83-48
Stone, Ann E79-112
Stone, Bill E79-113
Stone, John E69-62, E73-125
Stone, Joseph E81-45
Stone, Milburn E67-21
Stone, Noubar E83-71
Stone, Peter T69-7, T81-12
Stoned E80-88
Stoneman Family, The C67-7
Stop Action Playback E65-44
STOP THE WORLD—I WANT TO GET OFF T63-12
Stoppard, Tom T68-1, T76-1, T84-1
Storey, Ray E80-54
Stories of the Century E54-20
Storm Breaks, The E82-47
Storm in Summer, A E69-6, -12
"Story-Teller: A Session with Charles Laughton, The" G63-17
STORY THEATRE T71-3, -17
Strack, Larry E79-89, E81-92
Straight, Beatrice T53-5
Straigis, Tony T84-16
Stramsky, Mike E78-90
"Stranger in My House" G84-23
"Strangers in the Night" G67-1, -5, -26, -42
Strangers: The Story of a Mother & Daughter E78-16
Strasser, Robin E81-72
Straumer, Charles E59-18
Strauss, John E77-48
Strauss, Marilyn T78-1
Strauss, Peter E78-17
Strauss, Theodore H. E70-28, E76-55
"Strauss" G66-37, G75-39, G77-37

Index

Stravinsky, Igor G62-4, -34, G63-26, -30, -33, G68-37
"Stravinsky" G62-4, G63-26, -30, G66-38, G68-37, G71-33, -39, G81-47
Streep, Meryl E77-21
STREET SCENE T47-7
STREETCAR NAMED DESIRE, A T48-3, E83-29, -40, -49
Streisand, Barbra G64-2, -6, E64-8, G65-8, G66-6, T70-17, G78-3, -5, G81-6
Strenge, Walter E69-45
Strike, The E81-57
Stringer, Howard E79-97
Strong, Barrett G73-19
Strouse, Charles T61-9, T70-7, T77-13, G78-35
Struck, Duke E79-83
Struggle for Survival: Primal Man E73-122
Struthers, Sally E71-18, E78-14
Stucker, Len E78-90
Stucky, Lon E65-38, E71-69, E75-82
Studio One E51-3, E54-17, -22, -28, E55-32
Studs Lonigan E78-41
Styler, Adele E77-40
Styler, Burt E71-61, E77-40
Styne, Jule G65-24, T68-13
Su, K. E72-38
SUBJECT WAS ROSES, THE T65-1, -3
Submarine, The E69-41
"Suburban Attitudes in Country Verse G68-45
SUBWAYS ARE FOR SLEEPING T62-13
Sudhalter, Richard G83-57
Suffer the Little Children—An NBC News White Paper on Northern Ireland E71-30
Sugar Mama E78-12
Sughrue, John J. E64-15
Sullivan, Ed E70-70
Sullivan, Francis L. T55-3
Sullivan, William E79-113
Summer, Donna G79-22, G80-11, G84-36
SUMMER AND SMOKE T49-15
"Summer in the City" G74-7
Summer of My German Soldier E78-18
"Summer Place, Theme from A" G61-1, -40
Summer 67: What We Learned E67-8
"Summer Sketches '82" G84-7
Summers, Ted E75-64
Sumner, J.D. G82-36
"Sun of Latin Music" G76-32
SUNDAY IN THE PARK WITH GEORGE T84-16, -17
Sunday Morning E82-130

"Sunday Morning Coming Down" C70-4
Sundown E82-25
Sunnyland Slim G81-39
SUNRISE AT CAMPOBELLO T58-1, -2, -3, -6, -7, -8
Sunshine, Norman E75-98
Sunshine, William E73-123
Sunshine's on the Way E80-88
Superbowl XV E80-101
Superbowl XIV E79-107
Superbowl XIII E78-85, -90
Superbowl Today/Superbowl XII E77-105
Superfluous People E62-29
"Superman" G80-13, -39
Supersax G74-11
"Superstition" G74-19, -21
Support Your Local Mother E70-49
Surrender at Appomattox: Appointment with Destiny E72-36, -42
Survivor G83-13
Suski, Ed E83-59
Sutherland, Joan G62-29, G82-51
Sutton, Glenn G67-11
Sutton, Shaun E81-106
Swanson, Glen E74-54, E75-54, E82-99
Swanson, Robert L. E59-17
Swedish Television, Sweden E83-36
Sweeney, Gordon E74-83
SWEENEY TODD T79-7, -8, -10, -12, -13, -15, -16, -18, G80-40, -51
Sweeney Todd: Scenes from the Making of a Musical E81-104
SWEET BIRD OF YOUTH T76-4
SWEET CHARITY T66-13
Sweet Smell of Failure E69-35
Swerling, Jo T51-14
Swieden, Bruce G84-59
Swift, Lela E76-89, E78-75, E79-82
"Swing Dat Hammer" G61-20
Swing Out, Sweet Land E70-67
"Swingin'" C83-2
Swingle, Ward (See The Swingle Sisters)
Swingle Singers, The G64-26, -42, G65-28, G66-27, G70-38
"Swingle Sisters Going Baroque, The" G65-28
Swiss Broadcasting and Television (Zurich) E68-47
Swit, Loretta E79-19, E81-8
"Switched-On Bach" G70-34
Switched-On Symphony, The E69-44
Sybil E76-7, -23, -53, -62
Symphony of the Air G60-24
"Synchronicity" G84-13
Szeryng, Henryk G75-35, G76-36

Index

T

"TSOP" G75-23
TV Globo, Brazil E82-147
Tadros, Abdelnour E79-113
Taff, Russ G84-38
Taggart, Jill E83-33
Tail Gunner Joe E76-26, -54
Taillander, Jean E79-55
Taj Mahal, The E82-129, -135
Take Des Moines ... Please E72-74
TAKE HER, SHE'S MINE T62-5
TAKE ME ALONG T60-10
"Take Me Back" G76-28
Tale of Two Cities, A E80-65
Talent for Life: Jews of the Italian Renaissance, A E79-86
Tales of the Gold Monkey E82-41
"Talk About the Good Times" G71-25
TALLEY'S FOLLY T80-16
TAMBURLAINE THE GREAT T56-7
Tamburri, Kenneth E73-76
Tamburri, O. E65-37
Tamiris, Helen T50-16
Tandy, Jessica T48-3, T78-4, T83-4
Tanks E82-122
Tanzi, Rick E68-36
Tap Dance Kid, The E78-61, -92, T84-8, -14
"Tapestry" G72-2, -5
Tarr, Edward, Ensemble G69-31, -33
Tarses, Jay E72-63
Taste of Honey (group) G79-51
TASTE OF HONEY, A (play) T61-4
"Taste of Honey, A" (recording) G63-10, G66-1, -10, -24, -41
Tatarian, Harry E67-44
Tatashore, Fred E78-83
"Tatoo You" G82-55
Tattletales E76-88
Tatum, Art G74-13
Tavares G79-2
Taxi E78-1, -12, -32, E79-1, -24, -59, E80-1, -15, -17, -22, -26, -30, E81-13, -14, -31, E82-12, -19, -20
Taylor, Billy E82-130
Taylor, James G72-4, G78-4, G81-43, G83-45
Taylor, June E54-30
Taylor, Justis E79-86
Taylor, Kate G81-43
Taylor, Livingston G81-43
Taylor, Noel E64-22, E77-64
Taylor, Renee E72-62
Taylor, Ross E72-41

"Tchaikovsky" G59-20, G64-31, G82-47
TEA AND SYMPATHY T54-3
Teacher, Teacher E68-5
Teague, William E77-49, E78-35, E80-48
TEAHOUSE OF THE AUGUST MOON T54-1, -2, -6, -8, -19
Tebaldi, Renata G59-23
Teddy: CBS Reports E80-93
Teddy Kolleck's Jerusalem E79-102
Televise Radio Omroep Stichting, The Netherlands E78-94
Television Española (Madrid) E73-131
"Tell Me Something Good" G75-22
Tell Me Where It Hurts E73-80, -86
Tempest Live with the San Francisco Ballet, The E80-59
Temple University Chorus G68-40
Tempo, Nino G64-18
Temptations, The G69-20, G73-22, -23
"Tequila" G59-8
Ter–Arutunian, Rouben E57-26, T59-20
Terrible Joe Moran E83-18
Tewksbury, Peter E58-28
Texaco Star Theatre E49-4
Texas Boys Choir G67-35, G69-33
Thames Television, United Kingdom E82-145
Thanksgiving Story, The E73-79
Thanksgiving Visitor, The E68-11
That Certain Summer E72-26
THAT CHAMPIONSHIP SEASON T73-1, -6
"That Lovin' You Feelin' Again" G81-25
"That Nigger's Crazy" G75-24
"That Old Black Magic" G59-16
"That Was the Week that Was" G65-19, E65-45
Theatre Collection, New York City Museum, The T83-20
Theatre Development Fund T74-19
Theatre Guild, The T61-24
Theatre Guild – American Theatre Society, The T72-19
Theatre 1963 T63-7
"Theme from 'Shaft'" G72-7, -41
"Theme from Summer of '42" G72-30
"Theme from the French Connection" G73-7
"Theme from 'Z'" G71-7, -8
"Then and Now" G74-29
"There Goes My Everything" C67-2, -3, -4
"There Must Be a Better World Somewhere" G82-40
"(There's) No Gettin' Over Me" G82-25
"They Call Me Muddy Waters" G72-27
They've Killed President Lincoln E70-28

Thiederman, A. E81-38
Thief Is a Thief, A E67-43
Thiel, Ernest E78-90
"Think of One" G84-20
Third Avenue: Only the Strong Survive E80-94
Third Barry Manilow Special, The E78-42
30 Minutes E79-70, E80-67, E81-63
34th Annual Tony Awards, The E79-11
This Child Is Rated X: An NBC News White Paper on Juvenile Justice E71-24
"This Is a Recording" G72-22
"This Is It" G81-4
This Is My Night E80-29
This Is My Son E77-98
This Is the Life E73-127, E77-106, E79-86
This Is Your Life E53-10, E54-11
"This Masquerade" G77-1
This Old House E82-81
"This Time by Basie! Hits of the 50's and 60's" G64-15
"This Will Be" G76-20
Thom, Robert E62-20
Thomas, B.J. G78-28, G79-28, G80-33, G81-36, G82-35
Thomas, Dan E82-58
Thomas, Danny E54-4
Thomas, Dave E81-34
Thomas, Marlo E80-88
Thomas, Michael Tilson G76-41
Thomas, Richard E72-18
Thompson, Alex E79-88
Thompson, Sada T72-4, E77-17
Thompson, Trevor E81-92, E82-105
Thorn Birds, The E82-15, -21, -22, -30, -40, -48
Thorpe, Jerry E72-30
THOUSAND CLOWNS, A T63-5
Thousand Pardons, You're Dead, A E69-55
Thrasher, Ed G75-43
3M Company E69-65
3-2-1 Contact E79-88
THREEPENNY OPERA T56-22
Three's Company E83-16
"Threshold" G75-7
"Thrill Is Gone, The" G71-20
"Thriller" G84-2, -4, -59
Through the Looking Glass Darkly E73-128
"Thundering Herd" G75-12
Thurber, James T60-24
THURBER CARNIVAL, A T60-24
Thurman, Jim E72-11
Tick, Donald T83-1
Tijuana Brass G66-10, -24, G67-9
Tillis, Mel C76-1

Tillstrom, Burr E65-45, E70-52
Time for Beany E49-5, E50-5, E52-9
TIME OF THE CUCKOO T53-4
Time Out E79-88
TIME REMEMBERED T58-4, -21
Time Tunnel, The E66-35
Timex Presents Peggy Flemming at Sun Valley E70-33, -57
Timmens, Jim G78-37
Tinn, Arthur E77-105, E78-90, E80-99
Tinsley, Russ E76-43, E81-38
TINY ALICE T65-4
Tipton, Jennifer T77-17
Tischler, Stanford E75-59
Titus, Libby G81-43
Tjader, Cal G81-42
To All My Friends on Shore E71-59
To Be a Doctor: NBC Reports E80-94
To Die for Ireland E80-94
"To Russell, My Brother, Whom I Slept With" G69-21
To Soar and Never Falter E81-16
To Taste of Death But Once E70-46
Tocci, Tony E80-99
Today E67-16, E69-18, E70-19, E74-44
Todos Los Ninos Del Mundo E78-92
"Toga Brava Suite" G73-12
Tokyo Broadcasting Company E74-88
Tom Brown's Schooldays E72-7, -22
"Tom Dooley" G59-7
"Tom Jones" G64-22, E69-56
Tomlin, Lily G72-22, E73-84, G75-78, T77-20, E77-41
"Tommy" G74-43
"Tommy Dorsey/Frank Sinatra Sessions, Vols. 1, 2, & 3, The" G83-58
Tomorrow E73-18
Tomorrow's Farewell E81-45
Tompall C76-3
Tompkins, Joe I. E75-99, E76-65
Toms, Carl T75-15
Tonight Show Starring Johnny Carson, The E75-8, -67, E76-5, E77-5, E78-10
Tonight with Belafonte E59-11
Tonkin, Mel E66-28
Tonnesson, Kurt E78-39
Tony's Sister and Jim E80-26
Too Little, Too Late? E80-93
TOP BANANA T52-8
"Top Drawer" G84-19
Toplyn, Joseph E. E83-39
TORCH SONG TRILOGY T83-1, -2
Torino, Louis E72-40
Torme, Mel G83-19, G84-19
Torrance, Dean O. G72-42
Toto G83-1, -2, -59

Index

"Toto IV" G83-2, -55
TOUCH AND GO T50-16
Toulouse–Lautrec Is One of My Favorite Artists E70-32
Tour of the White House E61-28
TOVARISCH T63-11
Towey, Douglas E. E83-70
Town Like Alice, A E81-103
Townsend, Charles R. G75-44
TOYS IN THE ATTIC T60-5, -20
Tragedy of the Red Salmon E70-59, -66
Trammps G79-2
Travanti, Daniel E80-18, E81-9
"Travels" G84-22
TRAVESTIES T76-1, -2
Travilla E79-56
Travis, Larry E70-58
Travis, Merle G75-18
Travis, Neil E76-37
Trent, Buck C74-5, C76-9
Tresh, John E83-72
Treve Globo, Ltda., Brazil E81-105
Trevor, Claire E56-14
Trial by Fury E82-36, -59
Trial of Mary Lincoln, The E71-63
Trial That Sparked the Riots: CBS Reports, The E80-94
Triangle Factory Fire Scandal, The E78-51
Tribes E70-41, -43, -47
"Trilogy: Past, Present and Future" G81-55
Trimble, Tom E73-105
Trinitron Picture Tube E72-73
Trinity Square Repertory Company T81-20
"Trio, The" G75-11
TRIP TO BOUNTIFUL, THE T54-5
Trittipo, James E65-39, E67-49, E70-62
Triumph on Mt. Everest E83-39, -81
Troutman, James E71-41, E82-58
"Truly" G83-4
Truth or Consequences E50-14
Tsuno, Keiko E80-94
"Tubular Bells" G75-9
Tuck, Cecil E68-34
Tucker, Tanya G82-44
Tucker, Thomas E79-92
Tuckett, Phil E78-90, E79-110, E80-99, E83-75
Tuesday Movie of the Week E72-45
Tune, Tommy T74-9, T80-14, T82-15, T83-8, -14
Tunick, Johnathan E81-41
Tuning the Engine E80-88
Tunnel, The E62-7, -8, -9
Turn of the Screw, The E59-10
"Turn Your Love Around" G83-28
Turner, Ike & Tina G72-21

Turner, Ret E77-65, E83-60
Twelfth Night E57-26
XII Winter Olympic Games E75-21, -58, -64, -68
Twelve Angry Men E54-17, -22, -28
Twelve O'Clock High E64-18
Twentieth Century E59-5, E60-5
21st Century, The E67-13
$25,000 Pyramid, The E82-23
29th Annual Emmy Awards, The E76-33
26th Annual Grammy Awards E83-44
$20,000 Pyramid, The E75-11, -55, E76-91, E77-93, E78-74, E79-66, E80-74, -85
20/20 E80-93, E82-130
TWIGS T72-4
Twilight Zone E59-14, E60-17, -21
Twitty, Conway C72-8, G72-16, C73-8, C74-8, C75-8
"Two Days in November" G75-29
TWO FOR THE SEESAW T58-5
TWO GENTLEMEN OF VERONA T72-7, -12
Two Is the Number E63-14
Two of a Kind E82-55
TWO'S COMPANY T53-11
Tyne Tees Television Limited (Newcastle-upon-Tyne, England) E66-44
Tyson, Cecily E73-26, -30

U

U-Matic Video Cassette Concept E75-102
U.S. Open E80-99
U.S./Soviet Wheat Deal E72-69
U.S. Steel Hour E53-1, -13, E54-1
Uggams, Leslie T68-11, E82-91
Ulmer, Gary E78-49
ULYSSES IN NIGHTGOWN T74-17
"Uncle Albert/Admiral Halsey" G72-9
"Underground" G69-38
Undersea World of Jacques Cousteau, The E69-38, E70-59, -66, E71-23, -70, E73-122, -124
"Unfinished Masterpiece" G77-34
Unforgivable Secret, The E81-91
Unicorn Tales E77-96
"Unmistakably Lou" G78-23
UNSINKABLE MOLLY BROWN, THE T61-13
Unsinkable Sea Otter, The E71-23
Untiedt, Bud E79-113
"Until I Met You (Corner Pocket)" G82-21
Untouchables, The E59-7, -17, -18, -20
Up Close and Personals E79-108, -109, -110

Index

"Up, Up and Away" G68-1, -3, -30, -31, -32, -35
"Up Where We Belong" G83-6
Upstairs, Downstairs E73-5, E74-23, -47, E75-4, E76-3
Urbont, Jack E82-111
U'Ren, Jeff E80-99
Urethane E80-93
Ustinov, Peter E57-11, G60-10, E66-13, E69-12
Uttendaele, Tony E79-113

V

VD Blues E72-16
VW Beetle: The Hidden Danger E80-93
Vaccaro, Brenda E73-36
Vachon, Paul E82-47
Vadala, Joseph E75-100, E77-98
Valentin, Luis P. G61-37
Valentine, Karen E69-17
Valentine's Day Special E77-97
Van Bemmel, Teddy T61-23
Vandenort, Bill E80-99
Van Dyke, Dick T61-11, E63-11, E64-9, G65-17, E65-14
Van Fleet, Jo T54-5
Vanished Parts I and II E70-57
Vanity Fair E72-23
Van Lawick, Hugo E72-71
Van Runkle, Theodora E82-45
"Varese" G79-46
Varian Associates E76-74
"Variations on a Theme by Erik Satie" G70-9
Vaughan, Sarah E80-41, -52, G83-18
"Vaughan Williams" G73-46
Vaughn, Robert E77-20
"Velas" G82-7
Velasco, Richard E79-112
Velie, Grant E81-90
Venable, Jean E72-38
Venice Be Damned E71-30, -48
"Verdi" G63-29, G72-37, G78-45, G83-51, G84-56
Verdon, Gwen T54-13, T56-12, T58-12, T59-12, G60-18
Vereen, Ben T73-8
Verna: USO Girl E77-30
Verschore, Maurey E82-43
Versley, Tony E79-113
Verxier, Rene E78-92
Very Good Friends E77-84
Very Loud Family, A E83-26

"Very Special Love Song, A" C74-3, G75-14
Very, Very Special Place—NBC Weekend, A E79-102
Vicens, Joe E77-97
Victoria Regina E61-7, -11, -14
Victory at Sea E53-8, G60-28
Vienna Philharmonic Orchestra G60-27, G65-34, G67-36, G82-50
Vienna State Opera Chorus G73-34
Vienna Singverein G73-34
Vietnam Requiem E82-131, -134
Villa Alegre E78-92, E79-88
"Villa-Lobos" G72-35
Villafana, Irv E80-99
Vincens, Joseph E80-99
Vincent Van Gogh: A Self Portrait E61-19
Vincius Para Criancas or Arca De Noe E81-105
Viorst, Judith E69-51
"Virtuoso" G59-24
Visions E76-40
VISIT TO A SMALL PLANET, A T57-19
"Vivaldi" G78-41
Voegeli, Tom G83-35
Voigtlander, Ted E73-74, -75, E77-52, E78-36
Volk, Arthur E75-64, E79-112
Volpicelli, Lou E68-17
Volunteer, American Theatre Wing T50-20
Von Benge, Chris E82-139
von Karajan, Herbert G60-10, G65-34, G70-39, G79-39
von Stroheim, Josef E69-42, E74-61
Voorman, Klaus G67-38, G73-2
Voyage Round My Father, A E82-145
Voyage to the Bottom of the Sea E64-29, E65-40, -41, E66-30

W

WABC-TV (New York) E74-17
WBBM-TV (Chicago) E65-47, E75-101, E78-93
WCAU-TV (Philadelphia) E67-52
WCBS-TV (New York) E62-29
WCCO-TV (Minneapolis) E82-143
WDSU-TV (New Orleans) E64-34
WFIL-TV (Philadelphia) E68-45
WHA-TV (Madison, Wisconsin) E68-46
WJZ-TV (Baltimore) E67-52
WKRP in Cincinnati E80-32
WKY-TV (Oklahoma City) E73-128
WLW-TV (New Orleans) E67-54

Index 198

WRC-TV (Washington) E67-53
WTHR-TV (Indianapolis, Indiana) E81-101
WZZM-TV (Grand Rapids, Michigan) E71-74
Wadsworth School Boys Choir G72-39
Wagner, Jane E73-84, E75-78
Wagner, Lindsay E76-13
Wagner, Martin E77-97
Wagner, Michael E81-32
Wagner, Richard E72-42
Wagner, Robin T78-16
Wagner, Roger, Chorale G59-24
"Wagner" G63-28, G67-36, -41, G70-39, G83-52
Wagoner, Porter G67-21, C68-7, G68-23, C70-8, G70-28, C71-8
Waissman, Kenneth T83-1
Waite, Ric E76-46
Wake Up the Echoes: The History of Notre Dame Football E83-75
Walas, Len E79-89, E81-92
Waldman, Wendy G81-43
"Walk on the Water" G82-17
Walk Through the 20th Century with Bill Moyers, A E83-10
Walker, Bill E78-83
Walker, David E70-64
Walker, Joseph A. T74-1
Walker, Kathryn E75-31
Walker, Keaton S. E72-60, E76-72
Walker, Stanley G84-62
Walker, T-Bone G71-27
Walker, Vivienne E76-71
Walker, Zena T68-5
"Walking in Space" G70-13
"Wall, The" G81-53
Wallace, Governor George, shooting of E72-47, -70
Wallace, Chris E80-94
Wallace, Mike E70-26, E71-27, E72-68
Wallach, Eli T51-3, E66-21
Waller, Elizabeth E71-55
Wallop, Douglass T56-14
"Walls of Glass" G84-38
Walsh, David M. E74-72
Walsh, Tommie T80-14, T83-14
Walston, Ray T56-10
Walt Disney's Wonderful World of Color E62-6, -27
Walter, Jessica E74-25
Walter Cronkite's Universe E82-141
Walters, Barbara E74-44, E82-125
Watlers, John T60-23
Walters, Ron E78-50
Walton, Tony T73-16

"Walton" G74-40
Waltons, The E72-6, -18, -19, -27, -35, E73-22, -79, E74-30, -31, E75-25, -35, E76-19
"Wanna Be with You" G83-31
"Wanted—The Outlaws" C76-3
War and Peace E62-28
War of Children, A E72-8
"War Requiem" G64-34
War Song E71-39
War Window, The E76-40
Wardell, Don G83-58
Warden, Jack E71-14
Warfield, William G84-35
"Warm Breeze" G83-17
Warner, David E80-45
Warner, Don E73-70, E76-42
Warnes, Jennifer G83-6
Warren, Gene, Jr. E82-64
Warren, Mark E70-36
Warren, Rod E73-84, E75-78
Warwick, Breck E83-32
Warwick, Dionne G69-5, G71-5, G80-5, -26
Washington, Dinah G60-9
Washington, Grover, Jr. G82-22
Washington: Behind Closed Doors E77-20
Wasserman, Dale T66-7
Water E77-107
Watergate Affair, The E72-70
Watergate Coverage E73-113
Watergate: The White House Transcripts E73-113
Waters, Muddy G72-27, G73-29, G76-29, G78-33, G79-33, G80-38
Watson, Doc G74-29, G75-29, G80-24
Watson, Douglass E77-98, E79-75, E80-75
Watson, Merle G75-29, G80-24
Watts, Andre G64-41
Watts, Ernie G83-8
Watts, Robert E66-29
Wave, The E81-22
"Way We Were, The" G75-3, -31
Way It Was, The E77-102
Wayne, David T47-5, T54-2
Wayne, Don C74-4
Wayne, Paul E68-34
"We Come to Worship" G81-35
"We Dig Mancini" G66-26
"We Got Us" G61-25
"We Love You, Call Collect" G70-25
"We Shall Meet Again" G81-16
"We Sing Praises" G84-40
"We Want Miles" G83-20

Index

Weather Report G80-19
Weatherford, Bob E70-41, E83-32
Weaver, Dennis E58-17
Weaver, Dorothy E78-92, E80-88
Weaver, Fritz T70-2
Weaver, Sylvester L. 'Pat,' Jr. E66-46, E82-68
Webb, Daniel J. E79-92
Webb, Jim G68-3, G69-10
Webb, William E79-54
Webber, Andrew Lloyd T80-12, -13, G81-41, T83-13, G84-44
Webster, Don E71-29
Webster, Paul Francis G66-3
Webster, Tony E55-22, E56-20, E57-20
Wedgeworth, Ann T78-5
Wedlock, Hugh E67-35
Wednesday Night Movie of the Week E72-26
Weidman, Jerome T60-14
Weill, Kurt T47-8
Weinberger, Ed E74-64, E76-50
Weinstock, Jack T62-14
Weiskopf, Bob E70-50, E77-38
Weiss, Donna G82-3
Weiss, Jerry E78-39, E81-48
Weiss, Julie E83-61
Weiss, Larry C76-4
Weiss, Les E79-113
Weiss, Peter T66-1
Weiss, Wayne E79-108
Weissberg, Eric G74-18
Weissler, Barry and Fran T82-19
Weitz, Bruce E83-21
Weitzenhoffer, Max T78-19
Welch, Christopher T. E83-33
Welch, Ken E73-96, -97, E75-87, E80-29
Welch, Mike E76-39
Welch, Mitzi E73-96, -97, E75-87, E80-29
Welch, Robert E80-99
Welcome to Korea E75-59
Welcome to Palermo E82-122
Welk, Lawrence E80-38
"We'll Sing in the Sunshine" G65-21
We'll Win This World E82-55
Welles, Orson G77-27, G79-27, G82-34
Wellmen, Harold E. E57-24
Wells, Bob E74-66
Wells, John E80-99
Welsh, Tommy E82-47
Wendell, John E75-88
Wenig, Michael E72-40, E75-64
Wenman, Diana E79-89, E81-92, E82-105
Werner, Kenneth E. E80-94

West, Bernie E72-61
West, Dottie G65-13, C78-8, C79-8
West, John E54-34
West, Ray E78-35
West, Shelly C81-8
"West Meets East" G68-38
WEST SIDE STORY T58-17, -19, G61-8, G62-8, -23
Westin, Av E59-16
Westin, Robin E81-87
Westinghouse Corporation E69-63
Westinghouse Desilu Playhouse E58-35, E59-18, -20
Westlein, Richard E82-105
Westmore, Frank E71-56
Westmore, Michael E75-92, E83-62
Weston, Paul G61-16
Westwood Television Limited (Plymouth, England) E65-46
Wetzel, Stanley A. E82-60
Wexler, Connie E77-97
Wexler, Jerry G76-31
Wharton, John F. T74-19
"What a Diff'rence a Day Makes" G60-9
"What a Fool Believes" G80-1, -3, -14
"What a Friend" G79-30
What About Ronald Reagan E67-30
"What Are You Doing the Rest of Your Life?" G73-10
What Is Sonata Form? E64-4
"What Kind of Fool Am I?" G63-3
"What Now My Love" G67-9, -25
What Shall We Do About Mother?: CBS Reports E80-94
What's My Line? E52-10, E53-10, E58-10
"What's New" G84-9
Whedon, Tom E72-11
Wheeler, Hugh T73-12, T74-12, T79-12
Whelan, Aggie E73-122
Wheldon, Sir Huw E81-107
"When You're Hot, You're Hot" G72-15
"Where Is the Love?" G73-6, G76-19
"Where the Soul Never Dies" G77-29
WHERE'S CHARLEY? T49-10
Which Mother Is Mine E79-88
Whitaker, Jack E77-103
White, Betty E74-29, E75-33, E82-93
White, Chuck E80-63
White, Danny E79-33
White, Frank R. E73-70
White, Maurice (Also see Earth, Wind & Fire) G79-11
White, Michael T71-7
White, Miles T51-20, T53-20
White, Ruth E63-17
White, Theodore H. E66-36

Index

White Shadow E78-26
Whitehead, Robert T62-8, T84-19
Whitfield, Norman G73-19, G77-32
Whitmore, James T48-12, G76-25
Whitmore, Ken G66-42
Who Are the Debolts & Where Did They Get 19 Kids? E78-27
Who Do You Kill? E63-21
Who Killed Georgi Markov? E80-93
Who, What, When, Where, Why with Harry Reasoner E67-36
Who Will Love My Children? E82-27
Who Won What in America, a Few Minutes with Andy Rooney E79-96
Whorf, Christopher G75-43
Whorf, Richard T54-20
WHO'S AFRAID OF VIRGINIA WOOLF? T63-1, -2, -4, -6, -7, G64-17
WHO'S LIFE IS IT ANYWAY? T79-2
Why a Conductor E79-70
"Why I Oppose the War in Vietnam" G71-23
"Why Is There Air?" G66-18
Why Me? E83-62
"Why Not?" G84-21
Wiard, Tucker E77-50, E78-38, E81-30
"Wichita Lineman" G69-37
Wickline, Matt E83-39
Wide, Wide World E57-29
Wide, Wide World: In Concert E75-63
Wide World Concert E74-85
Wide World of Sports E70-53, E74-15, -39
Widhoff, Gene E70-60
Wiener, Ron E78-76, E81-80
Wight, Tom E72-40
Wilcox, Caroly E75-96, E80-86
Wilcox, Charlotte E82-38
Wilcox, Dan E69-62
Wilcox, John E83-81
Wilcox, Ken E82-51
"Wild and Crazy Guy, A" G79-26
Wild, Wild West E66-22
Wilder, Clinton T63-7
Wilhoit, Michael E83-32
Wilkes & Braun, Inc. G74-43
Wilkins, Nick E72-38
Wilkins, Rev. Robert G81-39
Wilkinson, Kenneth G73-42, G75-41, G78-46
Willcocks, David G64-33
William, R. E81-38
Williams, Big Joe G81-39
Williams, Darnell E82-86
Williams, Dave E69-44, E75-67
Williams, Deniece G83-45

Williams, Don C78-6, C81-3
Williams, Edward E55-30, E82-112
Williams, John (actor) T53-3
Williams, John (classical guitarist) G73-36
Williams, John (composer/conductor) E68-38, E71-66, G76-30, G78-8, -10, -34, G79-10, -34, G80-13, -39, G81-14, -40, G82-41, G83-7, -15, -42
Williams, Mason G69-9, -29
Williams, Pat G75-7, E79-40, E81-40
Williams, Paul G78-3
Williams, Robin G80-31
Williams, Sammy T76-9
Williams, Tennessee T51-6
Willman, Noel T62-7
"Willow Weep for Me" G70-12
Willowbrook Case: The People vs. the State of New York, The E74-17
Willson, Meredith T58-14, -15, G59-15
Wilmarth, Howard E81-43, E82-60
Wilson, Christine E78-44
Wilson, Dave E75-52
Wilson, Doug E68-17
Wilson, Elizabeth T72-5
Wilson, Flip E70-50, G71-22
Wilson, James E68-21
Wilson, Nancy G65-16
Wilson, Norris G75-14
Wilson, Pauline G81-43
Wimbledon '83 E83-68
Winchell, Paul G75-32
"Winchester Cathedral" G67-29
Windom, William E69-8
Winds of Kitty Hawk, The E78-35
Winds of War, The E82-34, -47, -64
"Winelight" G82-22
Wings G75-6, G80-10
WINGS T79-4
Winkle, Edward E69-47
Winkler, Harry E54-23
Winners E82-74
"Winnie the Pooh & Tigger Too" G75-32
Winningham, Mare E79-21
Winston, Stan E72-51
Winston Churchill, The Valiant Years E60-19, E61-25
Winter Olympics E59-19
Winterburn, Ted E79-108, E80-99
Winters, Marian T52-5
Winters, Shelly E63-14
Wiseman, Frederick E69-29
WISH YOU WERE HERE T53-13, -21
Wistrom, William H. E78-34, E81-38
With Ernie Kovaks E58-31
"With My Song I Will Praise Him" G81-34
Withers, Bill G72-18, G82-28

Index

"Without You" G73-4
Witness for the Prosecution T55-3, -5
Wittop, Freddy T64-21
"Wives and Lovers" G64-5
WIZ, THE T75-7, -9, -11, -12, -13, -14, -17, G76-31, G79-7
Wizards and Warriors E82-45
Wolcott, Joe E80-53
Woldin, Judd T74-7, G75-31
Wolf, Ben E66-38, E67-44, E68-36
Wolf, David E77-96
Wolf, Digby E67-35
Wolf, Harry E73-73, E75-70, E80-99
Wolf, Jack E72-44
Wolff, Perry E68-23, E79-96, E80-94, E82-133
Wolfson, Victor E60-19
Wollman, Howard E80-48
Wollner, Anthony E72-35
Wolper, David L. E83-66
Woman Named Golda, A E81-1, -5, -19
WOMAN OF THE YEAR T81-10, -11, -12, -13
Woman Who Willed a Miracle, The E82-73, -88, -97, -102
Women, The E83-37
Wonder, Stevie G74-2, -4, -19, -21, G75-2, -4, -19, -21, G77-2, -4, -23, -48
"Wonderful" G78-31
WONDERFUL TOWN T53-9, -12, -14, -15, -16, -17, -18, -19
Wonderful World of Burlesque, The E64-32
"Wonderfulness" G67-18
Wood, Barbara E81-92
Wood, John T76-2
Woodard, Alfre E83-20
Woods, Phil G76-12, G78-12, G83-16, G84-16
Woods, Robert G81-58, E82-84, G83-60
Woodside, Lyndon G78-38
Woodward, Charles T79-7
Woodward, Joanne E77-31
Woolery, Gerry E83-45
Woolery, Ted E83-45
Wooley, Sheb C68-10
Woolsey, Ralph E67-43
Working E81-53
World E80-93
World at War, The E73-115
World Championship Boxing (Ali/Spinks) E77-99
World News Roundup E57-6
World News Tonight E82-119, -120
World of Charlie Company, The E70-22
World Premiere E69-13, -36, -50
World Premiere NBC Monday Night at the Movies E70-14, -60

World University Games E83-72
World War III E81-51
"World's Greatest Blues Singer, The" G71-42
Worsham, Donald E80-49
Worth, Irene T65-4, T76-4
Worth, Merle E79-88
Wrestling E49-7
Wright, Betty G76-19
Wright, Robert T54-9
Wright, Wayne E78-90
Wulp, John T78-19
Wyatt, Jane E57-10, E58-12, E59-8
Wynette, Tammy C68-5, G68-11, C69-5, C70-5, G70-15
Wynn, Ed E49-1, -3
Wynn, Tracy Keenan E70-47, E73-81
Wyvern at War No. 2 E65-46

X

Xerox Corporation E65-48
Xerox Special E66-21, E67-18

Y

Yanok, George E75-78
Yant, James E77-48
Yates, Ascher E82-58
Yazbek, David E83-39
YEARS AGO T47-1
Years of Crisis E56-6
Yellen, Sherman E75-73
Yerkovich, Anthony E81-32
Yes, Virginia, There Is a Santa Claus E74-14
Yeston, Maury T82-13
Yohe, Tom E80-88
York, Paul E78-66
Yorkin, Bud E58-27, E59-13
Yorkshire Television Limited (London) E74-19, E77-109, E80-106
"You Are the Sunshine of My Life" G74-4
You Are There E55-34
You Can't Take It With You E78-48
"You Decorated My Life" G80-20
"You Don't Have to Be a Star (To Be in My Show)" G77-24
"You Gave Me Love (When Nobody Gave Me a Prayer)" G80-33
YOU KNOW I CAN'T HEAR YOU WHEN THE WATER'S RUNNING T68-2

Index

"You Light Up My Life" G78-3
"You Make Me Feel Like Dancing" G78-21
"You Need Me" G79-5
"You Should Hear How She Talks About You" G83-5
You'll Never Get Rich E55-2, -4, -22, -26
Young, Alan E50-2
Young, Dick E78-92
Young, Loretta E54-5, E56-8, E58-14
Young, Robert E56-7, E57-9, E69-10, E70-28
Young, Roger E79-25
Young, Victor E54-32
Young and the Restless, The E73-100, -105, E74-8, -52, E77-91, -97, E82-70
"Young, Gifted & Black" G73-20
Young Joe, The Forgotten Kennedy E77-49
Young People's Concert E60-6
Young People's Specials E82-110
YOUR ARM'S TOO SHORT TO BOX WITH GOD T77-11
Your Hit Parade E55-35, E56-27, E57-27
Your Show of Shows E51-6, E52-7
You're a Good Sport, Charlie Brown E75-18
"You've Got a Friend" G72-3, -4

Zak, John E81-90
Zal, Roxana E83-19
Zall, Andy E77-51, E78-56, E81-37
Zaltzberg, Charlotte T74-7
Zappia, Marco E70-42, E80-47
Zeffirelli, Franco T62-23
Zelinger, Gerald E80-63
Zemke, Ken E75-60
Zerbe, Anthony E75-36
Zetner, Si G62-15, -26
Ziegfeld: the Man and His Women E77-53, -73
Ziggy's Gift E82-7
Zink, Steve E75-72, E76-72, E79-88
Zipprodt, Patricia T65-20, T67-16
Zito, Torrie E81-41
Zizza, Bill E80-99
Zlotnik, Ed E79-112
Zoom E72-11, E73-11, E76-79
ZORBA T69-15, T84-10
Zubin and the I.P.O. E82-77, -94
Zuckerman, Pinchas G81-46, G82-48
Zuckerman, Joe E72-72
Zweibel, Alan E75-75, E76-52, E77-41
Zweig, Howard E79-89, E81-92, E82-105
Zwick, Edward E82-37

Z

Zaccaro, Anthony E80-99
Zaharuk, William E73-101